Corporate Finance

CFA® PROGRAM CURRICULUM • VOLUME 3

LEVEL II
2008

D1726577

PEARSON

Custom
Publishing

Cover photograph courtesy of Getty Images.

Printed in the United States of America

10 9 8 7 6 5 4 3 2

ISBN 0-536-34231-8

2006160831

AG/JS

Please visit our web site at *www.pearsoncustom.com*

PEARSON CUSTOM PUBLISHING
501 Boylston Street, Suite 900, Boston, MA 02116
A Pearson Education Company

CONTENTS

HOW TO USE THE CFA PROGRAM CURRICULUM

Congratulations on passing Level I of the Chartered Financial Analyst (CFA®) Program. This exciting and rewarding program of study reflects your desire to become a serious investment professional. You are participating in a program noted for its requirement of ethics and breadth of knowledge, skills, and abilities.

The credential you seek is respected around the world as a mark of accomplishment and dedication. Each level of the program represents a distinct achievement in professional development. Successful completion of the program is rewarded with membership in a prestigious global community of investment professionals. CFA charterholders are dedicated to life-long learning and maintaining currency with the ever-changing dynamics of a challenging profession.

The CFA examination measures your degree of mastery of the assigned CFA Program curriculum. Effective study and preparation based on that curriculum are keys to your success on the examination.

Curriculum Development

The CFA Program curriculum is grounded in the practice of the investment profession. CFA Institute regularly conducts a practice analysis survey of investment professionals around the world to determine the knowledge, skills, and abilities that are relevant to the profession. The survey results define the Candidate Body of Knowledge (CBOK™), an inventory of knowledge and responsibilities expected of the investment management professional at the level of a new CFA charterholder. The survey also determines how much emphasis each of the major topic areas receives on the CFA examinations.

A committee made up of practicing charterholders, in conjunction with CFA Institute staff, designs the CFA Program curriculum to deliver the CBOK to candidates. The examinations, also written by practicing charterholders, are designed to allow you to demonstrate your mastery of the CBOK as set forth in the CFA Program curriculum. As you structure your personal study program, you should emphasize mastery of the CBOK and the practical application of that knowledge. For more information on the practice analysis, CBOK, and development of the CFA Program curriculum, please visit www.cfainstitute.org/toolkit.

Organization

The Level II CFA Program curriculum is organized into 10 topic areas. Each topic area begins with a brief statement of the material and the depth of knowledge expected.

Each topic area is then divided into one or more study sessions. These study sessions—18 sessions in the Level II curriculum—should form the basic structure of your reading and preparation.

Each study session includes a statement of its structure and objective, and is further divided into specific reading assignments. The outline on the inside front cover of each volume illustrates the organization of these 18 study sessions.

The reading assignments are the basis for all examination questions, and are selected or developed specifically to teach the CBOK. These readings are drawn from textbook chapters, professional journal articles, research analyst reports, CFA Program-commissioned content, and cases. Many readings include problems and solutions as well as appendices to help you learn.

Reading-specific Learning Outcome Statements (LOS) are listed in the pages introducing each study session as well as at the beginning of each reading. These LOS indicate what you should be able to accomplish after studying the reading. We encourage you to review how to properly use LOS, and the descriptions of commonly used LOS "command words," at www.cfainstitute.org/toolkit. The command words signal the depth of learning you are expected to achieve from the reading. You should use the LOS to guide and focus your study, as each examination question is based on an assigned reading and one or more LOS. However, the readings provide context for the LOS and enable you to apply a principle or concept in a variety of scenarios. It is important to study the whole of a required reading.

Features of the Curriculum

► **Required vs. Optional Segments** - You should read all of the pages for an assigned reading. In some cases, however, we have reprinted an entire chapter or article and marked those parts of the reading that are not required as "optional." The CFA examination is based only on the required segments, and the optional segments are included only when they might help you to better understand the required segments (by seeing the required material in its full context). When an optional segment begins, you will see an icon and a solid vertical bar in the outside margin that will continue until the optional segment ends, accompanied by another icon. *Unless the material is specifically marked as optional, you should assume it is required.* Keep in mind that the optional material is provided strictly for your convenience and will not be tested. You should rely on the required segments and the reading-specific LOS in preparing for the examination.

► **Problems/Solutions** - *All questions and problems in the readings as well as their solutions (which are provided in an appendix at the end of each volume) are required material.* When appropriate, we have included problems after the readings to demonstrate practical application and reinforce your understanding of the concepts presented. The questions and problems are designed to help you learn these concepts. Many of the questions are in the same style and format as the actual CFA examination and will give you test-taking experience in that format. Examination questions that come from a past CFA examination are marked with the CFA logo in the margin.

2006 exam

► **Margins** - The wide margins in each volume provide space for your note-taking.

► **Two-color Format** - To enrich the visual appeal and clarity of the exhibits, tables, and text, the curriculum is printed in a two-color format.

► **Six-volume Structure** - For portability of the curriculum, the material is spread over six volumes.

► **Glossary and Index** - For your convenience, we have printed a comprehensive glossary and index in each volume. Throughout the curriculum, a **bolded blue** word in a reading denotes a term defined in the glossary.

Designing Your Personal Study Program

Create a Schedule - An orderly, systematic approach to examination preparation is critical. You should dedicate a consistent block of time every week to reading and studying. Complete all reading assignments and the associated problems and solutions in each study session. Review the LOS both before and after you study each reading to ensure that you have mastered the applicable content and can demonstrate the knowledge, skill, or ability described by the LOS and the assigned reading.

CFA Institute estimates that you will need to devote a minimum of 10–15 hours per week for 18 weeks to study the assigned readings. Allow a minimum of one week for each study session, and plan to complete them all at least 30–45 days prior to the examination. This schedule will allow you to spend the final four to six weeks before the examination reviewing the assigned material and taking multiple online sample examinations.

At CFA Institute, we believe that candidates need to commit to a *minimum* of 250 hours reading and reviewing the curriculum, and taking online sample examinations, to master the material. This recommendation, however, may substantially underestimate the hours needed for appropriate examination preparation depending on your individual circumstances, relevant experience, and academic background.

You will undoubtedly adjust your study time to conform to your own strengths and weaknesses, and your educational and professional background. You will probably spend more time on some study sessions than on others. You should allow ample time for both in-depth study of all topic areas and additional concentration on those topic areas for which you feel least prepared.

Candidate Preparation Toolkit - We have created the online toolkit to provide a single comprehensive location for resources and guidance for candidate preparation. In addition to in-depth information on study program planning, the CFA Program curriculum, and the online sample examinations, the toolkit also contains curriculum errata, printable study session outlines, sample examination questions, and more. Errata identified in the curriculum are corrected and listed periodically in the errata listing in the toolkit. We encourage you to use the toolkit as your central preparation resource during your tenure as a candidate. Visit the toolkit at www.cfainstitute.org/toolkit.

Online Sample Examinations - After completing your study of the assigned curriculum, use the CFA Institute online sample examinations to measure your knowledge of the topics and to improve your examination-taking skills. After each question, you will receive immediate feedback noting the correct response and indicating the assigned reading for further study. The sample examinations are designed by the same people who create the actual CFA examinations, and reflect the question formats, topics, and level of difficulty of the actual CFA examinations, in a timed environment. Aggregate data indicate that the CFA examination pass rate was higher among candidates who took one or more online sample examinations than among candidates who did not take the online sample examinations. For more information on the online sample examinations, please visit www.cfainstitute.org/toolkit.

Preparatory Providers - After you enroll in the CFA Program, you may receive numerous solicitations for preparatory courses and review materials. Although preparatory courses and notes may be helpful to some candidates, you should view these resources as *supplements* to the assigned CFA Program curriculum. The CFA examinations reference only the CFA Institute assigned curriculum—no preparatory course or review course materials are consulted or referenced.

Before you decide on a supplementary prep course, do some research. Determine the experience and expertise of the instructors, the accuracy and currency of their content, the delivery method for their materials, and the provider's claims of success. Most importantly, make sure the provider is in compliance with the CFA Institute Prep Provider Guidelines Program. Three years of prep course products can be a significant investment, so make sure you're getting a sufficient return. Just remember, there are no shortcuts to success on the CFA examinations. Prep products can enhance your learning experience, but the CFA curriculum is the key to success. For more information on the Prep Provider Guidelines Program, visit www.cfainstitute.org/cfaprog/resources/prepcourse.html.

SUMMARY

Every question on the CFA examination is based on specific pages in the required readings and on one or more LOS. Frequently, an examination question is also tied to a specific example highlighted within a reading or to a specific end-of-reading question/problem and its solution. To make effective use of the curriculum, please remember these key points:

1. All pages printed in the Custom Curriculum are required reading for the examination except for occasional sections marked as optional. You may read optional pages as background, but you will not be tested on them.

2. All questions/problems printed at the end of readings and their solutions in the appendix to each volume are required study material for the examination.

3. Make appropriate use of the CFA Candidate Toolkit, the online sample examinations, and preparatory courses and review materials.

4. Commit sufficient study time to cover the 18 study sessions, review the materials, and take sample examinations.

Feedback

At CFA Institute, we are committed to delivering a comprehensive and rigorous curriculum for the development of competent, ethically grounded investment professionals. We rely on candidate and member feedback as we work to incorporate content, design, and packaging improvements. You can be assured that we will continue to listen to your suggestions. Please send any comments or feedback to curriculum@cfainstitute.org. Ongoing improvements in the curriculum will help you prepare for success on the upcoming examinations, and for a lifetime of learning as a serious investment professional.

CORPORATE FINANCE

STUDY SESSIONS

Study Session 8   Corporate Finance
Study Session 9   Financing and Control Issues

TOPIC LEVEL LEARNING OUTCOME

The candidate should be able to demonstrate a working knowledge of capital budgeting concepts and analysis, the cost of capital and capital structure issues, dividend policy choice, and the market for corporate control. Candidates should understand the valuation implications of mergers and acquisitions and restructurings.

$4\frac{5}{8}$ 4

$5\frac{1}{2}$ $5\frac{1}{2}$ $-$ $\frac{3}{8}$

$5\frac{1}{2}$ $21\frac{3}{16}$ $-$ $\frac{1}{8}$

$20\frac{5}{8}$ $21\frac{3}{16}$ $-$ $\frac{1}{8}$

$17\frac{3}{8}$ $18\frac{1}{8}$ $+$ $\frac{7}{8}$

$19\frac{1}{2}$ $6\frac{1}{2}$ $6\frac{1}{2}$ $-$ $\frac{1}{2}$

$7\frac{1}{4}$ $6\frac{1}{2}$ $31\frac{1}{32}$ $-$ $\frac{1}{8}$

$15\frac{1}{16}$

1 $\frac{9}{16}$ $\frac{9}{16}$

$\frac{9}{16}$ $\frac{9}{16}$

$19\frac{1}{32}$ $7\frac{13}{16}$ $7\frac{15}{16}$

$7\frac{15}{16}$ $7\frac{13}{16}$ $7\frac{15}{16}$

$2\frac{5}{8}$ $2\frac{11}{32}$ $2\frac{1}{2}$ $+$

545 $2\frac{3}{4}$ $2\frac{1}{4}$ $2\frac{1}{4}$

327 $2\frac{3}{4}$ $2\frac{1}{4}$ $2\frac{1}{4}$

$6\frac{1}{8}$ $12\frac{1}{16}$ $11\frac{3}{8}$ $11\frac{3}{4}$ $+$

87 $33\frac{3}{4}$ 33 $33\frac{1}{8}$ $-$

902 $25\frac{5}{8}$ $24\frac{9}{16}$ $25\frac{3}{8}$ $+$

833 12 $11\frac{5}{8}$ $11\frac{7}{8}$ $+$

16 $10\frac{1}{2}$ $10\frac{1}{2}$ $10\frac{1}{2}$ $-$

78 $15\frac{5}{8}$ $15\frac{13}{16}$ $15\frac{7}{8}$ $-$

4508 $9\frac{1}{16}$ $8\frac{1}{4}$ $8\frac{7}{8}$ $+$

430 $11\frac{1}{4}$ $10\frac{1}{8}$ $10\frac{1}{2}$

$4\frac{1}{8}$

STUDY SESSION 8
CORPORATE FINANCE

This study session first presents capital budgeting analysis, focusing on the applications of concepts in the corporate finance decision-making process. These capital budgeting principles are critical for an analyst inside the firm preparing capital budgeting recommendations as well as for an external analyst estimating the value of the firm.

The second half of the study session covers capital structure and dividend policy. Included is a discussion of the Modigliani–Miller propositions relating to capital structure and dividend policy. The presentation of capital structure and dividend policy starts with the classic Modigliani–Miller propositions, and then relaxes their underlying assumptions by incorporating taxes and other market imperfections. Leverage and dividend policy help determine the risk and return characteristics of corporate stocks and bonds.

READING ASSIGNMENTS

Reading 31 Capital Budgeting
Reading 32 Capital Structure and Leverage
Reading 33 Dividends and Dividend Policy

LEARNING OUTCOMES

Reading 31: Capital Budgeting
The candidate should be able to:

a. compute the yearly cash flows of an expansion capital project and of a replacement capital project, and evaluate how the choice of depreciation method affects those cash flows;

b. discuss the effects of inflation on capital budgeting analysis;

c. evaluate and select the optimal capital project in situations of (1) mutually exclusive projects with unequal lives, using either the least common multiple of lives approach or the equivalent annual annuity approach, and (2) capital rationing;

d. explain how sensitivity analysis, scenario analysis, and Monte Carlo simulation can be used to assess the stand-alone risk of a capital project;

3

e. discuss the procedure for determining the discount rate to be used in valuing a capital project, and calculate a project's required rate of return using the CAPM;

f. discuss the types of real options, and evaluate a capital project using real options;

g. discuss common capital budgeting pitfalls;

h. calculate and interpret accounting income and economic income in the context of capital budgeting;

i. differentiate among, and evaluate a capital project using the following valuation models: economic profit (EP), residual income, and claims valuation.

Reading 32: Capital Structure and Leverage

The candidate should be able to:

a. define and explain leverage, business risk, sales risk, operating risk, and financial risk, and classify a risk, given a description;

b. calculate and interpret the degree of operating leverage, the degree of financial leverage, and the degree of total leverage;

c. characterize the operating leverage, financial leverage, and total leverage of a company given a description of it;

d. calculate the breakeven quantity of sales and determine the company's net income at various sales levels;

e. describe the effect of financial leverage on a company's net income and return on equity;

f. compare and contrast the risks of creditors and owners;

g. describe the objective of the capital structure decision;

h. discuss the Modigliani and Miller (MM) propositions concerning capital structure irrelevance and describe the relation between the cost of equity and financial leverage;

i. discuss the effect of taxes on the MM propositions, the cost of capital, and the value of a company;

j. identify and explain the costs of financial distress, the agency costs and net agency costs of equity, the costs of asymmetric information, and their relation to a company's optimal capital structure;

k. explain and diagram the static trade-off theory of the optimal capital structure;

l. compare the implications of the MM propositions, the pecking order theory of capital structure, and the static trade-off theory of capital structure;

m. explain the target capital structure and why actual capital structure may fluctuate around the target;

n. review the role of debt ratings in capital structure policy;

o. explain the factors an analyst should consider in evaluating the impact of capital structure policy on valuation;

p. discuss international differences in financial leverage and the implications for investment analysis.

Reading 33: Dividends and Dividend Policy

The candidate should be able to:

a. review cash dividends, stock dividends, stock splits, and reverse stock splits, and calculate and discuss their impact on a shareholder's wealth;

b. compare the impact on shareholder wealth of a share repurchase and a cash dividend of equal amount;

c. calculate the earnings per share effect of a share repurchase when the repurchase is made with borrowed funds and the company's after-tax cost of debt is greater (less) than its earnings yield;

d. calculate the book value effect of a share repurchase when the market value of a share is greater (less) than book value per share;

e. compare and contrast share repurchase methods;

f. review dividend payment chronology including declaration, holder-of-record, ex-dividend, and payment dates and indicate when the share price will most likely reflect the dividend;

g. summarize the factors affecting dividend payout policy;

h. calculate the effective tax rate on a dollar of corporate earnings distributed as a dividend using the double-taxation, split rate, and tax imputation systems;

i. discuss the types of information that dividend initiations, increases, decreases, and omissions may convey, and discuss cross-country differences in the signaling content of dividends;

j. compare and contrast the following dividend policies: residual dividend, longer-term residual dividend, dividend stability, and target payout ratio;

k. calculate a company's expected dividend using the variables in the target payout approach;

l. discuss the rationales for share repurchases and explain the signals that share repurchases may generate;

m. differentiate among the schools of thought on dividends (dividend irrelevance, dividend preference, and tax aversion), and discuss their implications for shareholder value and the price-to-earnings ratio;

n. demonstrate how the initiation of a regular dividend payout might affect the price-to-earnings multiple.

4⅛ +

5½ **5½ − ⁵⁄₈**

5½ 21¹³⁄₁₆ − ¼

20⅝ 21¹³⁄₁₆ − ⅞

17⅜ **18⅛ +** ⅞

18½ 6½ **6½ −** ½

7¼ 6½ **6½ −**

15⁄₁₆ 3¹⁄₃₂ −

1 9⁄₁₆ ⁹⁄₁₆

1⁄₃₂ 9⁄₁₆

7¹⁵⁄₁₆ 7¹³⁄₁₆ 7¹⁵⁄₁₆

2⅝ 2¹¹⁄₃₂ **2½ +**

2¾ 2¼ 2¼

6⅛ 12¹⁄₁₆ 11⅜ 11¼ +

87 33¾ 33 33¹⁄₁₆ −

602 25⅝ 24⁹⁄₁₆ 25⅜ +

833 12 11⅝ 11⅞ +

16 10½ 10½ 10½ −

78 15⅞ 15¹³⁄₁₆ 15⅞ −

4808 9¹⁄₁₆ 8¼ 8⅜ +

430 11¼ 10⅜

CAPITAL BUDGETING

by John D. Stowe and Jacques R. Gagné

LEARNING OUTCOMES

The candidate should be able to:

a. compute the yearly cash flows of an expansion capital project and of a replacement capital project, and evaluate how the choice of depreciation method affects those cash flows;

b. discuss the effects of inflation on capital budgeting analysis;

c. evaluate and select the optimal capital project in situations of (1) mutually exclusive projects with unequal lives, using either the least common multiple of lives approach or the equivalent annual annuity approach, and (2) capital rationing;

d. explain how sensitivity analysis, scenario analysis, and Monte Carlo simulation can be used to assess the stand-alone risk of a capital project;

e. discuss the procedure for determining the discount rate to be used in valuing a capital project, and calculate a project's required rate of return using the CAPM;

f. discuss the types of real options, and evaluate a capital project using real options;

g. discuss common capital budgeting pitfalls;

h. calculate and interpret accounting income and economic income in the context of capital budgeting;

i. differentiate among, and evaluate a capital project using the following valuation models: economic profit (EP), residual income, and claims valuation.

INTRODUCTION 1

Capital budgeting is the process that companies use for decision making on capital projects—those projects with a life of a year or more. This is a fundamental area of knowledge for financial analysts for many reasons.

▶ First, capital budgeting is very important for corporations. Capital projects, which make up the long-term asset portion of the balance sheet, can be so large that sound capital budgeting decisions ultimately decide the future of many corporations. Capital decisions cannot be reversed at a low cost, so mistakes are very costly. Indeed, the real capital investments of a company describe a company better than its working capital or capital structures, which are intangible and tend to be similar for many corporations.

► Second, the principles of capital budgeting have been adapted for many other corporate decisions, such as investments in working capital, leasing, mergers and acquisitions, and bond refunding.

► Third, the valuation principles used in capital budgeting are similar to the valuation principles used in **security analysis** and portfolio management. Many of the methods used by security analysts and portfolio managers are based on capital budgeting methods. Conversely, there have been innovations in security analysis and portfolio management that have also been adapted to capital budgeting.

► Finally, although analysts have a vantage point outside the company, their interest in valuation coincides with the capital budgeting focus of maximizing shareholder value. Because capital budgeting information is not ordinarily available outside the company, the analyst may attempt to estimate the process, within reason, at least for companies that are not too complex. Further, analysts may be able to appraise the quality of the company's capital budgeting process; for example, on the basis of whether the company has an accounting focus or an economic focus.

This reading is organized as follows: Section 2 presents the steps in a typical capital budgeting process. After introducing the basic principles of capital budgeting in Section 3, in Section 4 we discuss the criteria by which a decision to invest in a project may be made. Section 5 presents a crucial element of the capital budgeting process: organizing the cash flow information that is the raw material of the analysis. Section 6 looks further at cash flow analysis. Section 7 demonstrates methods to extend the basic investment criteria to address economic alternatives and risk. Finally, Section 8 compares other income measures and valuation models that analysts use to the basic capital budgeting model.

2 THE CAPITAL BUDGETING PROCESS

The specific capital budgeting procedures that a manager uses depend on the manager's level in the organization, the size and complexity of the project being evaluated, and the size of the organization. The typical steps in the capital budgeting process are as follows:

► Step One, Generating Ideas—Investment ideas can come from anywhere, from the top or the bottom of the organization, from any department or functional area, or from outside the company. Generating good investment ideas to consider is the most important step in the process.

► Step Two, Analyzing Individual Proposals—This step involves gathering the information to forecast cash flows for each project and then evaluating the project's profitability.

► Step Three, Planning the Capital Budget—The company must organize the profitable proposals into a coordinated whole that fits within the company's overall strategies, and it also must consider the projects' timing. Some projects that look good when considered in isolation may be undesirable strategically. Because of financial and real resource issues, scheduling and prioritizing projects is important.

► Step Four, Monitoring and Post-auditing—In a post-audit, actual results are compared to planned or predicted results, and any differences must be explained. For example, how do the revenues, expenses, and cash flows realized from an investment compare to the predictions? Post-auditing capital projects is important for several reasons. First, it helps monitor the forecasts and analysis that underlie the capital budgeting process. Systematic errors, such as overly optimistic forecasts, become apparent. Second, it helps improve business operations. If sales or costs are out of line, it will focus attention on bringing performance closer to expectations if at all possible. Finally, monitoring and post-auditing recent capital investments will produce concrete ideas for future investments. Managers can decide to invest more heavily in profitable areas and scale down or cancel investments in areas that are disappointing.

Planning for capital investments can be very complex, often involving many persons inside and outside of the company. Information about marketing, science, engineering, regulation, taxation, finance, production, and behavioral issues must be systematically gathered and evaluated. The authority to make capital decisions depends on the size and complexity of the project. Lower-level managers may have discretion to make decisions that involve less than a given amount of money, or that do not exceed a given **capital budget.** Larger and more complex decisions are reserved for top management, and some are so significant that the company's board of directors ultimately has the decision-making authority.

Like everything else, capital budgeting is a cost–benefit exercise. At the margin, the benefits from the improved decision making should exceed the costs of the capital budgeting efforts.

Companies often put capital budgeting projects into some rough categories for analysis. One such classification would be as follows:

1. Replacement projects. These are among the easier capital budgeting decisions. If a piece of equipment breaks down or wears out, whether to replace it may not require careful analysis. If the expenditure is modest and if not investing has significant implications for production, operations, or sales, it would be a waste of resources to overanalyze the decision. Just make the replacement. Other replacement decisions involve replacing existing equipment with newer, more efficient equipment, or perhaps choosing one type of equipment over another. These replacement decisions are often amenable to very detailed analysis, and you might have a lot of confidence in the final decision.

2. Expansion projects. Instead of merely maintaining a company's existing business activities, expansion projects increase the size of the business. These expansion decisions may involve more uncertainties than replacement decisions, and these decisions will be more carefully considered.

3. New products and services. These investments expose the company to even more uncertainties than expansion projects. These decisions are more complex and will involve more people in the decision-making process.

4. Regulatory, safety, and environmental projects. These projects are frequently required by a governmental agency, an insurance company, or some other external party. They may generate no revenue and might not be undertaken by a company maximizing its own private interests. Often, the company will accept the required investment and continue to operate. Occasionally, however, the cost of the regulatory/safety/environmental project is sufficiently high that the company would do better to cease operating altogether or to shut down any part of the business that is related to the project.

5. Other. The projects above are all susceptible to capital budgeting analysis, and they can be accepted or rejected using the net present value (NPV) or some other criterion. Some projects escape such analysis. These are either pet projects of someone in the company (such as the CEO buying a new aircraft) or so risky that they are difficult to analyze by the usual methods (such as some research and development decisions).

3 BASIC PRINCIPLES OF CAPITAL BUDGETING

Capital budgeting has a rich history and sometimes employs some pretty sophisticated procedures. Fortunately, capital budgeting relies on just a few basic principles. Capital budgeting usually uses the following assumptions:

1. Decisions are based on cash flows. The decisions are not based on accounting concepts, such as net income. Furthermore, intangible costs and benefits are often ignored because, if they are real, they should result in cash flows at some other time.

2. Timing of cash flows is crucial. Analysts make an extraordinary effort to detail precisely when cash flows occur.

3. Cash flows are based on opportunity costs. What are the incremental cash flows that occur with an investment compared to what they would have been without the investment?

4. Cash flows are analyzed on an after-tax basis. Taxes must be fully reflected in all capital budgeting decisions.

5. Financing costs are ignored. This may seem unrealistic, but it is not. Most of the time, analysts want to know the after-tax operating cash flows that result from a capital investment. Then, these **after-tax cash flows** and the investment outlays are discounted at the "required rate of return" to find the **net present value** (NPV). Financing costs are reflected in the required rate of return. If we included financing costs in the cash flows and in the discount rate, we would be double-counting the financing costs. So even though a project may be financed with some combination of debt and equity, we ignore these costs, focusing on the operating cash flows and capturing the costs of debt (and other capital) in the discount rate.

Capital budgeting cash flows are not accounting net income. Accounting net income is reduced by noncash charges such as accounting depreciation. Furthermore, to reflect the cost of debt financing, interest expenses are also subtracted from accounting net income. (No subtraction is made for the cost of equity financing in arriving at accounting net income.) Accounting net income also differs from economic income, which is the cash inflow plus the change in the market value of the company. Economic income does not subtract the cost of debt financing, and it is based on the changes in the market value of the company, not changes in its book value (accounting depreciation). We will further consider cash flows, accounting income, **economic income**, and other income measures at the end of this reading.

In assumption 5 above, we referred to the rate used in discounting the cash flows as the "required rate of return." The **required rate of return** is the discount rate that investors should require given the riskiness of the project. This discount rate is frequently called the "opportunity cost of funds" or the "cost of capital." If the company can invest elsewhere and earn a return of r, or if the company can repay its sources of capital and save a cost of r, then r is the company's opportunity cost of funds. If the company cannot earn more than its opportunity cost of funds on an investment, it should not undertake that investment. Unless an investment earns more than the cost of funds from its suppliers of capital, the investment should not be undertaken. The cost-of-capital concept is discussed more extensively elsewhere. Regardless of what it is called, an economically sound discount rate is essential for making capital budgeting decisions.

Although the principles of capital budgeting are simple, they are easily confused in practice, leading to unfortunate decisions. Some important capital budgeting concepts that managers find very useful are given below.

▶ A **sunk cost** is one that has already been incurred. You cannot change a sunk cost. Today's decisions, on the other hand, should be based on current and future cash flows and should not be affected by prior, or sunk, costs.

▶ An **opportunity cost** is what a resource is worth in its next-best use. For example, if a company uses some idle property, what should it record as the investment outlay: the purchase price several years ago, the current market value, or nothing? If you replace an old machine with a new one, what is the opportunity cost? If you invest $10 million, what is the opportunity cost? The answers to these three questions are, respectively: the current market value, the cash flows the old machine would generate, and $10 million (which you could invest elsewhere).

▶ An **incremental cash flow** is the cash flow that is realized because of a decision: the cash flow *with* a decision minus the cash flow *without* that decision. If opportunity costs are correctly assessed, the incremental cash flows provide a sound basis for capital budgeting.

▶ An **externality** is the effect of an investment on other things besides the investment itself. Frequently, an investment affects the cash flows of other parts of the company, and these externalities can be positive or negative. If possible, these should be part of the investment decision. Sometimes externalities occur outside of the company. An investment might benefit (or harm) other companies or society at large, and yet the company is not compensated for these benefits (or charged for the costs). **Cannibalization** is one externality. Cannibalization occurs when an investment takes customers and sales away from another part of the company.

▶ Conventional versus nonconventional cash flows—A **conventional cash flow** pattern is one with an initial outflow followed by a series of inflows. In a **nonconventional cash flow** pattern, the initial outflow is not followed by inflows only, but the cash flows can flip from positive to negative again (or even change signs several times). An investment that involved outlays (negative cash flows) for the first couple of years that were then followed by positive cash flows would be considered to have a conventional pattern. If cash flows change signs once, the pattern is conventional. If cash flows change signs two or more times, the pattern is nonconventional.

Several types of project interactions make the incremental cash flow analysis challenging. The following are some of these interactions:

▶ **Independent versus mutually exclusive projects. Independent projects** are projects whose cash flows are independent of each other. **Mutually exclusive projects** compete directly with each other. For example, if Projects A and B are mutually exclusive, you can choose A or B, but you cannot choose both. Sometimes there are several mutually exclusive projects, and you can choose only one from the group.

▶ **Project sequencing.** Many projects are sequenced through time, so that investing in a project creates the option to invest in future projects. For example, you might invest in a project today and then in one year invest in a second project if the financial results of the first project or new economic conditions are favorable. If the results of the first project or new economic conditions are not favorable, you do not invest in the second project.

▶ **Unlimited funds versus capital rationing.** An **unlimited funds** environment assumes that the company can raise the funds it wants for all profitable projects simply by paying the required rate of return. **Capital rationing** exists when the company has a fixed amount of funds to invest. If the company has more profitable projects than it has funds for, it must allocate the funds to achieve the maximum shareholder value subject to the funding constraints.

4 INVESTMENT DECISION CRITERIA

Analysts use several important criteria to evaluate capital investments. The two most comprehensive measures of whether a project is profitable or unprofitable are the net present value (NPV) and internal rate of return (IRR). In addition to these, we present four other criteria that are frequently used: the payback period, discounted payback period, average accounting rate of return (AAR), and profitability index (PI). An analyst must fully understand the economic logic behind each of these investment decision criteria as well as its strengths and limitations in practice.

4.1 Net Present Value

For a project with one investment outlay, made initially, the **net present value (NPV)** is the present value of the future after-tax cash flows minus the investment outlay, or

$$\text{NPV} = \sum_{t=1}^{n} \frac{\text{CF}_t}{(1 + r)^t} - \text{Outlay} \qquad \textbf{(31-1)}$$

where

CF_t = after-tax cash flow at time t

r = required rate of return for the investment

Outlay = investment cash flow at time zero

To illustrate the net present value criterion, we will take a look at a simple example. Assume that Gerhardt Corporation is considering an investment of €50 million in a capital project that will return after-tax cash flows of €16 million per year for the next four years plus another €20 million in year five. The required rate of return is 10 percent.

For the Gerhardt example, the NPV would be

$$NPV = \frac{16}{1.10^1} + \frac{16}{1.10^2} + \frac{16}{1.10^3} + \frac{16}{1.10^4} + \frac{20}{1.10^5} - 50$$

$$NPV = 14.545 + 13.223 + 12.021 + 10.928 + 12.418 - 50$$

$$NPV = 63.136 - 50 = €13.136 \text{ million}[1]$$

The investment has a total value, or present value of future cash flows, of €63.136 million. Since this investment can be acquired at a cost of €50 million, the investing company is giving up €50 million of its wealth in exchange for an investment worth €63.136 million. The investor's wealth increases by a net of €13.136 million.

Because the NPV is the amount by which the investor's wealth increases as a result of the investment, the **decision rule** for the NPV is as follows:

Invest if   NPV > 0
Do not invest if   NPV < 0

Positive NPV investments are wealth-increasing, while negative NPV investments are wealth-decreasing.

Many investments have cash flow patterns in which outflows may occur not only at time zero, but also at future dates. It is useful to consider the NPV to be the present value of all cash flows:

$$NPV = CF_0 + \frac{CF_1}{(1 + r)^1} + \frac{CF_2}{(1 + r)^2} + \ldots + \frac{CF_n}{(1 + r)^n}, \text{ or}$$

$$NPV = \sum_{t=0}^{n} \frac{CF_t}{(1 + r)^t}$$

(31-2)

In Equation 31-2, the investment outlay, CF_0, is simply a negative cash flow. Future cash flows can also be negative.

4.2 Internal Rate of Return

The **internal rate of return (IRR)** is one of the most frequently used concepts in capital budgeting and in security analysis. The IRR definition is one that all analysts know by heart. For a project with one investment outlay, made initially, the IRR is the discount rate that makes the present value of the future after-tax cash flows equal that investment outlay. Written out in equation form, the IRR solves this equation:

$$\sum_{t=1}^{n} \frac{CF_t}{(1 + IRR)^t} = Outlay$$

---

[1] Occasionally, you will notice some rounding errors in our examples. In this case, the present values of the cash flows, as rounded, add up to 63.135. Without rounding, they add up to 63.13627, or 63.136. We will usually report the more accurate result, the one that you would get from your calculator or computer without rounding intermediate results.

where IRR is the internal rate of return. The left-hand side of this equation is the present value of the project's future cash flows, which, discounted at the IRR, equals the investment outlay. This equation will also be seen rearranged as

$$\sum_{t=1}^{n} \frac{CF_t}{(1 + IRR)^t} - \text{Outlay} = 0 \qquad \textbf{(31-3)}$$

In this form, Equation 31-3 looks like the NPV equation, Equation 31-1, except that the discount rate is the IRR instead of r (the required rate of return). Discounted at the IRR, the NPV is equal to zero.

In the Gerhardt Corporation example, we want to find a discount rate that makes the total present value of all cash flows, the NPV, equal zero. In equation form, the IRR is the discount rate that solves this equation:

$$-50 + \frac{16}{(1 + IRR)^1} + \frac{16}{(1 + IRR)^2} + \frac{16}{(1 + IRR)^3} + \frac{16}{(1 + IRR)^4} + \frac{20}{(1 + IRR)^5} = 0$$

Algebraically, this equation would be very difficult to solve. We normally resort to trial and error, systematically choosing various discount rates until we find one, the IRR, that satisfies the equation. We previously discounted these cash flows at 10 percent and found the NPV to be €13.136 million. Since the NPV is positive, the IRR is probably greater than 10 percent. If we use 20 percent as the discount rate, the NPV is −€0.543 million, so 20 percent is a little high. One might try several other discount rates until the NPV is equal to zero; this approach is illustrated in Table 1:

TABLE 1	Trial and Error Process for Finding IRR
Discount Rate	**NPV**
10%	13.136
20%	−0.543
19%	0.598
19.5%	0.022
19.51%	0.011
19.52%	0.000

The IRR is 19.52 percent. Financial calculators and spreadsheet software have routines that calculate the IRR for us, so we do not have to go through this trial and error procedure ourselves. The IRR, computed more precisely, is 19.5197 percent.

The decision rule for the IRR is to invest if the IRR exceeds the required rate of return for a project:

Invest if   IRR > r
Do not invest if   IRR < r

In the Gerhardt example, since the IRR of 19.52 percent exceeds the project's required rate of return of 10 percent, Gerhardt should invest.

Many investments have cash flow patterns in which the outlays occur at time zero and at future dates. Thus, it is common to define the IRR as the discount rate that makes the present values of all cash flows sum to zero:

$$\sum_{t=0}^{n} \frac{CF_t}{(1 + IRR)^t} = 0 \tag{31-4}$$

Equation 31-4 is a more general version of Equation 31-3.

4.3 Payback Period

The **payback** period is the number of years required to recover the original investment in a project. The payback is based on cash flows. For example, if you invest $10 million in a project, how long will it be until you recover the full original investment? Table 2 below illustrates the calculation of the payback period by following an investment's cash flows and cumulative cash flows.

TABLE 2	Payback Period Example					
Year	**0**	**1**	**2**	**3**	**4**	**5**
Cash flow	−10,000	2,500	2,500	3,000	3,000	3,000
Cumulative cash flow	−10,000	−7,500	−5,000	−2,000	1,000	4,000

In the first year, the company recovers 2,500 of the original investment, with 7,500 still unrecovered. You can see that the company recoups its original investment between Year 3 and Year 4. After three years, 2,000 is still unrecovered. Since the Year 4 cash flow is 3,000, it would take 2/3 of the Year 4 cash flow to bring the cumulative cash flow to zero. So, the payback period is 3 years plus 2/3 of the Year 4 cash flow, or 3.67 years.

The drawbacks of the payback period are transparent. Since the cash flows are not discounted at the project's required rate of return, the payback period ignores the **time value of money** and the risk of the project. Additionally, the payback period ignores cash flows after the payback period is reached. In the table above, for example, the Year 5 cash flow is completely ignored in the payback computation!

Example 1 below is designed to illustrate some of the implications of these drawbacks of the payback period.

EXAMPLE 1

Drawbacks of the Payback Period

The cash flows, payback periods, and NPVs for Projects A through F are given in Table 3. For all of the projects, the required rate of return is 10 percent.

TABLE 3   Examples of Drawbacks of the Payback Period

| | Cash Flows | | | | | |
Year	Project A	Project B	Project C	Project D	Project E	Project F
0	−1,000	−1,000	−1,000	−1,000	−1,000	−1,000
1	1,000	100	400	500	400	500
2		200	300	500	400	500
3		300	200	500	400	10,000
4		400	100		400	
5		500	500		400	
Payback period	1.0	4.0	4.0	2.0	2.5	2.0
NPV	−90.91	65.26	140.60	243.43	516.31	7,380.92

Comment on why the payback period provides misleading information about the following:

1. Project A
2. Project B versus Project C
3. Project D versus Project E
4. Project D versus Project F

Solution 1: Project A does indeed pay itself back in one year. However, this result is misleading because the investment is unprofitable, with a negative NPV.

Solution 2: Although Projects B and C have the same payback period and the same cash flow after the payback period, the payback period does not detect the fact that Project C's cash flows within the payback period occur earlier and result in a higher NPV.

Solution 3: Projects D and E illustrate a common situation. The project with the shorter payback period is the less profitable project. Project E has a longer payback and higher NPV.

Solution 4: Projects D and F illustrate an important flaw of the payback period—that the payback period ignores cash flows after the payback period is reached. In this case, Project F has a much larger cash flow in Year 3, but the payback period does not recognize its value.

The payback period has many drawbacks—it is a measure of payback and not a measure of profitability. By itself, the payback period would be a dangerous criterion for evaluating capital projects. Its simplicity, however, is an advantage. The payback period is very easy to calculate and to explain. The payback period may also be used as an indicator of project liquidity. A project with a two-year payback may be more liquid than another project with a longer payback.

Because it is not economically sound, the payback period has no decision rule like that of the NPV or IRR. If the payback period is being used (perhaps as a measure of liquidity), analysts should also use an NPV or IRR to ensure that their decisions also reflect the profitability of the projects being considered.

4.4 Discounted Payback Period

The discounted payback period is the number of years it takes for the cumulative discounted cash flows from a project to equal the original investment. The discounted payback period partially addresses the weaknesses of the payback period. Table 4 gives an example of calculating the payback period and discounted payback period. The example assumes a discount rate of 10 percent.

TABLE 4	Payback Period and Discounted Payback Period					
Year	**0**	**1**	**2**	**3**	**4**	**5**
Cash flow (CF)	−5,000	1,500.00	1,500.00	1,500.00	1,500.00	1,500.00
Cumulative CF	−5,000	−3,500.00	−2,000.00	−500.00	1,000.00	2,500.00
Discounted CF	−5,000	1,363.64	1,239.67	1,126.97	1,024.52	931.38
Cumulative discounted CF	−5,000	−3,636.36	−2,396.69	−1,269.72	−245.20	686.18

The payback period is 3 years plus $500/1500 = 1/3$ of the fourth year's cash flow, or 3.33 years. The discounted payback period is between four and five years. The discounted payback period is 4 years plus $245.20/931.38 = 0.26$ of the fifth year's discounted cash flow, or 4.26 years.

The discounted payback period relies on discounted cash flows, much as the NPV criterion does. If a project has a negative NPV, it will usually not have a discounted payback period since it never recovers the initial investment.

The discounted payback does account for the time value of money and risk within the discounted payback period, but it ignores cash flows after the discounted payback period is reached. This drawback has two consequences. First, the discounted payback period is not a good measure of profitability (like the NPV or IRR) because it ignores these cash flows. Second, another idiosyncrasy of the discounted payback period comes from the possibility of negative cash flows after the discounted payback period is reached. It is possible for a project to have a negative NPV but to have a positive cumulative discounted cash flow in the middle of its life and, thus, a reasonable discounted payback period. The NPV and IRR, which consider all of a project's cash flows, do not suffer from this problem.

4.5 Average Accounting Rate of Return

The average accounting rate of return (AAR) can be defined as

$$AAR = \frac{\text{Average net income}}{\text{Average book value}}$$

To understand this measure of return, we will use a numerical example.

Assume a company invests $200,000 in a project that is depreciated straight-line over a five-year life to a zero salvage value. Sales revenues and **cash operating expenses** for each year are as shown in Table 5. The table also shows the annual income taxes (at a 40 percent tax rate) and the net income.

TABLE 5   Net Income for Calculating an Average Accounting Rate of Return

	Year 1	Year 2	Year 3	Year 4	Year 5
Sales	$100,000	$150,000	$240,000	$130,000	$80,000
Cash expenses	50,000	70,000	120,000	60,000	50,000
Depreciation	40,000	40,000	40,000	40,000	40,000
Earnings before taxes	10,000	40,000	80,000	30,000	−10,000
Taxes (at 40 percent)	4,000	16,000	32,000	12,000	−4,000[a]
Net income	6,000	24,000	48,000	18,000	−6,000

[a] Negative taxes occur in Year 5 because the earnings before taxes of −$10,000 can be deducted against earnings on other projects, thus reducing the tax bill by $4,000.

For the five-year period, the average net income is $18,000. The initial book value is $200,000, declining by $40,000 per year until the final book value is $0. The average book value for this asset is ($200,000 − $0) / 2 = $100,000. The average accounting rate of return is

$$AAR = \frac{\text{Average net income}}{\text{Average book value}} = \frac{18,000}{100,000} = 18\%$$

The advantages of the AAR are that it is easy to understand and easy to calculate. The AAR has some important disadvantages, however. Unlike the other capital budgeting criteria discussed here, the AAR is based on accounting numbers and not based on cash flows. This is an important conceptual and practical limitation. The AAR also does not account for the time value of money, and there is no conceptually sound cutoff for the AAR that distinguishes between profitable and unprofitable investments. The AAR is frequently calculated in different ways, so the analyst should verify the formula behind any AAR numbers that are supplied by someone else. Analysts should know the AAR and its potential limitations in practice, but they should rely on more economically sound methods like the NPV and IRR.

4.6 Profitability Index

The **profitability index** (PI) is the present value of a project's future cash flows divided by the initial investment. It can be expressed as

$$PI = \frac{PV \text{ of future cash flows}}{\text{Initial investment}} = 1 + \frac{NPV}{\text{Initial investment}} \qquad \textbf{(31-5)}$$

You can see that the PI is closely related to the NPV. The PI is the *ratio* of the PV of future cash flows to the initial investment, while an NPV is the *difference* between the PV of future cash flows and the initial investment. Whenever the NPV is positive, the PI will be greater than 1.0, and conversely, whenever the NPV is negative, the PI will be less than 1.0. The investment decision rule for the PI is as follows:

Invest if   PI > 1.0
Do not invest if   PI < 1.0

Because the PV of future cash flows equals the initial investment plus the NPV, the PI can also be expressed as 1.0 plus the ratio of the NPV to the initial investment, as shown in Equation 31-5 above. Example 2 illustrates the PI calculation.

EXAMPLE 2

Example of a PI Calculation

The Gerhardt Corporation investment (discussed earlier) had an outlay of €50 million, a present value of future cash flows of €63.136 million, and an NPV of €13.136 million. The profitability index is

$$PI = \frac{PV \text{ of future cash flows}}{\text{Initial investment}} = \frac{63.136}{50.000} = 1.26$$

The PI can also be calculated as

$$PI = 1 + \frac{NPV}{\text{Initial investment}} = 1 + \frac{13.136}{50.000} = 1.26$$

Because the PI > 1.0, this is a profitable investment.

The PI indicates the value you are receiving in exchange for one unit of currency invested. Although the PI is used less frequently than the NPV and IRR, it is sometimes used as a guide in capital rationing, which we will discuss later. The PI is usually called the profitability index in corporations, but it is commonly referred to as a "benefit-cost ratio" in governmental and not-for-profit organizations.

4.7 NPV Profile

The NPV profile shows a project's NPV graphed as a function of various discount rates. Typically, the NPV is graphed vertically (on the *y*-axis) and the discount rates are graphed horizontally (on the *x*-axis). The NPV profile for the Gerhardt capital budgeting project is shown in Example 3.

EXAMPLE 3

NPV Profile

For the Gerhardt example, we have already calculated several NPVs for different discount rates. At 10 percent the NPV is €13.136 million; at 20 percent the NPV is −€0.543 million; and at 19.52 percent (the IRR), the NPV is zero. What is the NPV if the discount rate is 0 percent? The NPV discounted at 0 percent is €34 million, which is simply the sum of all of the undiscounted cash flows. Table 6 and Figure 1 show the NPV profile for the Gerhardt example for discount rates between 0 percent and 30 percent.

TABLE 6   Gerhardt NPV Profile

Discount Rate	NPV (in € millions)
0%	34.000
5.00%	22.406
10.00%	13.136
15.00%	5.623
19.52%	0.000
20.00%	−0.543
25.00%	−5.661
30.00%	−9.954

FIGURE 1   Gerhardt NPV Profile

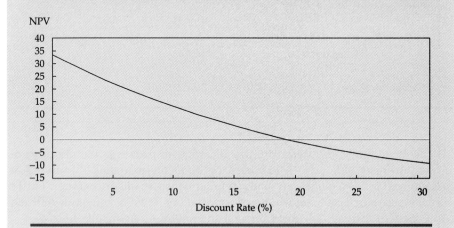

Three interesting points on this NPV profile are where the profile goes through the vertical axis (the NPV when the discount rate is zero), where the profile goes through the horizontal axis (where the discount rate is the IRR), and the NPV for the required rate of return (NPV is €13.136 million when the discount rate is the 10 percent required rate of return).

The NPV profile in Figure 1 is very well-behaved. The NPV declines at a decreasing rate as the discount rate increases. The profile is convex from the **origin** (convex from below). You will shortly see some examples in which the NPV profile is more complicated.

4.8 Ranking Conflicts between NPV and IRR

For a single conventional project, the NPV and IRR will agree on whether to invest or to not invest. For independent, conventional projects, no conflict exists between the decision rules for the NPV and IRR. However, in the case of two mutually exclusive projects, the two criteria will sometimes disagree. For example, Project A might have a larger NPV than Project B, but Project B has a higher IRR than Project A. In this case, should you invest in Project A or in Project B?

Differing cash flow patterns can cause two projects to rank differently with the NPV and IRR. For example, suppose Project A has shorter-term payoffs than Project B. This situation is presented in Example 4.

EXAMPLE 4

Ranking Conflict due to Differing Cash Flow Patterns

Projects A and B have similar outlays but different patterns of future cash flows. Project A realizes most of its cash payoffs earlier than Project B. The cash flows as well as the NPV and IRR for the two projects are shown in Table 7. For both projects, the required rate of return is 10 percent.

TABLE 7   Cash Flows, NPV, and IRR for Two Projects with Different Cash Flow Patterns

| | Cash Flows | | | | | | |
Year	0	1	2	3	4	NPV	IRR
Project A	−200	80	80	80	80	53.59	21.86%
Project B	−200	0	0	0	400	73.21	18.92%

If the two projects were not mutually exclusive, you would invest in both because they are both profitable. However, you can choose either A (which has the higher IRR) or B (which has the higher NPV).

Table 8 and Figure 2 show the NPVs for Project A and Project B for various discount rates between 0 percent and 30 percent.

TABLE 8	NPV Profiles for Two Projects with Different Cash Flow Patterns	
Discount Rate	NPV for Project A	NPV for Project B
0%	120.00	200.00
5.00%	83.68	129.08
10.00%	53.59	73.21
15.00%	28.40	28.70
15.09%	27.98	27.98
18.92%	11.41	0.00
20.00%	7.10	−7.10
21.86%	0.00	−18.62
25.00%	−11.07	−36.16
30.00%	−26.70	−59.95

FIGURE 2   NPV Profiles for Two Projects with Different Cash Flow Patterns

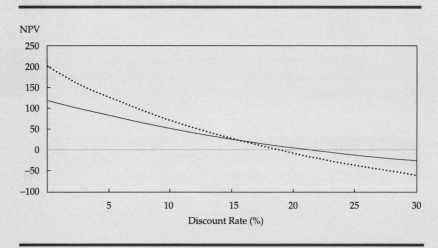

Note that Project B has the higher NPV for discount rates between 0 percent and 15.09 percent. Project A has the higher NPV for discount rates exceeding 15.09 percent. The crossover point of 15.09 percent in Figure 2 corresponds to the discount rate at which both projects have the same NPV (of 27.98). Project B has the higher NPV below the crossover point, and Project A has the higher NPV above it.

Whenever the NPV and IRR rank two mutually exclusive projects differently, as they do in the example above, you should choose the project based on the NPV. Project B, with the higher NPV, is the better project because of the **reinvestment** assumption. Mathematically, whenever you discount a cash flow at a particular discount rate, you are implicitly assuming that you can reinvest a cash flow at that same discount rate.[2] In the NPV calculation, you use a discount rate of 10 percent for both projects. In the IRR calculation, you use a discount rate equal to the IRR of 21.86 percent for Project A and 18.92 percent for Project B.

Can you reinvest the cash inflows from the projects at 10 percent, or 21.86 percent, or 18.92 percent? When you assume the required rate of return is 10 percent, you are assuming an opportunity cost of 10 percent—you are assuming that you can either find other projects that pay a 10 percent return or pay back your sources of capital that cost you 10 percent. The fact that you earned 21.86 percent in Project A or 18.92 percent in Project B does not mean that you can reinvest future cash flows at those rates. (In fact, if you can reinvest future cash flows at 21.86 percent or 18.92 percent, these should have been used as your required rate of return instead of 10 percent.) Because the NPV criterion uses the most realistic discount rate—the opportunity cost of funds—the NPV criterion should be used for evaluating mutually exclusive projects.

Another circumstance that frequently causes mutually exclusive projects to be ranked differently by NPV and IRR criteria is project scale—the sizes of the projects. Would you rather have a small project with a higher rate of return or a large project with a lower rate of return? Sometimes, the larger, low rate of return project has the better NPV. This case is developed in Example 5.

EXAMPLE 5

Ranking Conflicts due to Differing Project Scale

Project A has a much smaller outlay than Project B, although they have similar future cash flow patterns. The cash flows as well as the NPVs and IRRs for the two projects are shown in Table 9. For both projects, the required rate of return is 10 percent.

TABLE 9   Cash Flows, NPV, and IRR for Two Projects of Differing Scale

		Cash Flows					
Year	0	1	2	3	4	NPV	IRR
Project A	−100	50	50	50	50	58.49	34.90%
Project B	−400	170	170	170	170	138.88	25.21%

If they were not mutually exclusive, you would invest in both projects because they are both profitable. However, you can choose either Project A (which has the higher IRR) or Project B (which has the higher NPV).

[2] For example, assume that you are receiving $100 in one year discounted at 10 percent. The present value is $100/1.10 = $90.91. Instead of receiving the $100 in one year, invest it for one additional year at 10 percent, and it grows to $110. What is the present value of $110 received in two years discounted at 10 percent? It is the same $90.91. Because both future cash flows are worth the same, you are implicitly assuming that reinvesting the earlier cash flow at the discount rate of 10 percent has no effect on its value.

Table 10 and Figure 3 show the NPVs for Project A and Project B for various discount rates between 0 percent and 30 percent.

TABLE 10	NPV Profiles for Two Projects of Differing Scale	
Discount Rate	**NPV for Project A**	**NPV for Project B**
0%	100.00	280.00
5.00%	77.30	202.81
10.00%	58.49	138.88
15.00%	42.75	85.35
20.00%	29.44	40.08
21.86%	25.00	25.00
25.00%	18.08	1.47
25.21%	17.65	0.00
30.00%	8.31	−31.74
34.90%	0.00	−60.00
35.00%	−0.15	−60.52

FIGURE 3   NPV Profiles for Two Projects of Differing Scale

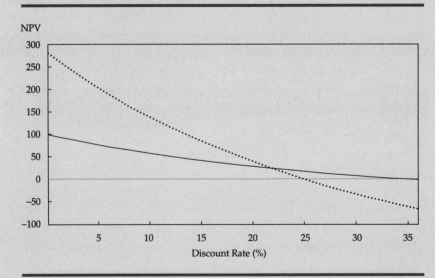

Note that Project B has the higher NPV for discount rates between 0 percent and 21.86 percent. Project A has the higher NPV for discount rates exceeding 21.86 percent. The crossover point of 21.86 percent in Figure 3 corresponds to the discount rate at which both projects have the same NPV (of 25.00). Below the crossover point, Project B has the higher NPV, and above it, Project A has the higher NPV. When cash flows are discounted at the 10 percent required rate of return, the choice is clear—Project B, the larger project, which has the superior NPV.

The good news is that the NPV and IRR criteria will usually indicate the same investment decision for a given project. They will usually both recommend acceptance or rejection of the project. When the choice is between two mutually exclusive projects and the NPV and IRR rank the two projects differently, the NPV criterion is strongly preferred. There are good reasons for this preference. The NPV shows the amount of gain, or wealth increase, as a currency amount. The reinvestment assumption of the NPV is the more economically realistic. The IRR does give you a rate of return, but the IRR could be for a small investment or for only a short period of time. As a practical matter, once a corporation has the data to calculate the NPV, it is fairly trivial to go ahead and calculate the IRR and other capital budgeting criteria. However, the most appropriate and theoretically sound criterion is the NPV.

4.9 The Multiple IRR Problem and the No IRR Problem

A problem that can arise with the IRR criterion is the "multiple IRR problem." We can illustrate this problem with the following nonconventional cash flow pattern:[3]

Time	0	1	2
Cash Flow	−1,000	5,000	−6,000

The IRR for these cash flows satisfies this equation:

$$-1,000 + \frac{5,000}{(1 + \text{IRR})^1} + \frac{-6,000}{(1 + \text{IRR})^2} = 0$$

It turns out that there are two values of IRR that satisfy the equation: IRR = 1 = 100% and IRR = 2 = 200%. To further understand this problem, consider the NPV profile for this investment, which is shown in Table 11 and Figure 4.

TABLE 11	NPV Profile for a Multiple IRR Example
Discount Rate	**NPV**
0%	−2,000.00
25%	−840.00
50%	−333.33
75%	−102.04
100%	0.00
125%	37.04
140%	41.67
150%	40.00
175%	24.79
200%	0.00
225%	−29.59
250%	−61.22

(Table continued on next page . . .)

---

[3] This example is adapted from Hirschleifer (1958).

TABLE 11 (continued)	
Discount Rate	**NPV**
300%	−125.00
350%	−185.19
400%	−240.00
500%	−333.33
1,000%	−595.04
2,000%	−775.51
3,000%	−844.95
4,000%	−881.62
10,000%	−951.08
1,000,000%	−999.50

FIGURE 4   NPV Profile for a Multiple IRR Example

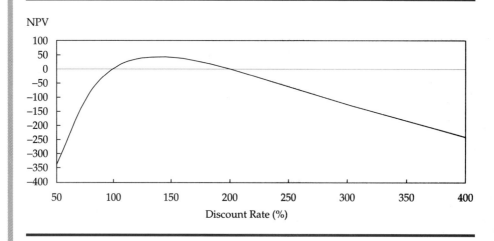

As you can see in the NPV profile, the NPV is equal to zero at IRR = 100% and IRR = 200%. The NPV is negative for discount rates below 100 percent, positive between 100 percent and 200 percent, and then negative above 200 percent. The NPV reaches its highest value when the discount rate is 140 percent.

It is also possible to have an investment project with no IRR. The "no-IRR problem" occurs with this cash flow pattern:[4]

Time	0	1	2
Cash Flow	100	−300	250

The IRR for these cash flows satisfies this equation:

$$100 + \frac{-300}{(1 + \text{IRR})^1} + \frac{250}{(1 + \text{IRR})^2} = 0$$

---

[4] This example is also adapted from Hirschleifer.

For these cash flows, no discount rate exists that results in a zero NPV. Does that mean this project is a bad investment? In this case, the project is actually a good investment. As Table 12 and Figure 5 show, the NPV is positive for all discount rates. The lowest NPV, of 10, occurs for a discount rate of 66.67 percent, and the NPV is always greater than zero. Consequently, no IRR exists.

TABLE 12 NPV Profile for a Project with No IRR	
Discount Rate	**NPV**
0%	50.00
25%	20.00
50%	11.11
66.67%	10.00
75%	10.20
100%	12.50
125%	16.05
150%	20.00
175%	23.97
200%	27.78
225%	31.36
250%	34.69
275%	37.78
300%	40.63
325%	43.25
350%	45.68
375%	47.92
400%	50.00

FIGURE 5 NPV Profile for a Project with No IRR

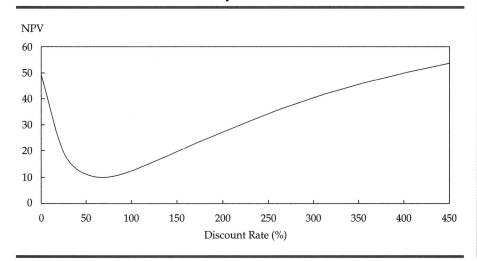

For conventional projects that have outlays followed by inflows—negative cash flows followed by positive cash flows—the multiple IRR problem cannot occur. However, for nonconventional projects, as in the example above, the multiple IRR problem can occur. The IRR equation is essentially an nth degree polynomial. An nth degree polynomial can have up to n solutions, although it will have no more real solutions than the number of cash flow sign changes. For example, a project with two sign changes could have zero, one, or two IRRs. Having two sign changes does not mean that you *will* have multiple IRRs; it just means that you *might*. Fortunately, most capital budgeting projects have only one IRR. Analysts should always be aware of the unusual cash flow patterns that can generate the multiple IRR problem.

4.10 Popularity and Usage of the Capital Budgeting Methods

Analysts need to know the basic logic of the various capital budgeting criteria as well as the practicalities involved in using them in real corporations. Before delving into the many issues involved in applying these models, we would like to present some feedback on their popularity.

The usefulness of any analytical tool always depends on the specific application. Corporations generally find these capital budgeting criteria useful. Two recent surveys by Graham and Harvey (2001) and Brounen, De Jong, and Koedijk (2004) report on the frequency of their use by U.S. and European corporations. Table 13 gives the mean responses of executives in five countries to the question "How frequently does your company use the following techniques when deciding which projects or acquisitions to pursue?"

TABLE 13	Mean Responses about Frequency of Use of Capital Budgeting Techniques				
	U.S.	U.K.	Netherlands	Germany	France
Internal rate of return[a]	3.09	2.31	2.36	2.15	2.27
Net present value[a]	3.08	2.32	2.76	2.26	1.86
Payback period[a]	2.53	2.77	2.53	2.29	2.46
Hurdle rate	2.13	1.35	1.98	1.61	0.73
Sensitivity analysis	2.31	2.21	1.84	1.65	0.79
Earnings **multiple** approach	1.89	1.81	1.61	1.25	1.70
Discounted payback period[a]	1.56	1.49	1.25	1.59	0.87
Real options approach	1.47	1.65	1.49	2.24	2.20
Accounting rate of return[a]	1.34	1.79	1.40	1.63	1.11
Value at risk	0.95	0.85	0.51	1.45	1.68
Adjusted present value	0.85	0.78	0.78	0.71	1.11
Profitability index[a]	0.85	1.00	0.78	1.04	1.64

Note: Respondents used a scale ranging from 0 (never) to 4 (always).

[a] These techniques were described in this section of the reading. You will encounter the others elsewhere.

Although financial textbooks preach the superiority of the NPV and IRR techniques, it is clear that several other methods are heavily used.[5] In the four European countries, the payback period is used as often as, or even slightly more often than, the NPV and IRR. In these two studies, larger companies tended to prefer the NPV and IRR over the payback period. The fact that the U.S. companies were larger, on average, partially explains the greater U.S. preference for the NPV and IRR. Other factors influence the choice of capital budgeting techniques. Private corporations used the payback period more frequently than did public corporations. Companies managed by an MBA had a stronger preference for the discounted cash flow techniques. Of course, any survey research also has some limitations. In this case, the persons in these large corporations responding to the surveys may not have been aware of all of the applications of these techniques.

These capital budgeting techniques are essential tools for corporate managers. Capital budgeting is also relevant to external analysts. Because a corporation's investing decisions ultimately determine the value of its financial obligations, the corporation's investing processes are vital. The NPV criterion is the criterion most directly related to stock prices. If a corporation invests in positive NPV projects, these should add to the wealth of its shareholders. Example 6 illustrates this scenario.

EXAMPLE 6

NPVs and Stock Prices

Freitag Corporation is investing €600 million in distribution facilities. The present value of the future after-tax cash flows is estimated to be €850 million. Freitag has 200 million outstanding shares with a current market price of €32.00 per share. This investment is new information, and it is independent of other expectations about the company. What should be the effect of the project on the value of the company and the stock price?

Solution: The NPV of the project is €850 million − €600 million = €250 million. The total market value of the company prior to the investment is €32.00 × 200 million shares = €6,400 million. The value of the company should increase by €250 million to €6,650 million. The price per share should increase by the NPV per share, or €250 million / 200 million shares = €1.25 per share. The share price should increase from €32.00 to €33.25.

The effect of a capital budgeting project's positive or negative NPV on share price is more complicated than Example 6 above, in which the value of the stock increased by the project's NPV. The value of a company is the value of its existing investments plus the net present values of all of its future investments. If an analyst learns of an investment, the impact of that investment on the stock price will depend on whether the investment's profitability is more or less than expected. For example, an analyst could learn of a positive NPV project, but if the project's profitability is less than expectations, this stock might drop in price on the news.

[5] Analysts often refer to the NPV and IRR as "discounted cash flow techniques" because they accurately account for the timing of all cash flows when they are discounted.

Alternatively, news of a particular capital project might be considered as a signal about other capital projects underway or in the future. A project that by itself might add, say, €0.25 to the value of the stock might signal the existence of other profitable projects. News of this project might increase the stock price by far more than €0.25.

The integrity of a corporation's capital budgeting processes is important to analysts. Management's capital budgeting processes can demonstrate two things about the quality of management: the degree to which management embraces the goal of shareholder wealth maximization, and its effectiveness in pursuing that goal. Both of these factors are important to shareholders.

5 CASH FLOW PROJECTIONS

In Section 4, we presented the basic capital budgeting models that managers use to accept or reject capital budgeting proposals. In that section, we assumed the cash flows were given, and we used them as inputs to the analysis. In Section 5, we detail how these cash flows are found for an "expansion" project. An expansion project is an independent investment that does not affect the cash flows for the rest of the company. In Section 6, we will deal with a "replacement" project, in which the cash flow analysis is more complicated. A replacement project must deal with the differences between the cash flows that occur with the new investment and the cash flows that would have occurred for the investment being replaced.

5.1 Table Format with Cash Flows Collected by Year

The cash flows for a conventional expansion project can be grouped into (1) the investment outlays, (2) after-tax operating cash flows over the project's life, and (3) terminal year after-tax non-operating cash flows. Table 14 gives an example of the cash flows for a capital project where all of the cash flows are collected by year.

The investment outlays include a $200,000 outlay for fixed capital items. This outlay includes $25,000 for nondepreciable land, plus $175,000 for equipment that will be depreciated straight-line to zero over five years. The investment in net working capital is the net investment in short-term assets required for the investment. This is the investment in **receivables** and inventory needed, less the short-term payables generated by the project. In this case, the project required $50,000 of current assets but generated $20,000 in current liabilities, resulting in a total investment in **net working capital** of $30,000. The total investment outlay at time zero is $230,000.

Each year, sales will be $220,000 and cash operating expenses will be $90,000. Annual depreciation for the $175,000 depreciable equipment is $35,000 (one-fifth of the cost). The result is an operating income before taxes of $95,000. Income taxes at a 40 percent rate are $0.40 \times \$95,000 = \$38,000$. This leaves operating income after taxes of $57,000. Adding back the depreciation charge of $35,000 gives the annual after-tax operating cash flow of $92,000.[6]

---

[6] Examining the operating cash flows in Table 14, we have a $220,000 inflow from sales, a $90,000 outflow for cash operating expenses, and a $38,000 outflow for taxes. This is an after-tax cash flow of $92,000.

TABLE 14 Capital Budgeting Cash Flows Example (Cash Flows Collected by Year)						
Year	**0**	**1**	**2**	**3**	**4**	**5**
Investment outlays:						
Fixed capital	−200,000					
Net working capital	−30,000					
Total	−230,000					
Annual after-tax operating cash flows:						
Sales		220,000	220,000	220,000	220,000	220,000
Cash operating expenses		90,000	90,000	90,000	90,000	90,000
Depreciation		35,000	35,000	35,000	35,000	35,000
Operating income before taxes		95,000	95,000	95,000	95,000	95,000
Taxes on operating income		38,000	38,000	38,000	38,000	38,000
Operating income after taxes		57,000	57,000	57,000	57,000	57,000
Add back: Depreciation		35,000	35,000	35,000	35,000	35,000
After-tax operating cash flow		92,000	92,000	92,000	92,000	92,000
Terminal year after-tax non-operating cash flows:						
After-tax salvage value						40,000
Return of net working capital						30,000
Total						70,000
Total after-tax cash flow	−230,000	92,000	92,000	92,000	92,000	162,000
Net present value at 10 percent required rate of return	162,217					
Internal rate of return	32.70%					

At the end of year five, the company will sell off the fixed capital assets. In this case, the fixed capital assets (including the land) are sold for $50,000, which represents a gain of $25,000 over the remaining book value of $25,000. The gain of $25,000 is taxed at 40 percent, resulting in a tax of $10,000. This leaves $40,000 for the fixed capital assets after taxes. Additionally, the net working capital investment of $30,000 is recovered, as the short-term assets (such as inventory and receivables) and short-term liabilities (such as payables) are no longer needed for the project. Total terminal year non-operating cash flows are then $70,000.

The investment project has a required rate of return of 10 percent. **Discounting** the future cash flows at 10 percent and subtracting the investment outlay gives an NPV of $162,217. The internal rate of return is 32.70 percent. Because the investment has a positive NPV, this project should be accepted. The IRR investment decision criterion would also recommend accepting the project because the IRR is greater than the required rate of return.

5.2 Table Format with Cash Flows Collected by Type

In the layout in Table 14, we essentially collected the cash flows in the columns, by *year*, and then found the NPV by summing the present values of the annual cash flows (at the bottom of each column). There is another way of organizing the same information. We could also find the NPV by finding the present values of the cash flows in Table 14 by rows, which are the *types* of cash flows. This approach is shown in Table 15:

TABLE 15	Capital Budgeting Cash Flows Example (Cash Flows Collected by Type)			
Time	Type of Cash Flow	Before-Tax Cash Flow	After-Tax Cash Flow	PV at 10%
0	Fixed capital	−200,000	−200,000	−200,000
0	Net working capital	−30,000	−30,000	−30,000
1–5	Sales minus cash expenses	220,000 − 90,000 = 130,000	130,000(1 − 0.40) = 78,000	295,681
1–5	Depreciation tax savings	None	0.40(35,000) = 14,000	53,071
5	After-tax salvage value	50,000	50,000 − 0.40(50,000 − 25,000) = 40,000	24,837
5	Return of net working capital	30,000	30,000	18,628
			NPV=	162,217

As Table 15 shows, the outlays in fixed capital and in net working capital at time zero total $230,000. For Years 1 though 5, the company realizes an after-tax cash flow for sales minus cash expenses of $78,000, which has a present value of $295,681. The depreciation charge results in a tax savings of $14,000 per year, which has a present value of $53,071. The present values of the after-tax salvage and of the return of net working capital are also shown in the table. The present value of all cash flows is an NPV of $162,217. Obviously, collecting the after-tax cash flows by year, as in Table 14, or by type, as in Table 15, results in the same NPV.

5.3 Equation Format for Organizing Cash Flows

The capital budgeting cash flows in the example project above were laid out in one of two alternative tabular formats. Analysts may wish to take even another approach. Instead of producing a table, you can also look at the cash flows using equations such as the following:

(1) Initial outlay: For a new investment:
　　Outlay = FCInv + NWCInv

where
　　　FCInv = Investment in new fixed capital
　　　NWCInv = Investment in net working capital

The above equation can be generalized for a replacement project (covered in Section 6.2), in which existing fixed capital is sold and provides some of the funding for the new fixed capital purchased. The outlay is then

$$\text{Outlay} = \text{FCInv} + \text{NWCInv} - \text{Sal}_0 + T(\text{Sal}_0 - B_0) \qquad \textbf{(31-6)}$$

where

Sal_0 = Cash proceeds (salvage value) from sale of old fixed capital
T = Tax rate
B_0 = Book value of old fixed capital

(2) Annual after-tax operating cash flow:

$$CF = (S - C - D)(1 - T) + D, \text{ or} \qquad \textbf{(31-7)}$$

$$CF = (S - C)(1 - T) + TD \qquad \textbf{(31-8)}$$

where

S = sales
C = cash operating expenses
D = depreciation charge

(3) Terminal year after-tax non-operating cash flow:

$$\text{TNOCF} = \text{Sal}_T + \text{NWCInv} - T(\text{Sal}_T - B_T) \qquad \textbf{(31-9)}$$

where

Sal_T = Cash proceeds (salvage value) from sale of fixed capital on **termination date**
B_T = Book value of fixed capital on termination date

The outlay in the example is found with Equation 31-6:

$$\text{Outlay} = 200,000 + 30,000 - 0 + 0 = \$230,000$$

For a replacement project, the old fixed capital would be sold for cash (Sal_0) and then there would be taxes paid on the gain (if $\text{Sal}_0 - B_0$ were positive) or a tax saving (if $\text{Sal}_0 - B_0$ were negative). In this example, Sal_0 and $T(\text{Sal}_0 - B_0)$ are zero because no existing fixed capital is sold at time zero.

Using Equation 31-7, we find that the annual after-tax operating cash flow is

$$
\begin{aligned}
CF &= (S - C - D)(1 - T) + D \\
&= (220,000 - 90,000 - 35,000)(1 - 0.40) + 35,000 = 95,000 \\
&\quad \times (0.60) + 35,000 \\
&= 57,000 + 35,000 = \$92,000
\end{aligned}
$$

Equation 31-7 is the project's **net income plus depreciation.** An identical cash flow results if we use Equation 31-8:

$$
\begin{aligned}
CF &= (S - C)(1 - T) + TD \\
&= (220,000 - 90,000)(1 - 0.40) + 0.40(35,000) \\
&= 130,000(0.60) + 0.40(35,000) = 78,000 + 14,000 = \$92,000
\end{aligned}
$$

Equation 31-8 is the after-tax sales and cash expenses plus the depreciation tax savings. The analyst can use either equation.

Equation 31-9 provides the terminal year non-operating cash flow:

$$\text{TNOCF} = \text{Sal}_T + \text{NWCInv} - T(\text{Sal}_T - B_T)$$
$$= 50{,}000 + 30{,}000 - 0.40(50{,}000 - 25{,}000)$$
$$= 50{,}000 + 30{,}000 - 10{,}000 = \$70{,}000$$

The old fixed capital (including land) is sold for \$50,000, but \$10,000 of taxes must be paid on the gain. Including the \$30,000 return of net working capital gives a terminal year non-operating cash flow of \$70,000.

The NPV of the project is the present value of the cash flows—an outlay of \$230,000 at time zero, an annuity of \$92,000 for five years, plus a single payment of \$70,000 in five years:

$$NPV = -230{,}000 + \sum_{t=1}^{5} \frac{92{,}000}{(1.10)^t} + \frac{70{,}000}{(1.10)^5}$$
$$= -230{,}000 + 348{,}752 + 43{,}465 = \$162{,}217$$

We obtain an identical NPV of \$162,217 whether we use a tabular format collecting cash flows by year, a tabular format collecting cash flows by type, or an equation format using Equations 31-6 through 31-9. The analyst usually has some flexibility in choosing how to solve a problem. Furthermore, the analysis that an analyst receives from someone else could be in varying formats. The analyst must interpret this information correctly regardless of format. An analyst may need to present information in alternative formats, depending on what the client or user of the information wishes to see. All that is important is that the cash flows are complete (with no cash flows omitted and none double-counted), that their timing is recognized, and that the discounting is done correctly.

6   MORE ON CASH FLOW PROJECTIONS

Cash flow analysis can become fairly complicated. Section 6 extends the analysis of the previous section to include more details on depreciation methods, replacement projects (as opposed to simple expansion projects), the use of spreadsheets, and the effects of inflation.

6.1 Straight-Line and Accelerated Depreciation Methods

Before going on to more complicated investment decisions, we should mention the variety of depreciation methods that are in use. The example in Section 5.1 assumed straight-line depreciation down to a zero salvage value. Most accounting texts give a good description of the straight-line method, the sum-of-years digits method, the double-declining balance method (and the 150 percent declining balance method), and the units-of-production and service hours method.[7]

---

[7] White, Sondhi, and Fried (2003) is a good example. Consult their Chapter 8, "Analysis of Long-Lived Assets: Part II—Analysis of Depreciation and Impairment," for review and examples.

Many countries specify the depreciation methods that are acceptable for tax purposes in their jurisdictions. For example, in the U.S., corporations use the **MACRS (modified accelerated cost recovery system)** for tax purposes. Under MACRS, real property (real estate) is usually depreciated straight-line over a 27.5- or 39-year life, and other capital assets are usually grouped into MACRS asset classes and subject to a special depreciation schedule in each class. These MACRS classes and the depreciation rates for each class are shown in Table 16.

For the first four MACRS classes (3-year, 5-year, 7-year, and 10-year), the depreciation is double-declining-balance with a switch to straight-line when optimal and with a half-year convention. For the last two classes (15-year and 20-year), the depreciation is 150 percent-declining-balance with a switch to straight-line when optimal and with a half-year convention. Take 5-year property in Table 16 as an example. With double-declining-balance, the depreciation each year is $2/5 = 40\%$ of the beginning-of-year book value. However, with a half-year convention, the asset is assumed to be in service for only six months during the first year, and only one-half of the depreciation is allowed the first year. After the

TABLE 16 Depreciation Rates under U.S. MACRS

	Recovery Period Class					
Year	3-Year	5-Year	7-Year	10-Year	15-Year	20-Year
1	33.33%	20.00%	14.29%	10.00%	5.00%	3.75%
2	44.45	32.00	24.49	18.00	9.50	7.22
3	14.81	19.20	17.49	14.40	8.55	6.68
4	7.41	11.52	12.49	11.52	7.70	6.18
5		11.52	8.93	9.22	6.93	5.71
6		5.76	8.93	7.37	6.23	5.28
7			8.93	6.55	5.90	4.89
8			4.45	6.55	5.90	4.52
9				6.55	5.90	4.46
10				6.55	5.90	4.46
11				3.29	5.90	4.46
12					5.90	4.46
13					5.90	4.46
14					5.90	4.46
15					5.90	4.46
16					2.99	4.46
17						4.46
18						4.46
19						4.46
20						4.46
21						2.25

first year, the depreciation rate is 40 percent of the beginning balance until Year 4, when straight-line depreciation would be at least as large, so we switch to straight-line. In Year 6, we have one-half of a year of the straight-line depreciation remaining because we assumed the asset was placed in service half-way through the first year.

Accelerated depreciation generally improves the NPV of a capital project compared to straight-line depreciation. For an example of this effect, we will assume the same capital project as in Table 14, except that the depreciation is MACRS 3-year property. When using straight-line, the depreciation was 20 percent per year ($35,000). The depreciation percentages for MACRS 3-year property are given in Table 16. The first-year depreciation is $0.3333 \times 175,000 = \$58,327.50$, second year depreciation is $0.4445 \times 175,000 = \$77,787.50$, third year depreciation is $0.1481 \times 175,000 = \$25,917.50$, fourth year depreciation is $0.0741 \times 175,000 = \$12,967.50$, and fifth year depreciation is zero. The impact on the NPV and IRR of the project is shown in Table 17.

As the table shows, the depreciation charges still sum to $175,000 (except for $2 of rounding), but they are larger in Years 1 and 2 and smaller in Years 3, 4, and 5. Although this method reduces operating income after taxes in Years 1 and

---

TABLE 17   Capital Budgeting Example with MACRS

Year	0	1	2	3	4	5
Investment outlays:						
Fixed capital	−200,000					
Net working capital	−30,000					
Total	−230,000					
Annual after-tax operating cash flows:						
Sales		220,000	220,000	220,000	220,000	220,000
Cash operating expenses		90,000	90,000	90,000	90,000	90,000
Depreciation		58,328	77,788	25,918	12,968	0
Operating income before taxes		71,673	52,213	104,083	117,033	130,000
Taxes on operating income (40%)		28,669	20,885	41,633	46,813	52,000
Operating income after taxes		43,004	31,328	62,450	70,220	78,000
Add back: Depreciation		58,328	77,788	25,918	12,968	0
After-tax operating cash flow		101,331	109,115	88,367	83,187	78,000
Terminal year after-tax non-operating cash flows:						
After-tax salvage value						40,000
Return of net working capital						30,000
Total						70,000
Total after-tax cash flows	−230,000	101,331	109,115	88,367	83,187	148,000
Net present value at 10% required rate of return	$167,403					
Internal rate of return	34.74%					

2 (and increases it in Years 3, 4, and 5), it reduces tax outflows in Years 1 and 2 and increases them later. Consequently, the after-tax operating cash flows (which were $92,000 per year) increase in early years and decrease in later years. This increases the NPV from $162,217 to $167,403, a difference of $5,186. The IRR also increases from 32.70 percent to 34.74 percent.[8]

The impact of accelerated depreciation can be seen without going through the complete analysis in Table 17. We previously showed in Table 15 that the present value of the depreciation tax savings (which was an annuity of $0.40 \times$ $35,000 = $14,000 a year for five years) was $53,071. The present value of the tax savings from accelerated depreciation is shown in Table 18.

TABLE 18	Present Value of Tax Savings from Accelerated Depreciation		
Year	Depreciation	Tax Savings	PV at 10%
1	$58,327.50	$0.40 \times$ $58,327.5 = $23,331	$21,210
2	$77,787.50	$0.40 \times$ $77,787.5 = $31,115	$25,715
3	$25,917.50	$0.40 \times$ $25,917.5 = $10,367	$7,789
4	$12,967.50	$0.40 \times$ $12,967.5 = $5,187	$3,543
5	$ 0	$0.40 \times$ $0 = $0	$0
Total present value			$58,257

By using the accelerated depreciation schedule, we increase the present value of the tax savings from $53,071 (from Table 15) to $58,257, an increase of $5,186. The tax deferral associated with the accelerated depreciation (compared to straight-line) adds $5,186 to the NPV of the project.

There are a myriad of tax and depreciation schedules that apply to investment projects around the world. These tax and depreciation schedules are also subject to change from year to year. To accurately assess the profitability of a particular capital project, it is vital to identify and apply the schedules that are relevant to the capital budgeting decision at hand.

6.2 Cash Flows for a Replacement Project

In Section 5.1, we evaluated the cash flows for an expansion project, basing our after-tax cash flows on the outlays, annual operating cash flows after tax, and salvage value for the project by itself. In many cases, however, investing in a project will be more complicated. Investing could affect many of the company's cash flows. In principle, the cash flows relevant to an investing decision are the incremental cash flows: the cash flows the company realizes *with* the investment compared to the cash flows the company would realize *without* the investment. For example, suppose we are investing in a new project with an outlay of $100,000

---

[8] This example assumes that the investment occurs on the first day of the tax year. If the outlay occurs later in the tax year, the depreciation tax savings for the tax years are unchanged, which means that the cash savings occur sooner, increasing their present values. The result is a higher NPV and IRR.

and we sell off existing assets that the project replaces for $30,000. The incremental outlay is $70,000.

A very common investment decision is a replacement decision, in which you replace old equipment with new equipment. This decision requires very careful analysis of the cash flows. The skills required to detail the replacement decision cash flows are also useful for other decisions in which an investment affects other cash flows in the company. We use the term "replacement" loosely, primarily to indicate that the cash flow analysis is more complicated than it was for the simpler expansion decision.

Assume we are considering the replacement of old equipment with new equipment that has more capacity and is less costly to operate. The characteristics of the old and new equipment are given below:

Old Equipment		New Equipment	
Current book value	$400,000		
Current market value	$600,000	Acquisition cost	$1,000,000
Remaining life	10 years	Life	10 years
Annual sales	$300,000	Annual sales	$450,000
Cash operating expenses	$120,000	Cash operating expenses	$150,000
Annual depreciation	$40,000	Annual depreciation	$100,000
Accounting salvage value	$0	Accounting salvage value	$0
Expected salvage value	$100,000	Expected salvage value	$200,000

If the new equipment replaces the old equipment, an additional investment of $80,000 in net working capital will be required. The tax rate is 30 percent, and the required rate of return is 8 percent.

The cash flows can be found by carefully constructing tables like Table 14 or by using Equations 31-6 through 31-9. The initial outlay is the investment in the new equipment plus the additional investment in net working capital less the after-tax proceeds from selling the old equipment:

$$\text{Outlay} = \text{FCInv} + \text{NWCInv} - \text{Sal}_0 + \text{T}(\text{Sal}_0 - \text{B}_0)$$
$$\text{Outlay} = 1{,}000{,}000 + 80{,}000 - 600{,}000$$
$$+ 0.3(600{,}000 - 400{,}000) = \$540{,}000$$

In this case, the outlay of $540,000 is $1,080,000 for new equipment and net working capital minus the after-tax proceeds of $540,000 the company receives from selling the old equipment. The incremental operating cash flows are

$$\text{CF} = (\text{S} - \text{C} - \text{D})(1 - \text{T}) + \text{D}$$
$$= \big[(450{,}000 - 300{,}000) - (150{,}000 - 120{,}000)$$
$$- (100{,}000 - 40{,}000)\big](1 - 0.30) + (100{,}000 - 40{,}000)$$
$$= (150{,}000 - 30{,}000 - 60{,}000)(1 - 0.30) + 60{,}000 = \$102{,}000$$

The incremental sales are $150,000, incremental cash operating expenses are $30,000, and incremental depreciation is $60,000. The incremental after-tax operating cash flow is $102,000 per year.

At the project termination, the new equipment is expected to be sold for $200,000, which constitutes an incremental cash flow of $100,000 over the $100,000 expected salvage price of the old equipment. Since the accounting salvage values for both the new and old equipment were zero, this gain is taxable at 30 percent. The company also recaptures its investment in net working capital. The terminal year after-tax non-operating cash flow is

$$
\begin{aligned}
\text{TNOCF} &= \text{Sal}_T + \text{NWCInv} - T(\text{Sal}_T - B_T) \\
&= (200{,}000 - 100{,}000) + 80{,}000 - 0.30 \\
&\quad \big[(200{,}000 - 100{,}000) - (0 - 0)\big] \\
&= \$150{,}000
\end{aligned}
$$

Once the cash flows are identified, the NPV and IRR are readily found. The NPV, found by discounting the cash flows at the 8 percent required rate of return, is

$$
\text{NPV} = -540{,}000 + \sum_{t=1}^{10} \frac{102{,}000}{1.08^t} + \frac{150{,}000}{1.08^{10}} = \$213{,}907
$$

The IRR, found with a financial calculator, is 15.40 percent. Because the NPV is positive, this equipment replacement decision is attractive. The fact that the IRR exceeds the 8 percent required rate of return leads to the same conclusion.

The key to estimating the incremental cash flows for the replacement is to compare the cash flows that occur with the new investment to the cash flows that would have occurred without the new investment. The analyst is comparing the cash flows with a particular course of action to the cash flows with an alternative course of action.

6.3 Spreadsheet Modeling

Although the examples in this reading can be readily solved with a financial calculator, capital budgeting is usually done with the assistance of personal computers and spreadsheets such as Microsoft Excel®. Spreadsheets are heavily used for several reasons. Spreadsheets provide a very effective way of building even complex models. Built-in spreadsheet functions (such as those for finding rates of return) are easy to use. The model's assumptions can be changed and solved easily. Models can be shared with other analysts, and they also help in presenting the results of the analysis. The example below shows how a spreadsheet can be used to solve a capital budgeting problem.

EXAMPLE 7

Capital Budgeting with a Spreadsheet

Lawton Enterprises is evaluating a project with the following characteristics:

► Fixed capital investment is $2,000,000.

► The project has an expected six-year life.

► The initial investment in net working capital is $200,000. At the end of each year, net working capital must be increased so that the cumulative investment in net working capital is one-sixth of the next year's projected sales.

- The fixed capital is depreciated 30 percent in Year 1, 35 percent in Year 2, 20 percent in Year 3, 10 percent in Year 4, 5 percent in Year 5, and 0 percent in Year 6.
- Sales are $1,200,000 in Year 1. They grow at a 25 percent annual rate for the next two years, and then grow at a 10 percent annual rate for the last three years.
- Fixed cash operating expenses are $150,000 for Years 1–3 and $130,000 for Years 4–6.
- Variable cash operating expenses are 40 percent of sales in Year 1, 39 percent of sales in Year 2, and 38 percent in Years 3–6.
- Lawton's marginal tax rate is 30 percent.
- Lawton will sell its fixed capital investments for $150,000 when the project terminates and recapture its cumulative investment in net working capital. Income taxes will be paid on any gains.
- The project's required rate of return is 12 percent.
- If taxable income on the project is negative in any year, the loss will offset gains elsewhere in the corporation, resulting in a tax savings.

1. Determine whether this is a profitable investment using the NPV and IRR.
2. If the tax rate increases to 40 percent and the required rate of return increases to 14 percent, is the project still profitable?

Solution to 1:

TABLE 19   Cash Flows for Lawton Investment (rounded to nearest $1,000)

Year	0	1	2	3	4	5	6
Fixed capital investment	−2,000						
NWC investments	−200	−50	−63	−31	−34	−38	
Sales		1,200	1,500	1,875	2,063	2,269	2,496
Fixed cash expenses		150	150	150	130	130	130
Variable cash expenses		480	585	713	784	862	948
Depreciation		600	700	400	200	100	0
Operating income before taxes		−30	65	613	949	1,177	1,417
Taxes on operating income		−9	20	184	285	353	425
Operating income after taxes		−21	45	429	664	824	992
Add back: Depreciation		600	700	400	200	100	0
After-tax operating cash flow		579	745	829	864	924	992
Salvage value							150
Taxes on salvage value							−45
Return of NWC							416
Total after-tax cash flows	−2,200	529	682	798	830	886	1,513
NPV (at r = 12 percent)	1,181						
IRR	26.60%						

Because the NPV of $1,181,000 is positive, the project is profitable for Lawton to undertake. The IRR investment decision rule also indicates that the project is profitable because the IRR of 26.60 percent exceeds the 12 percent required rate of return.

Solution to 2: The tax rate and required return can be changed in the spreadsheet model. When these changes are made, the NPV becomes $736,000 and the IRR becomes 24.02 percent. (The revised spreadsheet is not printed here.) Although profitability is lower, the higher tax rate and required rate of return do not change the investment decision.

6.4 Effects of Inflation on Capital Budgeting Analysis

Inflation affects capital budgeting analysis in several ways. The first decision the analyst must make is whether to do the analysis in "normal" terms or in "real" terms. Nominal cash flows include the effects of inflation, while real cash flows are adjusted downward to remove the effects of inflation. It is perfectly acceptable to do the analysis in either nominal or real terms, and sound decisions can be made either way. However, inflation creates some issues regardless of the approach.

The cash flows and discount rate used should both be nominal or both be real. In other words, nominal cash flows should be discounted at a nominal discount rate, and real cash flows should be discounted at a real rate. The real rate, just like real cash flows, has had the effect of inflation taken out. In general, the relationship between real and nominal rates is

$$(1 + \text{Nominal rate}) = (1 + \text{Real rate})(1 + \text{Inflation rate})$$

Inflation reduces the value of depreciation tax savings (unless the tax system adjusts depreciation for inflation). The effect of expected inflation is captured in the **discounted cash flow analysis**. If inflation is higher than expected, the profitability of the investment is correspondingly lower than expected. Inflation essentially shifts wealth from the taxpayer to the government. Higher-than-expected inflation increases the corporation's real taxes because it reduces the value of the depreciation tax shelter. Conversely, lower-than-expected inflation reduces real taxes (the depreciation tax shelters are more valuable than expected).

Inflation also reduces the value of fixed payments to bondholders. When bonds are originally issued, bondholders pay a price for the bonds reflecting their inflationary expectations. If inflation is higher than expected, the real payments to bondholders are lower than expected. Higher-than-expected inflation shifts wealth from bondholders to the issuing corporations. Conversely, if inflation is lower than expected, the real interest expenses of the corporation increase, shifting wealth from the issuing corporation to its bondholders.

Finally, inflation does not affect all revenues and costs uniformly. The company's after-tax cash flows will be better or worse than expected depending on how particular sales outputs or cost inputs are affected. Furthermore, contracting with customers, suppliers, employees, and sources of capital can be complicated as inflation rises.

The capital budgeting model accommodates the effects of inflation, although inflation complicates the capital budgeting process (and the operations of a business, in general).

7   PROJECT ANALYSIS AND EVALUATION

Assessing the opportunity costs and analyzing the risks of capital investments becomes more complex and sophisticated as you examine real cases. The first project interaction we examine in this section is that of comparing mutually exclusive projects with unequal lives. We will briefly describe other project interactions, but will not examine them in detail. We also examine the process of capital budgeting under capital rationing.

Up to this point, we have largely ignored the issue of accounting for risk. We will introduce risk analysis in two ways. The first is accounting for risk on a stand-alone basis. The second is accounting for risk on a systematic basis.

7.1 Mutually Exclusive Projects with Unequal Lives

We have previously looked at mutually exclusive projects and decided that the best project is the one with the greatest NPV. However, if the mutually exclusive projects have differing lives and the projects will be replaced (or replicated) repeatedly when they wear out, the analysis is more complicated. The analysis of a one-shot (one time only) investment differs from that of an investment chain (in which the asset is replaced regularly in the future).

For example, assume we have two projects with unequal lives of two and three years, with the following after-tax cash flows:

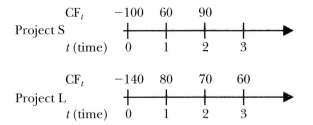

Both projects have a 10 percent required rate of return. The NPV of Project S is $28.93 and the NPV of Project L is $35.66. Given that the two projects are mutually exclusive, Project L, with the greater NPV, should be chosen.

However, let us now assume that these are not one-shot investments, but investments in assets that the company will need to replace when they wear out. Project S would be replaced every two years and Project L every three years. This situation is often referred to as a replacement chain. In this type of problem, you should examine the entire chain and not just the first link in the chain. If the projects are part of a replacement chain, examining the cash flows for only the initial investment for Projects S and L is improper because Project L provides cash flows during Year 3, when Project S provides none.

There are two logically equivalent ways of comparing mutually exclusive projects in a replacement chain. They are the "least common multiple of lives" approach and the "equivalent annual annuity" approach.

7.1.1 Least Common Multiple of Lives Approach

For the least common multiple of lives approach, the analyst extends the time horizon of analysis so that the lives of both projects will divide exactly into the horizon. For Projects S and L, the least common multiple of 2 and 3 is 6: The two-year project would be replicated three times over the six-year horizon and the three-year project would be replicated two times over the six-year horizon.[9] The cash flows for replicating Projects S and L over a six-year horizon are shown below.

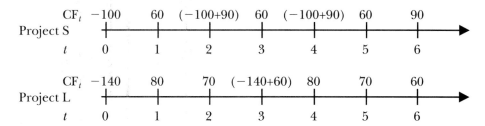

Discounting the cash flows for the six-year horizon results in an NPV for Project S of $72.59 and an NPV for Project L of $62.45. Apparently, investing in Project S and replicating the investment over time has a greater NPV than choosing Project L and replicating it. This decision is the reverse of the one we made when looking solely at the NPVs of the initial investments!

Because the NPV of a single investment represents the present values of its cash flows, you can also visualize the NPV of a replacement chain as the present value of the NPVs of each investment (or link) in the chain. For Projects S and L, the NPVs of each investment are shown on the timelines below:

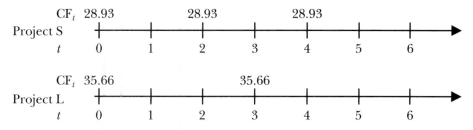

Investing in Project S is equivalent to receiving values of $28.93 at times 0, 2, and 4, while investing in Project L is equivalent to receiving values of $35.66 at times 0 and 3. The present values of these cash flow patterns are $72.59 for Project S and $62.45 for Project L. Discounting the NPVs of each investment in the chain is equivalent to discounting all of the individual cash flows in the chain.

7.1.2 Equivalent Annual Annuity Approach

The other method for properly evaluating a replacement chain is called the equivalent annual annuity (EAA) approach. The name for this approach is very descriptive. For an investment project with an outlay and variable cash flows in the future, the project NPV summarizes the equivalent value at time zero. For this same project, the EAA is the annuity payment (series of equal annual payments over the project's life) that is equivalent in value to the NPV.

Analysts can use a simple two-step procedure to find the EAA. The first step is to find the present value of all of the cash flows for an investment—the investment's NPV. The second step is to calculate an annuity payment that has a value equivalent to the NPV. For Project S above, we already calculated the NPV of the project over its two-year life to be $28.93. The second step is to find an annuity payment for the two-year life that is equivalent. For a two-year life and a 10 percent discount rate, a payment of $16.66 is the equivalent annuity.

---

[9] The least common multiple of lives is not necessarily the product of the two lives, as in the case of Projects S and L. For example, if two projects have lives of 8 and 10 years, the least common multiple of lives is 40 years, not 80. Both 8 and 10 are exactly divisible into 40.

The EAA for Project L is found by annuitizing its $35.66 NPV over three years, so the EAA for Project L is $14.34.

The decision rule for the EAA approach is to choose the investment chain that has the highest EAA, which in this case is Project S.

Given these two approaches to comparing replacement chains, which one should the analyst use? As a practical matter, the two approaches are logically equivalent and will result in the same decision.[10] Consequently, the analyst can choose one approach over the other based on personal preference. Or, if the audience for the analyst's work prefers to see the analysis using one approach, the analyst can simply produce the analysis in that format.

7.2 Capital Rationing

Capital rationing is the case in which the company's capital budget has a size constraint. For example, the capital budget is a fixed money amount. A fixed capital budget can place the company in several interesting situations. To illustrate these, we will assume that the company has a fixed $1,000 **capital budget** and has the opportunity to invest in four projects. The projects are of variable profitability.

In the first situation, the budget is adequate to invest in all profitable projects. Consider the four projects in Table 20.

TABLE 20 First Capital Rationing Example				
	Investment Outlay	**NPV**	**PI**	**IRR**
Project 1	600	220	1.37	15%
Project 2	200	70	1.35	16%
Project 3	200	−60	0.70	10%
Project 4	400	−100	0.75	8%

In this case, the company has two positive-NPV projects, Projects 1 and 2, which involve a total outlay of $800. Their total NPV is $290. The company should choose these projects, and it will have $200 in its capital budget left over. These excess funds can be used elsewhere in the company (moved to someone else's budget, used to pay dividends or repurchase shares, or used to pay down debt). If a manager is afraid to return the excess funds and chooses to invest in Project 3, the manager will consume the whole capital budget but reduce the total NPV to $230, essentially destroying $60 of wealth for the company.

A second case exists in which the company has more profitable projects than it can choose, but it is able to invest in the most profitable ones available. Continuing with the $1,000 capital budget, this second case is illustrated in Table 21.

---

[10] For Projects S and L, the NPVs of a replacement chain over the least common multiple of lives (six years) were $72.59 for Project S and $62.45 for Project L. If we discount the EAA for Project S ($16.66) and the EAA for Project L ($14.34) for six years (treating each as a six-year annuity), we have the same NPVs. Hence, the least common multiple of lives and EAA approaches are consistent with each other.

TABLE 21	Second Capital Rationing Example			
	Investment Outlay	**NPV**	**PI**	**IRR**
Project 5	600	300	1.50	16%
Project 6	200	80	1.40	18%
Project 7	200	60	1.30	12%
Project 8	200	40	1.20	14%

When the analyst has a fixed budget, the PI is especially useful because it shows the profitability of each investment per currency unit invested. If we rank these projects by their PIs, Projects 5, 6, and 7 are the best projects and we are able to select them. This selection results in a total NPV of $440. The IRRs, shown in the last column, are not a reliable guide to choosing projects under capital rationing because a high-IRR project may have a low NPV. Wealth maximization is best guided by the NPV criterion.

A third case exists in which the company has more profitable projects than it can choose, but it is not able to invest in the most profitable ones available. Assume the company cannot invest in fractional projects: It must take all or none of each project it chooses. Continuing with the $1,000 capital budget, this case is illustrated in Table 22.

TABLE 22	Third Capital Rationing Example			
	Investment Outlay	**NPV**	**PI**	**IRR**
Project 9	600	300	1.50	15%
Project 10	600	270	1.45	16%
Project 11	200	80	1.40	12%
Project 12	400	100	1.25	11%

In this example, an unlimited budget of $1,800 would generate a total NPV of $750. However, when the **budget constraint** is imposed, the highest NPV results from choosing Projects 9 and 12. The company is forced to choose its best project and its fourth-best project, as indicated by their relative PIs. Any other combination of projects either violates the budget or has a lower total NPV.

Capital rationing has the potential to misallocate resources. Capital markets are supposed to allocate funds to their highest and best uses, with the opportunity cost of funds (used as the discount rate for NPVs or the **hurdle rate** for IRRs) guiding this allocation process. Capital rationing violates market efficiency if society's resources are not allocated where they will generate the best returns. Companies that use capital rationing may be doing either "hard" or "soft" capital rationing. Under hard capital rationing, the budget is fixed and the managers cannot go beyond it. Under soft capital rationing, managers may be allowed to over-spend their budgets if they argue effectively that the additional funds will be deployed profitably.

In the case of hard rationing, choosing the optimal projects that fit within the budget and maximize the NPV of the company can be computationally intensive. Sometimes, managers use estimates and trial and error to find the optimal set of projects. The PI can be used as a guide in this trial and error process. Other times, the number of possibilities is so daunting that mathematical programming algorithms are used.

7.3 Risk Analysis of Capital Investments— Stand-Alone Methods

So far, we have evaluated projects by calculating a single NPV to decide whether a project is profitable. We took a single value, or **point estimate**, of each input into the model and combined the values to calculate the NPV.

Risk is usually measured as a dispersion of outcomes. In the case of stand-alone risk, we typically measure the riskiness of a project by the dispersion of its NPVs or the dispersion of its IRRs. Sensitivity analysis, scenario analysis, and simulation analysis are very popular stand-alone risk analysis methods. These risk measures depend on the variation of the project's cash flows.

To illustrate the stand-alone risk tools, we will use the following "base case" capital project:

Unit price	$5.00
Annual unit sales	40,000
Variable cost per unit	$1.50
Investment in fixed capital	$300,000
Investment in working capital	$50,000
Project life	6 years
Depreciation (straight-line)	$50,000
Expected salvage value	$60,000
Tax rate	40 percent
Required rate of return	12 percent

The outlay, from Equation 31-6, is $300,000 plus $50,000, or $350,000. The annual after-tax operating cash flow, from Equation 31-7, is

$$
\begin{aligned}
CF &= (S - C - D)(1 - T) + D \\
&= [(5 \times 40{,}000) - (1.50 \times 40{,}000) - (50{,}000)](1 - 0.40) + 50{,}000 \\
&= \$104{,}000
\end{aligned}
$$

The terminal year after-tax non-operating cash flow, from Equation 31-9, is

$$
\begin{aligned}
TNOCF &= Sal_6 + NWCInv - T(Sal_6 - B_6) \\
&= 60{,}000 + 50{,}000 - 0.40(60{,}000 - 0) = \$86{,}000
\end{aligned}
$$

The project NPV is

$$
NPV = -350{,}000 + \sum_{t=1}^{6} \frac{104{,}000}{1.12^t} + \frac{86{,}000}{1.12^6} = -350{,}000 + 471{,}157 = \$121{,}157
$$

7.3.1 Sensitivity Analysis

Sensitivity analysis calculates the effect on the NPV of changes in one input variable at a time. The base case above has several input variables. If we wish to do a sensitivity analysis of several of them, we must specify the changes in each that we wish to evaluate. Suppose we want to consider the following:

	Base Value	Low Value	High Value
Unit price	$5.00	$4.50	$5.50
Annual unit sales	40,000	35,000	45,000
Variable cost per unit	$1.50	$1.40	$1.60
Expected salvage value	$60,000	$30,000	$80,000
Tax rate	40%	38%	42%
Required rate of return	12%	10%	14%

We have changed each of six input variables. Table 23 shows the NPV calculated for the base case. Then the NPV is recalculated by changing one variable from its base case value to its high or low value.

TABLE 23   Sensitivity of Project NPV to Changes in a Variable

	Project NPV			
Variable	**Base Case**	**With Low Estimate**	**With High Estimate**	**Range of Estimates**
Unit price	$121,157	$71,820	$170,494	$98,674
Annual unit sales	$121,157	$77,987	$164,326	$86,339
Cost per unit	$121,157	$131,024	$111,289	$19,735
Salvage value	$121,157	$112,037	$127,236	$15,199
Tax rate	$121,157	$129,165	$113,148	$16,017
Required return	$121,157	$151,492	$93,602	$57,890

As Table 23 shows, the project's NPV is most sensitive to changes in the unit price variable. The project's NPV is least sensitive to changes in the salvage value. Roughly speaking, the project's NPV is most sensitive to changes in unit price and in unit sales. It is least affected by changes in cost per unit, salvage value, and the tax rate. Changes in the required rate of return also have a substantial effect, but not as much as changes in price or unit sales.

In a sensitivity analysis, the manager can choose which variables to change and by how much. Many companies have access to software that can be instructed to change a particular variable by a certain amount—for example, to increase or decrease unit price, unit sales, and cost per unit by 10 percent. The software then produces the changes in NPV for each of these changes. Sensitivity analysis can be used to establish which variables are most influential on the success or failure of a project.

7.3.2 Scenario Analysis

Sensitivity analysis calculates the effect on the NPV of changes in one variable at a time. In contrast, **scenario analysis** creates scenarios that consist of changes in several of the input variables and calculates the NPV for each scenario. Although corporations could do a large number of scenarios, in practice they usually do only three. They can be labeled variously, but we will present an example with "pessimistic," "most likely," and "optimistic" scenarios. Continuing with the basic example from the section above, the values of the input variables for the three scenarios are given in the table below.

TABLE 24 Input Variables and NPV for Scenario Analysis			
		Scenario	
Variable	**Pessimistic**	**Most Likely**	**Optimistic**
Unit price	$4.50	$5.00	$5.50
Annual unit sales	35,000	40,000	45,000
Variable cost per unit	$1.60	$1.50	$1.40
Investment in fixed capital	$320,000	$300,000	$280,000
Investment in working capital	$50,000	$50,000	$50,000
Project life	6 years	6 years	6 years
Depreciation (straight-line)	$53,333	$50,000	$46,667
Salvage value	$40,000	$60,000	$80,000
Tax rate	40%	40%	40%
Required rate of return	13%	12%	11%
NPV	−$5,725	$121,157	$269,685
IRR	12.49%	22.60%	34.24%

The most likely scenario is the same as the base case we used above for sensitivity analysis, and the NPV for the most likely scenario is $121,157. To form the pessimistic and optimistic scenarios, managers change several of the assumptions for each scenario. For the pessimistic scenario, several of the input variables are changed to reflect higher costs, lower revenues, and a higher required rate of return. As the table shows, the result is a negative NPV for the pessimistic scenario and an IRR that is less than the pessimistic scenario's 13 percent required rate of return. For the optimistic scenario, the more favorable revenues, costs, and required rate of return result in very good NPV and IRR.

For this example, the scenario analysis reveals the possibility of an unprofitable investment, with a negative NPV and with an IRR less than the cost of capital. The range for the NPV is fairly large compared to the size of the initial investment, which indicates that the investment is fairly risky. This example included three scenarios for which management wants to know the profitability of the investment for each set of assumptions. Other scenarios can be investigated if management chooses to do so.

7.3.3 Simulation (Monte Carlo) Analysis

Simulation analysis is a procedure for estimating a probability distribution of outcomes, such as for the NPV or IRR for a capital investment project. Instead of assuming a single value (a point estimate) for the input variables in a capital budgeting spreadsheet, the analyst can assume several variables to be stochastic, following their own **probability distributions**. By simulating the results hundreds or thousands of times, the analyst can build a good estimate of the distributions for the NPV or IRR. Because of the volume of computations, analysts and corporate managers rely heavily on their personal computers and specialized simulation software such as @RISK.[11] Example 8 presents a simple simulation analysis.

EXAMPLE 8

Capital Budgeting Simulation

Gouhua Zhang has made the following assumptions for a capital budgeting project:

- Fixed capital investment is 20,000; no investment in net working capital is required.
- The project has an expected five-year life.
- The fixed capital is depreciated straight-line to zero over a five-year life. The salvage value is normally distributed with an expected value of 2,000 and a standard deviation of 500.
- Unit sales in Year 1 are normally distributed with a mean of 2,000 and a standard deviation of 200.
- Unit sales growth after Year 1 is normally distributed with a mean of 6 percent and standard deviation of 4 percent. Assume the same sales growth rate for Years 2–5.
- The sales price is 5.00 per unit, normally distributed with a standard deviation of 0.25 per unit. The same price holds for all five years.
- Cash operating expenses as a percentage of total revenue are normally distributed with a mean and standard deviation of 30 percent and 3 percent, respectively.
- The discount rate is 12 percent and the tax rate is 40 percent.

1. What are the NPV and IRR using the expected values of all input variables?
2. Perform a simulation analysis and provide probability distributions for the NPV and IRR.

Solution to 1:

TABLE 25   Expected Cash Flows for Simulation Example

Time	0	1	2	3	4	5
Fixed capital	−20,000					
After-tax salvage value						1,200
Price		5.00	5.00	5.00	5.00	5.00
Output		2,000	2,120	2,247	2,382	2,525
Revenue		10,000	10,600	11,236	11,910	12,625
Cash operating expenses		3,000	3,180	3,371	3,573	3,787

(Table continued on next page . . .)

---

[11] @RISK is a popular and powerful risk analysis tool sold by Palisade Corporation. @RISK is an add-in for Microsoft Excel that allows simulation techniques to be incorporated into spreadsheet models.

TABLE 25 (continued)						
Time	0	1	2	3	4	5
Depreciation		4,000	4,000	4,000	4,000	4,000
Operating income before taxes		3,000	3,420	3,865	4,337	4,837
Taxes on operating income		1,200	1,368	1,546	1,735	1,935
Operating income after taxes		1,800	2,052	2,319	2,602	2,902
Depreciation		4,000	4,000	4,000	4,000	4,000
Total after-tax cash flow	−20,000	5,800	6,052	6,319	6,602	8,102
NPV (at r = 12 percent)	3,294					
IRR	18.11%					

Based on the point estimates for each variable (the mean values for each), which are shown in Table 25 above, Zhang should find the NPV to be 3,294 and the IRR to be 18.11 percent.

Solution to 2: Zhang performs a simulation using @RISK with 10,000 iterations. For each iteration, values for the five stochastic variables (price, output, output growth rate, cash expense percentage, and salvage value) are selected from their assumed distributions and the NPV and IRR are calculated. After the 10,000 iterations, the resulting information about the probability distributions for the NPV and IRR is shown in Figure 6 and Table 26.

FIGURE 6   Probability Distributions for NPV and IRR

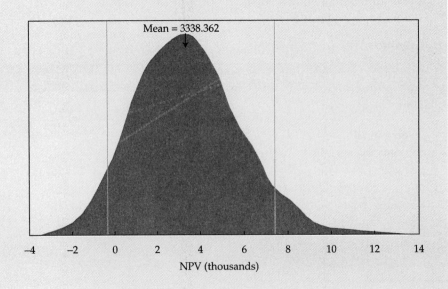

A. Distribution for NPV

B. Distribution for IRR

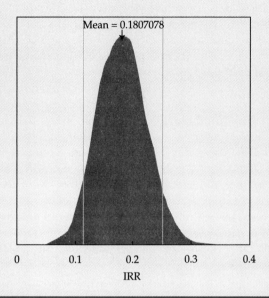

TABLE 26 Summary Statistics for NPV and IRR		
Statistic	**NPV**	**IRR**
Mean	3,338	18.07%
Standard deviation	2,364	4.18%
Skewness	0.2909	0.1130
Kurtosis	3.146	2.996
Median	3,236	18.01%
90% confidence interval	−3,779 to 7,413	11.38% to 25.13%

Correlations between Input Variables and NPV and IRR

Input Variable	**NPV**	**IRR**
Output	0.71	0.72
Output growth rate	0.49	0.47
Price	0.34	0.34
Cash expense proportion	−0.28	−0.29
Salvage value	0.06	0.05

As the figure shows, the distributions for the NPV and IRR are somewhat normal looking. The means and standard deviations for each are given in Table 26. Both distributions have a slight positive **skewness**, which means the distributions are **skewed** to the right. The two **kurtosis** values are fairly close to 3.0, which means that the distributions are not peaked or fat-tailed compared to the **standard normal distribution**. The median is the value at which 50 percent of the 10,000 outcomes fall on either side. The 90 percent confidence intervals show that 90 percent of the observations fall between −3,779 and 7,413 for the NPV and between 11.38 percent and 25.13 percent for the IRR. Although not shown in the table, 7.04 percent of the observations had a negative NPV and an IRR less than the 12 percent discount rate.

The means of the NPV and IRR from the simulation (in Table 26) are fairly close to their values calculated using point estimates for all of the input variables (in Table 25). This is not always the case, but it is here. The additional information from a simulation is the dispersions of the NPV and IRR. Given his assumptions and model, the simulation results show Zhang the distributions of NPV and IRR outcomes that should be expected. Managers and analysts often prefer to know these total distributions rather than just their mean values.

The correlations in Table 26 can be interpreted as sensitivity measures. Changes in the "output" variable have the highest correlation with NPV and IRR outcomes. The salvage value has the lowest (absolute value) correlation.

This capital budgeting simulation example was not very complex, with only five stochastic variables. The example's five input variables were assumed to be normally distributed—in reality, many other distributions can be employed. Finally, the randomly chosen values for each variable were assumed to be independent. They can be selected jointly instead of independently. Simulation techniques have proved to be a boon for addressing capital budgeting problems.

Sensitivity analysis, scenario analysis, and simulation analysis are well-developed stand-alone risk analysis methods. These risk measures depend on the variation of the project's cash flows. Market risk measures, presented in the next section, depend not only on the variation of a project's cash flows, but also on how those cash flows covary with (or correlate with) market returns.

7.4 Risk Analysis of Capital Investments— Market Risk Methods

When using market risk methods, the discount rate to be used in evaluating a capital project is the rate of return required on the project by a diversified investor. The discount rate should thus be a risk-adjusted discount rate, which includes a premium to compensate investors for risk.[12] This risk premium should reflect factors that are priced or valued in the marketplace. The two equilibrium models for estimating this **risk premium** are the capital asset pricing model (CAPM) and **arbitrage pricing theory (APT)**. We will discuss the **CAPM** as a way of finding risk-adjusted discount rates, although you should be aware that other methods can be used.

---

[12] Our approach to capital budgeting is to discount expected cash flows at a risk-adjusted cost of capital. An alternative approach, which is also conceptually sound, is the "certainty-equivalent method." In this method, certainty-equivalent cash flows (expected cash flows that are reduced to certainty equivalents) are valued by discounting them at a risk-free discount rate. The use of risk-adjusted discount rates is more intuitive and much more popular.

In the CAPM, total risk can be broken into two components: systematic risk and **unsystematic risk**. Systematic risk is the portion of risk that is related to the market and that cannot be diversified away. Unsystematic risk is non-market risk, risk that is idiosyncratic and that can be diversified away. Diversified investors can demand a risk premium for taking systematic risk, but not unsystematic risk.[13] Hence, the stand-alone risk measures—total risk measured by the dispersion of the NPV or the IRR—are inappropriate when the corporation is diversified, or, as is more likely, when the corporation's investors are themselves diversified.

In the capital asset pricing model, a project's or asset's "beta," or β, is generally used as a measure of systematic risk. The **security market line (SML)** expresses the asset's required rate of return as a function of β:

$$r_i = R_F + \beta_i[E(R_M) - R_F] \tag{31-10}$$

where

$$r_i = \text{required return for project or asset } i$$
$$R_F = \text{risk-free rate of return}$$
$$\beta_i = \text{beta of project or asset } i$$
$$[E(R_M) - R_F] = \textbf{market risk premium}, \text{ the difference between the}$$
$$\text{expected market return and the risk-free rate of return}$$

The project's required rate of return is equal to the risk-free rate plus a risk premium, where the risk premium is the product of the project beta and the market risk premium.

Here, the required rate of return (sometimes called a hurdle rate) is specific to the risk of the project. There is no one hurdle rate appropriate for all projects.

FIGURE 7   SML for Capital Budgeting Projects

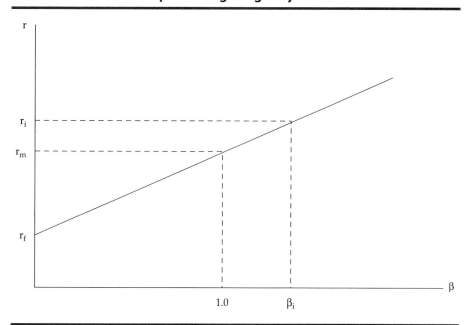

---

[13] The capital asset pricing model uses this intuition to show how **risky assets** should be priced relative to the market. While the CAPM assigns a single market risk premium for each security, the APT develops a set of risk premia. The CAPM and APT are developed in detail elsewhere in the CFA curriculum.

The security market line (SML) is graphed in Figure 7. This line indicates the required rate of return for a project, given its beta. The required rate of return can be used in two ways:

▶ The SML is used to find the required rate of return. The required rate of return is then used to find the NPV. Positive NPV projects are accepted and negative NPV projects are rejected.

▶ The SML is used to find the required rate of return. The project's IRR is compared to the required rate of return. If the IRR is greater than the required return, the project is accepted (this point would plot above the SML in Figure 7). If the IRR is less than the required rate of return (below the SML), the project is rejected.

Example 9 illustrates how the capital asset pricing model and the security market line are used as part of the capital budgeting process.

EXAMPLE 9

Using the SML to Find the Project Required Rate of Return

Premont Systems is evaluating a capital project with the following characteristics:

▶ The initial outlay is €150,000.
▶ Annual after-tax operating cash flows are €28,000.
▶ After-tax salvage value at project termination is €20,000.
▶ Project life is 10 years.
▶ The project beta is 1.20.
▶ The risk-free rate is 4.2 percent and the expected market return is 9.4 percent.

1. Compute the project NPV. Should the project be accepted?
2. Compute the project IRR. Should the project be accepted?

Solution to 1: The project required rate of return is

$$r_i = R_F + \beta_i[E(R_M) - R_F] = 4.2\% + 1.20(9.4\% - 4.2\%)$$
$$= 4.2\% + 6.24\% = 10.44\%$$

The cash flows discounted at 10.44 percent give an NPV of

$$\text{NPV} = -150,000 + \sum_{t=1}^{10} \frac{28,000}{1.1044^t} + \frac{20,000}{1.1044^{10}} = €26,252$$

The project should be accepted because it has a positive NPV.

Solution to 2: The IRR, found with a financial calculator, is 14.24 percent. The required rate of return, established with the SML as in the solution to Question 1 above, is 10.44 percent. Since the IRR exceeds the required rate of return, the project should be accepted. For a beta of 1.20, the IRR of 14.24 percent would plot above the SML.

Using project betas to establish required rates of return for capital projects is especially important when a project's risk differs from that of the company. The cost of capital for a company is estimated for the company as a whole—it is based on the average riskiness of the company's assets as well as its financial structure. The required rates of return of debt and equity are used to estimate the weighted (overall) average cost of capital (WACC) for the company. When a project under consideration is more risky or less risky than the company, the WACC should not be used as the project required rate of return.

For example, assume that the risk-free rate of return is 3 percent, the market return is 8 percent, and the company beta is 0.9. Assume also that the company is considering three projects: Project A with a 0.5 beta, Project B with a 0.9 beta, and Project C with a 1.1 beta. The required rates of return for the company and for each project are as follows:

Company	$3\% + 0.9(8\% - 3\%) = 7.5\%$
Project A	$3\% + 0.5(8\% - 3\%) = 5.5\%$
Project B	$3\% + 0.9(8\% - 3\%) = 7.5\%$
Project C	$3\% + 1.1(8\% - 3\%) = 8.5\%$

If management uses the company WACC as the required return for all projects, this rate is too high for Project A, making it less likely that Project A would be accepted. Project B has the same risk as the company, so it would be evaluated fairly. Using the WACC for Project C makes the error of using a discount rate that is too low, which would make it more likely that this high-risk project would be accepted. Whenever possible, it is desirable to use project-specific required rates of return instead of the company's overall required rate of return.

Market returns are readily available for publicly traded companies. The stock betas of these companies can then be calculated, and this calculation assists in estimating the companies' betas and WACC. Unfortunately, however, the returns for specific capital projects are not directly observable, and we have to use proxies for their betas. Frequently, we can employ the pure-play method, in which the analyst identifies other publicly traded stocks in the same business as the project being considered. The betas for the stocks of these companies are used to estimate a project beta. In the pure-play method, these proxy companies need to be relatively focused in the same line of business as the project. When the pure-play method is not possible, other methods, such as estimating accounting betas or cross-sectional regression analysis, are used.

7.5 Real Options

Real options are capital budgeting options that allow managers to make decisions in the future that alter the value of capital budgeting investment decisions made today. Instead of making all capital budgeting decisions now, at time zero, managers can wait and make additional decisions at future dates when these future decisions are contingent upon future economic events or information. These sequential decisions, in which future decisions depend on the decisions made today as well as on future economic events, are very realistic capital budgeting applications.

Real options are like financial options—they just deal with **real assets** instead of financial assets. A simple financial option could be a **call option** on a **share of stock**. Suppose the stock is selling for $50, the exercise (strike) price is $50, and the option expires in one year. If the stock goes up to $60, you exercise the option and have a gain of $10 in one year. If the stock goes down to $40, you do not exercise, and you have no gain. However, no gain is better than the $10 loss you would have had if you had purchased the stock at the beginning of the year. Real options, like financial options, entail the right to make a decision, but not the obligation. The corporation should exercise a real option only if it is value-enhancing.

Just as financial options are contingent on an underlying asset, real options are contingent on future events. The flexibility that real options give to managers can greatly enhance the NPV of the company's capital investments. The following are several types of these real options:

Timing Options   Instead of investing now, the company can delay investing. Delaying an investment and basing the decision on hopefully improved information that you might have in, say, a year could help improve the NPV of the projects selected.

Sizing Options   If after investing, the company can abandon the project when the financial results are disappointing, it has an **abandonment option**. At some future date, if the cash flow from abandoning a project exceeds the present value of the cash flows from continuing the project, managers should exercise the abandonment option. Conversely, if the company can make additional investments when future financial results are strong, the company has a **growth option** or an **expansion option**.

Flexibility Options   Once an investment is made, other operational flexibilities may be available besides abandonment or expansion. For example, suppose demand exceeds capacity. Management may be able to exercise a **price-setting option**. By increasing prices, the company could benefit from the excess demand, which it cannot do by increasing production. There are also **production-flexibility** options. Even though it is expensive, the company can profit from working overtime or from adding additional shifts. The company can also work with customers and suppliers for their mutual benefit whenever a demand–supply mismatch occurs. This type of option also includes the possibility of using different inputs or producing different outputs.

Fundamental Options   In cases like those above, there are options embedded in a project that can raise its value. In other cases, the whole investment is essentially an option. The payoffs from the investment are contingent on an underlying asset, just like most financial options. For example, the value of an oil well or refinery investment is contingent upon the price of oil. The value of a gold mine is contingent upon the price of gold. If oil prices are low, you may not drill a well. If oil prices are high, you go ahead and drill. Many R&D (research and development) projects also look like options.

There are several approaches to evaluating capital budgeting projects with real options. One of the difficulties with real options is that the analysis can be very complicated. Although some of the problems are simple and can be readily solved, many of them are so complex that they are expensive to evaluate or you may not have much confidence in the analysis. Four common sense approaches to real options analysis are presented below.

1. Use **DCF** analysis without considering options. If the NPV is positive without considering real options, and the project has real options that would simply add more value, it is unnecessary to evaluate the options. Just go ahead and make the investment.

2. Consider the Project NPV = NPV(based on DCF alone) − Cost of options + Value of options. Go ahead and calculate the NPV based on expected cash flows. Then simply add the value associated with real options. For example, if a project has a negative NPV based on DCF alone of $50 million, will the options add at least that much to its value?

3. Use **decision trees**. Although they are not as conceptually sound as option pricing models, decision trees can capture the essence of many sequential decision making problems.

4. Use option pricing models. Except for simple options, the technical requirements for solving these models may require you to hire special consultants or "quants." Some large companies have their own specialists.

The analyst is confronted with (1) a variety of real options that investment projects may possess and (2) a decision about how to reasonably value these options. Example 10 deals with production flexibility; in this case, an additional investment outlay gives the company an option to use alternative fuel sources.

EXAMPLE 10

Production-Flexibility Option

Sackley AquaFarms estimated the NPV of the expected cash flows from a new processing plant to be −$0.40 million. Sackley is evaluating an incremental investment of $0.30 million that would give management the flexibility to switch between coal, natural gas, and oil as an energy source. The original plant relied only on coal. The option to switch to cheaper sources of energy when they are available has an estimated value of $1.20 million. What is the value of the new processing plant including this real option to use alternative energy sources?

Solution: The NPV, including the real option, should be

$$\text{Project NPV} = \text{NPV(based on DCF alone)} - \text{Cost of options} + \text{Value of options}$$
$$\text{Project NPV} = -0.40 \text{ million} - 0.30 \text{ million} + 1.20 \text{ million}$$
$$= \$0.50 \text{ million.}$$

Without the flexibility offered by the real option, the plant is unprofitable. The real option to adapt to cheaper energy sources adds enough to the value of this investment to give it a positive NPV.

Two of the most valuable options are to abandon or expand a project at some point after the original investment. Example 11 illustrates the abandonment option.

EXAMPLE 11

Abandonment Option

Nyberg Systems is considering a capital project with the following characteristics:

▶ The initial outlay is €200,000.

▶ Project life is four years.

▶ Annual after-tax operating cash flows have a 50 percent probability of being €40,000 for the four years and a 50 percent probability of being €80,000.

▶ Salvage value at project termination is zero.

▶ The required rate of return is 10 percent.

▶ In one year, after realizing the first-year cash flow, the company has the option to abandon the project and receive the salvage value of €150,000.

1. Compute the project NPV assuming no abandonment.

2. What is the optimal abandonment strategy? Compute the project NPV using that strategy.

Solution to 1: The expected annual after-tax operating cash flow is $0.50(40,000) + 0.50(80,000) = €60,000$. The cash flows discounted at 10 percent give an NPV of

$$NPV = -200,000 + \sum_{t=1}^{4} \frac{60,000}{1.10^t} = -€9,808$$

The project should be rejected because it has a negative NPV.

Solution to 2: The optimal abandonment strategy would be to abandon the project in one year if the subsequent cash flows are worth less than the abandonment value. If at the end of the first year the low cash flow occurs, you can abandon for €150,000 and give up €40,000 for the following three years. The €40,000 annual cash flow, discounted for three years at 10 percent, has a present value of only €99,474, so you should abandon. Three years of the higher €80,000 cash flow has a present value of €198,948, so you should not abandon. After the first year, abandon if the low cash flow occurs, and do not abandon if the high cash flow occurs.

If the high cash flow occurs and you do not abandon, the NPV is

$$NPV = -200,000 + \sum_{t=1}^{4} \frac{80,000}{1.10^t} = €53,589$$

If you abandon when the low cash flow occurs, you receive the first year cash flow and the abandonment value and then no further cash flows. In that case, the NPV is

$$NPV = -200,000 + \frac{40,000 + 150,000}{1.10} = -€27,273$$

The expected NPV is then

$$NPV = 0.50(53,589) + 0.50(-27,273) = €13,158$$

Optimal abandonment raises the NPV by $13,158 - (-€9,808) = €22,966$.

A fundamental real option could be a gold mine or an oil well. Example 12 looks at the possibility of purchasing the rights to a gold mining property.

EXAMPLE 12

Erichmann Gold Mine

The Erichmann family has offered a five-year option on one of its small gold mining properties for $10 million. The current price of gold is $400 per ounce. The mine holds an estimated 500,000 ounces that could be mined at an average cost of $450 per ounce. The maximum production rate is 200,000 ounces per year. How would you assess the Erichmann family's offer?

Solution: A binomial option model can be built for the underlying price of gold. These binomial models are very common in assessing the value of financial options such as puts and **calls** on stocks, **callable bonds**, or mortgages with prepayment options. Whenever the price path for gold is above $450 per ounce, it might be attractive to commence mining. Of course, you would cease mining whenever the price is lower. With additional information about the volatility of gold prices and the risk-free interest rate, an expert could build this **binomial model** and value the real option. Comparing the value of this real option to its $10 million cost would enable you to make an investment decision.

A critical assumption of many applications of traditional capital budgeting tools is that the investment decision is made now, with no flexibility considered in future decisions. A more reasonable approach is to assume that the corporation is making sequential decisions, some now and some in the future. A combination of optimal current and future decisions is what will maximize company value. Real options analysis tries to incorporate rational future decisions into the assessment of current investment decision making. This future flexibility, exercised intelligently, enhances the value of capital investments. Some real options can be valued with readily available option pricing models, such as the binomial model or the Black–Scholes–Merton option pricing model.[14] Unfortunately, many real options are very complex and hard to value, which poses a challenge as the analyst tries to lay out the economic contingencies of an investment and assess their values. A real option, with the future flexibility it provides, can be an important piece of the value of many projects.

---

[14] Chapter 4 of Chance (2003) gives an excellent overview of option pricing models.

7.6 Common Capital Budgeting Pitfalls

Although the principles of capital budgeting may be easy to learn, applying the principles to real world investment opportunities can be challenging. Some of the common mistakes that managers make are listed in Table 27.

TABLE 27   Common Capital Budgeting Pitfalls

Not incorporating economic responses into the investment analysis

Misusing capital budgeting templates

Pet projects

Basing investment decisions on EPS, net income, or return on equity

Using IRR to make investment decisions

Bad accounting for cash flows

Overhead costs

Not using the appropriate risk-adjusted discount rate

Spending all of the investment budget just because it is available

Failure to consider investment alternatives

Handling sunk costs and opportunity costs incorrectly

Economic Responses   Economic responses to an investment often affect its profitability, and these responses have to be correctly anticipated. For example, in response to a successful investment, competitors can enter and reduce the investment's profitability. Similarly, vendors, suppliers, and employees may want to gain from a profitable enterprise. Companies that make highly profitable investments often find that a competitive marketplace eventually causes profitability to revert to normal levels.

Template Errors   Because hundreds or even thousands of projects need to be analyzed over time, corporations have standardized capital budgeting templates for managers to use in evaluating projects. This situation creates risks in that the template model may not match the project, or employees may input inappropriate information.

Pet Projects   Pet projects are projects that influential managers want the corporation to invest in. Ideally, pet projects will receive the normal scrutiny that other investments receive and will be selected on the strength of their own merits. Often, unfortunately, pet projects are selected without undergoing normal capital budgeting analysis. Or the pet project receives the analysis, but overly optimistic projections are used to inflate the project's profitability.

EPS, Net Income, or ROE   Managers sometimes have incentives to boost EPS, net income, or ROE. Many investments, even those with strong NPVs, do not boost these accounting numbers in the short run and may even reduce them. Paying attention to short-run accounting numbers can result in choosing projects that are not in the long-run economic interests of the business.

Basing Decisions on the IRR   The NPV criterion is economically sound. The IRR criterion is also sound for independent projects (with conventional cash flow patterns). If projects are mutually exclusive or competitive with each other, investing in projects based on the IRR will tend to result in choosing smaller, short-term projects with high IRRs at the expense of larger, longer-term, high NPV projects. Basing decisions on paybacks or accounting rates of return is even more dangerous. These measures can be economically unsound.

Bad Accounting for Cash Flows　In analyzing a complicated project, it is easy to omit relevant cash flows, double count cash flows, and mishandle taxes.

Overhead Costs　In large companies, the cost of a project must include the overhead it generates for such things as management time, information technology support, financial systems, and other support. Although these items are hard to estimate, over- or underestimating these overhead costs can lead to poor investment decisions.

Discount Rate Errors　The required rate of return for a project should be based on its risk. If a project is being financed with debt (or with equity), you should still use the project's required rate of return and not the cost of debt (or the **cost of equity**). Similarly, a high-risk project should not be discounted at the company's overall cost of capital, but at the project's required rate of return. Discount rate errors have a huge impact on the computed NPVs of long-lived projects.

Overspending and Underspending the Capital Budget　Politically, many managers will spend all of their budget and argue that their budget is too small. In a well-run company, managers will return excess funds whenever their profitable projects cost less than their budget, and managers will make a sound case for extra funds if their budget is too small.

Failure to Consider Investment Alternatives　Generating good investment ideas is the most basic step in the capital budgeting process, and many good alternatives are never even considered.

Sunk Costs and Opportunity Costs　Ignoring sunk costs is difficult for managers to do. Furthermore, not identifying the economic alternatives (real and financial) that are the opportunity costs is probably the biggest failure in much analysis. Only costs that change with the decision are relevant.

OTHER INCOME MEASURES AND VALUATION MODELS　　8

Capital budgeting was one of the first widespread applications of discounted cash flow analysis. In the basic capital budgeting model, the analyst values an investment by discounting future after-tax cash flows at the rate of return required by investors. Subtracting the initial investment results in the project's NPV. The future cash flows consist of after-tax operating cash flows plus returns of investment (such as salvage value and sale of working capital).

Analysts will employ and encounter other concepts of income and other valuation approaches besides this basic capital budgeting model. Because some of these other approaches are economically sound and widely employed, we will briefly describe some of them here. By considering these approaches, you can see the distinguishing features of each approach and that they should result in consistent valuations (if they are used correctly).

To facilitate the comparison of income measures and valuation models, we will employ as an example a simple company (the Granite Corporation) that invests in one project. The company goes out of business when that project expires. After evaluating that project with the NPV and IRR capital budgeting models, we will examine that same project using the following alternative methods:

▶ economic income and accounting income
▶ economic profit valuation
▶ residual income valuation
▶ claims valuation

Our purpose is to show how the various income measures and valuation methods are related to each other.

8.1 The Basic Capital Budgeting Model

The basic capital budgeting model (presented earlier) identifies the after-tax operating cash flows from an investment as well as non-operating cash flows (such as the initial investment or future recovery of invested capital or net working capital). Then, these cash flows are discounted at the required rate of return for the asset to establish the NPV.

The base-case capital budgeting project is the following. The company is going to invest $150,000 and generate sales for the next five years as shown in Table 28. Variable cash operating expenses will be 50 percent of sales each year, and fixed cash operating expenses are $20,000. Depreciation is straight-line to zero, $30,000 per year with a zero book value at the end of five years. The income tax rate is 40 percent. Salvage value is $10,000, which is taxable at 40 percent, leaving an after-tax salvage value of $6,000 at the end of five years. The required rate of return is 10 percent.

TABLE 28	Basic Capital Budgeting Example for Granite Corporation					
Year	0	1	2	3	4	5
Fixed capital investment	−150,000					
Sales		150,000	200,000	250,000	200,000	150,000
Variable cash expenses		75,000	100,000	125,000	100,000	75,000
Fixed cash expenses		20,000	20,000	20,000	20,000	20,000
Depreciation		30,000	30,000	30,000	30,000	30,000
Operating income before taxes		25,000	50,000	75,000	50,000	25,000
Taxes at 40 percent		10,000	20,000	30,000	20,000	10,000
Operating income after taxes		15,000	30,000	45,000	30,000	15,000
After-tax operating cash flow		45,000	60,000	75,000	60,000	45,000
Salvage value						10,000
Taxes on salvage value						4,000
After-tax salvage value						6,000
Total after-tax cash flow	−150,000	45,000	60,000	75,000	60,000	51,000
NPV (at r = 10 percent)	69,492					
IRR	26.27%					

The present value of the after-tax cash flows for Years 1–5 is $219,492. Subtracting the investment of $150,000 results in the NPV of $69,492. The IRR for the investment is 26.27 percent.

8.2 Economic and Accounting Income

Economic income and accounting income differ from the after-tax operating cash flows used in the basic capital budgeting model.

Economic income is the profit realized from an investment. For a given year, economic income is the investment's after-tax cash flow plus the change in the market value:

Economic income = Cash flow + Change in market value
Economic income = Cash flow + (Ending market value
　　　　　　　　　− Beginning market value)

or **(31-11)**

Economic income = Cash flow − (Beginning market value
　　　　　　　　　− Ending market value)
Economic income = Cash flow − Economic depreciation[15]

For the Granite Corporation, the cash flows are already calculated in Table 28. The beginning market value at time zero is the present value of the future after-tax cash flows at the 10 percent required rate of return, or $219,492. The market value at any future date is the present value of subsequent cash flows discounted back to that date. For the Granite Corporation, the cash flows, changes in market value, and economic incomes are shown in Table 29.

TABLE 29　Economic Income for Granite Corporation

Year	1	2	3	4	5
Beginning market value	219,492	196,441	156,086	96,694	46,364
Ending market value	196,441	156,086	96,694	46,364	0
Change in market value	−23,051	−40,356	−59,391	−50,331	−46,364
After-tax cash flow	45,000	60,000	75,000	60,000	51,000
Economic income	21,949	19,644	15,609	9,669	4,636
Economic rate of return	10%	10%	10%	10%	10%

In Year 1, the beginning value is $219,492 and the ending value is $196,441, so the change in value is −$23,051. The economic income is the cash flow plus the change in value, or $45,000 + (−$23,051) = $21,949. The economic income for Years 2–5 is found similarly. The economic rate of return is the year's economic income divided by its beginning market value. Notice that the economic

[15] These equations are conceptually identical because economic depreciation is the negative of the change in market value. For example, assume the cash flow is 10, the beginning market value is 30, and the ending market value is 25. Cash flow + Change in market value = Cash flow + (Ending market value − Beginning market value) = 10 + (25 − 30) = 5. Or, Cash flow − Economic depreciation = Cash flow − (Beginning market value − Ending market value) = 10 − (30 − 25) = 5.

rate of return is precisely 10 percent each year, which was the required rate of return on the project.

Accounting income for this company will differ from the economic income for two reasons. First, the accounting depreciation is based on the original cost of the investment (not the market value of the investment). Consequently, the accounting depreciation schedule does not follow the declines in the market value of an asset. Besides being based on accounting depreciation instead of economic depreciation, accounting net income is the after-tax income remaining after paying interest expenses on the company's debt obligations. In contrast, interest expenses are ignored when computing the economic income for an asset or the after-tax operating cash flows in the basic capital budgeting model. As explained in Section 3, the effects of financing costs are captured in the discount rate, not in the cash flows. In the capital budgeting model, if we included interest expenses in the cash flows, we would be double counting them.

To illustrate these differences, we will assume that the company borrows an amount equal to one-half of the value of the company, which is 50 percent of $219,492, or $109,746, and that it pays 8 1/3 percent interest each year on the beginning balance. With a 40 percent tax rate, the after-tax interest cost is 8 1/3% (1 − 0.40) = 5.0%. Because the Granite Corporation has a five-year life, it does not need to borrow or retain earnings for the future, and all cash flows will be distributed to bondholders and stockholders. Granite will maintain a 50 percent debt/value ratio on the company's debt, so bondholders will receive 8 1/3 percent interest on their beginning bond balance and the debt will also be amortized (paid down) whenever the value of the company goes down. Furthermore, after all operating costs, interest expenses, and taxes are paid, stockholders will receive all remaining cash flows each year as a cash dividend or share repurchase.[16]

The financial statements for the Granite Corporation are shown in Table 30.

The income statement for financial reporting purposes differs from that used in the capital budgeting model because the interest on debt obligations is now taken out as an expense before arriving at net income. The book value of the company's assets is based on the original accounting cost minus accumulated accounting depreciation. Note that the liabilities and net worth are also declining in the balance sheet. The liabilities decline each year, reflecting the amounts that were paid annually to reduce the principal of the loan. Notice, also, that the net worth is declining. Normally, the net worth of a company increases because beginning equity is increased by net retentions—the excess of net income over dividends paid. In this case, the company is shrinking and going out of business in five years, so the distributions to shareholders (which can be either cash dividends or share repurchases) exceed net income and net worth declines. The amounts that are paid each year to reduce debt and for dividends/share repurchases are shown in the financing section of the statement of cash flows.

Accounting measures of performance also can differ from economic measures of performance. Table 31 repeats the economic income and accounting income from Tables 29 and 30. The table also shows the economic rate of return each year and two popular accounting measures of performance: the return on equity (ROE = net income divided by beginning equity) and return on assets (ROA = EBIT divided by beginning assets).

---

[16] The assumptions may be unrealistic, but this is a very simple corporation.

TABLE 30 Condensed Financial Statements for Granite Corporation

Year	0	1	2	3	4	5
Balance sheets:						
Assets	150,000	120,000	90,000	60,000	30,000	0
Liabilities	109,746	98,221	78,043	48,347	23,182	0
Net worth	40,254	21,779	11,957	11,653	6,818	0
Income statements:						
Sales		150,000	200,000	250,000	200,000	150,000
Variable cash expenses		75,000	100,000	125,000	100,000	75,000
Fixed cash expenses		20,000	20,000	20,000	20,000	20,000
Depreciation		30,000	30,000	30,000	30,000	30,000
EBIT		25,000	50,000	75,000	50,000	25,000
Interest expense		9,146	8,185	6,504	4,029	1,932
EBT		15,854	41,815	68,496	45,971	23,068
Taxes at 40 percent		6,342	16,726	27,399	18,388	9,227
Net income before salvage		9,513	25,089	41,098	27,583	13,841
After-tax salvage value						6,000
Net income		9,513	25,089	41,098	27,583	19,841
Statements of cash flows:						
Operating cash flows:						
Net income		9,513	25,089	41,098	27,583	19,841
Depreciation		30,000	30,000	30,000	30,000	30,000
Total		39,513	55,089	71,098	57,583	49,841
Financing cash flows:						
Debt repayment		−11,525	−20,178	−29,696	−25,165	−23,182
Dividends/repurchases		−27,987	−34,911	−41,402	−32,417	−26,659
Total		−39,513	−55,089	−71,098	−57,583	−49,841
Investing cash flows		0	0	0	0	0
Total cash flows		0	0	0	0	0

TABLE 31 Economic Income, Accounting Income, and Rates of Return for Granite Corporation

Year	1	2	3	4	5
Economic income	21,949	19,644	15,609	9,669	4,636
Accounting income	9,513	25,089	41,098	27,583	19,841
Economic rate of return	10.00%	10.00%	10.00%	10.00%	10.00%
Return on equity (ROE)	23.63%	115.20%	343.71%	236.70%	291.00%
Return on assets (ROA)	16.67%	41.67%	83.33%	83.33%	83.33%

As Table 31 illustrates, economic and accounting incomes differ substantially. Over the five years, economic income is much less than accounting income, and the patterns certainly differ. In addition, the accounting rates of return, the ROE and ROA, for this admittedly unusual company are quite different from the economic rate of return.

8.3 Economic Profit, Residual Income, and Claims Valuation

Although the capital budgeting model is widely employed, analysts have used other procedures to divide up the cash flows from a company or project and then value them using discounted cash flow methods. We present three of these alternative models here: the economic profit model, the **residual income model**, and the claims valuation model. Used correctly, they are all consistent with the basic capital budgeting model and with each other.

8.3.1 Economic Profit

The first alternative method for measuring income and valuing assets is based on economic profit (EP).[17] Economic profit has been used in asset valuation as well as in performance measurement and management compensation. Its calculation is loosely as follows:

$$EP = NOPAT - \$WACC \qquad\qquad \textbf{(31-12)}$$

where

$$
\begin{aligned}
EP &= \text{Economic profit} \\
NOPAT &= \text{Net operating profit after tax} = \text{EBIT}(1 - \text{Tax rate}) \\
EBIT &= \text{Operating income before taxes, or Earnings before interest} \\
&\quad\ \text{and taxes} \\
\$WACC &= \text{Dollar cost of capital} = \text{WACC} \times \text{Capital} \\
WACC &= \text{Weighted average (or overall) cost of capital} \\
Capital &= \text{Investment}
\end{aligned}
$$

EP is a periodic measure of profit above and beyond the dollar cost of the capital invested in the project. The dollar cost of capital is the dollar return that the company must make on the project in order to pay the debt holders and the equity holders their respective required rates of return.[18]

For the Granite Corporation, for the first year, we have the following:

$$
\begin{aligned}
NOPAT &= \text{EBIT}(1 - \text{Tax rate}) = 25{,}000(1 - 0.40) = \$15{,}000 \\
\$WACC &= \text{WACC} \times \text{Capital} = 10\% \times 150{,}000 = \$15{,}000 \\
EP &= NOPAT - \$WACC = 15{,}000 - 15{,}000 = \$0
\end{aligned}
$$

---

[17] **Economic Value Added**® or EVA, trademarked by the consulting firm Stern Stewart & Company, is a well known commercial application of the economic profit approach. See Stewart (1991) and Peterson and Peterson (1996) for complete discussion.

[18] At Level I, you studied the relationship between the required rate of return on the project or WACC (here 10 percent), the rate of return required by debtholders (here 8 1/3 percent), and the rate of return required by equityholders (here 15 percent).

TABLE 32	EP for Granite Corporation				
Year	**1**	**2**	**3**	**4**	**5[b]**
Capital[a]	150,000	120,000	90,000	60,000	30,000
NOPAT	15,000	30,000	45,000	30,000	21,000
$WACC	15,000	12,000	9,000	6,000	3,000
EP	0	18,000	36,000	24,000	18,000

[a] Depreciation is $30,000 per year.

[b] The $6,000 after-tax gain from salvage is included in NOPAT in Year 5.

Table 32 shows the EP for all five years for the Granite Corporation.

EP is readily applied to valuation of an asset or a security. The NPV found by discounted cash flow analysis in the basic capital budgeting model will be equal to the present value of future EP discounted at the weighted average cost of capital.

$$NPV = \sum_{t=1}^{\infty} \frac{EP_t}{(1 + WACC)^t} \qquad \textbf{(31-13)}$$

This NPV is also called the **market value added (MVA)**.[19] So we have

$$NPV = MVA = \sum_{t=1}^{\infty} \frac{EP_t}{(1 + WACC)^t} \qquad \textbf{(31-14)}$$

Discounting the five years of EP for the Granite Corporation at the 10 percent WACC gives an NPV (and MVA) of $69,492. The total value of the company (of the asset) is the original investment of $150,000 plus the NPV of $69,492, or $219,492. The valuation using EP is the same as that found with the basic capital budgeting model.

8.3.2 Residual Income

Another method for estimating income and valuing an asset is the **residual income** method.[20] This method focuses on the returns to equity, where

Residual income = Net income − **Equity charge**,

or

$$RI_t = NI_t - r_e B_{t-1} \qquad \textbf{(31-15)}$$

where

RI_t = Residual income during period t

NI_t = Net income during period t

$r_e B_{t-1}$ = Equity charge for period t, which is the required rate of return on equity, r_e, times the beginning-of-period book value of equity, B_{t-1}

[19] Peterson and Peterson define MVA as the market value of the company minus the capital invested, which is an NPV.

[20] See Chapter 5 in Stowe, Robinson, Pinto, and McLeavey (2002) and Edwards and Bell (1961) for treatments of residual income analysis.

For the first year for the Granite Corporation, the net income is $9,513. The beginning book value of equity is $40,254 (from the balance sheet in Table 30), and the required rate of return on equity is 15 percent. Consequently, the residual income for Year 1 is:

$$RI_t = NI_t - r_e B_{t-1} = 9{,}513 - 0.15(40{,}254) = 9{,}513 - 6{,}038 = \$3{,}475$$

The residual income for all five years for Granite is shown in Table 33.

TABLE 33   Residual Income for Granite Corporation

Year	1	2	3	4	5[a]
NI_t	9,513	25,089	41,098	27,583	19,841
$r_e B_{t-1}$	6,038	3,267	1,794	1,748	1,023
RI_t	3,475	21,822	39,304	25,835	18,818

[a] The $6,000 after-tax gain from salvage is included in NI in Year 5.

Residual income, like EP, can also be applied to valuation of an asset or security. The NPV of an investment is the present value of future residual income discounted at the required rate of return on equity.

$$NPV = \sum_{t=1}^{\infty} \frac{RI_t}{(1 + r_e)^t} \qquad \text{(31-16)}$$

Discounting the residual income for the Granite Corporation at the 15 percent required rate of return on equity gives an NPV of $69,492. The total value of the company (of the asset) is the present value of the residual income, the original equity investment, plus the original debt investment:

PV of residual income	$69,492
Equity investment	40,254
Debt investment	109,746
Total value	$219,492

The value of the company is the original book value of its debt and equity plus the present value of the residual income (which is the project's NPV). Again, this is the same value we found with the basic capital budgeting model and with the EP model.

8.3.3 Claims Valuation

To value a company, the EP valuation approach essentially adds the present value of EP to the original investment. The residual income approach adds the present value of residual income to the original debt and equity investments in the company. Since the EP approach is from the perspective of all suppliers of capital, EP is discounted at the overall WACC. The residual income approach takes the perspective of equity investors, so residual income is discounted at the cost of equity.

The third and final alternative valuation approach that we present is to divide the operating cash flows between securityholder classes (in this example, debt and equity), and then value the debt and equity cash flows separately.

Balance Sheet

Assets	Liabilities
	Equity

The basic capital budgeting approach is to value the asset, which is on the left-hand side of the balance sheet above. The claims valuation approach values the liabilities and equity, the claims against the assets, which are on the right-hand side of the balance sheet. The value of the claims should equal the value of the assets.

For the Granite Corporation, the cash flows to debtholders are the interest payments and principal payments. These are valued by discounting them at the cost of debt, which is 8 1/3 percent. The cash flows to stockholders are the dividends and share repurchases, which are valued by discounting them at the 15 percent cost of equity. Table 34 lists the future cash flows for debt and equity.

TABLE 34	Payments to Bondholders and Stockholders of Granite Corporation				
Year	**1**	**2**	**3**	**4**	**5**
Interest payments	9,146	8,185	6,504	4,029	1,932
Principal payments	11,525	20,178	29,696	25,165	23,182
Total debt payments	20,671	28,363	36,199	29,194	25,114
Equity distributions	27,987	34,911	41,402	32,417	26,659

The present value of the total debt payments, discounted at the cost of debt, is $109,746. The value of the equity distributions, discounted at the cost of equity, is $109,746. The total value of the company is the combined value of debt and equity, which is $219,492.

In our example, the basic capital budgeting model, the economic profit model, the residual income model, and the claims valuation model all result in the same valuation of the company. In the real world, analysts must deal with many accounting complications. Some of these complications may include pension liability adjustments, valuations of marketable securities held, exchange rate gains and losses, and adjustments for leases, inventories, goodwill, deferred taxes, etc. In theory, all of the valuation models are equivalent. In practice, even with due diligence and care, analysts may prefer one approach over others and disagree about valuations.

There are other approaches to valuation that analysts use and run across. Two common ones are the free cash flow to the firm and **free cash flow to equity** approaches.[21] The free cash flow to the firm approach is fundamentally the same as the basic capital budgeting approach. The free cash flow to equity approach is related to the claims valuation approach. In corporate finance, corporate managers usually value an asset by valuing its total after-tax cash flows. Security analysts typically value equity by valuing the cash flows to stockholders. Real estate investors often evaluate real estate investments by valuing the cash flows to the equity investor after payments to creditors, which is like the claims valuation approach.

---

[21] The free cash flow to the firm and free cash flow to equity approaches are developed in Chapter 3 of Stowe, Robinson, Pinto, and McLeavey (2002).

SUMMARY

Capital budgeting is the process that companies use for decision making on capital projects—those projects with a life of a year or more. This reading developed the principles behind the basic capital budgeting model, the cash flows that go into the model, and several extensions of the basic model.

▶ Capital budgeting undergirds the most critical investments for many corporations—their investments in long-term assets. The principles of capital budgeting have been applied to other corporate investing and financing decisions and to security analysis and portfolio management.

▶ The typical steps in the capital budgeting process are: (1) generating ideas, (2) analyzing individual proposals, (3) planning the capital budget, and (4) monitoring and post-auditing.

▶ Projects susceptible to capital budgeting process can be categorized as: (1) replacement, (2) expansion, (3) new products and services, and (4) regulatory, safety and environmental.

▶ Capital budgeting decisions are based on incremental after-tax cash flows discounted at the opportunity cost of funds. Financing costs are ignored because both the cost of debt and the cost of other capital are captured in the discount rate.

▶ The net present value (NPV) is the present value of all after-tax cash flows, or

$$NPV = \sum_{t=0}^{n} \frac{CF_t}{(1+r)^t}$$

where the investment outlays are negative cash flows included in the CF_ts and where r is the required rate of return for the investment.

▶ The IRR is the discount rate that makes the present value of all future cash flows sum to zero. This equation can be solved for the IRR:

$$\sum_{t=0}^{n} \frac{CF_t}{(1+IRR)^t} = 0$$

▶ The payback period is the number of years required to recover the original investment in a project. The payback is based on cash flows.

▶ The discounted payback period is the number of years it takes for the cumulative discounted cash flows from a project to equal the original investment.

▶ The average accounting rate of return (AAR) can be defined as follows:

$$AAR = \frac{\text{Average net income}}{\text{Average book value}}$$

▶ The profitability index (PI) is the present value of a project's future cash flows divided by the initial investment:

$$PI = \frac{\text{PV of future cash flows}}{\text{Initial investment}} = 1 + \frac{NPV}{\text{Initial investment}}$$

► The capital budgeting decision rules are to invest if the NPV > 0, if the IRR > r, or if the PI > 1.0. There are no decision rules for the payback period, discounted payback period, and AAR because they are not always sound measures.

► The NPV profile is a graph that shows a project's NPV graphed as a function of various discount rates.

► For mutually exclusive projects that are ranked differently by the NPV and IRR, it is economically sound to choose the project with the higher NPV.

► The "multiple IRR problem" and the "no IRR problem" can arise for a project with nonconventional cash flows—cash flows that change signs more than once during the project's life.

► The fact that projects with positive NPVs theoretically increase the value of the company and the value of its stock could explain the popularity of NPV as an evaluation method.

► Analysts often organize the cash flows for capital budgeting in tables, summing all of the cash flows occurring at each point in time. These totals are then used to find an NPV or IRR. Alternatively, tables collecting cash flows by type can be used. Equations for the capital budgeting cash flows are as follows:

Initial outlay:
$$\text{Outlay} = \text{FCInv} + \text{NWCInv} - \text{Sal}_0 + T(\text{Sal}_0 - B_0)$$
Annual after-tax operating cash flow:
$$CF = (S - C - D)(1 - T) + D, \text{ or}$$
$$CF = (S - C)(1 - T) + TD$$
Terminal year after-tax non-operating cash flow:
$$\text{TNOCF} = \text{Sal}_T + \text{NWCInv} - T(\text{Sal}_T - B_T)$$

► Depreciation schedules affect taxable income, taxes paid, and after-tax cash flows, and therefore capital budgeting valuations.

► Spreadsheets are heavily used for capital budgeting valuation.

► When inflation exists, the analyst should perform capital budgeting analysis in "nominal" terms if cash flows are nominal and in "real" terms if cash flows are real.

► Inflation reduces the value of depreciation tax savings (unless the tax system adjusts depreciation for inflation). Inflation reduces the value of fixed payments to bondholders. Inflation usually does not affect all revenues and costs uniformly. Contracting with customers, suppliers, employees, and sources of capital can be complicated as inflation rises.

► Two ways of comparing mutually exclusive projects in a replacement chain are the "least common multiple of lives" approach and the "equivalent annual annuity" approach.

► For the least common multiple of lives approach, the analyst extends the time horizon of analysis so that the lives of both projects will divide exactly into the horizon. The projects are replicated over this horizon, and the NPV for the total cash flows over the least common multiple of lives is used to evaluate the investments.

► The equivalent annual annuity is the annuity payment (series of equal annual payments over the project's life) that is equivalent in value to the project's actual cash flows. Analysts find the present value of all of the cash flows for an investment (the NPV) and then calculate an annuity payment that has a value equivalent to the NPV.

▶ With capital rationing, the company's capital budget has a size constraint. Under "hard" capital rationing, the budget is fixed. In the case of hard rationing, managers use trial and error and sometimes mathematical programming to find the optimal set of projects. In that situation, it is best to use the NPV or PI valuation methods.

▶ Sensitivity analysis calculates the effect on the NPV of changes in one input variable at a time.

▶ Scenario analysis creates scenarios that consist of changes in several of the input variables and calculates the NPV for each scenario.

▶ Simulation (Monte Carlo) analysis is used to estimate probability distributions for the NPV or IRR of a capital project. Simulations randomly select values for stochastic input variables and then repeatedly calculate the project NPV and IRR to find their distributions.

▶ Risk-adjusted discount rates based on market risk measures should be used as the required rate of return for projects when the investors are diversified. The capital asset pricing model (CAPM) and arbitrage pricing theory (APT) are common approaches for finding market-based risk-adjusted rates.

▶ In the CAPM, a project's or asset's beta, or β, is used as a measure of systematic risk. The security market line (SML) estimates the asset's required rate of return as $r_i = R_F + \beta_i [E(R_M) - R_F]$.

▶ Project-specific betas should be used instead of company betas whenever the risk of the project differs from that of the company.

▶ Real options can be classified as (1) timing options; (2) sizing options, which can be abandonment options or growth (expansion) options; (3) flexibility options, which can be price-setting options or production-flexibility options; and (4) fundamental options. Simple options can be evaluated with decision trees; for more complex options, the analyst should use option pricing models.

▶ Economic income is the investment's after-tax cash flow plus the change in the market value. Accounting income is revenues minus expenses. Accounting depreciation, based on the original cost of the investment, is the decrease in the book (accounting) value, while **economic depreciation** is the decrease in the market value of the investment. Accounting net income is net of the after-tax interest expenses on the company's debt obligations. In computing economic income, financing costs are ignored.

▶ Economic profit is

$$EP = NOPAT - \$WACC$$

where NOPAT = Net operating profit after tax = EBIT$(1 - $ Tax rate$)$ and $WACC = Dollar cost of capital = WACC $\times$ Capital. When applied to the valuation of an asset or security, the NPV of an investment (and its market value added) is the present value of future EP discounted at the weighted average cost of capital.

$$NPV = MVA = \sum_{t=1}^{\infty} \frac{EP_t}{(1 + WACC)^t}$$

The total value of the company (of the asset) is the original investment plus the NPV.

▶ Residual income = Net income = Equity charge, or $RI_t = NI_t - r_e B_{t-1}$ where RI_t = Residual income during period t, NI_t = Net income during period t, r_e = the cost of equity, and B_{t-1} = the beginning-of-period book value of equity. The NPV of an investment is the present value of future residual income discounted at the required rate of return on equity:

$$\text{NPV} = \sum_{t=1}^{\infty} \frac{RI_t}{(1 + r_e)^t}$$

The total value of the company (of the asset) is the NPV plus the original equity investment plus the original debt investment.

▶ The claims valuation approach values an asset by valuing the claims against the asset. For example, an asset financed with debt and equity has a value equal to the value of the debt plus the value of the equity.

PRACTICE PROBLEMS FOR READING 31

1. FITCO is considering the purchase of new equipment. The equipment costs $350,000, and an additional $110,000 is needed to install it. The equipment will be depreciated straight-line to zero over a five-year life. The equipment will generate additional annual revenues of $265,000, and it will have annual cash operating expenses of $83,000. The equipment will be sold for $85,000 after five years. An inventory investment of $73,000 is required during the life of the investment. FITCO is in the 40 percent tax bracket and its cost of capital is 10 percent. What is the project NPV?

   A. $47,818.

   B. $63,658.

   C. $80,189.

   D. $97,449.

2. After estimating a project's NPV, the analyst is advised that the fixed capital outlay will be revised upward by $100,000. The fixed capital outlay is depreciated straight-line over an eight-year life. The tax rate is 40 percent and the required rate of return is 10 percent. No changes in cash operating revenues, cash operating expenses, or salvage value are expected. What is the effect on the project NPV?

   A. $100,000 decrease.

   B. $73,325 decrease.

   C. $59,988 decrease.

   D. No change.

3. When assembling the cash flows to calculate an NPV or IRR, the project's after-tax interest expenses should be subtracted from the cash flows for

   A. the NPV calculation, but not the IRR calculation.

   B. the IRR calculation, but not the NPV calculation.

   C. both the NPV calculation and the IRR calculation.

   D. neither the NPV calculation nor the IRR calculation.

4. Standard Corporation is investing $400,000 of fixed capital in a project that will be depreciated straight-line to zero over its ten-year life. Annual sales are expected to be $240,000, and annual cash operating expenses are expected to be $110,000. An investment of $40,000 in net working capital is required over the project's life. The corporate income tax rate is 30 percent. What is the after-tax operating cash flow expected in year one?

   A. $63,000.

   B. $92,000.

   C. $103,000.

   D. $130,000.

5. Five years ago, Frater Zahn's Company invested £38 million—£30 million in fixed capital and another £8 million in working capital—in a bakery. Today, Frater Zahn's is selling the fixed assets for £21 million and liquidating the investment in working capital. The book value of the fixed assets is £15 million and the marginal tax rate is 40 percent. The fifth year's after-tax non-operating cash flow to Frater Zahn's is *closest* to

A. £20.6 million.

B. £23.0 million.

C. £26.6 million.

D. £29.0 million.

The following information relates to Questions 6–8

McConachie Company is considering the purchase of a new 400-ton stamping press. The press costs $360,000, and an additional $40,000 is needed to install it. The press will be depreciated straight-line to zero over a five-year life. The press will generate no additional revenues, but it will reduce cash operating expenses by $140,000 annually. The press will be sold for $120,000 after five years. An inventory investment of $60,000 is required during the life of the investment. McConachie is in the 40 percent tax bracket.

6. What is the McConachie net investment outlay?
   A. $360,000.
   B. $400,000.
   C. $420,000.
   D. $460,000.

7. McConachie's annual after-tax operating cash flow is *closest* to
   A. $116,000.
   B. $124,000.
   C. $140,000.
   D. $164,000.

8. What is the terminal year after-tax non-operating cash flow at the end of year five?
   A. $108,000.
   B. $129,000.
   C. $132,000.
   D. $180,000.

The following information relates to Questions 9–14

Linda Pyle is head of analyst recruiting for PPA Securities. She has been very frustrated by the number of job applicants who, in spite of their stellar pedigrees, seem to have little understanding of basic financial concepts. Pyle has written a set of conceptual questions and simple problems for the human resources department to use to screen for the better candidates in the applicant pool. A few of her corporate finance questions and problems are given below.

▶ Concept 1. "A company invests in depreciable assets, financed partly by issuing fixed-rate bonds. If inflation is lower than expected, the value of the real tax savings from depreciation and the value of the real after-tax interest expense are both reduced."

▶ Concept 2. "Sensitivity analysis and scenario analysis are useful tools for estimating the impact on a project's NPV of changing the value of one capital budgeting input variable at a time."

▶ Concept 3. "When comparing two mutually exclusive projects with unequal lives, the IRR is a good approach for choosing the better project because it does not require equal lives."

▶ Concept 4. "Project-specific betas should be used instead of company betas whenever the risk of the project differs from that of the company."

Problem. "Fontenot Company is investing €100 in a project that is being depreciated straight-line to zero over a two-year life with no salvage value. The project will generate earnings before interest and taxes of €50 each year for two years. Fontenot's weighted average cost of capital and required rate of return for the project are both 12 percent, and its tax rate is 30 percent."

---

9. For Concept 1, the statement is correct regarding the effects on
   A. the real tax savings from depreciation, but incorrect regarding the real after-tax interest expense.
   B. the real after-tax interest expense, but incorrect regarding the real tax savings from depreciation.
   C. both the real tax savings from depreciation and the real after-tax interest expense.
   D. neither the real tax savings from depreciation nor the real after-tax interest expense.

10. For Concept 2, the statement is correct regarding
   A. sensitivity analysis, but not correct regarding scenario analysis.
   B. scenario analysis, but not correct regarding sensitivity analysis.
   C. both sensitivity analysis and scenario analysis.
   D. neither sensitivity analysis nor scenario analysis.

11. Are the statements identified as Concept 3 and Concept 4, respectively, correct?

	Concept 3	Concept 4
A.	No	No
B.	No	Yes
C.	Yes	No
D.	Yes	Yes

12. The after-tax operating cash flows in euros for the Fontenot Company are
- **A.** 70 in Year 1 and 70 in Year 2.
- **B.** 70 in Year 1 and 85 in Year 2.
- **C.** 85 in Year 1 and 70 in Year 2.
- **D.** 85 in Year 1 and 85 in Year 2.

13. The economic income in euros for the Fontenot Company is
- **A.** 9.11 in Year 1 and 17.24 in Year 2.
- **B.** 17.24 in Year 1 and 9.11 in Year 2.
- **C.** 17.76 in Year 1 and 24.89 in Year 2.
- **D.** 24.89 in Year 1 and 17.76 in Year 2.

14. The market value added (MVA) in euros for the Fontenot Company is *closest* to
- **A.** 38.87.
- **B.** 39.92.
- **C.** 43.65.
- **D.** 44.88.

The following information relates to Questions 15–20

The capital budgeting committee for Laroche Industries is meeting. Laroche is a North American conglomerate that has several divisions. One of these divisions, Laroche Livery, operates a large fleet of vans. Laroche's management is evaluating whether it is optimal to operate new vans for two, three, or four years before replacing them. The managers have estimated the investment outlay, annual after-tax operating expenses, and after-tax salvage cash flows for each of the service lives. Because revenues and some operating costs are unaffected by the choice of service life, they were ignored in the analysis. Laroche Livery's opportunity cost of funds is 10 percent. The table below gives the cash flows in thousands of Canadian dollars (C$).

Service Life	Investment	Year 1	Year 2	Year 3	Year 4	Salvage
2 years	−40,000	−12,000	−15,000			20,000
3 years	−40,000	−12,000	−15,000	−20,000		17,000
4 years	−40,000	−12,000	−15,000	−20,000	−25,000	12,000

Schoeman Products, another division of Laroche, has evaluated several investment projects and now must choose the subset of them that fits within its C$40 million capital budget. The outlays and NPVs for the six projects are given below. Schoeman cannot buy fractional projects, and must buy all or none of a project. The currency amounts are in millions of Canadian dollars.

Project	Outlay	PV of Future Cash Flows	NPV
1	31	34	13
2	15	21	6
3	12	16.5	4.5
4	10	13	3
5	8	11	3
6	6	8	2

Schoeman wants to determine which subset of the six projects is optimal.

A final proposal comes from the division Society Services, which has an investment opportunity with a real option to invest further if conditions warrant. The crucial details are as follows:

► The original project:
  ► an outlay of C$190 million at time zero
  ► cash flows of C$40 million per year for Years 1–10 if demand is "high"
  ► cash flows of C$20 million per year for Years 1–10 if demand is "low"
► The optional expansion project:
  ► an outlay of C$190 million at time one
  ► cash flows of C$40 million per year for Years 2–10 if demand is "high"
  ► cash flows of C$20 million per year for Years 2–10 if demand is "low"

▶ Whether demand is "high" or "low" in Years 1–10 will be revealed during the first year. The probability of "high" demand is 0.50, and the probably of "low" demand is 0.50.

▶ The option to make the expansion investment depends on making the initial investment. If the initial investment is not made, the option to expand does not exist.

▶ The required rate of return is 10 percent.

Society Services wants to evaluate its investment alternatives.

The internal auditor for Laroche Industries has made several suggestions for improving capital budgeting processes at the company. The internal auditor's suggestions are as follows:

Suggestion 1: "In order to put all capital budgeting proposals on an equal footing, the projects should all use the risk-free rate for the required rate of return."

Suggestion 2: "Because you cannot exercise both of them, you should not permit a given project to have both an abandonment option and an expansion/growth option."

Suggestion 3: "When rationing capital, it is better to choose the portfolio of investments that maximizes the company NPV than the portfolio that maximizes the company IRR."

Suggestion 4: "Project betas should be used for establishing the required rate of return whenever the project's beta is different from the company's beta."

---

15. What is the optimal service life for Laroche Livery's fleet of vans?

   A. Two years.

   B. Three years.

   C. Four years.

   D. Three and four years are equally attractive.

16. The optimal subset of the six projects that Schoeman is considering consists of Projects

   A. 1 and 5.

   B. 2, 3, and 4.

   C. 2, 3, and 5.

   D. 2, 4, 5, and 6.

17. What is the NPV (C$ millions) of the original project for Society Services without considering the expansion option?

   A. −6.11.

   B. −5.66.

   C. 2.33.

   D. 5.58.

18. What is the NPV (C$ millions) of the optimal set of investment decisions for Society Services including the expansion option?

   A. 1.83.

   B. 6.34.

   C. 9.17.

   D. 12.68.

19. Should the capital budgeting committee accept the internal auditor's first and second suggestions, respectively?

	Suggestion 1	Suggestion 2
A.	No	No
B.	No	Yes
C.	Yes	No
D.	Yes	Yes

20. Should the capital budgeting committee accept the internal auditor's third and fourth suggestions, respectively?

	Suggestion 3	Suggestion 4
A.	No	No
B.	No	Yes
C.	Yes	No
D.	Yes	Yes

The following information relates to Questions 21–26

Maximilian Böhm is reviewing several capital budgeting proposals from subsidiaries of his company. Although his reviews deal with several details that may seem like minutiae, the company places a premium on the care it exercises in making its investment decisions.

The first proposal is a project for Richie Express, which is investing $500,000, all in fixed capital, in a project that will have depreciation and operating income after taxes, respectively, of $40,000 and $20,000 each year for the next three years. Richie Express will sell the asset in three years, paying 30 percent taxes on any excess of the selling price over book value. The proposal indicates that a $647,500 terminal selling price will enable the company to earn a 15 percent internal rate of return on the investment. Böhm doubts that this terminal value estimate is correct.

Another proposal concerns Gasup Company, which does natural gas exploration. A new investment has been identified by the Gasup finance department with the following projected cash flows:

▶ Investment outlays are $6 million immediately and $1 million at the end of the first year.

▶ After-tax operating cash flows are $0.5 million at the end of the first year and $4 million at the end of each of the second, third, fourth, and fifth years. In addition, an after-tax outflow occurs at the end of the five-year project that has not been included in the operating cash flows: $5 million required for environmental cleanup.

▶ The required rate of return on natural gas exploration is 18 percent.

The Gasup analyst is unsure about the calculation of the NPV and the IRR because the outlay is staged over two years.

Finally, Dominion Company is evaluating two mutually exclusive projects: The Pinto grinder involves an outlay of $100,000, annual after-tax operating cash flows of $45,000, an after-tax salvage value of $25,000, and a three-year life. The Bolten grinder has an outlay of $125,000, annual after-tax operating cash flows of $47,000, an after-tax salvage value of $20,000, and a four-year life. The required rate of return is 10 percent. The net present value (NPV) and equivalent annual annuity (EAA) of the Pinto grinder are $30,691 and $12,341, respectively. Whichever grinder is chosen, it will have to be replaced at the end of its service life. The analyst is unsure about which grinder should be chosen.

Böhm and his colleague Beth Goldberg have an extended conversation about capital budgeting issues, including several comments listed below. Goldberg makes two comments about real options:

1. "The abandonment option is valuable, but it should be exercised only when the abandonment value is above the amount of the original investment."

2. "If the cost of a real option is less than its value, this will increase the NPV of the investment project in which the real option is embedded."

Böhm also makes several comments about specific projects under consideration:

A. "The land and building were purchased five years ago for $10 million. This is the amount that should now be included in the fixed capital investment."

B. "We can improve the project's NPV by using the after-tax cost of debt as the discount rate. If we finance the project with 100 percent debt, this discount rate would be appropriate."

C. "It is generally safer to use the NPV than the IRR in making capital budgeting decisions. However, when evaluating mutually exclusive projects, if the projects have conventional cash flow patterns and have the same investment outlays, it is acceptable to use either the NPV or IRR."

D. "You should not base a capital budgeting decision on its immediate impact on earnings per share (EPS)."

---

21. What terminal selling price is required for a 15 percent internal rate of return on the Richie project?

   A. $552,087.

   B. $588,028.

   C. $593,771.

   D. $625,839.

22. The NPV and IRR, respectively, of the Gasup Company investment are *closest* to

	NPV	IRR
A.	$509,600	21.4%
B.	$509,600	31.3%
C.	$946,700	21.4%
D.	$946,700	31.3%

23. Of the two grinders that the Dominion Company is evaluating, Böhm should recommend the

   A. Bolten grinder because its NPV is higher than the Pinto grinder NPV.

   B. Bolten grinder because its EAA is higher than the Pinto grinder EAA.

   C. Pinto grinder because its NPV is higher than the Bolten grinder NPV.

   D. Pinto grinder because its EAA is higher than the Bolten grinder EAA.

24. Are Goldberg's comments about real options correct?

	Comment #1 about Abandonment Value	Comment #2 about Increasing the NPV of the Investment Project
A.	No	No
B.	No	Yes
C.	Yes	No
D.	Yes	Yes

25. Is Böhm most likely correct regarding his

	Comment A about the $10 million capital investment?	Comment B about using the after-tax cost of debt?
A.	No	No
B.	No	Yes
C.	Yes	No
D.	Yes	Yes

26. Is Böhm most likely correct regarding his

	Comment C that it is acceptable to use either NPV or IRR?	Comment D about the immediate impact on EPS?
A.	No	No
B.	No	Yes
C.	Yes	No
D.	Yes	Yes

The following information relates to Questions 27–32

Barbara Simpson is a sell-side analyst with Smith Riccardi Securities. Simpson covers the pharmaceutical industry. One of the companies she follows, Bayonne Pharma, is evaluating a regional distribution center. The financial predictions for the project are as follows:

- ► Fixed capital outlay is €1.50 billion.
- ► Investment in net working capital is €0.40 billion.
- ► Straight-line depreciation is over a six-year period with zero salvage value.
- ► Project life is 12 years.
- ► Additional annual revenues are €0.10 billion.
- ► Annual cash operating expenses are reduced by €0.25 billion.
- ► The capital equipment is sold for €0.50 billion in 12 years.
- ► Tax rate is 40 percent.
- ► Required rate of return is 12 percent.

Simpson is evaluating this investment to see whether it has the potential to affect Bayonne Pharma's stock price. Simpson estimates the NPV of the project to be €0.41 billion, which should increase the value of the company.

Simpson is evaluating the effects of other changes to her capital budgeting assumptions. She wants to know the effect of a switch from straight-line to accelerated depreciation on the company's operating income and the project's NPV. She also believes that the initial outlay might be much smaller than initially assumed. Specifically, she thinks the outlay for fixed capital might be €0.24 billion lower, with no change in salvage value.

When reviewing her work, Simpson's supervisor provides the following comments. "I note that you are relying heavily on the NPV approach to valuing the investment decision. I don't think you should use an IRR because of the multiple IRR problem that is likely to arise with the Bayonne Pharma project. However, the equivalent annual annuity would be a more appropriate measure to use for the project than the NPV. I suggest that you compute an EAA."

---

27. Simpson should estimate the after-tax operating cash flow for Years 1–6 and 7–12, respectively, to be *closest* to

	Years 1–6	Years 7–12
A.	€0.31 billion	€0.21 billion
B.	€0.31 billion	€0.25 billion
C.	€0.35 billion	€0.21 billion
D.	€0.35 billion	€0.25 billion

28. Simpson should estimate the initial outlay and the terminal year non-operating cash flow, respectively, to be *closest* to

	Initial Outlay	Terminal Year Non-Operating Cash Flow
A.	€1.50 billion	€0.70 billion
B.	€1.50 billion	€0.90 billion
C.	€1.90 billion	€0.70 billion
D.	€1.90 billion	€0.90 billion

29. Is Simpson's estimate of the NPV of the project correct?

    A. Yes.

    B. No. The NPV is −€0.01 billion.

    C. No. The NPV is €0.34 billion.

    D. No. The NPV is €0.78 billion.

30. A switch from straight-line to accelerated depreciation would

    A. increase the NPV and decrease the first year operating income after taxes.

    B. increase the first year operating income after taxes and decrease the NPV.

    C. increase both the NPV and first year operating income after taxes.

    D. decrease both the NPV and first year operating income after taxes.

31. If the outlay is lower by the amount that Simpson suggests, the project NPV should increase by an amount *closest* to

    A. €0.09 billion.

    B. €0.14 billion.

    C. €0.17 billion.

    D. €0.24 billion.

32. How would you evaluate the comments by Simpson's supervisor about not using the IRR and about using the EAA?

	Comment about IRR	Comment about EAA
A.	Correct	Correct
B.	Correct	Incorrect
C.	Incorrect	Correct
D.	Incorrect	Incorrect

The following information relates to Questions 33–38

Mun Hoe Yip is valuing Pure Corporation. Pure is a simple corporation that is going out of business in five years, distributing its income to creditors and bondholders as planned in the financial statements below. Pure has a 19 percent cost of equity, 8-1/3 percent before-tax cost of debt, 12 percent weighted average cost of capital, and 40 percent tax rate, and it maintains a 50 percent debt/value ratio.

Yip is valuing the company using the basic capital budgeting method as well as other methods, such as EP, residual income, and claims valuation. Yip's research assistant, Linda Robinson, makes three observations about the analysis.

Observation 1: "The present value of the company's economic income should be equal to the present value of the discounted cash flows in the basic capital budgeting approach."

Observation 2: "The economic income each year is equal to the cash flow minus the economic depreciation."

Observation 3: "The market value added is the present value of the company's economic profit (EP), which equals the net worth of 77,973."

Year	0	1	2	3	4	5
Balance sheets						
Assets	200,000	160,000	120,000	80,000	40,000	0
Liabilities	122,027	107,671	88,591	64,222	33,929	0
Net worth	77,973	52,329	31,409	51,778	6,071	0
Income statements						
Sales		180,000	200,000	220,000	240,000	200,000
Variable cash expenses		90,000	100,000	110,000	120,000	100,000
Fixed cash expenses		20,000	20,000	20,000	20,000	20,000
Depreciation		40,000	40,000	40,000	40,000	40,000
EBIT		30,000	40,000	50,000	60,000	40,000
Interest expense		10,169	8,973	7,383	5,352	2,827
EBT		19,831	31,027	42,617	54,648	37,173
Taxes at 40 percent		7,932	12,411	17,047	21,859	14,869
Net income before salvage		11,899	18,616	25,570	32,789	22,304
After-tax salvage value						12,000
Net income		11,899	18,616	25,570	32,789	34,304
Statements of cash flows						
Operating cash flows						
Net income		11,899	18,616	25,570	32,789	34,304
Depreciation		40,000	40,000	40,000	40,000	40,000
Total		51,899	58,616	65,570	72,789	74,304

Year	0	1	2	3	4	5
Financing cash flows						
Debt repayment		14,357	19,080	24,369	30,293	33,929
Dividends/repurchases		37,542	39,536	41,201	42,496	40,375
Total		−51,899	−58,616	−65,570	−72,789	−74,304
Investing cash flows		0	0	0	0	0
Total cash flows		0	0	0	0	0

33. Economic income during year one is *closest* to

  A. 23,186.

  B. 29,287.

  C. 46,101.

  D. 51,899.

34. What is EP during year one?

  A. −12,101.

  B. −6,000.

  C. 6,000.

  D. 13,542.

35. What is residual income during year one?

  A. −2,916.

  B. 2,542.

  C. 8,653.

  D. 14,815.

36. What is the value of equity at time zero?

  A. 29,287.

  B. 44,055.

  C. 77,973.

  D. 122,027.

37. Are Robinson's first two observations, respectively, correct?

	Observation 1	Observation 2
A.	No	No
B.	No	Yes
C.	Yes	No
D.	Yes	Yes

38. Which of the following would be Yip's *most appropriate* response to Robinson's third observation?

   A. Your observation is correct.

   B. The market value added is not equal to the present value of EP, although the market value of equity is equal to 77,973.

   C. The market value added is equal to the present value of EP, which in this case is 44,055.

   D. The market value added is not equal to the present value of EP, and market value added is equal to 44,055.

Questions 39–44 relate to Carlos Velasquez

Carlos Velasquez, CFA, is a financial analyst with Embelesado, S.A., a Spanish manufacturer of sailboats and sailing equipment. Velasquez is evaluating a proposal for Embelesado to build sailboats for a foreign competitor that lacks production capacity and sells in a different market. The sailboat project is perceived to have the same risk as Embelesado's other projects.

The proposal covers a limited time horizon—three years—after which the competitor expects to be situated in a new, larger production facility. The limited time horizon appeals to Embelesado, which currently has excess capacity but expects to begin its own product expansion in slightly more than three years.

Velasquez has collected much of the information necessary to evaluate this proposal in Exhibits 1 and 2.

EXHIBIT 1	Selected Data for Sailboat Proposal (currency amounts in € millions)
Initial fixed capital outlay	60
Annual contracted revenues	60
Annual operating costs	25
Initial working capital outlay (recovered at end of the project)	10
Annual depreciation expense (both book and tax accounting)	20
Economic life of facility (years)	3
Salvage (book) value of facility at end of project	0
Expected market value of facility at end of project	5

EXHIBIT 2	Selected Data for Embelesado, S.A.
Book value of long-term debt/total assets	28.6%
Book value of equity/total assets	71.4%
Market value of long-term debt/market value of company	23.1%
Market value of equity/market value of company	76.9%
Coupon rate on existing long-term debt	8.5%
Interest rate on new long-term debt	8.0%
Cost of equity	13.0%
Marginal tax rate	35.0%
Maximum acceptable payback period	2 years

Velasquez recognizes that Embelesado is currently financed at its target capital structure and expects that the capital structure will be maintained if the sailboat project is undertaken. Embelesado's managers disagree, however, about the method that should be used to evaluate capital budgeting proposals.

One of Embelesado's vice presidents asks Velasquez the following questions:

1. Will projects that meet a corporation's payback criterion for acceptance necessarily have a positive net present value (NPV)?

2. For mutually exclusive projects, will the NPV and internal rate of return (IRR) methods necessarily agree on project ranking?

3. For the sailboat project, what will be the effects of using accelerated depreciation (for both book and tax accounting) instead of straight-line depreciation on (a) the NPV and (b) the total net cash flow in the terminal year?

4. Assuming a 13 percent discount rate, what will be the increase in the sailboat project's NPV if the expected market value of the facility at end of project is €15 million rather than €5 million?

2006 exam

39. The weighted average cost of capital for Embelesado is *closest* to

   A. 10.78%.

   B. 11.20%.

   C. 11.85%.

   D. 11.96%.

2006 exam

40. The total net cash flow (in € millions) for the sailboat project in its terminal year is *closest* to

   A. 33.00.

   B. 39.75.

   C. 43.00.

   D. 44.75.

2006 exam

41. The IRR for the sailboat project is *closest* to

   A. 18.5%.

   B. 19.7%.

   C. 20.3%.

   D. 24.7%.

2006 exam

42. The best responses that Velasquez can make to question #1 and question #2 are

	Question #1	Question #2
A.	No	No
B.	No	Yes
C.	Yes	No
D.	Yes	Yes

43. In response to question #3, what are the *most likely* effects on the NPV and the total net cash flow in the terminal year, respectively?

	NPV	Total Net Cash Flow in Terminal Year
A.	Increase	Increase
B.	Increase	Decrease
C.	Decrease	Increase
D.	Decrease	Decrease

44. In response to question #4, the increase in the sailboat project's NPV (in € millions) is *closest* to

- **A.** 4.50.
- **B.** 6.50.
- **C.** 6.76.
- **D.** 6.93.

$4\frac{5}{8}$ $4\frac{7}{}$

$5\frac{1}{2}$ $5\frac{1}{2}$ $-$ $\frac{5}{8}$

$5\frac{1}{2}$ $21\frac{3}{16}$ $-$ $\frac{1}{16}$

$20\frac{5}{8}$ $21\frac{3}{16}$ $-$ $\frac{1}{16}$

$17\frac{3}{8}$ $18\frac{1}{8}$ $+$ $\frac{7}{8}$

$6\frac{1}{2}$ $6\frac{1}{2}$ $-$ $\frac{1}{2}$

$7\frac{1}{4}$ $3\frac{1}{32}$ $-$ $\frac{1}{8}$

$\frac{15}{16}$

$\frac{9}{16}$ $\frac{9}{16}$

$\frac{9}{32}$ $7\frac{13}{16}$ $7\frac{15}{16}$

$7\frac{1}{16}$ $7\frac{13}{16}$ $7\frac{15}{16}$

$2\frac{5}{8}$ $2\frac{11}{32}$ $2\frac{1}{2}$ $+$

$2\frac{3}{4}$ $2\frac{1}{4}$ $2\frac{1}{4}$

$12\frac{1}{16}$ $11\frac{3}{8}$ $11\frac{3}{4}$ $+$

$33\frac{3}{4}$ 33 $33\frac{1}{16}$ $-$

602   $25\frac{5}{8}$ $24\frac{9}{16}$ $25\frac{5}{8}$ $+$

833   12 $11\frac{5}{8}$ $11\frac{7}{8}$ $+$

16 $10\frac{1}{2}$ $10\frac{1}{2}$ $10\frac{1}{2}$ $-$

78 $15\frac{5}{8}$ $15\frac{13}{16}$ $15\frac{7}{8}$ $-$

4808 $9\frac{1}{16}$ $8\frac{1}{4}$ $8\frac{5}{8}$ $+$

430   $11\frac{1}{4}$ $10\frac{5}{8}$

$4\frac{5}{8}$

CAPITAL STRUCTURE AND LEVERAGE

by Raj Aggarwal, Cynthia Harrington, Adam Kobor, and Pamela P. Peterson

LEARNING OUTCOMES

The candidate should be able to:

a. define and explain leverage, business risk, sales risk, operating risk, and financial risk, and classify a risk, given a description;

b. calculate and interpret the degree of operating leverage, the degree of financial leverage, and the degree of total leverage;

c. characterize the operating leverage, financial leverage, and total leverage of a company given a description of it;

d. calculate the breakeven quantity of sales and determine the company's net income at various sales levels;

e. describe the effect of financial leverage on a company's net income and return on equity;

f. compare and contrast the risks of creditors and owners;

g. describe the objective of the capital structure decision;

h. discuss the Modigliani and Miller (MM) propositions concerning capital structure irrelevance and describe the relation between the cost of equity and financial leverage;

i. discuss the effect of taxes on the MM propositions, the cost of capital, and the value of a company;

j. identify and explain the costs of financial distress, the agency costs and net agency costs of equity, the costs of asymmetric information, and their relation to a company's optimal capital structure;

k. explain and diagram the static trade-off theory of the optimal capital structure;

l. compare the implications of the MM propositions, the pecking order theory of capital structure, and the static trade-off theory of capital structure;

m. explain the target capital structure and why actual capital structure may fluctuate around the target;

n. review the role of debt ratings in capital structure policy;

o. explain the factors an analyst should consider in evaluating the impact of capital structure policy on valuation;

p. discuss international differences in financial leverage and the implications for investment analysis.

1 INTRODUCTION

This reading presents capital structure and leverage. **Leverage** is the use of fixed costs in a company's cost structure. The fixed costs that are operating costs (such as depreciation or rent) create operating leverage. Fixed costs that are financial costs (such as interest expense) create financial leverage. Analysts need to understand a company's use of leverage for three main reasons.

First, the degree of leverage is an important component in assessing a company's risk and return characteristics. Second, analysts may be able to discern a company's prospects from management's decisions about financing choices. Knowing how to interpret these signals also helps the analyst evaluate the quality of management's decisions. Third, the valuation of a company requires forecasting future cash flows and assessing the risk associated with those cash flows. The cost structure of a company affects its risk: The greater the company's fixed costs relative to its variable costs, the greater the potential volatility in its future earnings and, hence, cash flows. We refer to the use of fixed costs as leverage because these fixed costs act as a fulcrum for the company's earnings. Leverage can magnify earnings both up and down. The profits of highly leveraged companies might soar with small upturns in sales. But the reverse is also true: Small drops in revenue can rapidly lead to losses.

This reading also discusses the choice about how to finance (i.e., raise money for) a company's operations, which is the capital structure decision. Senior management makes the capital structure decision. The capital structure that is chosen will very often include the use of debt, which will affect the company's financial leverage. Thus, it is natural to discuss capital structure and leverage together. In this reading, therefore, we will:

► discuss and illustrate the business risk and financial risk of a company;
► show how to quantify these risks for a company or division using degrees of leverage;
► view how leverage affects a company's value; and
► learn how to evaluate a company's capital structure.

The reading is organized as follows: In Section 2, we introduce the concept of leverage. In Section 3, we discuss the sources of earnings volatility, including sales risk, operating risk, and financial risk, and explain quantitative measures of leverage. In Section 4, we discuss the company's capital structure decision and the choice of alternative sources of financing. In Section 5, we present important issues for the analyst, such as the role of debt rating in the capital structure decision and international differences in capital structure policies. We summarize this at the end of the reading.

LEVERAGE   2

Leverage increases the potential volatility of a company's earnings and cash flows and increases the risk of lending to or owning a company. Additionally, the valuation of a company and its equity is affected by the degree of leverage: The greater the leverage, the greater the risk and hence, the greater the discount rate applied in its valuation. Further, highly leveraged companies have a greater chance of incurring significant losses during downturns, thus accelerating conditions that lead to financial distress and bankruptcy.

Consider the simple example of two companies, Impulse Robotics, Inc., and Malvey Aerospace, Inc. These companies have the following performance for the period of study:[1]

TABLE 1	Impulse Robotics and Malvey Aerospace	
	Impulse Robotics	**Malvey Aerospace**
Revenues	$1,000,000	$1,000,000
Operating costs	700,000	750,000
Operating income	$300,000	$250,000
Financing expense	100,000	50,000
Net income	$200,000	$200,000

These companies have the same net income, but are they identical in terms of financial characteristics? Would we appraise these two companies at the same value? Not necessarily.

The risk associated with future earnings and cash flows of a company are affected by the company's cost structure. The **cost structure** of a company is the mix of variable and fixed costs. **Variable costs** fluctuate with the level of production and sales. Some examples of variable costs are the cost of goods purchased for resale, costs of materials or supplies, shipping charges, delivery charges, wages for hourly employees, sales commissions, and sales or production bonuses. **Fixed costs** are expenses that are the same regardless of the production and sales of the company. These costs include depreciation, rent, interest on debt, insurance, and wages for salaried employees.

---

[1] We are ignoring taxes for this example, but when taxes are included, the general conclusions remain the same.

Suppose that the cost structures of the companies differ in the following manner:

TABLE 2   Impulse Robotics and Malvey Aerospace

	Impulse Robotics	Malvey Aerospace
Number of units produced and sold	100,000	100,000
Sales price per unit	$10	$10
Variable cost per unit	$2	$6
Fixed operating cost	$500,000	$150,000
Fixed financing expense	$100,000	$50,000

The risk associated with these companies is different, although, as we saw in Table 1, they have the same net income. They have different operating and financing cost structures, resulting in differing potential volatility of net income.

For example, if the number of units produced and sold is different from 100,000, the net income of the two companies diverges. If 50,000 units are produced and sold, Impulse Robotics has a loss of $200,000 and Malvey Aerospace has $0 earnings. If, on the other hand, the number of units produced and sold is 200,000, Impulse Robotics earns $1 million whereas Malvey Aerospace earns $600,000. In other words, the swing in net income is greater for Impulse

FIGURE 1   Net Income for Different Numbers of Units Produced and Sold

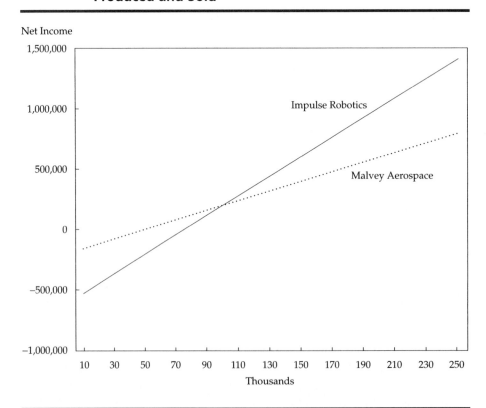

Robotics, which has higher fixed costs in terms of both fixed operating costs and fixed financing costs.

Impulse Robotics' cost structure results in more leverage than that of Malvey Aerospace. We can see this effect when we plot the net income of each company against the number of units produced and sold, as in Figure 1. The greater leverage of Impulse Robotics is reflected in the greater slope of the line representing net income. This means that as the number of units sold changes, Impulse Robotics experiences a greater change in net income than does Malvey Aerospace for the same change in units sold.

Companies that have more fixed costs relative to variable costs in their cost structures have greater variation in net income as revenues fluctuate and, hence, more risk.

BUSINESS RISK AND FINANCIAL RISK   **3**

Risk arises from both the operating and financing activities of a company. In the following, we address how that happens and the measures available to the analyst to gauge the risk in each case.

3.1 Business Risk and Its Components

Business risk is the risk associated with operating earnings. **Operating earnings** are uncertain because total revenues and many of the expenditures contributed to produce those revenues are uncertain. Revenues are affected by a large number of factors, including economic conditions, the actions of competitors, governmental regulation, and demographics. Therefore, prices of the company's goods or services or the quantity of sales may be different from what is expected. We refer to the uncertainty with respect to the price and quantity of goods and services as **sales risk.**

Operating risk is the risk attributed to the operating cost structure, in particular the use of fixed costs in operations. The greater the fixed operating costs relative to variable operating costs, the greater the operating risk. Business risk is therefore the combined risk of sales and operations. Companies that operate in the same line of business generally have similar business risk.

3.2 Sales Risk

Consider Impulse Robotics once again. Suppose that the forecasted number of units produced and sold in the next period is 100,000 but that the standard deviation of the number of units sold is 20,000. And suppose the price that the units sell for is expected to be $10 per unit but the standard deviation is $2. Contrast this situation with that of a company named Tolley Aerospace, Inc., which has the same cost structure but a standard deviation of units sold of 40,000 and a price standard deviation of $4.

If we assume, for simplicity's sake, that the fixed operating costs are known with certainty and that the units sold and price per unit follow a normal distribution, we can see the impact of the different risks on the operating income of the two companies through a simulation; the results are shown in Figure 2. Here, we see the differing distributions of operating income that result from the distributions of units sold and price per unit. So, even if the companies have the

FIGURE 2   Operating Income Simulations for Impulse Robotics and Tolley Aerospace

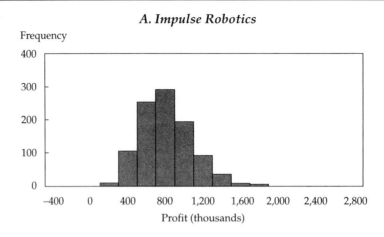

A. Impulse Robotics

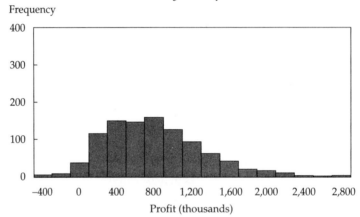

B. Tolley Aerospace

same cost structure, differing *sales risk* affects the potential variability of the company's profitability. In our example, Tolley Aerospace has a wider distribution of likely outcomes in terms of operating profit. This greater potential volatility in operating earnings means that Tolley Aerospace has more sales risk than Impulse Robotics.

3.3 Operating Risk

The greater the fixed component of costs, the more difficult it is for a company to adjust its operating costs to changes in sales. The mixture of fixed and variable costs depends largely on the type of business. Even within the same line of business, companies can vary their fixed and variable costs to some degree. We refer to the risk arising from the mix of fixed and variable costs as **operating risk**. The greater the fixed operating costs relative to variable operating costs, the greater the operating risk.

Next, we will look at how operating risk affects the variability of cash flows. A concept taught in **microeconomics** is **elasticity**, which is simply a measure of the sensitivity of changes in one item to changes in another. We can apply this concept to examine how sensitive a company's operating income is to changes in demand, as measured by unit sales. We will calculate the operating income elasticity, which we refer to as the **degree of operating leverage (DOL)**.

The degree of operating leverage is the ratio of the percentage change in operating income to the percentage change in units sold. We will simplify things and assume that the company sells all that it produces in the same period. Then,

$$\text{DOL} = \frac{\text{Percentage change in operating income}}{\text{Percentage change in units sold}} \quad \text{(32-1)}$$

Returning to Impulse Robotics, the price per unit is $10, the variable cost per unit is $2, and the **total fixed costs** are $500,000. If Impulse Robotics' output changes from 100,000 units to 110,000 units—an increase of 10 percent in the number of units sold—operating income changes from $300,000 to $380,000:[2]

TABLE 3	Operating Leverage of Impulse Robotics		
Item	Selling 100,000 Units	Selling 110,000 Units	Percentage Change
Revenues	$1,000,000	$1,100,000	+10.00%
less variable costs	200,000	220,000	+10.00%
less fixed costs	500,000	500,000	0.00%
Operating income	$300,000	$380,000	+26.67%

Operating income increases by 26.67 percent when units sold increases by 10 percent. What if the number of units *decreases* by 10 percent, from 100,000 to 90,000? Operating income is $220,000, representing a *decline* of 26.67 percent.

What is happening is that for a 1 percent change in units sold, the operating income changes by 2.67 times that percentage, in the same direction. If units sold increases by 10 percent, operating income increases by 26.7 percent; if units sold decreased by 20 percent, operating income would decrease by 53.3 percent.

We can represent the degree of operating leverage as given in Equation 32-1 in terms of the basic elements of the price per unit, variable cost per unit, number of units sold, and fixed operating costs. Operating income is

$$\begin{array}{l} \text{Operating} \\ \text{income} \end{array} = \left[\left(\begin{array}{c} \text{Price} \\ \text{per unit} \end{array} \right) \left(\begin{array}{c} \text{Number of} \\ \text{units sold} \end{array} \right) \right] - \left[\left(\begin{array}{c} \text{Variable cost} \\ \text{per unit} \end{array} \right) \left(\begin{array}{c} \text{Number of} \\ \text{units sold} \end{array} \right) \right]$$
$$- \left[\begin{array}{c} \text{Fixed operating} \\ \text{costs} \end{array} \right]$$

or

---

[2] We provide the variable and fixed operating costs for our sample companies used in this reading to illustrate the leverage and breakeven concepts. In reality, however, the financial analyst does not have these breakdowns but rather is faced with interpreting reported account values that often combine variable and fixed costs and costs for different product lines.

$$\underbrace{\begin{array}{c}\text{Operating}\\\text{income}\end{array} = \begin{pmatrix}\text{Number of}\\\text{units sold}\end{pmatrix}\left[\begin{pmatrix}\text{Price}\\\text{per unit}\end{pmatrix} - \begin{pmatrix}\text{Variable cost}\\\text{per unit}\end{pmatrix}\right]}_{\text{Contribution margin}}$$

$$- \begin{bmatrix}\text{Fixed operating}\\\text{costs}\end{bmatrix}$$

The **per unit contribution margin** is the amount that each unit sold contributes to covering fixed costs—that is, the difference between the price per unit and the variable cost per unit. That difference multiplied by the quantity sold is the **contribution margin**, which equals revenue minus variable costs.

How much does operating income change when the number of units sold changes? Fixed costs do not change; therefore, operating income changes by the contribution margin. The percentage change in operating income for a given change in units sold simplifies to

$$\text{DOL} = \frac{Q(P - V)}{Q(P - V) - F} \tag{32-2}$$

where Q is the number of units, P is the price per unit, V is the variable operating cost per unit, and F is the fixed operating cost. Therefore, $P - V$ is the per unit contribution margin and $Q(P - V)$ is the contribution margin.

Applying the formula for DOL using the data for Impulse Robotics, we can calculate the sensitivity to change in units sold from 100,000 units:

$$\begin{array}{c}\text{DOL @}\\\text{100,000 units}\end{array} = \frac{100,000(\$10 - \$2)}{100,000(\$10 - \$2) - \$500,000} = 2.67$$

A DOL of 2.67 means that a 1 percent change in units sold results in a $1\% \times 2.67 = 2.67\%$ change in operating income; a DOL of 5 means that a 1 percent change in units sold results in a 5 percent change in operating income, and so on.

Why do we specify that the DOL is at a particular quantity sold (in this case, 100,000 units)? Because the DOL is different at different numbers of units produced and sold. For example, at 200,000 units,

$$\begin{array}{c}\text{DOL @}\\\text{200,000 units}\end{array} = \frac{200,000(\$10 - \$2)}{200,000(\$10 - \$2) - \$500,000} = 1.45$$

We can see the sensitivity of the DOL for different numbers of units produced and sold in Figure 3. When operating profit is negative, the DOL is negative. At positions just below and just above the point where operating income is $0, operating income is at its most sensitive on a percentage basis to changes in units produced and sold. At the point at which operating income is $0 (at 62,500 units produced and sold in this example), the DOL is undefined because the denominator in the DOL calculation is $0. After this point, the DOL gradually declines as more units are produced and sold.

We will now look at a similar situation in which the company has shifted some of the operating costs away from fixed costs and into variable costs. Malvey

FIGURE 3   Impulse Robotics' Degree of Operating Leverage for Different Number of Units Produced and Sold

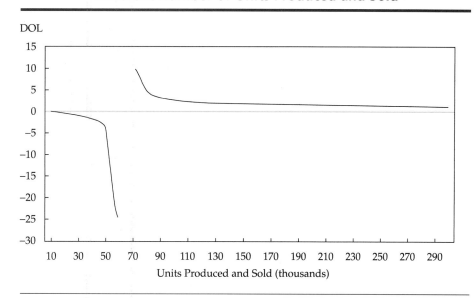

$P = \$10; \ V = \$2; \ F = \$500,000.$

Aerospace has a unit sales price of $10, a variable cost of $6 a unit, and $150,000 in fixed costs. A change in units sold from 100,000 to 110,000 (a 10 percent change) changes operating profit from $250,000 to $290,000, or 16 percent. The DOL in this case is 1.6:

$$\text{DOL @} \atop 100,000 \ \text{units} = \frac{100,000(\$10 - \$6)}{100,000(\$10 - \$6) - \$150,000} = 1.6$$

and the change in operating income is 16 percent:

$$\text{Percentage change} \atop \text{in operating income} = \text{DOL} \left(\text{Percentage change} \atop \text{in units sold} \right) = 1.6(10\%) = 16\%$$

We can see the difference in leverage in the case of Impulse Robotics and Malvey Aerospace companies in Figure 4. In Panel A, we see that Impulse Robotics has higher operating income than Malvey Aerospace when both companies produce and sell more than 87,500 units, but lower operating income than Malvey when both companies produce and sell less than 87,500 units.[3]

This example confirms what we saw earlier in our reasoning of fixed and variable costs: The greater the use of fixed, relative to variable, operating costs, the more sensitive operating income is to changes in units sold and, therefore, the more operating risk. Impulse Robotics has more operating risk because it has

---

[3] We can calculate the number of units that produce the same operating income for these two companies by equating the operating incomes and solving for the number of units. Let X be the number of units. The X at which Malvey Aerospace and Impulse Robotics generate the same operating income is the X that solves the following: $10X - 2X - 500,000 = 10X - 6X - 150,000$; that is, $X = 87,500$.

FIGURE 4 **Profitability and the DOL for Impulse Robotics and Malvey Aerospace**

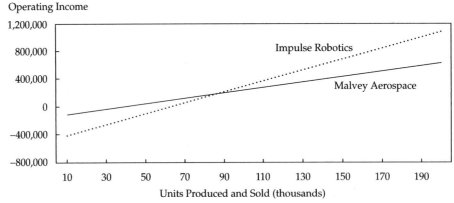

A. Operating Income and Number of Units Produced and Sold

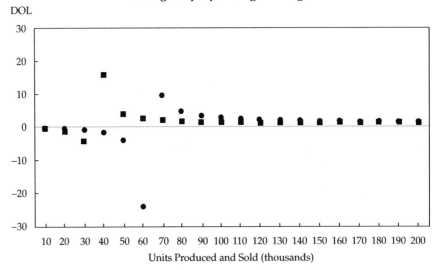

B. Degree of Operating Leverage

● Impulse Robotics   ■ Malvey Aerospace

Impulse Robotics: $P = \$10$; $V = \$2$; $F = \$500,000$.
Malvey Aerospace: $P = \$10$; $V = \$6$; $F = \$150,000$.

more operating leverage. However, as Panel B of Figure 4 shows, the degrees of operating leverage are similar for the two companies for larger numbers of units produced and sold.

Both sales risk and operating risk influence a company's business risk. And both sales risk and operating risk are determined in large part by the type of business the company is in. But management has more opportunity to manage and control operating risk than sales risk.

Suppose a company is deciding which equipment to buy to produce a particular product. The sales risk is the same no matter what equipment is chosen to produce the product. But the available equipment may differ in terms of the fixed and variable operating costs of producing the product. Financial analysts need to consider how the operating cost structure of a company affects the company's risk.

EXAMPLE 1

Calculating the Degree of Operating Leverage

Arnaud Kenigswald is analyzing the potential impact of an improving economy on earnings at Global Auto, one of the world's largest car manufacturers. Global is headquartered in Berlin. Two Global Auto divisions manufacture passenger cars and produce combined revenues of €93 billion. Kenigswald projects that sales will improve by 10 percent due to increased demand for cars. He wants to see how Global's earnings might respond given that level of increase in sales. He first looks at the degree of leverage at Global, starting with operating leverage.

Global sold 6 million passenger cars in 2003. The average price per car was €24,000, fixed costs associated with passenger car production total €15 billion per year, and variable costs per car are €14,000. What is the degree of operating leverage of Global Auto?

Solution:

$$\text{DOL @ 6 million units} = \frac{6 \text{ million}(€24,000 - €14,000)}{6 \text{ million}(€24,000 - €14,000) - €15 \text{ billion}}$$

$$= 1.333$$

For a 10 percent increase in cars sold, operating income increases by $1.333 \times 10\% = 13.33\%$.

Industries that tend to have high operating leverage are those that invest up front to produce a product but spend relatively little on making and distributing it. Software developers and pharmaceutical companies fit this description. Alternatively, retailers have low operating leverage because much of the cost of goods sold is variable.

Because most companies produce more than one product, the ratio of variable to fixed costs is difficult to obtain. We can get an idea of the operating leverage of a company by looking at the change in operating income in relation to changes in sales for the entire company. Although this approach does not provide a precise measure of operating risk, it can help provide a general idea of the sensitivity of operating earnings. For example, compare the relation between operating earnings and revenues for Abbott Laboratories, a pharmaceutical company, and Wal-Mart Stores, a discount retailer, as shown in Figure 5. Not only is the slope of a least-squares regression line greater for Abbott, but also note the higher volatility of observations around the regression.[4] We can see that operating earnings are more sensitive to changes in revenues for the higher-operating-leveraged Abbott as compared to the lower-operating-leveraged Wal-Mart Stores.

---

[4] A least-squares regression is a procedure for finding the best-fitting line through a set of data points by minimizing the squared deviations from the line.

FIGURE 5   Relation between Operating Earnings and Revenues

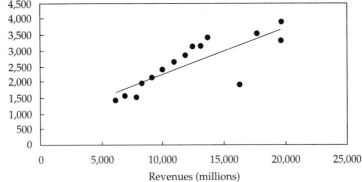

A. Abbott Laboratories Operating Earnings and Revenues, 1990-2004

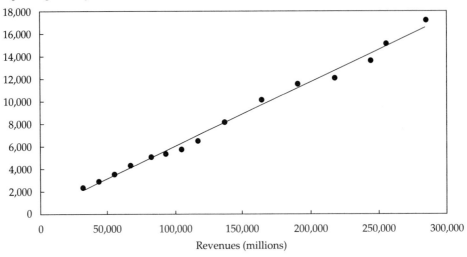

B. Wal-Mart Stores Operating Earnings and Revenues, 1990-2004

Sources: Abbott Laboratories 10-K filings and Wal-Mart Stores 10-K filings, various years.

3.4 Financial Risk

We can expand on the concept of risk to accommodate the perspective of owning a security. A security represents a claim on the income and assets of a business; therefore, the risk of the security goes beyond the variability of operating earnings to include how the cash flows from those earnings are distributed among the claimants—the creditors and owners of the business. The risk of a security is therefore affected by both business risk and financial risk.

Financial risk is the risk associated with how a company finances its operations. If a company finances with debt, it is legally obligated to pay the amounts that make up its debts when due. By taking on fixed obligations, such as debt and long-term leases, the company increases its financial risk. If a company finances its business with equity, generated either from operations (retained earnings) or from issuing new equity, it does not incur fixed obligations. The more fixed-cost obligations (e.g., debt) incurred by the company, the greater its financial risk.

We can quantify this risk in the same way we did for operating risk, looking at the sensitivity of the cash flows available to owners when operating income changes. This sensitivity, which we refer to as the **degree of financial leverage (DFL)**, is

$$DFL = \frac{\text{Percentage change in net income}}{\text{Percentage change in operating income}} \qquad \textbf{(32-3)}$$

Net income is equal to operating income, less interest and taxes.[5] If operating income changes, how does net income change? Consider Impulse Robotics. Suppose the interest payments are $100,000 and, for simplicity and wishful thinking, the tax rate is 0 percent: If operating income changes from $300,000 to $360,000, net income changes from $200,000 to $260,000:

TABLE 4   Financial Risk of Impulse Robotics (1)

	Operating Income of $300,000	Operating Income of $360,000	Percentage Change
Operating income	$300,000	$360,000	+20%
Less interest	100,000	100,000	0%
Net income	$200,000	$260,000	+30%

A 20 percent increase in operating income increases net income by $60,000, or 30 percent. What if, instead, the fixed financial costs are $150,000? A 20 percent change in operating income results in a 40 percent change in the net income, from $150,000 to $210,000:

TABLE 5   Financial Risk of Impulse Robotics (2)

	Operating Income of $300,000	Operating Income of $360,000	Percentage Change
Operating income	$300,000	$360,000	+20%
Less interest	150,000	150,000	0%
Net in come	$150,000	$210,000	+40%

Using more debt financing, which results in higher fixed costs, increases the sensitivity of owners' income. We can represent the sensitivity of owners' cash flows to a change in operating income, continuing the notation from before and including the fixed financial cost, C, and the tax rate, t, as

$$DFL = \frac{[Q(P - V) - F](1 - t)}{[Q(P - V) - F - C](1 - t)} = \frac{[Q(P - V) - F]}{[Q(P - V) - F - C]} \qquad \textbf{(32-4)}$$

---

[5] More complex entities than we have been using for our examples may also need to account for other income (losses) and extraordinary income (losses) together with operating income as the basis for earnings before interest and taxes.

As you can see in Equation 32-4, the factor that adjusts for taxes, $(1 - t)$, cancels out of the equation. In other words, the DFL is not affected by the tax rate.

In the case in which operating income is $300,000 and fixed financing costs are $100,000, the degree of financial leverage is

$$\text{DFL @ \$300,000 operating income} = \frac{\$300,000}{\$300,000 - \$100,000} = 1.5$$

If, instead, fixed financial costs are $150,000, the DFL is equal to 2.0:

$$\text{DFL @ \$300,000 operating income} = \frac{\$300,000}{\$300,000 - \$150,000} = 2.0$$

Again, we need to qualify our degree of leverage by the level of operating income because DFL is different at different levels of operating income.

The greater the use of financing sources that require fixed obligations, such as interest, the greater the sensitivity of net income to changes in operating income.

EXAMPLE 2

Calculating the Degree of Financial Leverage

Global Auto also employs debt financing. If Global can borrow at 8 percent, the interest cost is €40 billion. What is the degree of financial leverage of Global Auto if 6 million cars are produced and sold?

Solution: At 6 million cars produced and sold, operating income = €45 billion. Therefore:

$$\text{DFL @ €45 billion operating income} = \frac{€45 \text{ billion}}{€45 \text{ billion} - €40 \text{ billion}} = 9.0$$

For every 1 percent change in operating income, net income changes 9 percent due to financial leverage.

Unlike operating leverage, the degree of financial leverage is most often a choice by the company's management. Whereas operating costs are very similar among companies in the same industry, competitors may decide on differing capital structures.

Companies with a higher ratio of tangible assets to total assets may have higher degrees of financial leverage because lenders may feel more secure that their claims would be satisfied in the event of a downturn. In general, "old economy" businesses with plants, land, and equipment use more financial leverage than "new economy" businesses in technology and pharmaceuticals.

3.5 Total Leverage

The degree of operating leverage gives us an idea of the sensitivity of operating income to changes in revenues. And the degree of financial leverage gives us an idea of the sensitivity of owners' income to changes in operating income. But often we are concerned about the combined effect of both operating leverage and financial leverage. Owners are concerned about the combined effect because both factors contribute to the risk associated with their future cash flows. And financial managers, making decisions intended to maximize owners' wealth, need to be concerned with how investment decisions (which affect the operating cost structure) and financing decisions (which affect the capital structure) affect lenders' and owners' risk.

Look back on the example of Impulse Robotics. The sensitivity of owners' cash flow to a given change in units sold is affected by both operating and financial leverage. Consider using 100,000 units as the base number produced and sold. A 10 percent increase in units sold results in a 27 percent increase in operating income and a 40 percent increase in net income; a like decrease in units sold results in a similar decrease in operating income and net income.

TABLE 6 Total Leverage of Impulse Robotics			
	Units Produced and Sold		
	90,000	**100,000**	**110,000**
Revenues	$900,000	$1,000,000	$1,100,000
Less variable costs	180,000	200,000	220,000
Less fixed costs	500,000	500,000	500,000
Operating income	$220,000	$300,000	$380,000
Less interest	100,000	100,000	100,000
Net income	$120,000	$200,000	$280,000
Relative to 100,000 units produced and sold			
Percentage change in units sold	−10%		+10%
Percentage change in operating profit	−27%		+27%
Percentage change in net income	−40%		+40%

Combining a company's degree of operating leverage with its degree of financial leverage results in the **degree of total leverage (DTL)**, a measure of the sensitivity of the cash flows to owners to changes in the number of units produced and sold. Once again making the simplifying assumption that a company sells all that it produces in the same period,

$$DTL = \frac{\text{Percentage change in net income}}{\text{Percentage change in the number of units sold}} \quad \textbf{(32-5)}$$

or

$$DTL = \frac{Q(P-V)}{Q(P-V) - F} \times \frac{[Q(P-V) - F](1-t)}{[Q(P-V) - F - C](1-t)} \quad \textbf{(32-6)}$$

$$= \frac{Q(P-V)}{Q(P-V) - F - C} = DOL \times DFL$$

Suppose

Number of units sold $= Q = 100{,}000$
Price per unit $= P = \$10$
Variable cost per unit $= V = \$2$
Fixed operating cost $= F = \$500{,}000$
Fixed financing cost $= C = \$100{,}000$

Then,

$$\text{DTL} = \frac{100{,}000(\$10 - \$2)}{100{,}000(\$10 - \$2) - \$500{,}000 - \$100{,}000} = 4.0$$

which we could also have determined by multiplying the DOL, 2.67, by the DFL, 1.5. This means that a 1 percent increase in units sold will result in a 4 percent increase in net income; a 50 percent increase in units produced and sold results in a 200 percent increase in net income; a 5 percent decline in units sold results in a 20 percent decline in income to owners; and so on.

Because the DOL is relative to the base number of units produced and sold and the DFL is relative to the base operating earnings, DTL is different depending on the number of units produced and sold. We can see the DOL, DFL, and DTL for Impulse Robotics for different numbers of units produced and sold, beginning at the number of units for which the degrees are positive, in Figure 6.

In the case of operating leverage, the fixed operating costs act as a fulcrum. The greater the proportion of operating costs that are fixed, the more sensitive operating income is to changes in sales. In the case of financial leverage, the fixed financial costs, such as interest, act as a fulcrum. The greater the proportion of financing with fixed cost sources, such as debt, the more sensitive cash flows available to owners are to changes in operating income. Combining the effects of both types of leverage, we see that fixed operating and financial costs together increase the sensitivity of earnings to owners.

FIGURE 6   DOL, DFL, and DTL for Different Numbers of Units Produced and Sold

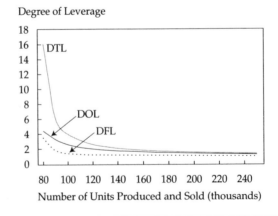

$P = \$10$, $V = \$2$, $F = \$500{,}000$, $C = \$100{,}000$.

3.6 Breakeven Rates and Expected Return

Looking back at Figure 1, we see that there is a number of units at which the company goes from being unprofitable to being profitable—that is, the number of units at which the net income is zero. This number is referred to as the breakeven point. The **breakeven point** is the number of units produced and sold at which the company's net income is zero—the point at which revenues are equal to costs.

Plotting revenues and total costs against the number of units produced and sold, as in Figure 7, indicates that the breakeven is at 75,000 units. At this number of units produced and sold, revenues are equal to costs and, hence, profit is zero.

We can calculate this breakeven point for Impulse Robotics and Malvey Aerospace. Consider that net income is zero when the revenues are equal to the expenses. We can represent this equality of revenues and costs as the following:

$$PQ = VQ + F + C$$

where

P is the price per unit
Q is the number of units produced and sold
V is the variable cost per unit
F is the fixed operating costs
C is the fixed financial cost

Therefore,

$$PQ_{BE} = VQ_{BE} + F + C$$

FIGURE 7   Impulse Robotics Break-Even

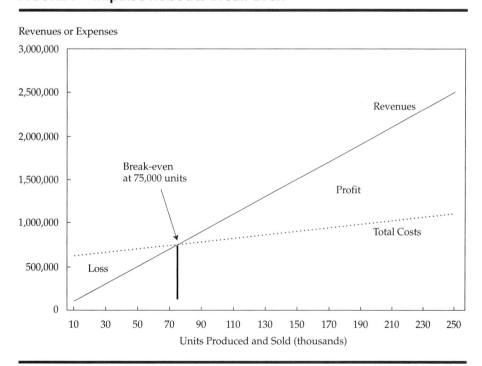

and the breakeven number of units, Q_{BE}, is[6]

$$Q_{BE} = \frac{F + C}{P - V}$$

(32-7)

In the case of Impulse Robotics and Malvey Aerospace, Impulse Robotics has a higher breakeven point:

Impulse Robotics: $Q_{BE} = \dfrac{\$500{,}000 + \$100{,}000}{\$10 - \$2} = 75{,}000$ units

Malvey Aerospace: $Q_{BE} = \dfrac{\$150{,}000 + \$50{,}000}{\$10 - \$6} = 50{,}000$ units

This means that Impulse Robotics must produce and sell more units to achieve a profit. So, while the higher-leveraged Impulse Robotics has a greater breakeven point relative to Malvey Aerospace, the profit that Impulse Robotics generates beyond this breakeven point is greater than that of Malvey Aerospace. Therefore, leverage has its rewards in terms of potentially greater profit, but it also increases risk.

EXAMPLE 3

Calculating the Degree of Total Leverage

Continuing from Example 2, Global Auto's total leverage is

$$\text{DTL@}_{\text{6 million units}} = \text{DOL@}_{\text{6 million units}} \times \text{DFL@}_{\text{€45 million operating income}}$$

$$\text{DTL@}_{\text{6 million units}} = \frac{6 \text{ million}(\text{€24,000} - \text{€14,000})}{6 \text{ million }(\text{€24,000} - \text{€14,000}) - \text{€15 billion}}$$
$$\times \frac{\text{€45 billion}}{\text{€45 billion} - \text{€40 billion}}$$

$$\text{DTL@}_{\text{6 million units}} = 1.333 \times 9.0 = 12$$

Given Global Auto's operating and capital structures, a 1 percent change in unit sales changes net income by 12 percent.

We can also specify the breakeven in terms of the operating profit, which we refer to as the **operating breakeven**, Q_{OBE}. In this case, the equality is set for revenues and operating costs and the breakeven number of units, Q_{OBE}, is

$$PQ_{OBE} = VQ_{OBE} + F$$

$$Q_{OBE} = \frac{F}{P - V}$$

---

[6] You will notice that we did not consider taxes in our calculation of the breakeven point. This is because at the point of breakeven, taxable income is zero.

For the two companies in our example, Impulse Robotics and Malvey Aerospace, the operating breakevens are 62,500 and 37,500 units, respectively:

$$\text{Impulse Robotics:} \quad Q_{OBE} = \frac{\$500,000}{\$10 - \$2} = 62,500 \text{ units}$$

$$\text{Malvey Aerospace:} \quad Q_{OBE} = \frac{\$150,000}{\$10 - \$6} = 37,500 \text{ units}$$

Again, Impulse Robotics has a higher breakeven point in terms of the number of units produced and sold.

EXAMPLE 4

Calculating the Breakeven Point

Continuing with his analysis, Kenigswald considers the effect of a possible downturn on Global Auto's earnings. He divides the fixed costs of €15 billion by the per unit contribution margin:

$$Q_{OBE} = \frac{\text{€15 billion}}{\text{€24,000} - \text{€14,000}} = 1,500,000 \text{ cars}$$

The operating breakeven for Global is 1,500,000 cars, or €36 billion in revenues. We calculate the total breakeven by dividing fixed operating costs, plus interest costs, by the contribution margin:

$$Q_{BE} = \frac{\text{€15 billion} + \text{€40 billion}}{\text{€24,000} - \text{€14,000}} = \frac{\text{€55 billion}}{\text{€10,000}} = 5,500,000 \text{ cars}$$

Considering the degree of total leverage, Global's total breakeven is 5.5 million cars, or revenues of €132 billion.

We can verify these calculations by constructing an income statement for the breakeven sales (in € billions):

	1,500,000 Cars	5,500,000 Cars
Revenues	€36	€132
Variable operating costs	21	77
Fixed operating costs	15	15
Operating income	**€0**	€40
Fixed financial costs	40	40
Net income	−€40	**€0**

As business expands or contracts beyond or below breakeven points, fixed costs do not change. The breakeven points for companies with low operating and financial leverage are less important than those for companies with high leverage. Companies with greater total leverage must generate more revenue to cover fixed operating and financing costs. The farther unit sales are from the breakeven point for high-leverage companies, the greater the magnifying effect of this leverage.

EXAMPLE 5

The Leveraging Role of Debt

Consider the Capital Company, which is expected to generate $1.5 million in revenues and $0.5 million in operating earnings next year. Currently, the Capital Company does not use debt financing and has assets of $2 million.

Suppose Capital were to change its capital structure, buying back $1 million of stock and issuing $1 million in debt. If we assume that interest on debt is 5 percent and income is taxed at a rate of 30 percent, what is the effect of debt financing on Capital's net income and return on equity if operating earnings may vary as much as 40 percent from expected earnings?

TABLE 7   Return of Equity of Capital Company

No Debt Shareholders' Equity = $2 Million	Expected Operating Earnings, less 40%	Expected Operating Earnings	Expected Operating Earnings, plus 40%
Earnings before interest and taxes	$300,000	$500,000	$700,000
Interest expense	0	0	0
Income before taxes	$300,000	$500,000	$700,000
Taxes	90,000	150,000	210,000
Net income	$210,000	$350,000	$490,000
Return on equity[7]	10.5%	17.5%	24.5%

Debt to Total Assets = 50% Shareholders' Equity = $1 Million	Expected Operating Earnings, less 40%	Expected Operating Earnings	Expected Operating Earnings, plus 40%
Earnings before interest and taxes	$300,000	$500,000	$700,000
Interest expense	50,000	50,000	50,000
Income before taxes	$250,000	$450,000	$650,000
Taxes	75,000	135,000	195,000
Net income	$175,000	$315,000	$455,000
Return on equity	17.5%	31.5%	45.5%

Depicting a broader array of capital structures and operating earnings, ranging from an operating loss of $500,000 to operating earnings of $2 million, Figure 8 shows the effect of leverage on the return on equity for Capital Company.

---

[7] Recall that ROE is calculated as Net income/Shareholders' equity.

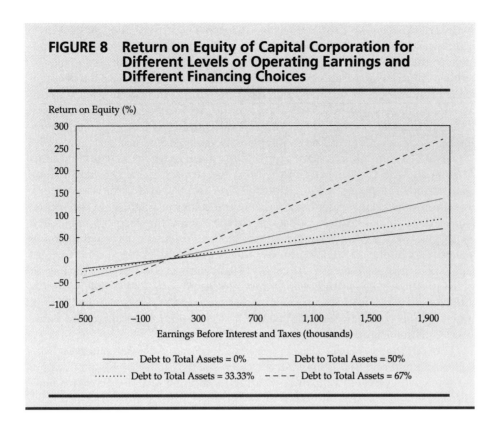

FIGURE 8   Return on Equity of Capital Corporation for Different Levels of Operating Earnings and Different Financing Choices

Business is generally an uncertain venture. Changes in the macroeconomic and competitive environments that influence sales and profitability are typically hard to discern and forecast. The larger the proportion of debt in the financing mix of a business, the greater is the likelihood that it will face default. Similarly, the greater the proportion of debt in the capital structure, the more earnings are magnified upward in improving economic times. The bottom line? The greater the leverage, the greater the risk of ownership for equityholders.

3.7 The Risks of Creditors and Owners

As we discussed earlier, business risk refers to the effect of economic conditions as well as the level of operating leverage. Uncertainty about demand, output prices, and costs are among the many factors that affect business risk. When conditions change for any of these factors, companies with higher business risk experience more volatile earnings. Financial risk is the additional risk that results from the use of debt and **preferred stock**. The degree of financial risk grows with greater use of debt. Who bears this risk?

The risk for providers of equity and debt capital differs because of the relative rights and responsibilities associated with the use of borrowed money in a business. Lenders have priority claims on assets, so they have greater security. In return for lending money to a business, lenders require the payment of interest and principal when due. These contractual payments to lenders must be made regardless of the profitability of the business. A business must satisfy these claims in a timely fashion or face the pain of bankruptcy should it default. In return for their higher priority in claims, lenders get predefined yet limited returns.

In contrast, equity providers claim whatever is left over after all expenses, including debt service, have been paid. So, unlike the fixed and known commitments to the lenders, what is left over for the owners may be a great deal or may be nothing. In exchange for this risk, providers of equity capital exercise the decision-making power over the business, including the right to hire, guide, and if necessary, fire managers. Equityholders also have the right to declare what portion of the business earnings they will take out as dividends. In public companies, ownership rights are usually exercised through an elected board of directors.

Legal codes in most countries provide for these rights, as well as conditions for companies to file for bankruptcy. Most bankruptcy codes provide in some form for two categories of bankruptcies. One form provides for a temporary protection from creditors so that a viable business may reorganize. In the United States, the U.S. Bankruptcy Code sets the terms for the form of negotiated **reorganization** of a company's capital structure that allows it to remain a going concern in Chapter 11.[8] For businesses that are not viable, the second form of bankruptcy process allows for the orderly satisfaction of the creditors' claims. In the United States, this form of bankruptcy is referred to as **liquidation**,[9] Whereas both types of bankruptcy lead to major dislocations in the rights and privileges of owners, lenders, employees, and managers, it is in this latter category of bankruptcy that the original business ceases to exist.

The difference between a company that reorganizes and emerges from bankruptcy and one that is liquidated is often the difference between operating and financial leverage. Companies with high operating leverage have less flexibility in making changes, and bankruptcy protection does little to help reduce operating costs. Companies with high financial leverage use bankruptcy laws and protection to change their capital structure and, once the restructuring is complete, can emerge as ongoing concerns.

EXAMPLE 6

Chapter 11 Reorganization and Owens Corning

The world's largest manufacturer of glass fiber insulation, Owens Corning Corporation of Toledo, Ohio, filed for Chapter 11 bankruptcy on 5 October 2000, as it faced growing asbestos liability claims. With revenues exceeding $6 billion per year, Owens Corning was one of the largest corporations ever afforded bankruptcy protection by the U.S. courts.

From 1952 to 1972, Owens Corning produced an asbestos-containing high-temperature pipe coating called Kaylo, and at the time of its bankruptcy filing, it had received more than 460,000 asbestos personal injury claims and had paid or agreed to pay more than $5 billion for asbestos-related awards and settlements, legal expenses, and claims processing fees. While the company had assets of $7 billion and liabilities of $5.7 billion, the trust fund it set aside to pay those claims appeared inadequate.

The company's stock traded at between $15 and $25 per share in the year prior to the announcement; the price fell to $1 per share when Owens Corning declared bankruptcy and admitted that it had been overwhelmed by the asbestos liabilities.

---

[8] U.S. Code, Title 11—Bankruptcy, Chapter 11—Reorganization. Companies filing for bankruptcy under this code are referred to as having filed for Chapter 11 bankruptcy.

[9] U.S. Code, Title 11—Bankruptcy, Chapter 7—Liquidation.

EXAMPLE 7

Chapter 7 and Webvan Do Not Deliver

Since the peak of the NASDAQ in March of 2000, many technology companies have found either that they cannot raise enough capital to implement their business plans or that they have an untenable business plan. Some have simply shut their doors and gone out of business, while others have filed for bankruptcy. Either way, these companies have left many unsatisfied creditors.

For example, Webvan.com was a start-up company in the late 1990s that raised over $1.2 billion in equity, $375 million of which came from an IPO in November 1999. It had very ambitious business plans to build a series of warehouses and deliver groceries to fulfill customer orders placed over the Internet. Webvan.com, however, faced a number of challenges, including a downturn in the economy, and quickly ran through its capital.

Webvan.com filed for Chapter 11 bankruptcy protection in July 1999 and reported that it owed $106 million to creditors. By the time it began liquidation under **Chapter 7** in January 2002, it reported that the value of its liquidated assets totaled only $25 million, leaving its creditors to receive pennies on the dollar and its investors to receive little or nothing for their $1.2 billion investment in the company.

Whereas the ability to file for bankruptcy is important to the economy, the goal of the analyst is to avoid ownership of companies that are heading toward this extreme step, as well as to be able to evaluate opportunities among companies already in bankruptcy. Under both Chapter 7 and Chapter 11, providers of equity capital generally lose all value during the bankruptcy. On the other hand, debtholders typically receive at least a portion of their capital, but the payments of principal and interest are delayed during the period of bankruptcy protection.

THE CAPITAL STRUCTURE DECISION   4

A company's **capital structure** is the mix of debt and equity that a company uses to finance its business. The goal of a company's capital structure decision is to determine the financial leverage or capital structure that maximizes the value of the company by minimizing the average cost of capital. The weighted average cost of capital (WACC) is given by the average of the marginal costs of financing for each type of financing used. For a company with both debt and equity in its capital structure for which interest expense is tax deductible at a rate t, the WACC is

$$\text{WACC} = \left(\frac{D}{V}\right) r_d (1 - t) + \left(\frac{E}{V}\right) r_e$$

where r_e is the cost of equity, r_d is the before-tax cost of debt, and t is the marginal tax rate.[10] Variables E and D denote the market value of the shareholders' equity

---

[10] For simplicity, this discussion ignores preferred stock. Additionally, (D/V) and (E/V) have been substituted for w_d and w_e, respectively.

and the outstanding debt, respectively, and the value of the company is given by $V = D + E$. You will notice that we use the term "marginal" with respect to both the cost of capital and the tax rate. The cost of capital is a marginal cost: what it costs the company to raise additional capital. Therefore, the cost of equity, the cost of debt, and the tax rate that we use throughout the remainder of this reading are marginal: the cost or tax rate for additional capital.

In this section, we first consider the theoretical relationship between leverage and a company's value. We then examine the practical relationship between leverage and company value in equal depth.

4.1 Proposition I without Taxes: Capital Structure Irrelevance

In now-classic papers, Nobel Prize–winning economists Franco Modigliani and Merton Miller argued the important theory that, given certain assumptions, a company's choice of capital structure does not affect its value.[11] The assumptions relate to expectations and markets:

1. Investors agree on the expected cash flow from a given investment.[12]
2. Bonds and shares of stock are traded in a perfect capital market.[13]

Implicit in the perfect market assumption is that bankruptcy has no costs.

Consider the capital of a company to be a pie you can split any number of ways, but the size of the pie remains the same. Likewise, Modigliani and Miller reason, the amount and risk of the aggregate returns to debtholders and equityholders of a company do not change with changes in capital structure. They use the concept of arbitrage to demonstrate their point: If the value of an unlevered company—that is, a company without any debt—is not equal to that of a levered company, investors could make an arbitrage profit and this profit taking would force the values to be equivalent.

The importance of the Modigliani and Miller theory is that it demonstrates that managers cannot create value simply by changing the company's capital structure. Consider why this might be true. The operating earnings of a business are available to the providers of its capital. In an all-equity company (that is, a company with no debt), all of the operating earnings are available to the equityholders and the value of the company is the present value of these operating earnings. If, on the other hand, a company is partially financed by debt, these operating earnings are split between the providers of capital: the equityholders and the debtholders. Under market equilibrium, the sum of the values of debt and equity in such a case should equal the value of the all-equity company. In other words, the value of a company is determined solely by its cash flows, not by the relative reliance on debt and equity capital.

This principle does not change the fact of the relative risks of leverage to debtholders versus equityholders. Adding leverage does increase the risk faced by the equityholders. In such a case, equityholders are compensated for this extra risk by receiving a larger proportion of the operating earnings, with the

---

[11] Modigliani and Miller (1958, 1963).

[12] All investors have the same expectations with respect to the cash flows from an investment in bonds or stocks. In other words, expectations are homogeneous.

[13] A perfect capital market is one in which any two investments with identical cash flow streams must trade for the same price.

debtholders receiving a smaller portion, as they face less risk. Indeed, in equilibrium, the increase in equity returns is exactly offset by increases in the risk and the associated increase in the required rate of return on equity, so that there is no change in the value of the company.

Modigliani and Miller (MM) first illustrated the capital structure irrelevance proposition under the condition of no taxes:

> *MM Proposition I:*
> The market value of a company is not affected by the capital structure of the company.

In other words, the value of the company levered (V_L) is equal to the value unlevered (V_U), or $V_L = V_U$.

To understand this proposition, we can think about two companies with the same expected, perpetual cash flows and uncertainty and, hence, the same discount rate applied to value these cash flows. Even if the companies have different capital structures, these two companies must have the same present value using discounted cash flow models. If capital structure changes were to have any effect on a company's value, there would exist an arbitrage opportunity to make endless profits.

In a perfect market, investors can substitute their own leverage for a company's leverage by borrowing or lending appropriate amounts in addition to holding shares of the company. Because this process is costless for investors (remember, we assumed no transaction costs), a company's financial leverage should have no impact on its value. Therefore, a company's capital structure is irrelevant in perfect markets if taxes are ignored.

4.2 Proposition II without Taxes: Higher Financial Leverage Raises the Cost of Equity

Modigliani and Miller's second proposition focuses on the cost of capital of the company:

> *MM Proposition II:*
> The cost of equity is a linear function of the company's debt to equity ratio.

Assuming that financial distress has no costs and that debtholders have prior claim to assets and income relative to equityholders, the cost of debt is less than the cost of equity. According to this proposition, as the company increases its use of debt financing, the cost of equity rises. The net effect of the increased use of a cheaper source of capital and the rising cost of equity is that there is *no* change in the company's overall cost of capital. Again, Modigliani and Miller argue that the relative amount of debt versus equity does not affect the overall value of the company. This is because despite the low cost of using debt financing, the more debt in the capital structure, relative to equity, the riskier the equity capital.

The risk of the equity depends on two factors: the risk of the company's operations (business risk) and the degree of financial leverage (financial risk). Business risk determines the cost of capital, whereas the capital structure determines financial risk.

The **weighted average cost of capital (WACC)**, *ignoring taxes*, is

$$r_a = \left(\frac{D}{V}\right)r_d + \left(\frac{E}{V}\right)r_e$$

where

r_a is the weighted average cost of capital of the company
r_d is the before-tax marginal cost of debt capital
r_e is the marginal cost of equity capital
D is the value of debt
E is the value of equity
V is the value of the company, which is equal to $D + E$

We can rearrange the weighted average cost of capital to solve for the cost of equity:

$$r_e = r_a + (r_a - r_d)\left(\frac{D}{E}\right)$$

More than four decades later, the MM theory still provides the foundation for discussions about company value as it relates to capital structure. Higher leverage does not create value. As shown in the above equation, as the debt/equity ratio increases, the cost of equity capital also increases.

Just as we can express the beta of any investment portfolio as a market-value weighted average of the betas of the investments in that portfolio, we can express the systematic risk of each of the sources of a company's capital in a similar manner.[14] In other words, we can represent the systematic risk of the assets of the entire company as a weighted average of the systematic risk of the company's debt and equity:

$$\beta_a = \left(\frac{D}{V}\right)\beta_d + \left(\frac{E}{V}\right)\beta_e$$

where β_a is the asset's systematic risk, or **asset beta**, β_d is the beta of debt, and β_e is the equity beta. The asset beta represents the amount of the risk that cannot be diversified away by investing in assets that are not perfectly correlated with one another.

According to Modigliani and Miller, the company's cost of capital does not depend on its capital structure but rather is determined by the business risk of the company. On the other hand, as the level of debt rises, the risk of the company's defaulting on its debt increases. These costs are borne by the equityholders. So, as the proportionate use of debt rises, the equity's beta, β_e also rises. By reordering the formula of β_a to solve for β_e we get

$$\beta_e = \beta_a + (\beta_a - \beta_d)\left(\frac{D}{E}\right)$$

In the next section, we look at the decision to use debt financing given the taxes and market imperfections found in the real world.

4.3 Taxes, the Cost of Capital, and the Value of the Company

Taxes are the first practical consideration in modifying the results of the MM propositions. Because interest is deductible from income for tax purposes in most countries, the use of debt provides a tax shield that translates into savings

---

[14] Hamada (1972).

that enhance the value of a company. Indeed, ignoring other practical realities of costs of financial distress and bankruptcy, the value of the company increases with increasing levels of debt. In effect, by making the interest costs deductible for income taxes, the government subsidizes companies' use of debt. The actual cost of debt is reduced by the level of the company's tax benefit:

After-tax cost of debt = Before-tax cost of debt $\times$ (1 − Marginal tax rate)

Or, representing the after-tax cost of debt as r_d^*,

$$r_d^* = r_d(1 - t)$$

where t is the marginal tax rate. By introducing corporate tax, we adjust the weighted average cost of capital formula to reflect the impact of the tax benefit:

$$r_a = \left(\frac{D}{V}\right) r_d(1 - t) + \left(\frac{E}{V}\right) r_e$$

or

$$r_a = \left(\frac{D}{V}\right) r_d^* + \left(\frac{E}{V}\right) r_e$$

We can rearrange this equation to solve for the cost of equity:

$$r_e = r_a + (r_a - r_d^*)\left(\frac{D}{E}\right)$$

Therefore, the cost of equity is equal to the return on the company as a whole, plus an adjustment for financial leverage.

This tax shield afforded by debt financing adds value to a company. In fact, the value of a levered company is the value of an unlevered (i.e., all-equity) company plus the value of the tax shield, td:[15]

$$V_L = V_U + td$$

Therefore, if taxes are considered but financial distress and bankruptcy costs are not, debt financing is highly advantageous, and in the extreme, a company's optimal capital structure is all debt.

We can see the effect of taxes on the cost of capital in Figure 9. Here, we see that if there are no taxes, as shown in Panel B, the cost of capital is constant at r_a. If, on the other hand, interest is tax deductible, the cost of capital declines for ever-increasing use of debt financing, as shown in Panel C.

---

[15] Note that the annual tax saving is $r_d \cdot td$. Expressing its present value in the form of an annuity, we get PV(tax saving) $= r_d \cdot td / r_d = td$.

FIGURE 9   Modigliani and Miller Propositions

A. Value of the Company and Cost of Capital for Propositions without and with Taxes

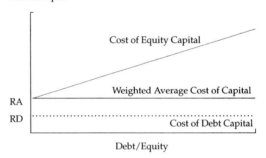

	Without Taxes	With Taxes
Proposition I	$V_L = V_U$	$V_L = V_U + tD$
Proposition II	$R_A = \left(\dfrac{D}{V}\right)R_D + \left(\dfrac{E}{V}\right)R_E$	$R_A = \left(\dfrac{D}{V}\right)R_D(1-t) + \left(\dfrac{E}{V}\right)R_E$

B. Costs of Capital if There Are No Taxes

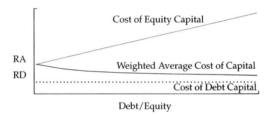

C. Costs of Capital if There Are Taxes

EXAMPLE 8

The After-Tax Cost of Debt

Payment People, a provider of temporary accounting workers, is considering an $85 million acquisition. The company could raise capital by selling either debt or equity. If the company finances the acquisition with debt at 8 percent interest, what is the after-tax cost of issuing debt if the company's marginal tax rate is 34 percent?

Solution: Annual interest expense on $85 million at 8 percent is $6.8 million. The $6.8 million is deducted from income, saving $2,312,000 in taxes. The after-tax interest cost is $6.8 million − $2.312 million = $4.488 million. The before-tax cost of debt is 8 percent; the after-tax cost of debt is

After-tax cost of debt = $4.488 million / $85 million = 5.28%, or
0.08(1 − 0.34) = 0.0528, or 5.28%.

EXAMPLE 9

The Cost of Equity

Hotel chain Hostales Vacaciones finances land purchases for new hotels through debt financing. The company is opening in ten locations for a total cost of 500 million pesos. The company is considering the cost of equity versus debt for its financing needs. The company has a cost of capital of 13 percent, a debt to equity ratio of 0.5, debt costs of 9 percent, and a tax rate of 32 percent. What is the company's cost of equity with and without the consideration of taxes?

Solution:

Without taxes

$$r_e = r_a + (r_a - r_d)\left(\frac{D}{E}\right)$$
$$r_e = 13\% + [(13\% - 9\%)(0.5)] = 0.15, \text{ or } 15\%$$

With taxes

$$r_e = r_a + (r_a - r_d^*)\left(\frac{D}{E}\right)$$
$$r_e = 13\% + [(13\% - 6.12\%)(0.5) = 0.1644, \text{ or } 16.44\%$$

Miller (1977) introduced another aspect into the benefit from tax deductibility of interest on debt. He argued that if investors face different tax rates on dividend and interest income for their personal taxes, this situation may reduce the advantage of debt financing somewhat. If investors face a higher rate of tax on income from debt investments relative to stock investments, they will demand a higher return on debt—and, hence, a higher cost of debt—than if there were no differential personal taxes in order to compensate for the personal tax on the income from the bond investment.[16]

From these examples with taxes, we can see that the more a company borrows, the greater the company's value. In practice, however, the value of a levered company is affected by more than the interest due on the debt. Things get more complicated once we introduce factors such as the cost of financial distress, agency costs, and asymmetric information. We address these additional factors next.

4.4 Costs of Financial Distress

The downside of operating and financial leverage is that earnings are magnified downward during economic slowdowns. Lower or negative earnings put companies under stress, and this **financial distress** adds costs—both explicit and **implicit costs**—to a company. Even before taking the drastic step of filing for bankruptcy, companies under stress may lose customers, creditors, suppliers, and valuable employees to more secure competitors.

---

[16] It can be argued that there is a higher personal tax on debt income because debt instruments typically provide investors with taxable interest periodically, whereas taxable income from stock investments could, conceivably, be lower because the tax consequences of investing in non-dividend-paying stocks are deferred until the stock is sold.

EXAMPLE 10

Costs of Financial Distress

Enron is an extreme example of the loss of value due to financial distress. Up until its demise in 2001, Enron was a large player in the natural gas industry. Events leading up to the eventual bankruptcy protection filing caused investors to flee the common stock as creditors refused new lending. Enron went from a favored to a disdained company in record time.

According to a company presentation made ten days after its 2 December 2001 bankruptcy filing, the company's common stock price plunged from $80 per share to $1 per share prior to the bankruptcy announcement, losing $25 billion in market value.[17] This loss in value was due to a number of factors, including:

► investors' and creditors' lost confidence;

► financial market reaction from a lack of access to capital markets;

► current maturities greatly exceeding operating cash flow because of the inability to refinance debt;

► nervous trade creditors;

► Dynegy pulling out of the merger on 28 November 2001; and

► the bond ratings downgrade on 28 November 2001.

Cash bankruptcy expenses listed in the bankruptcy filing documents totaled $17.3 million, though the bankruptcy costs including accountants', advisors', and lawyers' fees were over $500 million by November of 2003.[18]

The expected cost of financial distress is composed of two key ingredients: (1) the costs of financial distress and bankruptcy and (2) the likelihood of financial distress. We can classify the costs of financial distress into direct and indirect costs. Direct costs of financial distress include the actual cash expenses associated with the bankruptcy process, such as legal and **administrative fees**. Indirect costs of financial distress include forgone investment opportunities, impaired ability to conduct business, and agency costs associated with the debt during periods in which the company is near or in bankruptcy.

Companies whose assets have a ready secondary market have lower costs associated with financial distress. Companies with safe, tangible assets, such as airlines, shipping companies, and steel manufacturers, incur lower costs from financial distress because such assets are usually more readily marketable. On the other hand, companies with few tangible assets, such as high-tech growth companies, pharmaceutical companies, information technology companies, and others in the service industry, have less to liquidate and therefore have a higher cost associated with financial distress.

The probability of bankruptcy increases as the degree of leverage increases. The probability of bankruptcy for a given company depends on how the fixed costs of debt service interact with the instability of the business environment and the **reserves** available to the company to delay bankruptcy. In other words, the

---

[17] Enron Corporation Organizational Meeting, 12 December 2001.

[18] *Houston Business Journal*, 19 November 2003.

probability of bankruptcy depends, in part, on the company's business risk. Other factors that affect the likelihood of bankruptcy include the company's corporate governance structure and the management of the company.

4.5 Agency Costs

Agency costs are the costs associated with the fact that all public companies and the larger private companies are managed by nonowners. Agency costs result from the inherent conflicts of interest between managers and equity owners. The smaller the stake that managers have in the company, the less is their share in bearing the cost of excessive perquisite consumption or not giving their best efforts in running the company. This conflict has been called the agency costs of equity. Given that outside shareholders are aware of this conflict, they will take actions to minimize the loss, such as requiring audited financial statements. The net agency costs of equity therefore have three components:[19]

1. **Monitoring costs.** These are the costs borne by owners to monitor the management of the company and include the expenses of the annual report, board of director expenses, and the cost of the annual meeting.

2. **Bonding costs.** These are the costs borne by management to assure owners that they are working in the owners' best interest. These include the implicit cost of noncompete employment contracts and the explicit cost of insurance to guarantee performance.

3. **Residual loss.** This consists of the costs that are incurred even when there is sufficient monitoring and bonding, because monitoring and bonding mechanisms are not perfect.

The better a company is governed, the lower the agency costs. Good governance practices translate into higher shareholder value, reflecting the fact that managers' interests are better aligned with those of shareholders. Additionally, agency theory posits that a reduction in net agency costs of equity results from an increase in the use of debt versus equity. That is, there is an agency cost savings associated with the use of debt. Similarly, the more financially leveraged a company is, the less freedom managers have to either take on more debt or untowardly spend cash. This is the foundation of Michael Jensen's **free cash flow hypothesis.**[20] Higher debt levels discipline managers by forcing them to make fixed debt service payments and by reducing the company's free cash flow.[21]

4.6 Costs of Asymmetric Information

Asymmetric information arises from the fact that managers have more information about a company's performance and prospects (and future investment opportunities) than do outsiders such as owners and creditors. Whereas all companies have a certain level of insider information, companies with comparatively high asymmetry in information are those with complex products like high-tech companies, companies with little transparency in financial accounting information, or companies with lower levels of institutional ownership. Providers

---

[19] Jensen and Meckling (1976) provide this breakdown of agency costs.

[20] Jensen (1986).

[21] Harvey, Lins, and Roper (2004) observe that this discipline is especially important in emerging markets, in which there is a tendency to overinvest.

of both debt and equity capital demand higher returns from companies with higher asymmetry in information because there is a greater likelihood of agency costs in companies with higher asymmetry in information.

Some degree of asymmetric information always exists because investors never know as much as managers and other insiders. Consequently, investors often closely watch manager behavior for insight into insider opinions on the company's future prospects. Being aware of this scrutiny, managers take into account how their actions might be interpreted by outsiders. The signaling model of capital structure suggests a pecking order to financing decisions. When a company is presented with a new investment opportunity, management must choose the best way to pay for the project. Management wants to optimize return on the investment at the lowest risk.

The **pecking order theory**, developed by Myers and Majluf, suggests that managers choose methods of financing that range from the least visible signals up the scale to the most visible—public offerings of equity.[22] The least visible form of financing is no external financing at all—that is, internally generated funds. If internal financing is insufficient, managers next prefer debt, and finally equity. Another implication of the work of Myers and Majluf is that financial managers tend to issue equity when they believe the stock is overvalued but are reluctant to issue equity if they believe the stock is undervalued. Hence, the issuance of stock is interpreted by investors as a negative signal.

We can read the signals that managers provide in their choice of financing method. For example, commitments to fixed payments, such as dividends and debt service payments, may be interpreted as the company's management having confidence in the company's future prospects of making payments. Such signals are considered too costly for poorly performing companies to afford. Alternatively, the signal of raising money at the top of the pecking order and issuing equity at the bottom of the pecking order holds other clues. If, for instance, the company's cost of capital increases after an equity issuance, we may interpret this effect as an indication that management needed capital beyond what comes cheaply; in other words, this is a negative signal regarding the company's future prospects.

4.7 The Optimal Capital Structure According to the Static Trade-Off Theory

Companies make decisions about financial leverage that weigh the value-enhancing effects of leverage from the tax deductibility of interest against the value-reducing impact of the costs of financial distress or bankruptcy, agency costs, and asymmetric information. Putting together all the pieces of the theory of Modigliani and Miller, along with the taxes, costs of financial distress, agency costs, and asymmetric information, we see that as financial leverage is increased, there comes a point beyond which further increases in value from value-enhancing effects are offset completely by value-reducing effects. This point is known as the **optimal capital structure**. In other words, the optimal capital structure is that capital structure at which the value of the company is maximized.

Considering only the tax shield provided by debt and the costs of financial distress, the expression for the value of a leveraged company becomes

$$V_{\text{L}} = V_{\text{U}} + td - \text{PV}(\text{Costs of financial distress}) \tag{32-8}$$

---

[22] Myers and Majluf (1984).

Equation 32-8 represents the **static trade-off theory of capital structure**. It results in an optimal capital structure such that debt composes less than 100 percent of a company's capital structure. We diagram this optimum in Figure 10.

The static trade-off theory of capital structure is based on balancing the expected costs from financial distress against the tax benefits of debt service payments, as shown in Panel A of Figure 10. Unlike the Modigliani and Miller proposition of no optimal capital structure, or a structure with almost all debt when the tax shield is considered, static trade-off theory puts forth an optimal capital structure with an optimal proportion of debt. Optimal debt usage is found at the point where any additional debt would cause the costs of financial distress to increase by a greater amount than the benefit of the additional tax shield.

We cannot say precisely at which level of debt financing a company reaches its optimal capital structure. The optimal capital structure depends on the company's business risk, combined with its tax situation, corporate governance, and financial accounting information transparency, among other factors. However, what we can say, based on this theory, is that a company should consider a number of factors, including its business risk and the possible costs of financial distress, in determining its capital structure.

A company's management uses these tools to decide the level of debt appropriate for the company. The tax benefit from the deductibility of the interest expense on debt must be balanced against the risk associated with the

FIGURE 10 Tradeoff Theory with Taxes and Cost of Financial Distress

A. Value of the Company and the Debt-Equity Ratio

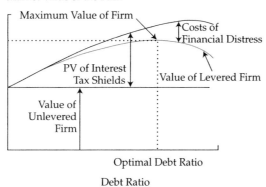

B. Cost of Capital and the Debt-Equity Ratio

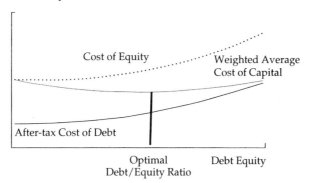

EXAMPLE 11

Financial Leverage and the Cost of Capital

The Chuang Ho Company provides copper wired components for cellular telephone manufacturers globally. Chuang Ho currently has no debt and has assets of 3 billion SGD. The company's business has matured and it now expects operating earnings of 20,000 SGD per year, indefinitely. Alex Ahn, the company's CFO, wants to evaluate a target leverage structure and uses a scenario approach to evaluate the cost of capital for the present 0 percent debt and possible 50 percent debt or 80 percent debt. Chuang Ho's marginal tax rate is 35 percent. Ahn has gathered the following information regarding costs of capital:

▶ The cost of equity rises with increased levels of debt from 15 percent to 18 percent to 24 percent.
▶ The company can borrow at 12 percent on 50 percent debt, or at 16 percent on 80 percent debt.

Which capital structure is expected to have the lowest cost of capital?

Solution: First, calculate the cost of capital under the three scenarios:

TABLE 8 Chuang Ho Company

	Leverage		
	No Debt	**50% Debt**	**80% Debt**
Assets	$3,000,000,000	$3,000,000,000	$3,000,000,000
Debt	$0	$1,500,000,000	$2,400,000,000
Equity	$3,000,000,000	$1,500,000,000	$600,000,000
Debt/equity ratio	0	1	4
Proportion of debt	0%	50%	80%
Proportion of equity	100%	50%	20%
Before-tax cost of debt	—	12%	16%
Cost of equity	15%	18%	24%
After-tax cost of debt	—	7.8%	10.4%
Weighted average cost of capital	15.0%	12.9%	13.1

Of the three capital structures that we are evaluating, the cost of capital is lowest for 50 percent debt.

use of debt. The extent of financial leverage used should thus depend on owners' and management's appetites for risk, as well as the stability of the company's business environment. Indeed, as we show in Panel B of Figure 10, as the proportion of debt in a business rises, the costs of both debt and equity are likely to rise to offset the higher risks associated with higher levels of debt. These cost increases reduce or even negate the cost savings due to the greater use of debt, the cheaper source of financing. The result is a U-shaped weighted average cost of capital curve.

When the company does indeed recognize that it has a most appropriate or best capital structure, it may adopt this as its **target capital structure**. Because management may exploit short-term opportunities in one or another financing source and because market-value fluctuations continuously affect the company's capital structure, a company's capital structure at any point in time may differ from the target. Nevertheless, so long as the assumptions of the analysis and the target are unchanged, analysts and management should focus on the target capital structure.

PRACTICAL ISSUES IN CAPITAL STRUCTURE POLICY

5

5.1 Debt Ratings

Debt ratings are an important consideration in the practical management of leverage. As leverage rises, rating agencies tend to lower the ratings of the company's debt to reflect the higher credit risk resulting from the increasing leverage. Lower ratings signify higher risk to both equity and debt capital providers, who therefore demand higher returns.

Most large companies pay one or more rating services to rate their bonds. Debt issues are rated for creditworthiness by public rating agencies. The rating agencies include Moody's, Standard & Poor's, and Fitch. Rating agencies perform a financial analysis of the company's ability to pay the promised cash flows, as well as an analysis of the bond's **indenture**, the set of complex legal documents associated with the issuance of debt instruments.

FIGURE 11 Bond Ratings by Moody's, Standard & Poor's, and Fitch

	Moody's	Standard & Poor's	Fitch	
Highest quality	Aaa	AAA	AAA	
High quality	Aa	AA	AA	Investment grade
Upper medium grade	A	A	A	
Medium grade	Baa	BBB	BBB	
Speculative	Ba	BB	BB	
Highly speculative	B	B	B	
Substantial risk	Caa	CCC	CCC	Speculative grade
Extremely speculative	Ca			
Possibly in default	C			
Default		D	DDD-D	

**FIGURE 12   Yields on Aaa and Baa Rated Corporate Bonds,
1984–2005**

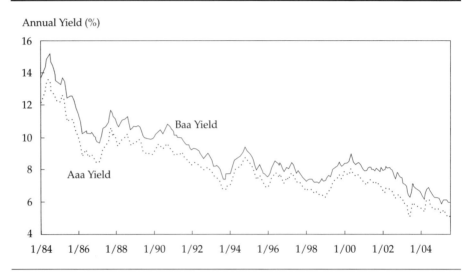

Source: Board of Governors of the Federal Reserve System, release H.15.

These agencies evaluate the wealth of information about the issuer and the bond, including the bond's characteristics and indenture, and provide investors with an assessment of the company's ability to pay the interest and principal on the bond as promised. We provide the bond rating classifications in Figure 11. Though there is significant agreement in ratings among the three major services, some disagreements do occur. For example, Standard & Poor's reduced the credit rating of General Motors to speculative grade in early May of 2005, but Moody's did not do so until late August of 2005.

In practice, most managers consider the company's debt rating in their policies regarding capital structure. Managers must be mindful of their company's bond ratings because the cost of capital is tied closely to bond ratings. Consider the difference in the yields on Aaa and Baa rated corporate bonds, as shown in Figure 12. Typically, a difference of 100 basis points exists between the yields of Aaa and Baa bonds, though this spread widens in economic recessions.[23] The cost of debt increases significantly when a bond's rating drops from **investment grade** to speculative. For example, when the rating of General Motors' unsecured 7.2 percent bond maturing in 2011 was changed by Moody's from Baa to Ba, the bond's price fell by over 7.5 percent and its yield rose from 7.541 percent to 9.364 percent.

5.2 Evaluating Capital Structure Policy

In evaluating a company's capital structure, the financial analyst must look at the capital structure of the company over time, the capital structure of competitors that have similar business risk, and company-specific factors, such as the quality of corporate governance, that may affect agency costs, among other factors.[24]

---

[23] The Board of Governors of the Federal Reserve System H15 series of Aaa and Baa corporate yields shows an average spread of 119 basis points between Aaa and Baa rated bonds, on average, from 1919 to mid-2005. The largest spread occurred in 1932, with 565 bps, and the lowest spread occurred in 1966, with a 32 bp difference.

[24] Good corporate governance should lower the net agency costs of equity.

The financial analyst is not privy to the company's target capital structure but rather can evaluate the company's ability to handle its financial obligations and the potential role of costs of financial distress in determining how much financial leverage a company can handle.

A common goal of capital structure decisions is to finance at the lowest cost of capital. Analysts can use a scenario approach to assess this point for a particular company, starting with the current cost of capital for a company and considering various changes to answer the following questions:

1. What happens to the cost of capital as the debt ratio is changed?
2. At what debt ratio is the cost of capital minimized and company value maximized?
3. What will happen to the company value and stock price if the company moves toward its optimal capital structure?

5.3 Leverage in an International Setting

Despite the fact that Modigliani and Miller tell us that under several conditions the market value of a company is independent of its capital structure, we know that a company's capital structure is indeed relevant in the real world due to the effects of taxation, the costs of financial distress, and agency costs. The static trade-off theory suggests that the optimal level of leverage should be the level at which the value of the company is maximized; this is the level of debt financing at which any additional debt increases the costs of financial distress by an amount greater than the benefit from interest deductibility.

A company's capital structure largely depends on company-specific factors such as the probability of bankruptcy, profitability, quality and structure of assets, and growth opportunities. Beyond these factors, the company's industry affiliation, as well as the characteristics of the country where the company operates, can account for differences in capital structure also.

The general business environment differs from one country to another, and researchers show that country-specific factors have explanatory power that is similar to or even greater than that of the company's industry affiliation in determining a company's capital structure.[25] Drawing conclusions from the comparison of financial leverage indicators of a U.S.-based energy company and a Japanese energy company is not meaningful if we do not take country-specific differences into account. Tradition, tax policy, and regulation may largely explain the different degrees of leverage in the two countries.

In examining the capital structure and debt maturity structure of corporations in an international context, researchers generally find that differences in the capital structures exist between developed and emerging markets, as well as across the developed countries. Moreover, the debt maturity structure—another important capital structure decision—also tends to vary across the international setting. Therefore, when analysts focus on the capital structure of companies in an international setting, they must consider both the relative use of debt and the maturity structure of debt. In fact, short-term and long-term debt ratios follow very different patterns in an international comparison:

▶ Taking total debt into account, companies in France, Italy, and Japan tend to be more highly levered than companies in the United States and the United Kingdom.

---

[25] See, for example, Fan, Titman, and Twite (2004).

► Focusing on the use of long-term debt, on the other hand, a different picture emerges: North American companies tend to use more long-term debt than do Japanese companies.

► Companies in developed markets typically use more long-term debt and tend to have higher long-term debt to total debt ratios compared to their emerging market peers.

Beyond the pure comparison of the capital structures, it is equally or even more important to identify and understand the country-specific factors that explain the cross-country differences.[26] Three major types of factors may be used to explain most capital structure differences in an international comparison:

1. *Institutional and legal environment.* These factors represent the legal and regulatory environment in which companies operate, as well as the requirements related to financial reporting. These institutional factors—including taxation, accounting standards, and even the presence or lack of corruption—may affect a company's optimal capital structure.

2. *Financial markets and banking sector.* These factors include characteristics of the banking sector, as well as the size and activity of the financial markets. Financial institutions are crucial for companies' access to financing.

3. *Macroeconomic environment.* These factors capture the general economic and business environment, addressing the influence of economic growth and inflation on the capital structure.

5.3.1 Institutional and Legal Environment

Taxation, financial legislation, the content of laws (e.g., bankruptcy law), and the quality of their enforcement all differ from one country to another. These differences may influence the capital structures of companies and explain many of the differences that we observe across countries.

The apparent conflict of interest between the companies' management and outside investors has already been addressed as the **agency problem**. This problem is, in fact, one of the key determinants of a company's ability to obtain capital; hence, agency costs are one of the major factors determining the capital structure. This conflict may be mitigated by carefully prepared contracts. The quality of investors' legal protections depends on both the content and the enforcement of the contracts and laws. As a result, we expect to see higher financial leverage in those countries that have weaker legal systems. Further, in countries with weaker legal systems, we expect a greater use of short-term debt financing versus long-term debt financing. Researchers find that companies operating in countries with an efficient legal system tend to use more long-term debt than short-term debt and exhibit lower leverage than comparable companies in countries with weaker legal systems.

Some researchers assume that legal systems based on common law offer external capital providers (both equity and debt providers) with better protection compared to the legal systems of civil-law countries. Common law originated in England and is also followed in other countries, such as the United States, Canada, Australia, New Zealand, Singapore, India, and Malaysia. Civil law, on the other hand,

---

[26] We should note, however, that the conclusions drawn in different studies are not always consistent with each other. The results of empirical studies, in fact, may depend on several factors, such as the set of countries and companies taken into the data sample, the analyzed historical period, the hypotheses that the researchers intended to test, and even the definition of leverage that they considered.

has origins going back to ancient Rome; the countries of continental Europe and most of the rest of the world have legal systems based on this tradition. Researchers find mixed and limited evidence that companies operating in common-law countries tend to have longer debt maturity structures compared to their peers in civil-law countries and use less debt and more equity in their capital structure.

Similar to the rationale described in the case of legal system efficiency, a high level of information asymmetry between insiders and outsiders encourages a greater use of debt relative to equity, as well as a greater reliance on short-term debt than on long-term debt in the capital structure. This is likely due to the fact that enforcing the debt contract is easier than enforcing the less clearly contracted shareholders' rights. Auditors and financial analysts can help in reducing information asymmetries and increase the level of transparency.[27] Researchers confirm that the presence of auditors and analysts is associated with lower financial leverage. The importance of auditors is usually strongest in emerging markets, whereas the presence of analysts is more important in developed markets.

As we discussed earlier, taxes affect the capital structure decision by lowering the cost of debt financing to the issuer in those jurisdictions in which interest expense is tax deductible. In the absence of agency and bankruptcy costs, the benefit from the tax deductibility of interest encourages companies to use debt financing instead of equity financing. However, if dividend income is taxed at lower rates than interest income, some of the advantage of debt versus equity financing may be reduced from the corporate perspective because the price at which equity can be sold should reflect that advantage. Taxes are an important factor in a company's capital structure decision.

Researchers find mixed results on the effect of the corporate tax rate on capital structures, but they find that personal tax rates do matter. Because the tax treatment of dividends differs across countries, researchers can examine the importance of different tax treatments of dividend income.[28] They find that companies in countries that have lower tax rates on dividend income also have less debt in their capital structures.[29]

5.3.2 Financial Markets and Banking Sector

The size, activity, and liquidity of capital markets are crucial for corporations' access to capital. Several researchers have analyzed the impact of capital markets' characteristics on companies' capital structures. Some find that liquid and active capital markets affect companies' debt maturity structure. Specifically, they find that companies in countries that have liquid and active capital markets tend to use more long-term debt with longer debt maturity. Researchers attribute this finding to the heightened external monitoring of companies by market participants in active markets.[30]

The banking sector is one of the primary sources of funds for the corporate sector in many countries, and its role is especially significant in countries that do not have a corporate bond market. The importance of the banking sector relative to the capital markets can vary from one country to another, however. Countries with a common-law tradition, where the shareholders' rights are stronger, tend to be more market-based, whereas civil-law countries tend to be more

---

[27] Fan et al.

[28] Fan et al.

[29] A lower dividend tax burden can be achieved in countries that apply dividend tax relief (e.g., Austria, Belgium, Thailand, and Turkey) or dividend imputation (e.g., Canada, France, Germany, Italy, United Kingdom, and Mexico).

[30] See Demirguc-Kunt and Maksimovic (1998).

bank-based. Because the relationship between a bank and a company is stronger and closer than between a company and a bondholder, banks can handle information asymmetries more efficiently. This effect may partly explain why civil-law countries are more bank-oriented.

However, researchers' findings are mixed regarding the effect of the banking system. Some researchers claim that banks have no effect on companies' financial leverage and that the difference between the bank-oriented and market-oriented countries is more reflected by the relative importance of public financing (i.e., stock and bonds) and private financing (i.e., bank loans).[31] On the other hand, some researchers find that companies in bank-based countries exhibit higher financial leverage compared to those that operate in market-based countries.[32]

The presence of institutional investors may also affect the companies' capital structure choice. Some institutional investors may have preferred habitats, and this preference may affect companies' debt maturity structure. Insurance companies and pension plans, for example, may prefer investing in long-term debt securities in order to match the interest rate risk of their long-term liabilities. Researchers find limited results regarding the influence of preferred habitats; companies in countries that have more institutional investors in their markets tend to have less short-term and more long-term debt and somewhat lower debt to equity ratios.[33]

5.3.3 Macroeconomic Environment

Inflation is a widely recognized macroeconomic indicator. High inflation has a negative impact on both the level of the debt financing and the desired debt maturity.[34] Companies in higher-inflation countries usually exhibit lower levels of financial leverage, rely more on equity financing, and have a shorter debt maturity structure compared to their peers in lower-inflation countries.

Researchers have also found that the growth in gross domestic product is associated with longer debt maturity in developed markets. In addition, researchers focusing on developing countries find that companies in countries with high growth rely more on equity financing.[35]

5.3.4 Conclusions

Financial analysts must consider country-specific factors when analyzing and comparing companies that operate in different countries. We have summarized these factors in Figure 13.

These factors include the differences in the business and legal environments in other countries, taxes, and macroeconomic factors, among others. Companies' optimal capital structures may differ simply as a consequence of these many country-specific differences. In addition to presenting challenges for international financial and credit analysis, these international differences in debt ratios present some challenges in developing debt policies for the foreign subsidiaries of multinational companies. Theory provides little guidance, and corporate practices in this area seem to vary widely.

---

[31] Rajan (1995).

[32] See, for example, Claessens, Djankov, and Nevova (2001).

[33] See, for example, Fan et al. and Domowitz, Glen, and Madhavan (2000).

[34] See, for example, Demirguc-Kunt and Maksimovic (1999), Domowitz et al., and Fan et al.

[35] See Domowitz et al.

FIGURE 13 Country-Specific Factors and Their Assumed Impacts on the Companies' Capital Structure

Country-Specific Factor	If a Country	. . . Then D/E Ratio Is Potentially	. . . And Debt Maturity Is Potentially
Institutional framework			
Legal system efficiency	Is more efficient	Lower	Longer
Legal system origin	Has common law as opposed to civil law	Lower	Longer
Information intermediaries	Has auditors and analysts	Lower	Longer
Taxation	Has taxes that favor equity	Lower	
Banking system, financial markets			
Equity and bond markets	Has active bond and stock markets		Longer
Bank-based or market-based country	Has a bank-based financial system	Higher	
Investors	Has large institutional investors	Lower	Longer
Macroeconomic environment			
Inflation	Has high inflation	Lower	Shorter
Growth	Has high GDP growth		Longer

SUMMARY

In this reading, we have reviewed the fundamentals of business risk, financial risk, and selection of sources of financing.

▶ Many companies have goals for maintaining a certain credit rating, and these goals are influenced by the relative costs of debt financing among the different rating classes.

▶ In evaluating a company's capital structure, the financial analyst must look at the capital structure of the company over time, the capital structure of competitors that have similar business risk, and company-specific factors, such as the quality of corporate governance, that may affect agency costs, among other factors.

▶ Good corporate governance and accounting transparency should lower the net agency costs of equity.

▶ When comparing capital structures of companies in different countries, an analyst must consider a variety of characteristics that might differ and affect both the typical capital structure and the debt maturity structure. The major characteristics fall into three categories: institutional and legal environment, financial markets and banking sector, and macroeconomic environment.

PRACTICE PROBLEMS FOR READING 32

1. If two companies have identical operating risk, they also have identical

   A. business risk.

   B. sales risk.

   C. total leverage.

   D. sensitivity of operating earnings to changes in the number of units produced and sold.

2. Operating leverage is a measure of the

   A. sensitivity of net earnings to changes in operating earnings.

   B. sensitivity of net earnings to changes in sales.

   C. sensitivity of fixed operating costs to changes in variable costs.

   D. sensitivity of earnings before interest and taxes to changes in the number of units produced and sold.

3. The Fulcrum Company produces decorative swivel platforms for home televisions. If Fulcrum produces 40 million units, it estimates that it can sell them for $100 each. The variable production costs are $65 per unit, whereas the fixed production costs are $1.05 billion. Which of the following statements is true?

   A. The Fulcrum Company produces a positive operating income if it produces and sells more than 25 million swivel platforms.

   B. The Fulcrum Company's degree of operating leverage is 1.333.

   C. If the Fulcrum Company increases production and sales by 5 percent, its operating earnings are expected to increase by 20 percent.

   D. Increasing the fixed production costs by 10 percent will result in a lower sensitivity of operating earnings to changes in units produced and sold.

4. Increases and decreases in the level of sales are due to business risk. The business risk of a particular company is characterized by

   A. the ratio of debt to equity in the capital structure.

   B. the level of risk assumed by the debt providers.

   C. operating leverage and uncertainty about demand, output prices, and competition.

   D. uncertainty about credit ratings, government debt, interest rates, and the demand for the domestic currency.

5. Consider two companies that operate in the same line of business and have the same degree of operating leverage: the Basic Company and the Grundlegend Company. The Basic Company has no debt in its capital structure, but the Grundlegend Company has a capital structure that consists of 50 percent debt. Which of the following statements is true?

   A. The Grundlegend Company has a degree of total leverage that exceeds that of the Basic Company by 50 percent.

   B. The Grundlegend Company has the same sensitivity of net earnings to changes in earnings before interest and taxes as the Basic Company.

   C. The Grundlegend Company has the same sensitivity of earnings before interest and taxes to changes in sales as the Basic Company.

   D. The Grundlegend Company has the same sensitivity of net earnings to changes in sales as the Basic Company.

6. Myundia Motors now sells 1 million units at ¥3,529 per unit. Fixed operating costs are ¥1,290 million and variable operating costs are ¥1,500 per unit. If the company pays ¥410 million in interest, the levels of sales at the operating and total breakeven points are, respectively

	Operating	Total
A.	¥1,500,000,000	¥2,257,612,900
B.	¥2,243,671,760	¥2,956,776,737
C.	¥2,975,148,800	¥3,529,000,000
D.	¥2,257,612,900	¥3,529,000,000

7. Juan Alavanca is evaluating the risk of two companies in the machinery industry: The Gearing Company and Hebelkraft, Inc. Alavanca used the latest fiscal year's financial statement and interviews with managers of the respective companies to gather the following information:

	The Gearing Company	Hebelkraft, Inc.
Number of units produced and sold	1 million	1.5 million
Sales price per unit	$200	$200
Variable cost per unit	$120	$100
Fixed operating cost	$40 million	$90 million
Fixed financing expense	$20 million	$20 million

Based upon this information, the total breakeven points for The Gearing Company and Hebelkraft, Inc. are

A. 0.75 million and 1.1 million units, respectively.

B. 1 million and 1.5 million units, respectively.

C. 1.5 million and 0.75 million units, respectively.

D. 1.0 million units for both companies.

8. If there are homogeneous expectations, an efficient market, and no taxes, transactions costs, or bankruptcy costs, the Modigliani and Miller Proposition I states that

A. bankruptcy risk rises with more leverage.

B. managers cannot increase the value of the company by adding debt.

C. the value of a company is the product of leverage, taxes, and imperfect markets.

D. managers cannot add value by employing tax-saving strategies.

9. If managers justified a choice of optimal capital structure using Modigliani and Miller's Proposition II without taxes, they would contend that

A. taxes increase the value of debt.

B. taxes increase the value of equity.

C. debt is riskier than equity, so it is more costly.

D. the cost of equity increases with increasing proportionate use of debt in the capital structure.

10. Suppose the cost of capital of the Gadget Company is 10 percent. If Gadget has a capital structure that is 50 percent debt and 50 percent equity, its before-tax cost of debt is 5 percent, and its marginal tax rate is 20 percent, then its cost of equity capital is *closest* to

   A. 10 percent.

   B. 12 percent.

   C. 14 percent.

   D. 16 percent.

11. The current weighted average cost of capital for Van der Welde, a South African mining company, is 10 percent. The company announced a stock offering that raises the marginal cost of capital to 13 percent. The company is *most likely* signaling that

   A. debt financing is cheaper than equity.

   B. equity financing is cheaper than debt.

   C. the company's debt/equity ratio has moved beyond the optimal range.

   D. the company's prospects are improving.

12. The financial literature generally finds that

   A. companies in the United States and United Kingdom tend to have higher financial leverage ratios (taking total debt into account) compared to their peers in Japan, France, or Italy.

   B. companies in the United States tend to use long-term financing more intensively than their peers in Japan.

   C. companies in emerging markets tend to use long-term financing more intensively than their peers in the developed markets.

   D. country-specific factors have no explanatory power regarding companies' financing structures.

13. The corporate debt maturity structure is typically longer in those countries where

   A. the legal system is weak.

   B. capital markets are passive and illiquid.

   C. inflation is low.

   D. economic growth is low.

14. Financial leverage ratios tend to be higher in those countries where

   A. the legal system is inefficient.

   B. the presence of information intermediaries (e.g., auditors) is significant.

   C. the tax burden on dividends is low.

   D. inflation is high.

15. According to the pecking order theory

   A. new debt is preferable to new equity.

   B. new equity is preferable to internally generated funds.

   C. new debt is preferable to internally generated funds.

   D. new equity is always preferable to other sources of capital.

16. According to the static trade-off theory,
  A. the amount of debt a company has is irrelevant.
  B. debt should be used only as a last resort.
  C. debt will not be used if a company's tax rate is high.
  D. companies have an optimal level of debt.

The following information relates to Questions 17–22

Barbara Andrade is a generalist in equity analysis for Greengable Capital Partners, a major global asset manager. The investment committee relies on her input for a variety of equity recommendations. She has a background as an analyst in the finance department of an entertainment company, so she is often asked to evaluate a variety of issues relating to that industry.

Greengable owns a significant position with a large gain in Mosely Broadcast Group. On a regular quarterly conference call, Brian Hunsaker, Greengable's growth portfolio manager, feels that Mosely's CFO may adjust the company's capital structure to include more debt. Concerned that any changes in the capital structure will impact the value of Greengable's holdings, Hunsaker asks Andrade to evaluate the impact of such a change.

To begin the analysis, Andrade first compiles the following current information relating to Mosely:

Yield to maturity on debt	8.00%
Market value of debt	$100 million
Number of shares of common stock	10 million
Price per share of common stock	$30
Weighted average cost of capital	10.82%
Marginal tax rate	35%

Additionally, Andrade determines that increased levels of debt will result in higher costs of both debt and equity to reflect increased credit risk and more financial leverage. Based on comparisons with similar companies in the industry, Andrade estimates that for the following debt-to-total capital ratios, the corresponding costs of debt and cost of equity will be:

Debt-to-Total Capital Ratio	Cost of Debt	Cost of Equity
20%	7.7%	12.5%
30%	8.4%	13.0%
40%	9.3%	14.0%
50%	10.4%	16.0%

17. The current after-tax cost of debt for Mosely is *closest* to

   A. 2.80%.

   B. 5.20%.

   C. 7.65%.

   D. 10.80%.

18. With consideration of taxes, Mosely's current cost of equity capital is *closest* to

    A. 8.25%.

    B. 10.05%.

    C. 11.76%.

    D. 12.69%.

19. Based on the information above, what debt-to-total capital ratio would minimize Mosely's weighted average cost of capital?

    A. 20%.

    B. 30%.

    C. 40%.

    D. 50%.

20. An increase in the marginal tax rate to 40 percent would

    A. result in a lower cost of debt capital.

    B. result in a higher cost of debt capital.

    C. not affect the company's cost of capital.

    D. increase both the cost of Mosely's equity capital and the cost of its debt capital.

21. According to the static trade-off theory of capital structure, an increase in Mosely's debt ratio

    A. would result in a lower market value of the company.

    B. would result in a higher market value of the company.

    C. would have no impact on the market value of the company.

    D. could cause either an increase or decrease in the market value of the company.

22. According to the pecking order theory, Mosely would use the following ranking in raising capital

	First Choice	Last Choice
A.	Debt	Internally generated funds
B.	Internally generated funds	Debt
C.	Internally generated funds	A new public equity issue
D.	Debt	Internally generated funds

DIVIDENDS AND DIVIDEND POLICY

by George H. Troughton and Catherine E. Clark

LEARNING OUTCOMES

The candidate should be able to:

a. review cash dividends, stock dividends, stock splits, and reverse stock splits, and calculate and discuss their impact on a shareholder's wealth;

b. compare the impact on shareholder wealth of a share repurchase and a cash dividend of equal amount;

c. calculate the earnings per share effect of a share repurchase when the repurchase is made with borrowed funds and the company's after-tax cost of debt is greater (less) than its earnings yield;

d. calculate the book value effect of a share repurchase when the market value of a share is greater (less) than book value per share;

e. compare and contrast share repurchase methods;

f. review dividend payment chronology including declaration, holder-of-record, ex-dividend, and payment dates and indicate when the share price will most likely reflect the dividend;

g. summarize the factors affecting dividend payout policy;

h. calculate the effective tax rate on a dollar of corporate earnings distributed as a dividend using the double-taxation, split rate, and tax imputation systems;

i. discuss the types of information that dividend initiations, increases, decreases, and omissions may convey, and discuss cross-country differences in the signaling content of dividends;

j. compare and contrast the following dividend policies: residual dividend, longer-term residual dividend, dividend stability, and target payout ratio;

k. calculate a company's expected dividend using the variables in the target payout approach;

l. discuss the rationales for share repurchases and explain the signals that share repurchases may generate;

> **m.** differentiate among the schools of thought on dividends (dividend irrelevance, dividend preference, and tax aversion), and discuss their implications for shareholder value and the price-to-earnings ratio;
>
> **n.** demonstrate how the initiation of a regular dividend payout might affect the price-to-earnings multiple.

1   INTRODUCTION

One of the longest running and most debated issues in corporate finance is whether a company's decision about the level of its dividends has an impact on the value of its equity. Essentially, a company has three choices with respect to its earnings in any given year: 1) it could reinvest the earnings back into the business, 2) it could pay the earnings out to the shareholders in the form of dividends, or 3) it could repurchase outstanding shares. In reality, most large companies do some combination of the three. For example, in recent decades, large companies in Germany, Great Britain, and the United States paid out dividends that often ranged from 20 percent to 60 percent of their earnings. Japan and some other developing nations had significantly lower dividend payout ratios.

We emphasize in this reading that the overriding consideration in determining a company's dividend payout policy is whether it has positive net present value (NPV) reinvestment opportunities. In addition, a country's income taxes on corporate profits, shareholder income, and capital gains play an important role. Furthermore, traditions, transaction costs for new share issues, and shareholder preferences enter the picture. Finally, dividends are often read in the market place as sending a signal regarding the company's short- and long-term prospects.

This reading is organized as follows: In Section 2, we discuss how cash and stock dividends are paid and how shares are repurchased. In Section 3, we present the chronology of dividend payment procedures, including record date, ex-dividend date, and payment date. In Section 4, we discuss the factors affecting a company's payout policy including taxation, flotation costs, debt covenants and other institutional restrictions, the clientele effect, and the information content of dividends. This leads to a discussion in Section 5 of alternative dividend policies once a company is committed to paying a dividend. We look at the residual, stable, and target cash dividend approaches, as well as whether companies appear to be changing dividend policies. In Section 6, we explore the question of whether dividends matter or are irrelevant, and in Section 7, we touch briefly on the valuation implications of dividends. The last section summarizes the reading.

FORMS OF DIVIDENDS

Companies can pay dividends in a number of ways. Cash dividends can be distributed to shareholders through regular, extra, special, or liquidating dividends. Other forms include stock dividends, stock splits, and share repurchases. In this section, we will explore the different forms that dividends can take and their impact on both the shareholder and the issuing company.

2.1 Regular Dividends

Many companies choose to distribute dividends on a regular schedule. Most U.S. and Canadian companies pay quarterly dividends. Some non-North American companies, such as Samsung (Korea), Bayer AG (Germany), and Sony (Japan) distribute **regular dividends** either semi-annually or annually. In each case, the intention is to distribute among shareholders a portion of a company's profits on a regularly recurring basis.

Most companies that pay regular dividends strive to maintain—or better yet, increase—their dividends on a regular basis. A record of consistent dividends over a very long period of time is important to many companies and many shareholders. The higher standard of consistently increasing dividends is a goal that a substantial number of companies seek to attain and a significant portion of shareholders value.

Regular dividends, and especially increasing regular dividends, also signal to investors that their company is growing and willing to share the gains with their shareholders. Perhaps more importantly, management can use dividend announcements to communicate confidence in the future. An increase in the regular dividend (especially if it is unexpected) will likely have a more positive effect on the share price than could be explained by the increased monetary value of the dividend.

However, some interpret rising dividends or the payment of any dividends as a tacit sign of lack of sufficient growth opportunities, that is, as a sign that the company is unable to profitably reinvest all its earnings. In general, though, failing to increase a regular dividend over a long period of time, or worse yet, cutting it, is often an indication that all is not well at the company.

2.1.1 Dividend Reinvestment Plans (DRIPs)

Some companies have in place a system that allows shareholders to automatically reinvest their dividends into the purchase of additional company shares. Shareholders must register to sign up for the **dividend reinvestment plan**. The advantages for the company are numerous: It retains the cash otherwise sent out to the shareholder; it reduces the transaction costs of making the payments; and it accumulates more equity capital while saving the underwriting costs of a new share issue. The advantages to the shareholder are twofold: It allows accumulation of shares using **cost averaging**, and the shareholder's additional investments are in a company he has already deemed a good investment. The additional shares are purchased with no transaction costs, and some companies offer the additional benefit of purchasing shares at a discount (usually 3–5 percent) to the market price.

A disadvantage to the shareholder is the extra bookkeeping involved in jurisdictions in which capital gains are taxed. Shares purchased through a dividend reinvestment plan change the average cost basis for capital gains tax purposes. If the share price is higher (lower) than the original purchase price, it will increase (decrease) the average cost basis. Either way, the average shareholder is left with an accounting situation that is complicated. A further perceived disadvantage to the shareholder is that the cash dividend is fully taxed in the year received even when reinvested, which means the shareholder is paying tax on cash not actually received.

2.2 Extra (or Special) Dividends

Extra (or special) dividends occur when a company does not have a regular dividend policy or rate or it wants to make a one-time extra payment.[1] Extra dividends are generally viewed as nonrecurring payments to shareholders brought about by special circumstances. Typically, companies in more cyclical industries would be likely to use this form of dividend payment. When times are bad and earnings are down, cash that would otherwise have gone to dividends can be conserved. But when times are good and earnings are up, the companies can "share the wealth" with their shareholders by issuing a special dividend. Some companies in **cyclical industries** choose to declare a small regular dividend and then, when circumstances warrant, declare an extra dividend at the end of the year. While "extra" implies that this dividend is in addition to a more regular base of dividends, extra dividend, irregular dividend, and special dividend are terms used interchangeably. In the past, certain automobile companies were among those that regularly used the extra dividend. Ford and GM declared moderate regular quarterly dividends and used the "**extra dividend**" at the end of the year to reflect particularly good earnings years.

2.3 Liquidating Dividends

A **liquidating dividend** occurs when a company dissolves its business and distributes the proceeds to its shareholders. Alternatively, a liquidating dividend could refer to the sale of part of a company's business for cash that is distributed to the shareholders. In either case, the distribution would be treated as a capital gain for tax purposes.

2.4 Stock Dividends

Another form of dividend used by some companies is the stock dividend. Here the company does not send cash to its shareholders, but distributes a certain percentage (typically 2–10 percent) of additional shares to each shareholder. The shareholders' total cost basis remains the same but the cost per share held is reduced. For example, if a shareholder owns 100 shares at a price of $10 per share, the total cost base would be $1,000. After a 5 percent stock dividend, the total cost basis would be the same $1,000 but the cost basis per share would become (approximately) $9.52 on the 105 shares now held ($9.52 = $1,000/105).

Superficially, the stock dividend might seem an improvement on the cash dividend from both the shareholders' and the company's point of view. Each shareholder ends up with more shares, which didn't have to be paid for, and the company didn't have to spend any actual money issuing a dividend. Furthermore,

---

[1] In *The Wall Street Journal's* Dividend News Section, extra or special dividends are referred to as irregular dividends.

the shareholder postpones any tax due until the stock is ultimately sold. However, the stock dividend does nothing to change the value of each shareholder's ownership position in the company since along with shares outstanding, earnings per share (and other per share data) are also adjusted. For example, a company with a billion dollar market capitalization before issuing a stock dividend will still be a company with a billion dollar market capitalization after the stock dividend: The decrease in the share price should be exactly offset by the increase in the number of shares outstanding.

Table 1 shows the impact of a 3 percent stock dividend to a shareholder who owns 10 percent of a company with a market value of $20 million.[2] As one can see, the market value of the shareholder's wealth does not change, assuming an unchanged P/E. In addition, a stock dividend and, as the reader will see shortly, a stock split do not alter a company's asset base or earning power.

TABLE 1	Illustration of the Effect of a Stock Dividend	
	Before Dividend	**After Dividend**
Shares outstanding	1,000,000	1,030,000
Earnings per share	$1.00	$0.97 (1/1.03)
Stock price	$20.00	$19.4175 (20 × 0.9709)
P/E	20	20
Total market value	$20 million	$20 million (1,030,000 × $19.4175)
Shares owned	100,000 (10% × 1,000,000)	103,000 (10% × 1,030,000)
Ownership value	$2,000,000 (100,000 × $20)	$2,000,000 (103,000 × $19.4175)

In contrast to financial theorists, companies that regularly pay stock dividends see some advantages to this form of dividend payment. From the company's point of view, more shares outstanding broaden the shareholder base. With more shares outstanding, there is a higher probability that more individual shareholders will own the stock, almost always a plus for companies. Market folklore has it that a lower stock price will attract more investors, all else equal. U.S. companies often view the optimal share price as $20 to $80. Assuming a growing company, a systematic stock dividend will be more likely to keep the stock in the "optimal" range. For example, Tootsie Roll Industries has issued a 3 percent dividend every year since 1966 in addition to its regular quarterly dividend. When the company pays the same **dividend rate** on the new shares as they did on the old shares, a shareholder's dividend income has increased.

A stock dividend has no effect on a company's capital structure (its mix of sources of financing) because it leaves the market values of equity and debt unchanged. This is a difference between cash and stock dividends. Cash dividends transfer assets from the company to shareholders, thereby reducing the assets of the company and the market value of its equity. As a result, cash dividends increase leverage (i.e., the proportion of financing provided by debt) from what it was before the payment of the dividend. An increase in leverage

---

[2] The table rounds intermediate calculations to only four decimal places. Final results ignore rounding errors.

could decrease the market value of existing bonds, and bondholders usually seek to protect their position through certain restrictions on the payment of cash dividends, as discussed in more detail in Section 4.3.

Another difference between a cash dividend and a stock dividend is its accounting treatment on the books of the corporation. By shifting retained earnings (equal to the market value of the additional stock being distributed) to the capital account, a stock dividend merely reclassifies certain amounts of shareholders' equity on the balance sheet, whereas a cash dividend represents a cash outflow and a reduction in shareholders' equity.

2.5 Stock Splits

Stock splits are similar to stock dividends, in that each shareholder ends up with more shares but no change in his percent ownership of the company. For example, if a company announces a three-for-one stock split, each shareholder will be issued two additional shares for each share owned, so that the end result will be three shares for each one share previously owned. In the process, though, earnings and dividends (and all other per share data) will decline by two thirds, leaving the P/E, dividend yield, and market value all unchanged. While two-for-one and three-for-one stock splits are the most common, unusual splits such as five-for-four or seven-for-three are not unheard of. It is important for each shareholder to recognize that their wealth is unchanged by the stock split (just as it was for a stock dividend, all else equal). Following is an example of a six-for-five split and its impact on stock price, earnings per share, dividends per share, **dividend yield**, P/E, and market value.

TABLE 2 Before and After a Six-for-Five Stock Split		
	Before Split	**After Split**
Number of shares outstanding	4 million	4.8 million
Stock price	$40.00	$33.33 [$40 / (6/5)]
Earnings per share	$1.50	$1.25 [$1.50 / (6/5)]
Dividends per share	$0.50	$0.4167 [$0.50 / (6/5)]
Dividends yield	1.25%	1.25% ($0.4167/$33.33)
P/E	26.7	26.7 ($33.33/$1.25)
Market value of company	$160 million	$160 million

As one can see, a six-for-five stock split is basically the same as a 20 percent stock dividend, since all per share data have been reduced by 20 percent. The only difference is in the accounting treatment on the books of the company: Stock splits are accounted for as a reduction in the **par value** of the shares, whereas stock dividends are a transfer from retained earnings to equity capital. A company may announce a stock split at any time. Typically it is after a period in which the stock has risen either for reasons specific to that company or, just as likely, during a general rise in the stock market in which the company's stock has done well. Investor folklore has it that an announcement of a stock split is viewed as a positive sign for future stock gains by some investors. However, announced stock splits more often merely recognize that the stock has risen enough to justify a stock split, and return the stock price to the "optimal" range of $20 to $80 per share.

In mid 1999 when its stock was selling for about $90 per share, Enron announced a two-for-one stock split. Over the next year the stock doubled before the company plunged into bankruptcy in 2001. Ameritrade had two stock splits in 1999, a two-for-one in March and a three-for-one in August. The stock commenced to fall from over $60 per share (adjusted) to less than $3 per share in 2002. Even two of the largest companies in the world (as measured by market value), General Electric and Microsoft, saw their stocks decline significantly during the three years after their 1999 stock splits. In each of these above cases, the stock was split after a significant rise but was not, in and of itself, a meaningful predictor of future price action.

Much less common than stock splits are reverse stock splits. A **reverse stock split** increases share price and reduces the number of shares outstanding—again, with no change to the underlying fundamentals. Just as a rising stock price might indicate an upcoming stock split, so, too, a dramatically falling stock price might signal a forthcoming reverse stock split. Reverse stock splits are typically one-for-a much larger number, with the objective of getting the stock closer (this time *up*) to the optimal $20 to $80 range. Reverse stock splits are perhaps most common for companies coming out of bankruptcy (where a one-for-thirty or one-for-fifty reverse stock split would not be unusual) or when the share price declines to a low value (for example, in the United States many institutional investors do not regard stocks selling below $5 per share as investment grade). AT&T Corporation had a 1-for-5 reverse split in November 2002 that brought its stock price up from approximately $5 (adjusting for a liquidating dividend paid on the same date) to about $28.

2.6 Share Repurchases

A **share repurchase** (or buyback) is a transaction in which a company buys back its own shares. Unlike stock dividends and stock splits, share repurchases use corporate cash. Hence, share repurchases can be viewed as an alternative to cash dividends. Shares that have been issued and subsequently repurchased become **treasury shares (treasury stock)**, which are not considered for dividends, voting, or computing earnings per share. Treasury shares may be reissued later, typically for employee stock options. When used for stock options, repurchased shares reduce or prevent earnings per share dilution but do not increase earnings per share.

Share repurchases have been around for a long time, but it is only in the last twenty years that they have been used extensively. In the early 1980s, cash dividends were approximately five times greater than the market value of share repurchases. For a number of years in the bull market of the late 1990s, the value of share repurchases was greater than the value of cash dividends in the United States.

A share repurchase should be equivalent to the payment of cash dividends of equal amount in their effect on shareholders' wealth, all other things being equal. "All other things being equal" in this context is shorthand for assumptions that the taxation and information content of cash dividends and share repurchases do not differ. (We shall discuss the information content of dividends in a subsequent section.) Understanding this baseline equivalence result permits more advanced analysis to explore the result's sensitivity to various modifications to the "all other things being equal" assumption. For example, in Section 5.4 we will discuss the advantage share repurchases may have over cash dividends when the tax rate on dividend income is higher than that on capital gains. Example 1 demonstrates the claim of equivalence in the "all other things being equal" case.

EXAMPLE 1

The Equivalence of Share Repurchases and Cash Dividends

Waynesboro Chemical Industries, Inc. (WCII) has 10,000,000 shares outstanding with a current market value of $20 per share. WCII's Board of Directors is considering two ways of distributing WCII's current $50,000,000 free cash flow to equity. The first method involves paying a cash dividend of $50,000,000/10,000,000 = $5 per share. The second method involves repurchasing $50,000,000 worth of shares. For simplicity, we make the assumptions that dividends are received when the shares go ex-dividend and that any quantity of shares can be bought at the market price of $20 per share. We also assume that the taxation and information content of cash dividends and share repurchases do not differ. How would the wealth of a shareholder be affected by WCII's choice of method in distributing the $50,000,000?

Cash dividend. After the shares go ex-dividend, a shareholder of a single share would have $5 in cash (the dividend) and a share worth $20 − $5 = $15. The ex-dividend value of $15 can be demonstrated as the market value of equity after the distribution of $50,000,000, divided by the number of shares outstanding after the dividend payment, or [(10,000,000) ($20) − $50,000,000]/10,000,000 = $150,000,000/10,000,000 = $15. (The payment of a cash dividend of course has no effect on the number of shares outstanding.) Total wealth from ownership of one share is therefore $5 + $15 = $20.

Share repurchase. With $50,000,000 WCII could repurchase $50,000,000/$20 = 2,500,000 shares. The post-repurchase share price would be unchanged at $20, which can be calculated as the market value of equity after the $50,000,000 share repurchase, divided by the shares outstanding after the share repurchase, or [(10,000,000)($20) − $50,000,000]/(10,000,000 − 2,500,000) = $150,000,000/7,500,000 = $20. Total wealth from ownership of one share is therefore $20, exactly the same as in the case of a cash dividend. It is irrelevant for a shareholder's wealth whether the shareholder actually sold the share back to the WCII in the share repurchase: If the one share was sold, $20 in cash would be realized; if the share was not sold, its market value of $20 would count equally towards the shareholder's wealth.

The assumption made in Example 1 that the company repurchases shares at the market price is an important one. Example 2 illustrates that if a company repurchases shares from an individual shareholder at a negotiated price representing a premium over the market price, the remaining shareholders' wealth is reduced.

EXAMPLE 2

A Share Repurchase that Transfers Wealth

While considering the choice between cash dividends and a share repurchase at the market price of $20 per share, WCII becomes aware that Kirk Parent recently purchased a major position in its outstanding shares with the intention of influencing the business operations of WCII in ways the current board does not approve. An advisor to the board has suggested approaching Parent privately with an offer to buy back $50,000,000 worth of shares from him at $25 per share, which is a $5 premium over the current market price. The board of WCII declines to do so because of the effect of such a repurchase on its other shareholders. Determine the effect of the proposed share repurchase on the wealth of shareholders other than Parent.

Solution: With $50,000,000 WCII could repurchase $50,000,000/$25 = 2,000,000 shares from Parent. The post-repurchase share price would be $18.75, which can be calculated as the market value of equity after the $50,000,000 share repurchase divided by the shares outstanding after the share repurchase, or $[(10,000,000)($20) - $50,000,000]/(10,000,000 - 2,000,0000) = $150,000,000/8,000,000 = 18.75. Shareholders other than Parent would lose $20 - $18.75 = 1.25 for each share owned. Although this share repurchase would conserve total wealth (including Parent's), it effectively transfers wealth to Parent from the other shareholders.

The theme of Example 1 was that, as the baseline result, a company should not expect to create or destroy shareholder wealth merely by its choice of method in distributing money to shareholders. In Example 1, the market price per share of $20 was not affected by the share repurchase. We can interpret $20 as the product of expected EPS and a forward price-to-earnings ratio, or as the product of book value per share and the price-to-book ratio. A share repurchase may affect the terms in these products (e.g., EPS and price-to-earnings) but, if it does, Example 1 suggests that the changes should be offsetting. Examples 3 and 4 illustrate the types of analysis we can conduct on the effect of share repurchases on EPS and book value per share (BVPS).

EXAMPLE 3

Share Repurchases Using Borrowed Funds: The Effect on EPS When the After-Tax Cost of Borrowing Equals E/P

Jensen Industries plans to borrow $12 million which it will use to repurchase shares. The following information is given:

- share price at time of buyback: $60
- EPS before buyback = $3
- earnings yield (E/P) = $3/$60 = 5%
- after-tax cost of borrowing = 5%
- shares outstanding = 2.2 million
- planned buyback: 200,000 shares

Calculate the EPS after the buyback.

Solution: EPS after buyback = Earnings less After-tax cost of funds/Shares outstanding after buyback.

= [$6.6 million − (200,000 shares × $60 × 0.05)]/2 million shares

= [$6.6 million − ($0.6 million)]/2 million shares

= $6.0 million/2 million shares

= $3.00

With the after-tax cost of borrowing equal to the earnings yield (E/P) of the shares, the share repurchase has no effect on the company's EPS.

In Example 3, the share repurchase produced no change in EPS because the shares' earnings yield of 5% equaled its after-tax cost of borrowing. We can also see that if the after-tax cost of borrowing were greater than 5%, earnings after the buyback would be less than $6 million so that EPS after the buyback would be less than $3.00. On the other hand, after-tax cost of borrowing less than 5% would increase EPS to a level above $3.00. In summary, a share repurchase may increase, not affect, or reduce EPS, depending on whether the after-tax cost of the funds used to accomplish the repurchase is less than, equal to, or greater than the earnings yield of the shares (E/P) before the repurchase. A share repurchase may cause the price-to-earnings ratio to change as well. For example, if a share repurchase causes a company's financial leverage to change, the financial risk of the company's earnings stream changes and the price-to-earnings ratio post-repurchase may change from its pre-repurchase level to reflect the change in risk.

EXAMPLE 4

The Effect of Share Repurchase on Book Value per Share

Company A and Company B stocks sell at $20 a share and each company has 10 million shares outstanding. Both companies have announced a $5 million buyback. The only difference is that Company A has a market price per share greater than its book value per share, while Company B has a market price per share less than its book value per share:

▶ Company A has book value of equity of $100 million and BVPS of $100 million/10 million shares = $10. *The market price per share of $20 is greater than BVPS of $10.*

▶ Company B has a book value of equity of $300 million and BVPS of $300 million / 10 million shares = $30. *The market price per share of $20 is less than BVPS of $30.*

Both companies:

▶ Buy back 250,000 shares at the market price per share ($5 million buyback/$20 per share = 250,000).

▶ Are left with 9.75 million shares outstanding (10 million pre-buyback shares − 0.25 million repurchased = 9.75 million shares).

After the share repurchase:

▶ Company A's shareholders' equity at book value falls to $95 million
($100 million − $5 million) and its *book value per share decreases* from
$10 to $9.74 (shareholders' equity/shares outstanding = $95
million/9.75 million shares = $9.74).

▶ Company B's shareholders' equity at book value falls to $295 million
($300 million − $5 million) and its *book value per share increases* from
$30 to $30.26 (shareholders' equity/shares outstanding = $295
million/9.75 million = $30.26).

Example 4 shows that book value per share will either increase or decrease
depending on whether share price is higher or lower than BVPS. When share
price is greater than BVPS, BVPS will decrease after a share repurchase; when
share price is less than BVPS, BVPS will increase after a share repurchase. Still
worth underlining is that if shares are repurchased at market price, we would not
expect the balance sheet effect just illustrated to affect shareholders' wealth, all
other things being equal.

2.7 Repurchase Methods

There are three main ways that companies repurchase shares:

1. **Buy in the open market**. This is the most common method of repurchase,
   with the company buying "from time to time, as conditions warrant in the
   open market." This gives the company optimum flexibility and, in many
   shareholders' minds, acts to set a **floor** on the price of the shares. The latter
   is not always the case, but all other things being equal, an outstanding
   authorized share repurchase probably does function as a support for the
   share price.

2. **Buy back a fixed number of shares at a fixed price**. Sometimes a company
   will make a *tender offer* to repurchase a specific number of shares, typically at
   a premium to the current market. Shareholders may subscribe to the offer
   agreeing to sell their shares at the pre-determined price. If more shares are
   subscribed than the total repurchase, the company will typically buy back a
   pro rata amount from each shareholder.

3. **Repurchase by direct negotiation**. On occasion a company will negotiate
   with a major shareholder to buy back its shares, often at a premium to the
   market price. Example 2 illustrated this practice. The company may do this
   to keep a large block of shares from overhanging the market (and thus acting to dampen the share price). In some of the more infamous cases,
   unsuccessful takeover attempts have ended with the company buying back
   the would-be suitor's shares in what is referred to as a greenmail transaction, often to the detriment of remaining shareholders.[3]

---

[3] **Greenmail** is the purchase of the accumulated shares of a hostile investor by a company that is
targeted for takeover by that investor, usually at a substantial premium over market price.

2.8 Dividend Forms outside the United States

To provide a perspective on dividends, our discussion thus far has been limited to the United States. Laws, customs, and other considerations, all of which can vary from country to country, influence the forms that dividends take. Legal restrictions affect some forms of dividends. Stock repurchases, so common in recent years in the United States, are discouraged or even prohibited in some countries. Repurchases in the open market could be viewed as an attempt at company manipulation of its own stock. In fact, the U.S. Securities and Exchange Commission (SEC) held such a view until it adopted a safe harbor for company repurchases in 1982.

Companies may also consider their competitive environment when contemplating dividends and the form that a prospective dividend might take. In smaller capitalization markets, a company may feel that returning cash to its shareholders is not in its best interest. Some managements worry that a shareholder would take the cash (from either a cash dividend or repurchased shares) and invest it in a competitor of the company, thus possibly hurting the company's competitive position.

3 DIVIDEND PAYMENT CHRONOLOGY

In the previous section, we saw that dividends can take several forms. Once a company's Board of Directors votes a dividend, a fairly standard dividend chronology is set in motion. Below we provide an explanation of dividend payment chronology in the United States. Since the payment chronology is determined by rules set by exchanges in various countries, there are some country-to-country differences; but declaration dates, ex-dividend dates, and record dates are common on most exchanges. Furthermore, the shares of most large non-U.S. companies trade on the New York Stock Exchange (NYSE) and thus must meet the chronology described below. For example, the five largest publicly held non-U.S. companies, BP (UK), DaimlerChrysler (Germany), Toyota (Japan), Royal Dutch (Netherlands/UK) and Total (France), as well as 354 other global companies, trade on the NYSE as American Depository Securities (ADS). Canadian companies such as Royal Bank of Canada, Alcan, Nortel Networks, EnCana, and Canadian National Railway trade like U.S. shares on the NYSE.

3.1 Declaration Date

The first date on the time line is the **declaration date**, the day that the corporation issues a statement declaring a specific dividend. Whether it is a regular, irregular, special, liquidating, or stock dividend, all begin with a company's Board of Directors authorizing its payment. In Japan and several European countries, the company's shareholders must approve the payment. At the time of the declaration, the company will state the **holder-of-record date** and the **payment date**. Typically, business publications will list dividends declared during the previous day (for daily publications) or week (for weekly publications) under the heading "Dividends Reported" including the period for which the dividend applies (e.g. monthly, quarterly, special), the dollar amount of the dividend (to six decimal points if applicable), the payable date, and the record date.

3.2 Ex-Dividend Date

After the declaration date, the next pertinent date is the **ex-dividend date** (also referred to as the ex-date). This is the first date that a share trades without (i.e. "ex") the dividend. For a share traded on the ex-dividend date, the seller will receive the dividend. In order to have a claim on that dividend, the share must be bought no later than the last business day *before* the ex-dividend date. This is the last day a share trades "**cum dividend,**" or with the dividend, and the last day that the buyer of the share will receive the dividend. For example, in the United States, if the ex-date is Tuesday, December 26th, shares must be bought by Friday, December 22nd, to receive the dividend (markets are closed on Christmas Day, Monday, December 25th, and are not open on Saturday and Sunday). Trading ex-dividend refers to shares that no longer carry the right to the next dividend payment. This trading day is often designated in the share price tables of business publications with an *x* in the volume column. This indicates that the money value of the upcoming dividend has been subtracted from the previous day's closing price. For example, if a share closed at $20 on the day before the ex-date and the upcoming dividend is $0.25, then on the ex-date (all other things being equal) the shares will start the trading day at $19.75. If it closes at $20 for that day, it will show a gain of $0.25 for the day, even though the closing price is the same as it was the day before.

3.3 Holder-of-Record Date

The **holder-of-record date** (also called the owner-of-record date, shareholder-of-record date, **record date**, or date of record) is two business days after the ex-dividend date. This is the date that a shareholder listed on the corporation's books will be deemed to have ownership of the shares for purposes of receiving the upcoming dividend. While the shareholder-of-record date is determined by the corporation, the ex-date is determined by the exchange on which the shares trade. Currently, the ex-date is two business days before the record date. In our example above, if the ex-date were Tuesday, December 26th, the record date would be Thursday, December 28th. Not too many years ago, there were four or five business days between the ex- and the record dates. The shorter time frame no doubt is due to technological improvements in handling share transactions and mirrors the fewer number of days stipulated between trade and settlement dates for share transactions.

3.4 Payment Date

The final pertinent date on the dividend chronology is the **payment date** (also called the payable date). This is the day that the company actually mails out (or, more recently, electronically transfers) the dividend payment. As discussed earlier, the company typically states the payment date when the dividend declaration is made. Unlike other pertinent dates, such as the ex-date and record date which are only on business days, the payment date is just as likely to be on a weekend or holiday as not. For example, a company may list its payment dates as March 15th, June 15th, September 15th, and December 15th even though some of those dates will inevitably fall on a Saturday, Sunday, or holiday.

3.5 Interval between Key Dates in the Dividend Payment Chronology

The time between the ex-date and the record date is fixed (currently at two days) but the time between the other pertinent dates is determined by each company and can vary substantially. For example, record dates are typically anywhere from a week to a month after the declaration date for most normal dividends, but can be much longer for less-commonly occurring dividends such as irregular dividends, special dividends, liquidating dividends, and stock dividends. Likewise, the time between the record date and the payment date is typically anywhere from a few days to a month or more. However, most companies follow a fairly set routine for their dividends, especially for regular quarterly dividends. Some business publications such as *Value Line* include in their individual company reports the approximate dates of a company's next dividend meeting, its ex-date, and payment date. Exhibit 1 portrays a typical time-line for dividend chronology.

EXHIBIT 1	Typical Timeline for Dividend Chronology

3.5.1 *Impact on Indirect Shareholders*

For those who own shares through open-end, closed-end, and **exchange-traded funds (ETFs)**, the dividend chronology is generally the same as for those who own shares directly. That is, on the ex-dividend date for any shares in the fund portfolio, the price of those shares will nominally fall by the value of the dividend, and on the payment date the company will send an electronic transfer for the value of the dividend to the fund. However, most funds only declare their dividends (the total dividends and interest received by the portfolio less management fees and expenses) to fund owners on a periodic basis. No doubt, this is for logistical purposes, because accounting for each fund's shareholder payments on a frequent pro-rata basis would not be cost effective. Therefore, equity funds typically distribute dividend income on a periodic basis, usually quarterly or annually. For example, for the Vanguard funds, those with a relatively higher dividend yield (the Wellington Balanced Fund, Index 500, and Value Index Fund) generally distribute dividends quarterly, while those funds with a relatively lower dividend yield (the small-cap, growth, and international funds) generally distribute dividends once a year, usually in December. Paralleling the ex-dividend concept, on the dividend distribution date, the price of the fund will be decreased by the value of the dividends being distributed. The fund owner can then either receive the dividends in cash or reinvest them in additional shares of the fund. For example, if a fund has a net asset value of $20 on January 15th and is distributing $1 in dividends on the 16th, the net asset value of the fund will drop $1 to $19 (all other things being equal) on the 16th. The total value to each fund shareholder is still $20 ($19 in share value and $1 in dividends) although the dividend distribution is a taxable event to the fund shareholder. Under U.S. tax law, regulated investment companies are not taxed on fund income as long as 90 percent of such income (after fees) is passed on to the fund shareholder.

FACTORS AFFECTING DIVIDEND PAYOUT POLICY

In this section we explore six factors affecting a company's decision to pay dividends—its **dividend payout policy**. Some factors are external to the company, such as taxation, while other factors are more company-specific, such as possible restrictions on dividend payments and flotation costs. Shareholder preference for current income versus capital gains and the so-called clientele effect are also discussed. We also look at the information content of dividends—how dividends can be used as a signaling device by management.

4.1 Taxation of Dividends

Taxation is an important factor in all investment decisions, because it is the after-tax return that is most relevant to investors. Different countries tax corporate dividends in a wide variety of ways, and even within a single country it can be quite complex. In addition, as a major fiscal policy tool that is subject to politics, governments have a tendency to "re-address" tax issues, sometimes with great frequency, thereby complicating the issue even more. As with other aspects of taxation, governments use the taxation of dividends to address a variety of goals: either to encourage or discourage the retention or distribution of corporate earnings; to redistribute income; or to address other political, social, and/or investment goals.

Most developed markets tax shareholder investment income. Some tax both capital gains and dividend income. Others tax dividends but not capital gains. Hong Kong is an exception in that it levies no tax on either dividends or capital gains.

For the global investor, foreign taxes can be just as important as domestic taxes. Foreign tax credits in the investor's home country also may figure importantly into the overall taxation issue. For example, GlaxoSmithKline PLC (GSK) is a giant pharmaceutical company based in the United Kingdom. In 2003, the United Kingdom withheld approximately 5 percent of GSK's dividend, but U.S. shareholders were generally able to claim a tax credit for the amount withheld by the United Kingdom on their U.S. tax return.

4.1.1 Taxation Methods

We will look at three main systems of taxation that impact dividends: the **double taxation**, **split-rate**, and **imputation** tax systems. Other tax systems can be a combination of these.

The United States is often described as an example of a *double taxation* system. Corporate earnings are taxed regardless of whether they will be distributed as dividends or retained at the corporate level, and dividends are taxed again at the individual shareholder level. (In fact, for many U.S. investors, there is triple taxation of dividends because many states also levy a tax on dividend income.) In 2003, taxes on the shareholders' dividends were lowered from a maximum of 39.6 percent (the highest marginal income tax rate) to a maximum of 15 percent. At the same time, the tax on long-term capital gains was also reduced to the same 15 percent (from a 20 percent maximum rate). Table 3 depicts the double taxation system using the highest marginal rate on dividends in the United States both before and after the 2003 tax law change.[4]

---

[4] Under current U.S. tax law both dividend and capital gains tax rates are scheduled to return to pre-2003 levels in 2009.

TABLE 3 Double Taxation of Dividends at Different Personal Tax Rates (per $100)		
	39.6%	**15%**
Net income before taxes	$100	$100
Corporate tax rate	35%	35%
Net income after tax	$65	$65
Dividend assuming 100% payout	$65	$65
Shareholder tax	$25.74	$9.75
Net dividend to Shareholder	$39.26	$55.25
Double tax rate per $ of dividend	60.7%	44.8%

While there is still double taxation of dividends in the example, the net tax rate on a dollar of income distributed in dividends has declined from 61 percent to 45 percent: a decline of about 26 percent. Though U.S. investors clearly prefer the lower preferential tax rate for dividends, it is not clear whether they would prefer a higher or lower payout, because the current tax rate is the same on both dividends and long-term capital gains for most shareholders. Later we will discuss a company's decision with respect to the dividend payout ratio.

Other countries, such as Germany, have a *split-rate* system of corporate taxes. A split-rate system taxes earnings to be distributed as dividends at a different rate than earnings to be retained. Corporate profits distributed as dividends are taxed at a lower rate than those retained in the business. This offsets the higher taxation of dividends at the individual level compared with taxation of capital gains. The following table depicts this split-rate tax system for dividends.

TABLE 4 Taxation of Dividends Based on Split Rate System (per €100)	
Pretax earnings	€200
Pretax earnings retained	100
35% tax on retained earnings	35
Pretax earnings allocated to dividends	100
20% tax on earnings allocated to dividends	20
Dividends distributed	80
Shareholder tax rate	35%
After tax dividend to shareholder	$[(1 - 0.35) \times 80] = 52$
Effective tax rate on dividend	$[20\% + (80 \times 0.35)] = 48\%$

The split-rate tax system would lead shareholders in a low tax bracket to prefer a higher payout, since distributed income is taxed less. Alternatively, those shareholders in higher brackets would prefer a lower payout, with more funds retained, since capital gains receive a preferential tax treatment. Canada and Japan have a tax credit system that would have a similar effect.

A third major taxation system is the *imputation* tax system, which imputes, or attributes, taxes at only one level of taxation. The United Kingdom, New Zealand, and Australia have a form of the imputation system. For countries using an **imputation tax system,** taxes on dividends are effectively levied only at the shareholder rate. Taxes are paid at the corporate level but they are *attributed* to the shareholder. Shareholders deduct from their tax bill their portion of taxes paid by the company. If the shareholder's tax bracket were lower than the company's, the shareholder would receive a tax credit equal to the difference between the two rates. If the shareholder's tax bracket is higher than the company's, the shareholder pays the difference between the two rates. The following table depicts the taxation of dividends based on the tax imputation system for both a low marginal-rate shareholder and a high marginal-rate shareholder.

TABLE 5 Taxation of Dividends Based on Tax Imputation System ($Australian)		
	Marginal Shareholder Tax Rate	
	15%	47%
Pretax income	$100	$100
Taxes at 30% corporate tax rate	30	30
Net income after tax	70	70
Dividend assuming 100% payout	70	70
Shareholder taxes	15	47
Less tax credit for corporate payment	30	30
Tax due from shareholder	(15)	17
Effective tax rate on dividend	15/100 = 15%	47/100 = 47%

Here, as with the split-rate system, shareholders in lower tax brackets would prefer higher payouts, since they actually receive a tax credit for the difference between the corporate rate and their individual rate.

4.1.2 Shareholder Preference for Current Income versus Capital Gains

All other things being equal, one could expect that the lower the tax rate on dividends the higher the level of dividends. But other tax issues also impinge on this issue. As mentioned earlier, the trade-off between taxes on dividends and taxes on capital gains is an important part of the equation. Even if dividends were to be taxed at a lower rate than capital gains, it is not clear that shareholders would necessarily prefer higher dividends. After all, capital gains taxes don't have to be paid until the shares are sold, whereas taxes on dividends must be paid in the year received, even if reinvested. In addition, in some countries such as the United States, shares held at the time of death benefit from a *step-up* valuation to the death date. Finally, tax-exempt institutions such as pension funds and endowment funds are major shareholders in most industrial countries. Such institutions are typically exempt from both taxes on dividends and taxes on capital gains. Hence, all other things being equal, they are indifferent as to whether their return comes in the form of current dividends or capital gains.

4.2 Flotation Costs on New Issues versus Retaining Earnings

Another factor affecting a company's decision to pay dividends is the flotation costs on new issues versus retained earnings. **Flotation cost** is the percentage cost of new common share issuance, and reflects the fees paid to investment bankers as well as other costs of share issuance. It is typically higher for smaller companies and smaller share issues. Because of flotation costs, the cost of new equity capital is always higher than the cost of retained earnings. Therefore, many companies will not pay a dividend while issuing new shares in order to fund projects with positive NPVs. Issuing shares to fund the payment of dividends would be unprofitable.

EXAMPLE 5

A Company that Needs to Reinvest All Profits

Boar's Head Spirits Ltd., based in the United Kingdom, has estimated profits of £500 million. The company's financial analyst has calculated its cost of capital as 12 percent. The same analyst has evaluated modernization and expansion projects with a positive NPV that would require £800 million. The cost of positive NPV projects exceeds estimated profits by £300 million (£800 million − £500 million). Boar's Head does not want to increase its long-term debt in the next year. Hence, in this simplified example, the company would not pay dividends because free cash flow is not positive.

Because the company has unfunded positive NPV projects, it should consider issuing new shares incurring flotation costs of perhaps 5–7 percent of the new issue. The company would not, however, issue shares to fund the payment of dividends.

4.3 Restrictions on Dividend Payments

The ability of a company to even consider paying a dividend is often affected by restrictions, both formal and informal. In some countries there is a legal restriction, known as the **impairment of capital rule**, which states that dividends cannot exceed retained earnings. More typical are formal restrictions resulting from debt covenants, which can be anything that the company and the lender agree to. Here, certain minimum figures are set for such constraints as interest coverage, **current ratio**, and net worth, before any dividend payments may be considered.

Informal restrictions can also figure into a company's decision to pay dividends. Cash flow is an important one. Some companies will continue to pay a regularly scheduled dividend even when earnings are down and the payout ratio exceeds the company's target payout ratio. It is also not unusual for a company's dividend to exceed its earnings for a brief period. But most companies are loath to pay out dividends that exceed their cash flow from operations unless the company is in a liquidation mode.

Industry life cycle may also act as an implicit restriction on dividend payments. Many companies in the technology-related industries have negative net income, although positive EBITDA (earnings before interest, taxes, depreciation, and amortization). Even profitable biotechnology companies, or any company with an assumed high growth rate, might well be viewed negatively for instituting a dividend, because shareholders could interpret a dividend as a lack of investment opportunities for the company. Banks, on the other hand, typically have a dividend yield that exceeds that of the overall market. For example, in late 2004 the shares of Barclay's Bank (U.K.), Citigroup (U.S.), and UBS (Switzerland) yielded 4.3 percent, 3.4 percent, and 2.8 percent, respectively.

4.4 Clientele Effect

Another factor affecting a company's decision to pay dividends is the clientele effect. The **clientele effect** is the preference some investors have for shares that exhibit certain characteristics. For example, investors with low or no tax exposure are assumed to be attracted to companies with high or relatively high dividend yields. Retired investors typically have a preference for higher current income; they usually prefer to hold stocks with a higher dividend yield. On the other hand, other investor groups, such as younger workers with a long time horizon, might favor industries and companies that reinvest a high proportion of their earnings for long term capital growth and therefore prefer stocks with little or no dividends.

The tax status of the investor is an important component of this clientele effect. As discussed earlier, tax-exempt entities such as pension funds, university **endowments**, or charitable foundations would reasonably have a higher preference for current income (and, therefore, dividends) than would higher-taxed individuals who would rather defer tax payments through capital gains.

Institutional investors, including certain mutual funds, banks, and insurance companies, will only invest in companies that pay at least some dividend. Some even require (either officially or unofficially) a specific minimum dividend yield. As dividend yields fell during the bull market of the 1990s, this requirement was often altered to accept stocks with dividend yields in the top quartile (or half) of their stock universe. Trusts and foundations may be under a restriction that stipulates that only income (i.e., interest and dividends) may be distributed to beneficiaries.

Some individual investors use a self-control device of "only spending the dividends, not the principal" in order to preserve their capital.[5] Furthermore, in some jurisdictions, there are *legal lists* or *approved lists of equity investments* for institutions such as insurance companies and trusts for individuals. Such legal lists typically mandate that permissible investments consist of only companies that pay dividends. Often, such restrictive lists are intended to serve as a proxy discouraging high-risk stocks. All of this suggests that a clientele effect does exist and that a preference for dividends is one way in which the equity market can be segmented.

The question of whether different industries attract different investors can be partially addressed by looking at the dividend yield of major industry groups. Exhibit 2 shows the dividend yield for five of the S&P 500 industry groups: Utilities, Financial, Energy, Health Care, and Information Technology.

---

[5] See Hersh Shefrin and Meir Statman, "Explaining Investor Preference for Cash Dividends," *Journal of Financial Economics*, 1984.

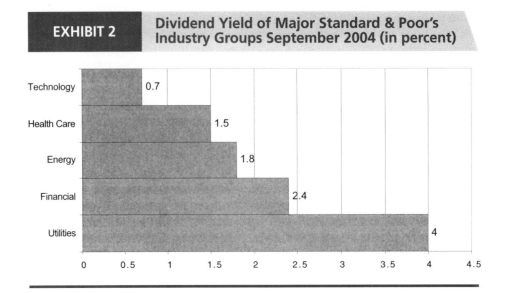

EXHIBIT 2 **Dividend Yield of Major Standard & Poor's Industry Groups September 2004 (in percent)**

As is evident, there is a dramatic difference in dividend yields for these five industries, with Utilities having the highest yield and Technology having a miniscule one. The clientele effect would suggest that certain investors might be drawn to certain industry groups because of the dividend yield.

4.5 Signaling Effect: The Information Content of Dividends

A final factor affecting dividend payout policy is the information content of dividends. The implication is that a company's board of directors and/or management uses its dividend policy to signal investors about how the company is *really* doing. Empirical studies support the thesis that dividend initiation or increases are associated with future earnings growth, and a dividend omission or reduction are associated with future earnings problems.[6] Members of both the board and management are, after all, the ultimate insiders, and it is likely that no other group has better information about future earnings and cash flow. A dividend declaration can help resolve some of the information asymmetry between insiders and outsiders. Therefore, a company's decision to initiate, maintain, increase, or cut a dividend can often convey much more information than could words alone.

Good examples of this are companies that regularly increase their dividend. Many companies take pride in their record of consistently increasing dividends on a regular basis over a long period of time. It is an important tool to let shareholders know that the future is good and that the company has a desire to share its increasing fortunes with its shareholders. For example, ExxonMobil has consistently increased its dividend on a yearly basis over the past two decades. While the company's earnings, cash flow, payout, and yield have fluctuated over this

---

[6] For example, see Harry DeAngelo, Linda DeAngelo, and Douglas Skinner, "Reversal of Fortune: Dividend Signals and the Disappearance of Sustained Earnings Growth," *Journal of Financial Economics*, 1986.

time, dividends have continued to increase each year, signaling to the market that the company's long-term outlook is intact. Unlike other companies in its peer group whose dividends have more closely reflected current movements in the fortunes of the oil industry, for ExxonMobil to cut dividends, or even fail to increase the yearly dividend, would send a meaningful (and negative) signal to investors about the future of the company. Anecdotal evidence for a signaling effect is also found on the Standard & Poor's web site. As of September 2004, S&P found 58 companies in the S&P 500 Index that are "Dividend Aristocrats" in that they have increased their dividend for 25 consecutive years. These companies span various industries and include General Electric, Pfizer, Procter & Gamble, and Wal-Mart. Mergent has established a list of Canadian and European companies that are called Dividend Achievers. These companies include Novartis (Switzerland), Barclays (U.K.), Unilever (Netherlands), Imperial Oil (Canada), and Thompson (Canada).[7] Companies that consistently increase their dividends seem to share certain characteristics:

▶ Dominant or niche positions in their industry; in Michael Porter's terms they have a competitive advantage.

▶ Global operations.

▶ Relatively high returns on assets.

▶ Relatively low debt ratios (unlikely to be affected by debt covenants).

Dividend cuts or omissions present a powerful signaling component. For many companies under financial or operating stress, the dividend declaration date is viewed with more than usual interest. Will they cut the dividend? Will they omit the dividend altogether? In these instances, merely holding the dividend or not cutting it as much as expected is viewed as good news, although in retrospect there are plenty of instances where the dividend should have been cut or omitted and was not. Some companies hang in to the bitter end and only omit the dividend as they file for bankruptcy, sending what turned out to be a most erroneous signal to the market.

In some instances, though, management can attempt to send a positive signal by cutting the dividend (this, admittedly, is more difficult). In 1993, IBM, long the giant of mainframe computers and having maintained an enviable record of dividend increases over the years, announced a more than 50 percent cut in its dividend, explaining that their intention was to shift its business by strongly investing in non-mainframe technology and consulting services to improve future returns. While the message was met with varying reactions, it was, in retrospect, a positive signal, and those who paid attention were richly rewarded. Likewise, in 2003 Schering-Plough, a leading U.S.-based pharmaceutical company, suffered a triple blow to its worldwide position including loss of patent on its leading drug, Claritin; a U.S. Food and Drug Administration (FDA) consent degree; and legal actions by government prosecutors related to sales and marketing. In April 2003 Fred Hassan was appointed Chairman and CEO. Mr. Hassan is generally credited with the turnaround in Pharmacia that was later merged in Pfizer. He announced a six to eight year plan to transform Schering-Plough that included a 68 percent cut in the quarterly dividend. As of late 2004, the jury is still out regarding Schering-Plough's prospective turnaround.

Another even more complicated example of the signaling content of dividends can be found in Microsoft's initial dividend declaration. As we saw from

---

[7] *Barron's*, November 1, 2004, p. 37.

Exhibit 2, technology companies have among the lowest dividend yields. This makes sense. By their very nature (most would argue), technology companies are on the cutting edge; they have high R&D requirements, and those that are profitable have high returns on assets. All of this would suggest low (or no) dividend payments, because funds would much better be spent on investing in new product development that will maintain high returns. But in the mid 1990s, as Microsoft's phenomenal growth and dominance of its industry continued, net cash grew to tens of billions of dollars and many wondered if the company could effectively use its cash "hoard," and if it were time for Microsoft to pay a dividend.

In late 2003, Microsoft declared its first annual dividend of $0.06 per share, equaling about 7 percent of its yearly cash flow, less than two percent of its net cash position, and representing a yield of 0.3 percent. Then, in the summer of 2004, the company increased its annual dividend to $0.32 per share and announced a special year-end dividend of $3.00 a share. Clearly, the signaling effect was more important than the actual cash impact on either the company or its investors. The stock market viewed these declarations with mixed feelings. Some viewed that Microsoft was signaling an interest in broadening its investor focus and in sharing its wealth with shareholders. The clientele effect, discussed earlier, would suggest that Microsoft's dividend opened up a whole new group of potential shareholders, possibly increasing demand for the company's shares. On the other hand, others viewed the dividend declaration as an admission that it was becoming a mature company—that it could no longer reap the high returns from reinvesting. The future growth prospects for the stock, they would argue, had been diminished. In any event, few could argue that the 2003–2004 dividend declarations by Microsoft were not signals of some importance. It is interesting to speculate that taxes had some impact on Microsoft's dividend decision. Bill Gates and other Microsoft insiders were among those who had their tax rate on dividend income reduced from 39.6 percent in 2002 to 15 percent in 2003 and 2004.

4.5.1 Cross-Country Differences in Signaling Content

It should be noted that there is often a cultural or country-specific element to the signaling aspect of dividends. For example, where U.S. investors often infer significant signals in long-term expectations from even minute changes in a dividend, Japanese investors are much less likely to regard even large changes in dividend policy as a message from management about future prospects. U.S. companies are typically reluctant to reduce a regular dividend, because it almost always gives a signal that "all is not well." However, in some Asian markets, a dividend cut is not necessarily viewed as an unfavorable sign and therefore companies are freer to raise and lower their dividends depending on circumstances.

Furthermore, dividends are larger and considered more important in some markets than in others. When investing in the global marketplace, investors will find that the contribution of dividends to total return will vary considerably. As discussed earlier in this reading, most of the world's largest companies trade on the New York Stock Exchange either as American depository shares (ADS) or ordinary shares. For example, the five largest non-U.S. companies had the following dividend yields (in US$) in October 2004: BP (U.K.) 2.9 percent, Daimler-Chrysler (Germany) 4.3 percent, Toyota (Japan) 1.5 percent, Royal Dutch (Holland/U.K.) 4.0 percent, and Total (France) 2.7 percent. Canadian companies trade as ordinary shares. Representative Canadian dividend yields (in US$) were Bank of Nova Scotia 3.7 percent, Thomson 2.2 percent, and EnCana 0.8 percent.

An investor who wanted to gain some insight into the relative importance of dividends around the world might look at the gross dividend yield on the FTSE Global Equity Indexes.

TABLE 6	**Gross Dividend Yield on Selected FTSE Index Funds (October 2004)**

Regions	
FTSE Global Large Cap	2.1%
FTSE North America Large Cap	1.9%
FTSE Developed Europe Large Cap	2.8%
FTSE Asia Pacific Large Cap (ex-Japan)	2.9%
FTSE All Emerging Large Cap	2.7%
Specific countries	
FTSE U.K. All Cap	3.1%
FTSE U.S.A. All Cap	1.7%
FTSE Japan (Large/Mid Cap)	0.9%

Source: Financial Times, 12 October 2004, p. 30.

4.6 Conclusion

There are several factors affecting a company's decision to pay dividends. We have examined some of them in this section, but it is not possible to argue that one is more dominant than another. Indeed, it is more likely that multiple factors affect dividend policy, with customs, laws, taxes, shareholder preferences, and management signaling interacting to affect a given company's actions.

DIVIDEND POLICIES   5

In the last section, we considered factors affecting a company's decision to pay dividends or not. In this section we look more closely at how the amount of the dividend is actually determined. **Dividend payout policy** is the strategy that companies follow in determining the amount and timing of dividend payments over time to shareholders. Our starting point is the residual dividend approach, one of the gold standards of corporate finance theory. Next we consider a dividend policy that results in a more stable dividend over time. The target payout ratio is then examined as an approach to dividend policy. We then discuss share repurchase as an alternative to the payment of dividends.

5.1 Residual Dividend Approach

The **residual dividend approach** is perhaps the most logical and intuitively appealing of all possible dividend policies, and can be defined as the payment of dividends resulting from earnings less funds necessary to finance the equity portion of the company's capital budget.

Recall that the NPV for any potential investment project is the net present value of all cash inflows minus the net present value of all cash outflows. When the NPV is positive, the investment should be undertaken, and when the NPV is negative, the project should be rejected. The company uses its weighted average cost of capital (WACC) as its discount rate. The company's optimal capital budget will include all positive NPV projects. The company then finances the equity portion of these projects with retained earnings. What is left over—the residual—is distributed to shareholders as a dividend. In essence, a company should reinvest earnings only when it can earn a higher rate of return on the shareholder's money than the shareholder could earn on his own by investing in equivalent-risk assets. If the company cannot earn such a return, the company should pay the earnings out in the form of dividends.

The following table depicts how the residual dividend approach might work. We look at the implied residual dividend given a company with earnings of $100 million, a target debt/equity ratio of 30/70, and three prospective capital spending plans of $50 million, $100 million, and $150 million.

TABLE 7	Residual Dividend Approach for a Target Debt/Equity Ratio of 30/70 (dollars in millions)		
	$50 in Capital Spending	**$100 in Capital Spending**	**$150 in Capital Spending**
Earnings	$100	$100	$100
Target D/E	30/70	30/70	30/70
Capital spending	$50	$100	$150
Financed from new debt	$0.3 \times 50 = \$15$	$0.3 \times 100 = \$30$	$0.3 \times 150 = \$45$
Financed from retained earnings	$0.7 \times 50 = \$35$	$0.7 \times 100 = \$70$	$(0.7 \times 150 > 100) = \$100$
Financed from new equity	$0	$0	$5
Residual cash flow = residual dividend	$100-\$35 = \$65$	$100-\$70 = \$30$	$100-\$100 = \$0$
Implied payout ratio	$65/100 = 65\%$	$30/100 = 30\%$	$0/100 = 0\%$

It should be pointed out that under the residual dividend approach, the only retained earnings the company has available are from the current year's operations, since all previous years' earnings have been either spent on capital projects or paid out as dividends to shareholders. Also, it can be noted that in the final column of the above table, the $150 million in capital spending requires $105 million in equity ($150 million × 0.70), which is greater than the total earnings of $100 million. Therefore, financing from new equity would be required. If the target debt/equity ratio were maintained, new equity issues would incur flotation costs. The cost of capital would be higher, and potentially fewer projects would have a positive NPV.

As can be seen from the above table, various capital spending plans result in dramatically different implied dividend payments. Payout ratios, too, range from a zero payment of dividends under the highest capital spending plan, to a 65 percent payout ratio under the lowest capital spending plan.

EXAMPLE 6

Determining Dividends Using the Residual Dividend Approach

Acree Products uses the residual dividend approach in determining its dividend policy. Using the following information, calculate the expected dividend:

- ► earnings: $1.6 million
- ► debt: $20 million
- ► capital budget: $1 million
- ► optimal capital structure: 25/75 debt/equity

Solution:

$$\begin{aligned}
\text{Expected dividend} &= \text{Earnings} - (\text{Capital budget} \times \text{Equity percent}) \\
&= 1.6 \text{ mil} - (1.0 \text{ mil} \times 0.75) \\
&= \$850{,}000
\end{aligned}$$

The residual dividend approach definitely has advantages to the company. It is intuitively appealing to use funds generated to profitably maintain and grow the business, and only return what is left over—the residual—to the owners of the company. The residual dividend approach also allows the company to more freely determine attractive investments independent of dividend considerations.

A major disadvantage of the residual dividend approach is that it results in widely fluctuating dividends. Not only will earnings vary with the economic cycle and innumerable company-specific events, but also the optimal capital budget will fluctuate with interest rates, investment opportunities, and a plethora of other investment inputs. This uncertainty about future dividend levels implies a higher level of perceived risk by the investor, thereby increasing the investor's required rate of return (k) and lowering the expected value of the stock, as can be seen in the following familiar constant growth dividend discount model equation:

$$V = D_1 / (k - g)$$

where

V = the value of a share of common stock today

D_1 = the expected dividend per share for Year 1, assumed to be paid at the end of the year

k = the required rate of return on the stock

g = the expected growth rate of dividends

The implication is that if future annual dividends are uncertain, as they would be under the residual dividend approach, then the value of the share (V) might decline (all other things being equal) as k increases.

To take advantage of the benefits of the residual approach while reducing its negative implications, many companies will forecast their optimal capital budget for the next five or ten years. The residual from that process will be allocated to dividends and paid out on a steadier, more even basis over the same period. A relatively new approach over the last twenty years is for companies to use this longer-term residual approach to allocate all funds designated for shareholders—including both cash dividends and share repurchases—paying out a more stable cash dividend to shareholders and allocating a more flexible amount to share repurchases.

5.2 Stable Dividend Policy

In many instances, both management and shareholders prefer more stability in their stream of dividends than strict adherence to the residual dividend approach would allow. Companies that employ a stable dividend approach are likely to look more toward a forecast of their long-run sustainable earnings in determining their dividend policy. In addition, over the last three decades when inflation has become a more important consideration, dividend stability has come to mean stability *in the rate of increase* in dividends.

Many companies pride themselves on a long record of gradually and consistently rising dividends. For example, following is the earnings and dividend record of La-Z-Boy Inc. since 1993.

TABLE 8	Earnings and Dividends of La-Z-Boy Inc. 1993–2004			
	Earnings per Share	**Change in Earnings**	**Dividends per Share**	**Change in Dividends**
1993	$0.63	26%	$0.21	5%
1994	$0.67	6%	$0.23	10%
1995	$0.71	6%	$0.25	9%
1996	$0.83	17%	$0.26	4%
1997	$0.91	10%	$0.28	8%
1998	$1.24	36%	$0.30	7%
1999	$1.60	29%	$0.32	7%
2000	$1.19	(26%)	$0.35	9%
2001	$1.23	3%	$0.36	3%
2002	$1.67	36%	$0.39	8%
2003	$1.09	(35%)	$0.40	3%
2004e	$0.99	(9%)	$0.44	10%

Source: Value Line.

As one can see from the above example, dividends over this period have increased at a fairly consistent, real rate, even while earnings have experienced considerable variability.

5.3 Target Payout Ratio

Many companies have a target payout ratio as the basis for their dividend policy. A **payout ratio** is the percentage of total earnings paid out in dividends in any given year (in per-share terms, DPS/EPS). A **target payout ratio** is a strategic corporate goal representing the long-term proportion of earnings that the company intends to distribute to shareholders as dividends.

Companies may, on occasion, state publicly their target payout ratio. What is more likely is that the company will use its dividend policy to move toward a dividend payout target.

In a classic study on this subject in the mid 1950s, John Lintner[8] drew three basic conclusions: 1) Companies have a target payout ratio, based on long-run, sustainable earnings; 2) they prefer to move toward this goal in smaller, incremental steps; and 3) cutting or eliminating a dividend should only be done in extreme circumstances or as a last resort.

While the resulting Lintner regression model has many variables, a simplified version can be used to show how a company in certain circumstances could incrementally move toward its target payout ratio.[9] In instances when the payout ratio is below the target payout ratio and earnings are expected to increase, the product of the increase in earnings, the target payout ratio, and the adjustment factor (1 divided by the number of years over which the adjustment in dividends should take place) will result in an estimated increase in the dividend. For example, given a current dividend of $0.40, a target payout ratio of 50 percent, an adjustment factor of 0.2 (i.e. the adjustment is to occur over five years), and an earnings increase from $1.00 to $1.50, the expected increase in dividends would be

= Increase in earnings × Target payout ratio × Adjustment factor
= $0.50 × 0.5 × 0.2
= $0.05 Increase in dividends

Therefore, even though earnings increased 50 percent from $1.00 to $1.50, the dividend would only incrementally increase by about 13 percent from $0.40 to $0.45.

Using this example, it can be noted that if in the following year earnings fell from $1.50 to $1.00, the dividend might well be increased by up to $0.05 per share, as the implied new dividend of $0.50 would still be moving the company toward its target payout ratio of 50 percent. Even if earnings were to fall further or even experience a loss, the company would be reluctant to cut or eliminate the dividend (unless its estimate of sustainable earnings or target payout ratio were lowered) opting, rather, to maintain the current dividend until future earnings increases justified an increase in the dividend.

EXAMPLE 7

Determining Dividend Using a Target Payout Adjustment Approach

Last year Luna Inc. had earnings of $2.00 per share and paid a regular dividend of $0.40. For the current year, the company anticipates earnings of $2.80. It has a 30 percent target payout ratio and uses a 5-year period to adjust the dividend. Compute the expected dividend for the current year.

---

[8] John Lintner, "Distribution of Incomes of Corporations Among Dividends, Retained Earnings, and Taxes," *American Economic Review*, 1956.

[9] Ronald Lease et al., *Dividend Policy: Its Impact on Firm Value*, Boston: Harvard Business School Press, 2000, p. 124.

Solution:

Expected dividend = Last dividend + (Expected increase in earnings
                    × Target payout ratio × Adjustment factor)

= $0.40 + [($2.80 − $2.00) × 0.3 × (1/5)]

= $0.40 + ($0.80 × 0.3 × 0.2)

= $0.45

Thus, while earnings are expected to increase by 40 percent, the increase in the dividend would be 12.5 percent.

5.4 Share Repurchase

In earlier parts of this reading we discussed the mechanics of share repurchase and showed that share repurchases were equivalent to cash dividends of equal amount in their effect on shareholders' wealth, all other things being equal. For some companies, share repurchase is intended to prevent the earnings per share dilution that would result from the exercise of employee stock options. Whether stated or not, many companies endeavor to buy back at least as many shares as were issued in the exercise of stock options—even though the options are exercised at lower prices than the repurchase price. Otherwise, share repurchase can be considered part of a company's dividend policy. In this section we consider the advantages and disadvantages of substituting a share repurchase program for the payment of a regular or extra cash dividend.

The main advantage of share repurchase over cash dividend occurs in those jurisdictions that tax shareholder dividends at higher rates than shareholder capital gains. This argument is now much less powerful in the United States as its tax code now taxes shareholder dividends and capital gains at the same rate. Furthermore, the U.S. tax code prohibits "routine" repurchase, as it could be tax avoidance. Other countries tax share repurchases at the same rate as dividends. Some jurisdictions have actually prohibited company share repurchase. An analyst should evaluate a company's share repurchase policy based on the tax circumstances of the company's home country as well as the investor's home country.

In principle, share repurchase sends the same signal to shareholders as does a cash dividend: Your company does not have sufficient reinvestment opportunities for the amount of cash flow generated. Shareholders have to consider why a company is shrinking its equity base. An alternative view is that management thinks its company's shares are undervalued.

5.4.1 Reasons for Share Repurchase

A company may decide to repurchase its shares for a variety of reasons. Perhaps the best reason is that the company views its own shares as an excellent investment. While the company's stock market judgment can be just as good or bad as any other market participant, there is no question that the company has more information about itself than does any other entity, and is therefore the ultimate insider. For many years, the oil industry has been a large purchaser of its own shares, as investment returns in their current operations (through a share purchase) were an attractive alternative to drilling for new sources of oil. In one five-year period, ExxonMobil spent more than $30 billion in repurchasing its own shares while it has also paid out $30 billion in cash dividends.

Another closely related reason for announcing a share repurchase is to signal to the investment community that the outlook for the company is good even if the share price is declining. Management has confidence in the company's future and believes that its stock is undervalued. An unexpected announcement of a meaningful buyback can often have the same positive impact on share price as would a better-than-expected earnings report or other similarly encouraging event. In the days following the global stock market crash of October 1987, a number of prominent companies announced huge buybacks in an effort to halt the slide in the price of their shares and show confidence in the future. It may have been an important aspect in the relatively quick stock market rebound. As indicated earlier, some investment analysts take issue with the notion that share repurchase sends positive signals.

A third reason for buying back shares is to alter the company's capital structure by decreasing the equity component. Borrowing money to buy back shares intensifies this shift.

EXAMPLE 8

Share Repurchase to Increase Financial Leverage

Canadian Holdings Inc. (CHI) is evaluating the impact of a buyback of $C7 million or 10 percent of the market value of its common stock. The estimated impact on CHI's capital structure depends on whether it has the cash on hand to make the buyback or if it has to borrow to finance the purchase.

TABLE 9   Estimated Impact on Capital Structure (in millions of $C)

| | | | After Buy-Back | | | |
| | Before Buyback | | All Cash | | All Debt | |
	$C	%	$C	%	$C	%
Debt	$ 30	30%	$30	32%	$ 37	37%
Equity (at market)	$ 70	70%	$63	68%	$ 63	63%
Total Cap	$100	100%	$93	100%	$100	100%

Canadian Holdings' beginning debt/equity ratio was 30/70. If Canadian Holdings uses borrowed funds to repurchase equity, the debt/equity ratio at market will increase to 37/63, which is significantly more than if it used excess cash (32/68).

Finally, a company could use both a regular cash dividend and a periodic share repurchase policy as a supplement to cash dividends. This policy is particularly apt in years where there are large and extraordinary increases in cash flow that are not expected to continue in future years. In this way, share repurchase becomes a substitute for an extra cash dividend. Such a policy could smooth out dividends similar to the target payout policy. Grullon and Michaely found that U.S. companies used repurchases as a substitute for cash dividends and that companies often initiate payouts through repurchases rather than cash dividends.[10] Share buybacks are more flexible than cash dividends, as repurchases are not a long-term commitment.

While all of the preceding can be the stated or unstated reasons for share repurchases, in general, buybacks are larger when the economy is strong and companies have more cash. During recessions, when company coffers are not as full, buybacks typically fall. This is perhaps the biggest disadvantage of share repurchases: They occur in the greatest number when times are good, and concurrently, when share prices are relatively high. Were shareholders' interests best served in 2000–2001 when high technology companies bought back their shares when the NASDAQ was at 5000? To carry this one step further, some companies may actually endanger their future viability by embarking on a highly leveraged repurchase endeavor. This is most likely for companies that have been threatened with large holdings by "aggressive" shareholders. More than one company has been eased into bankruptcy by increasing its debt burden to repurchase the shares of a potential hostile takeover suitor.

Example 9, in which a company initiates a cash dividend, integrates a number of themes related to cash dividends, stock dividends, and share repurchases.

EXAMPLE 9

Scottsville Instruments' Dividend Policy Decision

Scottsville Instruments, Inc. (SCII), is a U.S.-based emerging leader in providing medical testing equipment to the pharmaceutical and biotechnology industries. SCII's **primary markets** are growing and the company is spending $100 million a year on research and development to enhance its competitive position. SCII is highly profitable and has substantial positive free cash flow after funding positive NPV projects. During the past three years, SCII has made significant share repurchases. Subsequent to the reduction in the tax rate on cash dividends to 15 percent in the United States, SCII management has begun to consider the initiation of an annual dividend of $0.40 per share. Based on estimated earnings per share of $3.20, this dividend would represent a payout ratio (DPS/EPS) of 0.125 or 12.5 percent. The proposal that will be brought before the Board is the following:

"Proposed: Scottsville Instruments, Inc. will institute a $0.40 per share annual dividend to be paid quarterly beginning in the next fiscal year."

The company's Board of Directors will formally consider the dividend proposal at its next meeting in one month's time. Although some directors favor the dividend initiation proposal, other directors, led by William Marshall, are skeptical of it. Marshall has stated:

"The initiation of a cash dividend will suggest to investors that SCII is no longer a growth company."

---

[10] Gustavo Grullon and Roni Michaely, "Dividends, Share Repurchases, and the Substitution Hypothesis," *Journal of Finance,* 2002.

As a counterproposal, Marshall has offered his support for the initiation of an annual 2 percent stock dividend. Elise Tashman, a director who is neutral to both the cash and stock dividend ideas, has told Marshall the following:

"The initiation of a cash dividend will have no effect on the value of the firm to shareholders. Likewise, a 2 percent stock dividend should also be value neutral to our shareholders."

Table 10 presents selected *pro forma* financials of SCII, if the directors approve the initiation of a cash dividend.

**TABLE 10   Scottsville Instruments, Inc.
Pro Forma Financial Data Assuming Cash Dividend
(in millions, except for ratios and percentages)**

Income Statement

Sales	$1,200
Earnings before Taxes	140
Taxes	35
Net income	105

Statement of Cash Flows

Cash flow from operations	$135
Cash flow from investing activities:	(84)
Cash flow from financing activities:	
Debt repayment	(4)
Share repurchase	(32)
Proposed dividend	(15)
Estimated change in cash	0

Ratios

Current ratio	2.1
Debt/Equity (at market)	0.27
Interest Coverage	10.8x
ROA	10.0%
ROE	19.3%
P/E	20x
E/P	5.0%

Five-Year Forecasts

Sales growth	8% annually
Earnings growth	11% annually
Projected cost of capital	10%

Using the proceeding information, address the following:

1. Critique Marshall's statement.
2. Justify Tashman's statement concerning stock dividends.
3. Identify and explain the dividend policy approach that the proposed $0.40 a share cash dividend reflects.

Solution to 1: The following points argue against the thesis of Marshall's statement:
▶ As discussed in the text, dividend initiations and increases are on average associated with higher future earnings growth.
▶ Forecasted sales and earnings growth are relatively high.

> ▶ SCII still has considerable positive NPV projects available to it, as shown by the cash flow from investing activities of negative $84 million. This fact is consistent with a company with substantial current growth opportunities.

> ▶ For several years SCII has been making share repurchases, so investors are already cognizant that management is distributing cash to shareholders. The initiation of a dividend as a continuation of that policy is less likely to be interpreted as an information signaling event.

> **Solution to 2:** A stock dividend has no effect on shareholder wealth. A shareholder owns the same percentage of the company and its earnings as it did before the stock dividend. All other things being equal, the price of a stock will decline to reflect the stock dividend, but the decline will be exactly offset by the greater number of shares owned.

> **Solution to 3:** As shown in the Statement of Cash Flows, the $0.40 annual dividend reflects a total amount of $15 million, fully using SCII's free cash flow after acceptance of positive NPV projects, as shown in the Statement of Cash Flows. This reflects a residual dividend policy approach.

5.5 Are Dividend Policies Changing?

In the late 1990s, some financial analysts claimed that the historical role of dividends was "disappearing." This was a period characterized by its enthusiasts as the "New Era Economy," and by its critics as "Irrational Exuberance." It was highlighted in most of the developed world by several years of rising share prices, particularly in the more speculative industries. Companies that were barely profitable (and sometimes unprofitable) obtained larger market capitalizations than very profitable companies in unglamorous industries. At its peak, almost 40 percent of the S&P Index's market value was composed of companies in the technology and telecommunications sectors. This phenomenon was not limited to the United States, as Nortel Networks had the highest market capitalization in Canada in 2000 and companies such as Nokia in Finland and SAP in Germany were market leaders.

Proponents of New Era investing argued that dividends were a trivial, if not an unwelcome component of total return for investors more interested in capital gains. Investor preference for or aversion to dividends is a mercurial argument. The more interesting issue is whether corporations were changing their dividend policies. Fama and French[11] investigated the case for disappearing dividends. They found a large decline in the number of U.S. based industrial companies that paid dividends from 1978 to 1998. But the aggregate payout ratio in the 1990s was about 40 percent; within the 40–60 percent range typical of the 1960–1998 period. Fama and French argued that the decline in dividends was related to the large number of relatively unprofitable companies that were assuming prominence in the stock market. The following exhibit shows the relatively stable dividend payout range for all U.S. corporations from 1979–2003. In fact, the graph would seem to argue that companies follow the target payout approach.

---

[11] Eugene Fama and Kenneth French, "Disappearing Dividends: Changing Firm Characteristics or Lower Propensity to Pay?" *Journal of Financial Economics*, 2001.

EXHIBIT 3	Net Dividends as a Percent of Corporate Profits after Tax for U.S. Corporations 1979–2003

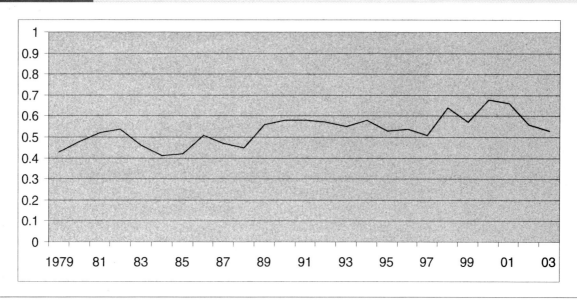

Source: Economic Report Of The President 2004, Washington: U.S. Government Printing Office, 2004, p. 389.

DeAngelo, DeAngelo, and Skinner[12] enhanced Fama and French's argument by showing that even though fewer corporations were paying dividends, the largest 100 companies in the United States increased their inflation-adjusted dividends by 23 percent from 1978 to 2000. What appears to be happening is that there are two tiers of companies. The first tier is composed of approximately 100 large, extremely profitable companies that have a fairly stable payout ratio of around 42 percent. The second tier is composed of two types of non-dividend payers: financially troubled marginally profitable or money losing companies, and/or companies related to technology where companies typically use share repurchase as a substitute for dividends.

In the period following the severe developed-country stock market decline in the early 2000s, investors began to question reported earnings, balance sheets, and cash flows as corporate scandals revealed management shenanigans to over inflate revenues, use accruals to understate expenses, and hide liabilities off-balance sheet. An argument can be made that dividends are more important than ever since it is the one number that a shareholder can trust. Earnings per share and even cash flow per share can be manipulated by management, but dividend checks can be cashed.

THE DIVIDEND CONTROVERSY: DO DIVIDENDS MATTER?

6

For the last forty years, leading financial theorists have argued over whether dividends and dividend policy matter to a company's shareholders. The first school

---

[12] Harry DeAngelo, Linda DeAngelo, and Douglas Skinner, "Are Dividends Disappearing? Dividend Concentration and the Consolidation of Earnings," *Journal of Financial Economics*, 2004.

of thought is that dividends are irrelevant. The second school says that dividends do matter because investors prefer them and higher dividend payouts are likely to increase the value of a company's shares. The third school says that dividends do matter, but a company's high dividend payout ratio will lead to a lower share price because dividend income is often taxed at a higher rate than capital gains.

6.1 Dividends Are Irrelevant

In a 1961 paper, Miller and Modigliani (MM) argued that in a world without taxes and transaction costs, a company's dividend policy would have no impact on its cost of capital or shareholder wealth.[13] Their argument begins by assuming a company has a given capital budget (e.g., it accepts all projects with a positive NPV), and that its current capital structure and debt ratio are optimal. Hence, if the company decided to pay out all its earnings in dividends, it would have to issue new shares of common stock to finance its capital budget. The value of the newly issued shares would exactly offset the value of the dividend. So if the company paid out a dividend that represented a 5 percent dividend yield (dividend per share/price per share), its share price would drop 5 percent to represent the dilution resulting from the new shares. If a common stock in Australia were priced at A\$20 before an A\$1 dividend, the implied new price would be A\$19. The shareholder has assets worth A\$20 if the dividend were not paid, and assets worth A\$20 if the stock drops to A\$19 and a A\$1 dividend is paid.

Further embellishing MM's theory is the concept of a "homemade dividend." If a shareholder really wanted or needed income, he or she could construct their own dividend policy by selling sufficient shares to create their own dividend. Using the Australian example above, assume the company did not pay the A\$1 dividend and the stock remained at A\$20. A holder of 1000 shares who desired A\$1000 in income could sell 50 shares at A\$20 reducing his/her holdings to 1950 shares.

In the real world, there are market imperfections that create some problems for MM's dividend irrelevance propositions. First, there are transaction costs because a company issuing new shares would incur flotation costs (typically 4 percent to 10 percent of the capital raised, depending on the size of the company and the size of the issue). Second, a shareholder selling shares to create a homemade dividend would incur transaction costs and, in some countries, capital gains taxes (of course, he would also incur taxes on cash dividends in most countries). Furthermore, selling shares on a periodic basis to create a stream of dividends over time can be problematic when equities are volatile. Some shareholders will be reluctant to create a dividend when share price is low because they would have to sell off more shares.

6.2 Dividends Matter: Investors Prefer Dividends

Traditionalists such as Myron Gordon,[14] John Lintner,[15] and Benjamin Graham argued that investors prefer a dollar of dividends to a dollar of reinvested earnings.

---

[13] Merton H. Miller and Franco Modigliani, "Dividend Policy, Growth, and the Valuation of Shares," *Journal of Business*, October 1961.

[14] Myron Gordon, "Optimal Investment and Financing Policy," *Journal of Finance*, May 1963.

[15] John Lintner, "Dividends, Earnings, Leverage, Stock Prices and the Supply of Capital to Corporations," *Review of Economics and Statistics*, August 1962.

Graham's viewpoint was that "... the typical dollar of reinvestment has less economic value to the shareholder than a dollar paid in dividends."[16] Gordon, Lintner, and Graham's argument is similar to the "bird in the hand" analogy. Because a dollar of dividends is more certain than a dollar of capital gains, a company that pays dividends will have a lower cost of equity capital. As indicated in the section on the residual dividend approach, in the constant growth dividend discount model, investors will often use a lower discount rate for a company that pays dividends than for a company that does not pay dividends.

EXAMPLE 10

Dividends and P/Es

Splashco Inc. is an international oil service company headquartered in Calgary, Alberta, Canada. It has a good record of earnings growth over the last 20 years, albeit subject to the ups and downs of oil and gas production. It has never paid dividends but has used its considerable cash flow to repurchase shares. Institutional investors in both Canada and the United States have indicated that they think Splashco would sell at a price/earnings multiple more similar to its competitors if it instituted regular dividend payments. John Petrowitz, CFA of Splashco's Treasurer's office has been asked to present the case for a dividend to the company's Board of Directors. He starts his analysis with the fact that Splashco typically sells at a P/E of 12–15x current earnings per share as compared to 17–20x for its competitors. He decides to use the constant growth dividend discount model to make his case.[17]

$$P = D_1 / (k - g)$$

where

P = share price (at fair value)
D_1 = the expected dividend for Year 1
k = the required rate of return on the stock
g = the expected growth rate of dividends

Dividing both sides of the equation by E_1 where E_1 = next year's estimated earnings per share, the result is

$$P/E_1 = (D_1/E_1) / (k - g)$$

Constant growth is estimated at 8 percent. The implied required rate of return for Splashco has been 12 percent, but Petrowitz thinks the initiation of a dividend would lower the required rate of return to 11 percent, close to the average of its competitors. If Splashco had a target

---

[16] Benjamin Graham, David Dodd, et al. *Security Analysis*, 4th edition, New York: McGraw-Hill, 1962, p. 486.

[17] Frank Reilly and Keith Brown, *Investment Analysis and Portfolio Management*, 7th edition, Mason, OH: 2003, pp. 388–391.

payout ratio of 50 percent and next year's earnings were C$2.00, the P/E_1 would be

$$P/E_1 = (1.00/2.00)/(0.11 - 0.08)$$
$$= 0.50/0.03$$
$$= 16.7x$$

Petrowitz concludes that if Splashco initiated a C$1.00 dividend, it might alleviate some investor concern about what the company would do with its earnings and its P/E might increase from 12–15x to 16–17x.

Real world market imperfections also bolster the "higher payouts lead to higher share prices" argument. There appear to be specific clienteles who desire to live off their wealth, but selling off shares periodically to produce homemade dividends is cumbersome and a taxable event. In some jurisdictions, trusts and institutions are precluded from spending principal. Miller and Modigliani would rebut this argument by saying that different dividend policies will attract different clienteles and assuming both types of clients are active in the market place, the value of the company will be unaffected by dividend policy.

6.3 Dividends Matter: Investors Are Tax Averse to Dividends

In the United States and several other countries, dividend income has traditionally been taxed at higher rates than capital gains. In the 1970s, tax rates on dividend income in the United States were as high as 70 percent while the long-term capital gains rate was 35 percent. Even as recently as 2002, U.S. tax rates were as high as 39.1 percent on dividends and 20 percent on long-term capital gains. A good argument could be that in a high dividend tax country, investors would prefer companies that pay low dividends and reinvest earnings in growth opportunities. Presumably, any growth in earnings would translate into a higher P/E. If a company lacked growth opportunities sufficient to consume its annual retained earnings, it should repurchase shares. Taken to its extreme, this school of thought would advocate a *zero* payout ratio. Here again some real world market imperfections muddy the waters, as tax law often precludes companies from the accumulation of excess earnings and restricts share repurchase if it appears to be an ongoing event such as in lieu of payment of dividends.

As already discussed, effective in 2003 the playing field between dividends and long- term capital gains in the United States was leveled, with both dividends and long-term capital gains being taxed at 15 percent. This neutralized tax environment should provide financial researchers with a fertile laboratory to clarify some of the dividend controversy.

7   VALUATION IMPLICATIONS OF DIVIDENDS

In a world without market imperfections, Miller and Modigliani describe a market where both corporations and shareholders would be unconcerned with dividend policies. In an MM world there are no valuation implications of dividends. Shareholder value is created by investing in profitable projects, not by manipulating the debt/equity ratio on the balance sheet or by financing dividend payments with new equity issues. But looking at the real world, this reading has established the existence of market imperfections. In addition, some investors are led, by logic or custom, to prefer dividends. When valuing equities in various countries, investors should factor both market imperfections and market preferences into the **valuation process.**[18]

First and foremost on the list of market imperfections is taxation, and in particular any differential in the way dividends are taxed as compared to capital gains. Almost all countries tax corporate profits and some tax them twice when profits are paid out in dividends. If a government taxes dividends at high rates, it encourages low payouts. At the limit, a 100 percent tax on dividends would lead to a zero payout ratio. The United States reduced the highest tax rate on dividends from 39.1 percent to 15 percent and equalized the tax rate on dividends and long term capital gains. Researchers are already finding evidence that more companies have initiated dividend payments, and existing dividend payers have increased dividends more than would be associated with a typical period of profit recovery.[19]

In some countries, there are restrictions on the payment of dividends and de facto requirements to pay dividends in order to obtain admission to institutional legal lists or screens. Some investors become part of a clientele for dividend paying shares, while others have no preference for dividends.

We discussed the information content of dividends (signaling effect). Boards of directors and management send important information about the future prospects of their company by increasing and decreasing the dividend. In a world where the quality of accounting information is suspect, investors would do well to heed management's signals.

Finally, ownership structure and ensuing agency problems provide a possible explanation of country differences in dividend policy.[20] Dividends assume a larger role in the valuation process in certain jurisdictions. Dividend payments are higher in Canada, Great Britain, the United States, and some parts of Europe. They are lower in Japan and in developing countries. There may be more than tradition to explain these differences. For example, ownership of public corporations in the United States, Canada, and Great Britain tends to be diffuse rather than concentrated; corporations finance operations through capital markets. Companies in Asia and developing markets often have large family shareholder control and finance operations using banks and insurance companies rather than through capital markets. There is a natural conflict of interest between owners and management in countries that have dispersed ownership. This agency cost can be alleviated by the payment of dividends. Payment of dividends restricts management's ability to reinvest earnings in negative NPV projects just to build empires. Dividends thus discipline management to be more careful with the shareholders' money. In countries where founding families still control large blocks of shares and there are close links between financial institutions and industrial corporations, there is less need of discipline because the "insiders" are less likely to act imprudently with their own money.

---

[18] For practical application of how analysts use dividends and dividend policy in equity valuation, see John Stowe, Thomas Robinson, Jerald Pinto and Dennis McLeavey, *Analysis of Equity Investments: Valuation*, Charlottesville, VA: AIMR, 2002.

[19] Raj Chetty and Emmanuel Saez, "Do Dividends Respond to Taxes? Preliminary Evidence from the 2003 Dividend Tax Cut" NBER Working Paper 10572, June 2004.

[20] William Megginson, *Corporate Finance Theory*, Reading, MA: Addison-Wesley, 1997, pp. 374–378.

So what can we conclude about the link between dividends and valuation? Unfortunately, the evidence is contradictory as shown by a myriad of studies over the years. It is difficult to show an exact relationship between dividends and value because there are so many variables affecting value. In the paragraphs above, we have presented factors that would seem to explain why some companies put emphasis on dividends and others do not. Financial theory proclaims that reinvestment opportunities should be the dominant factor. Indeed, no matter where they are located in the world, smaller, fast-growing companies pay out little or none of their earnings. Regardless of jurisdiction, more mature companies with fewer reinvestment opportunities tend to pay dividends. For these mature companies, taxes, laws, tradition, signaling, ownership structure, and attempts to reconcile agency conflicts all seem to play a role in determining the dividend payout ratio. At a minimum, in looking at a company, an analyst should evaluate whether a given company's dividend policy matches its reinvestment opportunities, clientele preferences, and legal/financial environment.

SUMMARY

The dividend policy of a company affects the form in which shareholders receive the return on their investment and is a prominent decision of a company's board of directors. This reading has made the following points:

▶ Dividends can take the form of regular or special cash payments, stock dividends, or stock splits. Only cash dividends are payments to shareholders. Stock dividends and splits merely carve equity into smaller pieces.

▶ A share repurchase is equivalent to the payment of a cash dividend of equal amount in its effect on shareholders' wealth, all other things being equal.

▶ If a company has to fund a share repurchase with debt and its after-tax cost of debt is greater than the earning yield, earnings per share will decline. If the buyback market price is greater than the book value, the book value will decline.

▶ Share repurchases can be accomplished in the open market, through a tender offer to all shareholders, or by a direct negotiation with a major shareholder. The latter is not likely to positively affect share price.

▶ The key dates for a cash dividend are the declaration date, the ex-date, the shareholder-of-record date, and the payment date. Share price will reflect the dividend as of record date and, all else being equal, share price will be reduced by the amount of the dividend on the ex-date.

▶ Under double taxation systems, dividends are taxed at both the corporate and shareholder level. Under split rate taxation systems, corporate profits are taxed at different rates depending on whether the profits are retained or paid out in dividends. Under tax imputation systems, a shareholder receives a credit on dividends for the tax paid on corporate profits.

▶ Companies with debt outstanding often are restricted in the amount of dividends they can pay because of debt covenants, and formal and informal traditions in industries and countries. Some institutions require that a company pay a dividend in order to be on their "approved" list. If a company funds capital expenditures by borrowing while paying earnings out in dividends, it will incur flotation costs on new issues.

▶ The clientele effect assumes that different classes of investors have differing preferences for dividend income. Those who prefer dividends will tend to invest in higher yielding shares.

▶ The signaling effect assumes that declaration of dividends provide information to current and prospective shareholders as to the prospects of the company. Initiating a dividend or increasing a dividend sends a positive signal, while cutting a dividend or omitting a dividend sends a negative signal.

▶ Using a residual dividend approach, a company first compares its capital expenditure requirements to its net income and whatever is left is paid out to shareholders in the form of cash dividends. An advantage of the residual approach is that all positive NPV opportunities have the first priority.

▶ In a strict residual approach, the amount of the annual dividend is equal to annual earnings minus the capital budget times the percent of the capital budget to be financed through retained earnings.

▶ Using a stable dividend approach, a company tries to align its dividend growth rate to the company's long-term earnings growth rate. Dividends may increase even in years when earnings decline, and dividends will increase at a lower rate than earnings in boom years. A longer-term **residual** approach is a combination of residual and stable policies, where the **company maintains the dividend at some level and increases the dividend** periodically. With a target approach, the company has a goal of **maintaining** the dividend payout within a range; the dividend will increase with **the company's long-term sustainable growth rate**, but the increase will be in incremental steps.

▶ In the target payout adjustment approach, the expected dividend is **equal** to last year's dividend per share, plus [(this year's expected increase in earnings per share) × (the target payout ratio) × (an annual adjustment factor)].

▶ Companies can repurchase shares in lieu of increasing cash dividends. **This** policy is often justified in jurisdictions where dividends are taxed at **higher** rates than capital gains. Companies can also pay regular cash dividends **supplemented** by share repurchases. In years of extraordinary increases **in** earnings, share repurchase becomes a substitute for increasing dividends, smoothing out potentially volatile payout ratios.

▶ Share repurchases can signal that company officials think their **shares are** undervalued. On the other hand, share repurchases could send a **negative** signal that the company has few positive NPV opportunities. Share repurchases can also lower debt ratings.

▶ Considering aggregate corporate dividend payout ratios, dividend **policy** has remained within historical levels in recent years. A large number **of** companies with little or no earnings and/or questionable financials **make it** appear that dividends are "disappearing."

▶ There are three general theories on investor preference for dividends. **The** first, MM, argues that in a no-tax, no-market world, dividends are **irrelevant.** The "bird-in-the-hand" theory contends that investors value a dollar of **dividends** today more than uncertain capital gains in the future. The **third** theory argues that investors are tax averse to cash dividends and would **prefer** companies buy back shares, especially when the tax rate on **dividends is** greater than the tax rate on capital gains.

▶ Miller and Modigliani demonstrate that shareholders who want **dividends** could create their own homemade dividends by periodically selling **off part** of their holdings.

▶ According to those who argue that dividends do matter, a company **could** increase its price/earnings ratio by initiating a cash dividend. The **initiation** of a dividend results in a higher P/E by reducing the spread between **the** company's required rate of return and its expected growth rate **using a** constant growth dividend discount model.

PRACTICE PROBLEMS FOR READING 33

1. Would a cash dividend, compared to a stock dividend, most likely result in a higher

	debt/equity ratio?	current ratio?
A.	No	No
B.	No	Yes
C.	Yes	No
D.	Yes	Yes

2. In a recent presentation, Doug Pearce made two statements about dividends:

- ▶ "A stock dividend should increase share price, all other things being equal."
- ▶ "One practical concern with a stock split is that it will reduce the firm's price-to-earnings ratio."

Are Pearce's comments about the effects of the stock dividend and stock split correct or incorrect?

	Stock Dividend	Stock Split
A.	Correct	Correct
B.	Correct	Incorrect
C.	Incorrect	Correct
D.	Incorrect	Incorrect

3. Devon Ltd. common shares sell at $40 a share and its estimated price/earnings ratio (P/E) is 32x. If Devon borrows funds to repurchase shares at its cost of capital of 5 percent, its EPS will

A. increase.

B. decrease.

C. remain the same.

D. increase initially but decline in future years.

4. The following calendar dates in Column 1 are potentially significant dates in a typical dividend chronology. Column 2 lists descriptions of these potentially significant dates (in random order).

Column 1	Column 2
Friday, 10 June	A. Holder-of-record date
Thursday, 23 June	B. Declaration date
Friday, 24 June	C. Payment date
Sunday, 26 June	D. Not a significant date
Tuesday, 28 June	E. Ex-date
Sunday, 10 July	F. Last day shares trade cum dividend

Match the significance of these typical dividend chronology dates by placing the correct letter of the description by the appropriate date. Use the template for your answer.

Dividend Chronology

Friday, 10 June	
Thursday, 23 June	
Friday, 24 June	
Sunday, 26 June	
Tuesday, 28 June	
Sunday, 10 July	

---

5. Assume that a company is based in a country that has no taxes on dividends and capital gains. The company is considering either paying a special dividend or repurchasing its own shares. Shareholders of the company would have

   A. greater wealth if the company paid a special cash dividend.

   B. greater wealth if the company repurchased its shares.

   C. the same wealth under either a cash dividend or share repurchase program.

   D. less wealth under either a cash dividend or share repurchase program.

6. Aiken Instruments (AIK) has recently declared a regular quarterly dividend of $0.50, payable on 12 November, to holders of record on 1 November. 28 October is the ex-date. Which date below would be the last day an investor purchasing AIK shares would receive the quarterly dividend?

   A. 27 October.

   B. 28 October.

   C. 1 November.

   D. 12 November.

7. WL Corporation is located in a jurisdiction that has a 40 percent corporate tax rate on pretax income and a 30 percent personal tax rate on dividends. WL distributes all its after-tax income to shareholders. What is the effective tax rate on WL pretax income distributed in dividends?

   A. 42 percent.

   B. 52 percent.

   C. 58 percent.

   D. 70 percent.

8. The clientele effect implies that

   A. high tax bracket investors are indifferent to dividends.

   B. investors prefer high dividend paying shares.

   C. investors have varying preferences regarding dividends.

   D. low tax bracket investors are indifferent to dividends.

9. Which of the following factors would *not* tend to be associated with company having a low dividend payout ratio?

   A. Restrictive debt covenants.

   B. High flotation costs on new equity issues.

   C. High tax rates on dividends.

   D. Low growth prospects.

10. Which of the following is *most* likely to signal negative information concerning a firm?

   A. Share repurchase.

   B. Increase in the payout ratio.

   C. Decrease in the quarterly dividend rate.

   D. A two-for-one stock split.

11. Berkshire Gardens Inc. uses a target payout adjustment approach in paying its annual dividend. Last year Berkshire had earnings per share of $3.00 and paid a dividend of $0.60 a share. This year it estimates earning at $4.00 a share. What is its dividend per share for this year if it has a 25 percent target payout ratio and uses a five-year period to adjust its dividend?

   A. $0.65.

   B. $0.72.

   C. $0.80.

   D. $0.85.

12. Investors may prefer companies that repurchase their shares instead of paying a cash dividend when

   A. capital gains are taxed at higher rates than dividends.

   B. capital gains are taxed at lower rates than dividends.

   C. capital gains are taxed at the same rate as dividends.

   D. the company needs more equity to finance capital expenditures.

13. Sophie Chan owns 100,000 shares of PAT Company. PAT is selling for €40 per share, so her investment is worth €4,000,000. Chan reinvests the gross amount of all dividends received to purchase additional shares. If PAT pays a €1.50 dividend, Chan's new share ownership after reinvesting dividends at the ex-dividend price is closest to

   A. 103,450.

   B. 103,600.

   C. 103,750.

   D. 103,900.

14. Mary Young intends to take a position in Megasoft Industries once Megasoft begins paying regular dividends with a special dividend of C$4 on 2 December. The ex-date for the dividend is 10 November, and the holder-of-record date is 12 November. What is the last possible date for Mary to purchase her shares if she wants to receive the dividend?

   A. 9 November.

   B. 10 November.

   C. 11 November.

   D. 12 November.

15. The Apex Corp. has a target debt/equity ratio of 40/60. Its capital budget for next year is estimated at $40 million. Estimated net income is $30 million. What would its dividend be using the residual dividend approach?

  A. $6 million.

  B. $12 million.

  C. $14 million.

  D. $18 million.

16. Which of the following scenarios best reflects a stable dividend policy?

  A. Maintaining a constant dividend payout ratio of 40 percent to 50 percent.

  B. Maintaining the dividend at $1.00 a share for several years.

  C. Increasing the dividend at the company's long term earnings growth rate of 5 percent.

  D. Paying special dividends when earnings are abnormally high.

17. Match the phases in Column A with the corresponding dividend theory in Column B. Note that you may use the answers in Column B more than once.

Column A	Column B
1. Bird in the hand	a) dividends matter
2. Homemade dividends	b) dividends are irrelevant
3. High tax rates on dividends	
4. No transaction costs	

18. Which of the following assumptions is *not* required for Miller and Modigliani's (MM) dividend theory?

  A. Shareholders have no transaction costs when buying and selling shares.

  B. There are no taxes.

  C. There are no flotation costs on new issues.

  D. Markets are inefficient.

The following information relates to Questions 19–25

Janet Wu is treasurer of Wilson Paper Company, a manufacturer of paper products for the office and school markets. Wilson Paper is selling one of its divisions for $70 million cash. Wu is considering whether to recommend a special dividend of $70 million, or a repurchase of 2 million shares of Wilson common stock in the open market. She is reviewing some possible effects of the buyback with the company's financial analyst. Wilson has a long-term record of gradually increasing earnings and dividends. Wilson's board has also approved capital spending of $15 million to be entirely funded out of this year's earnings.

Book value of equity	$750 million ($30 a share)
Shares outstanding	25 million
12-month trading range	$25–$35
Current share price	$35
After-tax cost of borrowing	7 percent
Estimated full year earnings	$25 million
Last year's dividends	$9 million
Target debt/equity (market value)	35/65

19. Assume that Wilson Paper could buy back its shares at the current market price. A $70 million buyback would result in a book value per share that

   A. increases.

   B. decreases.

   C. remains unchanged.

   D. may remain unchanged or increase.

20. In investors' minds, Wilson's share buyback could be a signal that

   A. the company is decreasing its financial leverage.

   B. the company has more investment opportunities than it could fund internally.

   C. the company lacks good investment opportunities.

   D. the company's share price is too high.

21. Assume that Wilson Paper funds its capital spending out of its estimated full year earnings. Using the residual dividend approach, determine Wilson's implied dividend payout ratio.

   A. 36 percent.

   B. 40 percent.

   C. 60 percent.

   D. 72 percent.

22. Suppose the sale of the division did not occur and Wilson Paper had to raise $70 million in new funds at the company's after-tax cost of borrowing in order to fund the buyback. The expected earnings per share following the share repurchase is *closest* to

   A. $0.80.

   B. $0.87.

   C. $1.09.

   D. $1.15.

23. Wilson's buyback is most likely to be dilutive to earnings per share if

   A. the after-tax cost of borrowing is lower than the earnings yield.

   B. the after-tax cost of borrowing is higher than the earnings yield.

   C. book value is less than market value.

   D. book value is higher than the buyback price.

24. If a company borrows to finance a share repurchase, the likely result is

   A. an increase in the market value of the company.

   B. an increase in the market value of debt offset by a decrease in the market value of equity.

   C. an increase in the market value of equity offset by a decrease in the market value of debt.

   D. no change in the market value or debt/equity ratio.

25. The most likely tax environment where Wilson Paper's shareholders would prefer that Wilson repurchase its shares (share buybacks) instead of paying dividends is when

   A. there is no tax on shareholder dividends or capital gains.

   B. the tax rate on capital gains and dividends is the same.

   C. capital gains tax rates are higher than dividend income tax rates.

   D. capital gains tax rates are lower than dividend income tax rates.

STUDY SESSION 9
CORPORATE FINANCE:
Financing and Control Issues

This study session presents two major organizational topics of corporate finance. First, corporate governance covers the system of principles and policies used to manage the conflicts of interest between different groups of stakeholders of a corporation. Second, mergers and acquisitions and corporate restructurings, which redistribute ownership and control, are assessed.

READING ASSIGNMENTS

Reading 34 Corporate Governance
Reading 35 Mergers and Acquisitions

LEARNING OUTCOMES

Reading 34: Corporate Governance
The candidate should be able to:

a. explain corporate governance, discuss the objectives and the core attributes of an effective corporate governance system, and evaluate whether a company's corporate governance has those attributes;

b. compare and contrast the major business forms and describe the conflicts of interest associated with each;

c. discuss the conflicts that arise in agency relationships, including manager–shareholder conflicts and director–shareholder conflicts;

d. describe the responsibilities of the board of directors, and explain the qualifications and core competencies that an investment analyst should look for in the board of directors;

e. illustrate effective corporate governance practice as it relates to the board of directors, and evaluate the strengths and weaknesses of a company's corporate governance practice;

f. describe the elements of a company's statement of corporate governance policies that investment analysts should assess;

g. discuss the valuation implications of corporate governance.

Reading 35: Mergers and Acquisitions

The candidate should be able to:

a. categorize merger and acquisition (M&A) activities based on forms of integration and types of mergers;

b. explain the common motivations behind M&A activity;

c. illustrate how earnings per share (EPS) bootstrapping works and calculate a company's post-merger EPS;

d. discuss the relation between merger motivations and types of mergers based on industry lifecycles;

e. contrast merger transaction characteristics by form of acquisition, method of payment, and attitude of target management;

f. distinguish and describe pre-offer and post-offer takeover defense mechanisms;

g. summarize U.S. antitrust legislation;

h. calculate the Herfendahl-Hirschman Index (HHI) and evaluate the likelihood of an antitrust challenge for a given business combination;

i. compare and contrast the three major methods for valuing a target company including the advantages and disadvantages of each;

j. calculate free cash flows for a target company and estimate the company's intrinsic value based upon discounted cash flow analysis;

k. estimate the intrinsic value of a company using comparable company analysis;

l. estimate the intrinsic value of a company using comparable transaction analysis;

m. evaluate a merger bid, calculate the estimated post-merger value of an acquirer, and calculate the gains accrued to the target shareholders versus the acquirer shareholders;

n. explain the effects of price and payment method on the distribution of risks and benefits in a merger transaction;

o. describe the empirical evidence related to the distribution of benefits in a merger;

p. define, compare, and contrast divestitures, equity carve-outs, spin-offs, split-offs, and liquidation;

q. discuss the major reasons for divestitures.

CORPORATE GOVERNANCE

by Rebecca Todd McEnally and Kenneth Kim

LEARNING OUTCOMES

The candidate should be able to:

a. explain corporate governance, discuss the objectives and the core attributes of an effective corporate governance system, and evaluate whether a company's corporate governance has those attributes;

b. compare and contrast the major business forms and describe the conflicts of interest associated with each;

c. discuss the conflicts that arise in agency relationships, including manager–shareholder conflicts and director–shareholder conflicts;

d. describe the responsibilities of the board of directors, and explain the qualifications and core competencies that an investment analyst should look for in the board of directors;

e. illustrate effective corporate governance practice as it relates to the board of directors, and evaluate the strengths and weaknesses of a company's corporate governance practice;

f. describe the elements of a company's statement of corporate governance policies that investment analysts should assess;

g. discuss the valuation implications of corporate governance.

INTRODUCTION 1

The modern corporation is a very efficient and effective means of raising capital, obtaining needed resources, and generating products and services. These and other advantages have caused the corporate form of business to become the dominant one in many countries. The corporate form, in contrast to other business forms, frequently involves the separation of ownership and control of the assets of the business. The ownership of the modern, public corporation is typically diffuse; it has many owners, most with proportionally small stakes in the company, who are distant from, and often play no role in, corporate decisions. Professional managers control and deploy the assets of the corporation. This separation of ownership (shareholders) and control (managers) may result in a number of conflicts of interest between managers and shareholders. Conflicts of interest can also arise that affect creditors as well as other stakeholders such as employees and suppliers. In order to remove or at least minimize such conflicts of interest, corporate governance structures have been developed and implemented in corporations. Specifically, **corporate governance** is the system of principles, policies, procedures, and clearly defined responsibilities and accountabilities used by stakeholders to overcome the conflicts of interest inherent in the corporate form.

The failure of a company to establish an effective system of corporate governance represents a major operational risk to the company and its investors.[1] Corporate governance deficiencies may even imperil the continued existence of a company. Consequently, to understand the risks inherent in an investment in a company, it is essential to understand the quality of the company's corporate governance practices. It is also necessary to continually monitor a company's practices, because changes in management, the composition of its board of directors, the company's competitive and market conditions, or mergers and acquisitions, can affect them in important ways.

A series of major corporate collapses in North America, Europe, and Asia, nearly all of which involved the failure or direct override by managers of corporate governance systems, have made it clear that strong corporate governance structures are essential to the efficient and effective functioning of companies and the financial markets in which they operate. Investors lost great amounts of money in the failed companies. The collapses weakened the trust and confidence essential to the efficient functioning of financial markets worldwide.

Legislators and regulators responded to the erosion of trust by introducing strong new regulatory frameworks. These measures are intended to restore the faith of investors in companies and the markets, and, very importantly, to help prevent future collapses. Nevertheless, the new regulations did not address all outstanding corporate governance problems and were not uniform across capital markets. Thus, we may expect corporate governance-related laws and regulations to further evolve.

---

[1] An **operational risk** is the risk of loss from failures in a company's systems and procedures, or from external events.

The reading is organized as follows: Section 2 presents the objectives of corporate governance systems and the key attributes of effective ones. Section 3 addresses forms of business and conflicts of interest, and Section 4 discusses two major sources of governance problems. In Section 5 we discuss standards and principles of corporate governance, providing three representative sets of principles from current practice. Section 6 addresses environmental, social, and governance factors, and Section 7 touches on the valuation implications of the quality of corporate governance.

CORPORATE GOVERNANCE: OBJECTIVES AND GUIDING PRINCIPLES

2

The modern corporation is subject to a variety of conflicts of interest. This fact leads to the following two major objectives of corporate governance:

▶ to eliminate or mitigate conflicts of interest particularly those between managers and shareholders; and

▶ to ensure that the assets of the company are used efficiently and productively and in the best interests of its investors and other stakeholders.

How then can a company go about achieving those objectives? The first point is that it should have a set of principles and procedures sufficiently comprehensive to be called a corporate governance system. No single system of effective corporate governance applies to all firms in all industries worldwide. Different industries and economic systems, legal and regulatory environments, and cultural differences may affect the characteristics of an effective corporate governance system for a particular company. However, there are certain characteristics that are common to all sound corporate governance structures. The core attributes of an effective corporate governance system are:

▶ delineation of the *rights* of shareholders and other core stakeholders;

▶ clearly defined manager and director governance *responsibilities* to stakeholders;

▶ identifiable and measurable *accountabilities* for the performance of the responsibilities;

▶ *fairness* and equitable treatment in all dealings between managers, directors, and shareholders; and

▶ complete *transparency* and accuracy in disclosures regarding operations, performance, risk, and financial position.

These core attributes form the foundation for systems of good governance, as well as for the individual principles embodied in such systems. Investors and analysts should determine whether companies in which they may be interested have these core attributes.

3

FORMS OF BUSINESS AND CONFLICTS OF INTEREST

The goal of for-profit businesses in any society is simple and straightforward: to maximize their owners' wealth. This can be achieved through strategies that result in long-term growth in sales and profits. However, pursuing wealth maximization involves taking risks. A business itself is risky for a variety of reasons. For example, there may be demand uncertainty for its products and/or services, economic uncertainty, and competitive pressures. Financial risk is present when a business must use debt to finance operations. Thus, continued access to sufficient capital is an important consideration and risk for businesses. These risks, and the inherent conflicts of interests in businesses, increase the need for strong corporate governance.

A firm's ability to obtain capital and to control risk is perhaps most influenced by the manner in which it is organized. Three of the predominant forms of business globally are the sole **proprietorship**, the partnership, and the corporation. Hybrids of these three primary business forms also exist, but we do not discuss them here because they are simply combinations of the three main business forms. With regard to the three primary business forms, each has different advantages and disadvantages. We will discuss each of them, the conflicts of interest that can arise in each, and the relative need for strong corporate governance associated with each form. However, a summary of the characteristics is provided in Table 1.

TABLE 1 Comparison of Characteristics of Business Forms

Characteristic	Sole Proprietorship	Partnership	Corporation
Ownership	Sole owner	Multiple owners	Unlimited ownership
Legal requirements and regulation	Few; entity easily formed	Few; entity easily formed	Numerous legal requirements
Legal distinction between owner and business	None	None	Legal separation between owners and business
Liability	Unlimited	Unlimited but shared among partners	Limited
Ability to raise capital	Very limited	Limited	Nearly unlimited
Transferability of ownership	Non-transferable (except by sale of entire business)	Non-transferable	Easily transferable
Owner expertise in business	Essential	Essential	Unnecessary

3.1 Sole Proprietorships

The **sole proprietorship** is a business *owned and operated* by a single person. The owner of the local cleaner, restaurant, beauty salon, or fruit stand is typically a sole proprietor. Generally, there are few, if any, legal formalities involved in establishing a sole proprietorship and they are relatively easy to start. In many jurisdictions, there are few, if any, legal distinctions between the sole proprietor and the business. For example, tax liabilities and related filing requirements for sole proprietorships are frequently set at the level of the sole proprietor. Legitimate business expenses are simply deducted from the sole proprietor's taxable income.

Sole proprietorships are the most numerous form of business worldwide, representing, for example, approximately 70 percent of all businesses in the United States, by number.[2] However, because they are usually small-scale operations, they represent the smallest amount of market capitalization in many markets. Indeed, the difficulties of the sole proprietor in raising large amounts of capital, coupled with **unlimited liability** and lack of transferability of ownership, are serious impediments to the growth of a sole proprietorship.

From the point of view of corporate governance, the sole proprietorship presents fewer risks than the corporation because the manager and the owner are one and the same. Indeed, the major corporate governance risks are those faced by creditors and suppliers of goods and services to the business. These stakeholders are in a position to be able to demand the types and quality of information that they need to evaluate risks before lending money to the business or providing goods and services to it. In addition, because they typically maintain direct, recurring business relations with the companies, they are better able to monitor the condition and risks of the business, and to control their own exposure to risk. Consequently, we will not consider sole proprietorships further in this reading.

3.2 Partnerships

A **partnership**, which is composed of more than one owner/manager, is similar to a sole proprietorship. For the most part, partnerships share many of the same advantages and disadvantages as the sole proprietorship. Two obvious advantages of a partnership over a sole proprietorship are the pooling together of **financial capital** of the partners and the sharing of business risk among them. However, even these advantages may not be as important as the pooling together of service-oriented expertise and skill, especially for larger partnerships. Some very large international partnerships operate in such fields as real estate, law, investment banking, architecture, engineering, advertising, and accounting. Note also that larger partnerships may enjoy competitive and economy-of-scale benefits over sole proprietorships.

Partners typically overcome conflicts of interest internally by engaging in partnership contracts specifying the rights and responsibilities of each partner. Conflicts of interest with those entities outside the partnership are similar to those for the sole proprietorship and are dealt with in the same way. Hence, we will not consider these conflicts further in this reading.

---

[2] William J. Megginson, *Corporate Finance Theory* (Reading, MA: Addison-Wesley, 1997), p. 40.

3.3 Corporations

Corporations represent less than twenty percent of all businesses in the United States but generate approximately ninety percent of the country's business revenue.[3] The percentage is lower elsewhere, but growing. The **corporation** is a legal entity, and has rights similar to those of a person. For example, a corporation is permitted to enter into contracts. The chief officers of the corporation, the executives or top managers, act as agents for the firm and are legally entitled to authorize corporate activities and to enter into contracts on behalf of the business.

There are several important and striking advantages of the corporate form of business. First, corporations can raise very large amounts of capital by issuing either stocks or bonds to the investing public. A corporation can grant ownership stakes, common stock, to individual investors in exchange for cash or other assets. Similarly, it can borrow money, for example, bonds or other debt from individual or institutional investors, in exchange for interest payments and a promise to pay back the principal of the loan. Shareholders are the owners of the corporation, and any profits that the corporation generates accrue to the shareholders.

A second advantage is that corporate owners need not be experts in the industry or management of the business, unlike the owners of sole proprietorships and partnerships where business expertise is essential to success. Any individual with sufficient money can own stock. This has benefits to both the business and the owners. The business can seek capital from millions of investors, not only in domestic markets but worldwide.

Among the most important advantages of the corporate form is that stock ownership is easily transferable. Transferability of shares allows corporations to have unlimited life. A final and extremely important advantage is that shareholders have **limited liability**. That is, they can lose only the money they have invested, nothing more.

The corporate form of business has a number of disadvantages, however. For example, because many corporations have thousands or even millions of non-manager owners, they are subject to more regulation than are partnerships or sole proprietorships. While regulation serves to protect shareholders, it can also be costly to shareholders as well. For example, the corporation must hire accountants and lawyers to deal with accounting and other legal documents to comply with regulations. Perhaps the most significant disadvantage with the corporation (and the one most critical to corporate governance) is the difficulty that shareholders have in monitoring management and the firm's operations. As a sole proprietor of a small business, the owner will be able to directly oversee such day-to-day business concerns as inventory levels, product quality, expenses, and employees. However, it is impossible for a shareholder of a large corporation such as General Motors or International Business Machines to monitor business activities and personnel, and to exert any control rights over the firm. In fact, a shareholder of a large firm may not even feel like an owner in the usual sense, especially because corporations are owned by so many other shareholders, and because most owners of a large public corporation hold only a relatively small stake in it.

Agency relationships arise when someone, an agent, acts on behalf of another person, the principal. In a corporation, managers are the agents who act on behalf of the owners, the shareholders. If a corporation has in place a diligent management team that works in the best interests of its shareholders and other stakeholders, then the problem of passive shareholders and bondholders becomes a non-issue. In real life, unfortunately, management may not always

---
[3] Megginson, 1997.

work in the stakeholders' best interests. Managers may be tempted to see to their own well-being and wealth at the expense of their shareholders and others to whom they owe a fiduciary duty. This is known as an **agency problem**, or the **principal-agent problem**. The money of shareholders, the principals, is used and managed by agents, the managers, who promise that the firm will pursue wealth-maximizing business activities. However, there are potential problems with these relationships, which we will discuss next.

SPECIFIC SOURCES OF CONFLICT: AGENCY RELATIONSHIPS

4

Conflicts among the various constituencies in corporations have the potential to cause problems in the relationships among managers, directors, shareholders, creditors, employees, and suppliers. However, we will concentrate here on the relationships between (1) managers and shareholders, and (2) directors and shareholders. These two relationships are the primary focus of most systems of corporate governance. However, to the extent that strong corporate governance structures are in place and effective in companies, the agency conflicts among other stakeholders are mitigated as well. For example, managers are responsible for maximizing the wealth of the shareholders and minimizing waste (including excessive compensation and perquisite consumption). To the extent that managers do so, the interests of employees and suppliers are more likely to be met because the probability increases that sufficient funds will be available for payment of salaries and benefits, as well as for goods and services. In this section, we will describe these agency relationships, discuss the problems inherent in each, and will illustrate these agency problems with real-world examples. An understanding of the nature of the conflicts in each relationship is essential to a full understanding of the importance of the provisions in codes of corporate governance.

4.1 Manager–Shareholder Conflicts

From the point of view of investors, the manager–shareholder relationship is the most critical one. It is important to recognize that firms and their managers, the shareholders' agents, obtain operating and investing capital from the shareholders, the owners, in two ways. First, although shareholders have a 100 percent claim on the firm's net income, the undistributed net income (the earnings remaining after the payment of dividends) is reinvested in the company. We normally term this reinvested income retained earnings. Second, the firm can issue stock to obtain the capital, either through an initial public offering (IPO) if the firm is currently privately owned, or through a seasoned equity offering (SEO) if the firm already has shares outstanding. By whatever means the firm obtains equity capital, shareholders entrust management to use the funds efficiently and effectively to generate profits and maximize investors' wealth.

However, although the manager is responsible for advancing the shareholder's best interests, this may not happen. For example, management may use funds to try to expand the size of the business to increase their job security, power, and salaries without consideration of the shareholders' interests. In addition, managers may also grant themselves numerous and expensive perquisites which are treated as ordinary business expenses. Managers enjoy these benefits, and shareholders bear the costs. This is a serious agency problem and, unfortunately, there are a number of recent real-world examples of their occurrence in corporations.

Managers also may make other business decisions, such as investing in highly risky ventures, that benefit themselves but that may not serve the company's investors well. For example, managers who hold substantial amounts of executive stock options will receive large benefits if risky ventures pay off, but will not suffer losses if the ventures fail. By contrast, managers whose wealth is closely tied to the company and who are therefore not well diversified may choose to not invest in projects with a positive expected net present value because of excessive risk aversion. The checks and balances in effective corporate governance systems are designed to reduce the probability of such practices.

The cases of Enron (bankruptcy filing: 2001, in the United States) and Tyco (resignation of CEO: 2002, in the United States) make clear that in the absence of the checks and balances of strong and effective corporate governance systems, investors and others cannot necessarily rely upon managers to serve as stewards of the resources entrusted to them. Example 1, dealing with Enron, illustrates the problems that can ensue from a lack of commitment to a corporate governance system. Example 2, dealing with Tyco, illustrates a case in which there were inadequate checks and balances to the power of a CEO.

EXAMPLE 1

Corporate Governance Failure (1)

Enron was one of the world's largest energy, commodities, and services companies. However, it is better known today as a classic example of how the conflicts of interest between shareholders and managers can harm even major corporations and their shareholders. Enron executives, with the approval of members of the board of directors, overrode provisions in Enron's code of ethics and corporate governance system that forbade any practices involving self-dealing by executives. Specifically, Enron's chief financial officer set up off-shore partnerships in which he served as general partner. As an Enron executive, he was able to make deals with these partnerships on behalf of Enron. As a general partner of the partnerships, he received the enormous fees that the deals generated.[4]

The partnerships served other useful purposes. For example, they made it possible to hide billions of dollars in Enron debt off of the company's balance sheet, and generated artificial profits for Enron. Thus, disclosure of the company's rapidly deteriorating financial condition was delayed, preventing investors and creditors from obtaining information critical to the valuation and riskiness of their securities. At the same time, Enron executives were selling their own stock in the company.

These egregious breaches of good governance harmed both Enron's outside shareholders and their creditors. The bonds were becoming riskier but the creditors were not informed of the deteriorating prospects. The exorbitant fees the executives paid themselves came out of the shareholders' earnings, earnings that were already overstated by the artificial profits. Investors did not receive full information about the problems in the company until well after the collapse and the company's bankruptcy filing, by which time their stock had lost essentially all of its value.

[4] William C. Powers, Jr., Raymond S. Troubh, and Herbert S. Winokur, Jr., *Report of Investigation by the Special Investigative Committee of the Board of Directors of Enron Corp.*, February 1, 2002.

Most, if not all, of the core attributes of good governance were violated by Enron's managers, but especially the responsibility to deal fairly with all stakeholders, including investors and creditors, and to provide full transparency of all material information on a timely basis.

EXAMPLE 2

Corporate Governance Failure (2)

Tyco provides another well-known example of a corporate governance failure. The CEO of Tyco used corporate funds to buy home decorating items, including a $17,000 dollar traveling toilette box, a $445 pin cushion, and a $15,000 umbrella stand. He also borrowed money from the company's employee loan program to buy $270 million dollars worth of yachts, art, jewelry, and vacation estates. Then, in his capacity as CEO, he forgave the loan. All told, the CEO may have looted the firm, and thereby its shareholders, of over $600 million dollars.[5]

It is instructive that in court proceedings in the Tyco case, the CEO and his representatives have not argued that he did not do these things, but rather that it was not illegal for him to do so.

Tyco is a striking example of excessive perquisite consumption by a CEO.

The role of complete transparency in sound corporate governance, including understandable and accurate financial statements, cannot be overestimated. Without full information, investors and other stakeholders are unable to evaluate the company's financial position and riskiness, whether the condition is improving or deteriorating, and whether insiders are aggrandizing themselves, or making poor business decisions, to the detriment of long-term investors.

Two additional cases illustrate how false, misleading, or incomplete corporate disclosure may harm investors and other stakeholders.

EXAMPLE 3

Corporate Governance Failure (3)

The Italian firm, Parmalat, was one of the world's largest dairy foods suppliers. The founders and top executives of Parmalat were accused of fictitiously reporting the existence of a $4.9 billion bank account so that the company's enormous liabilities would appear less daunting.[6] By hiding the true financial condition of the firm, the executives were able to continue borrowing. The fraud perpetrated by Parmalat's largest shareholders and executives hurt Parmalat's creditors as well as the shareholders. Parmalat eventually defaulted on a $185 million bond payment in November 2003 and the company collapsed shortly thereafter.

---

[5] Mark Maremont and Laurie Cohen, "How Tyco's CEO Enriched Himself," *The Wall Street Journal*, August 7, 2002, p. A1.

[6] Gail Edmondson, 2004, "How Parmalat Went Sour," *Business Week*, July 12, 2004.

> ### EXAMPLE 4
>
> #### Corporate Governance Failure (4)
>
> During the late 1990s, Adelphia, the fifth-largest provider of cable entertainment in the United States, and the company's founders embarked on an aggressive acquisition campaign to increase the size of the company. During this time, the size of Adelphia's debt more than tripled from $3.5 billion to $12.6 billion. However, the founders also arranged a $2.3 billion personal loan which Adelphia guaranteed, but this arrangement was not fully disclosed to Adelphia's other stakeholders.[7] In addition, it is alleged that fictitious transactions were recorded to boost accounting profits.[8] These actions by Adelphia's owners were harmful to all of Adelphia's non-founder stakeholders, including investors and creditors. The company collapsed in bankruptcy in 2002.

The severity of the agency problems of the companies discussed in Examples 1 through 4 does not represent the norm, although the potential for serious conflicts of interest between shareholders and managers is inherent in the modern corporation. Strong corporate governance systems provide mechanisms for monitoring managers' activities, rewarding good performance and disciplining those in a position of responsibility for the company to make sure they act in the interests of the company's stakeholders.

4.2 Director–Shareholder Conflicts

Corporate governance systems rely on a system of checks and balances between the managers and investors in which the board of directors plays a critical role. The purpose of boards of directors in modern corporations is to provide an intermediary between managers and the owners, the shareholders. Members of the board of directors serve as agents for the owners, the shareholders, a mechanism designed to represent the investors and to ensure that their interests are being well-served. This intermediary generally is responsible for monitoring the activities of managers, approving strategies and policies and making certain that these serve investors' interests. The board is also responsible for approving mergers and acquisitions, approving audit contracts and reviewing the audit and financial statements, setting managers' compensation including any incentive or performance awards, and disciplining or replacing poorly performing managers.

The conflict between directors and shareholders arises when directors come to identify with the managers' interests rather than those of the shareholders. This can occur when the board is not independent, for example, or when the members of the board have business or personal relationships with the managers that bias their judgment or compromise their duties to the shareholders. If members of the board have consulting agreements with the company, serve as major lenders to the firm, are members of the manager's family, or are from the circle of close friends, their objectivity may be called into question. Many corporations

---

[7] John Nofsinger and Kenneth Kim, *Infectious Greed* (Prentice Hall Financial Times, 2003), pp. 60–61.

[8] Jerry Markon and Robert Frank, 2002, "Five Adelphia Officials Arrested on Fraud Charges," *The Wall Street Journal*, July 25, page A3.

have been found to have inter-linked boards. For example, one or more senior managers from one firm may serve as directors in the companies of their own board members, frequently on compensation committees. Another ever-present problem is the frequently overly generous compensation paid to directors for their services. Excessive compensation may incline directors to accommodate the wishes of management rather than attend to the concerns of investors.

All of the examples cited in this section involve compliant or less than independent board members. In Section 5 we formulate the most important points to check in evaluating a company's corporate governance system.

CORPORATE GOVERNANCE EVALUATION 5

An essential component of the analysis of a company and its risk is a review of the quality of its corporate governance system. This evaluation requires an assessment of issues relating to the board of directors, managers, and shareholders. Ultimately, the long-term performance of a company is dependent upon the quality of managers' decisions and their commitment to applying sound management practice. However, as one group concerned with the issues observes, "by analyzing the state of corporate governance for a given company, an analyst or shareholder may ascertain whether the company is governed in a manner that produces better management practices, promotes higher returns on shareholder capital, or if there is a governance and/or management problem which may impair company performance."[9]

In the following sections we provide a set of guidelines for evaluating the quality of corporate governance in a company. We reiterate that there is no single system of governance that is appropriate for all companies in all industries worldwide. However, this core set of global best practices is being applied in financial markets in Europe, Asia, and North America. They represent a standard by which corporate practices may be evaluated.

The information and corporate disclosure available in a specific jurisdiction will vary widely. However, most large financial markets and, increasingly, smaller ones require a substantial amount of information be provided about companies' governance structures and practices. In addition, a few regulatory jurisdictions will require a subset of the criteria we shall give as part of **registration**, exchange listing, or other requirements.

The analyst should begin by carefully reviewing the requirements in effect for the company. Information is generally available in the company's required filings with regulators. For example, in the United States, such information is provided in the 10-K report, the annual report, and the Proxy Statement (SEC Form DEF 14A). All of these are filed with the U.S. Securities and Exchange Commission (U.S. SEC), are available on the U.S. SEC website, usually are available on the company's website, and are provided by the company to current investors as well as on request. In Europe, the company's annual report provides some information. However, in an increasing number of EU countries, companies are required to provide a report on corporate governance. This report typically will provide information on board activities and decisions, whether the company has abided by its relevant national code, and explain why it departed from the code, if it has. In addition, the announcement of the

---

[9] New York Society of Securities Analysts, *Corporate Governance Handbook*, September 22, 2003. New York City. p. 1.

company's annual general meeting should disclose the issues on the agenda that are subject to shareholder vote. The specific sources of information will differ by jurisdiction and company.

5.1 The Board of Directors

Boards of directors are a critical part of the system of checks and balances that lie at the heart of corporate governance systems. Board members, both individually and as a group, have the responsibility to:

► establish corporate values and governance structures for the company to ensure that the business is conducted in an ethical, competent, fair, and professional manner;

► ensure that all legal and regulatory requirements are met and complied with fully and in a timely fashion;

► establish long-term strategic objectives for the company with a goal of ensuring that the best interests of shareholders come first and that the company's obligations to others are met in a timely and complete manner;

► establish clear lines of responsibility and a strong system of accountability and performance measurement in all phases of a company's operations;

► hire the chief executive officer, determine the compensation package, and periodically evaluate the officer's performance;

► ensure that management has supplied the board with sufficient information for it to be fully informed and prepared to make the decisions that are its responsibility, and to be able to adequately monitor and oversee the company's management;

► meet frequently enough to adequately perform its duties, and meet in extraordinary session as required by events; and

► acquire adequate training so that members are able to adequately perform their duties.

Depending upon the nature of the company and the industries within which the company operates, these responsibilities will vary; however these general obligations are common to all companies.

In summarizing the duties and needs of boards of directors, *The Corporate Governance of Listed Companies: A Manual for Investors*[10] states:

> Board members owe a duty to make decisions based on what ultimately is best for the long-term interests of shareowners. In order to do this effectively, board members need a combination of three things: independence, experience and resources.
>
> **First**, a board should be composed of at least a majority of independent board members with the autonomy to act independently from management. Board members should bring with them a commitment to take an unbiased approach in making decisions that will benefit the company and long-term shareowners, rather than simply voting with management. **Second**, board members who have appropriate experience and expertise relevant to the Company's business are best able to evaluate what is in the best interests of shareowners. Depending on the nature of

---

[10] *The Corporate Governance of Listed Companies: A Manual for Investors*, CFA Institute Centre for Financial Market Integrity, CFA Institute, 2005, p. 11.

the business, this may require specialized expertise by at least some board members. **Third**, there need to be internal mechanisms to support the independent work of the board, including the authority to hire outside consultants without management's intervention or approval. This mechanism alone provides the board with the ability to obtain expert help in specialized areas, to circumvent potential areas of conflict with management, and to preserve the integrity of the board's independent oversight function. [Emphasis added]

In the following sections we detail the attributes of the board that an investor or investment analyst must assess.

5.1.1 Board Composition and Independence

The board of directors of a corporation is established for the primary purpose of serving the best interests of the outside shareholders in the company. Other stakeholders including employees, creditors, and suppliers are usually in a more powerful position to oversee their interests in the company than are shareholders. The millions of outside investors cannot, individually or collectively, monitor, oversee, and approve management's strategies and policies, performance, and compensation and consumption of perquisites.

The objectives of the board are to see that company assets are used in the best long-term interests of shareholders and that management strategies, plans, policies, and practices are designed to achieve this objective. In a recent amendment to the *Investment Company Act of 1940* rules, the U.S. SEC argues that a board must be "an independent force in [company] affairs rather than a passive affiliate of management. Its independent directors must bring to the boardroom a high degree of rigor and skeptical objectivity to the evaluation of [company] managements and its plans and proposals, particularly when evaluating conflicts of interest."[11]

Similarly, the *Corporate Governance Handbook*[12] observes:

> Board independence is essential to a sound governance structure. Without independence there can be little accountability. In the words of Professor Jeffrey Sonnenfeld of Yale University, "The highest performing companies have extremely contentious boards that regard dissent as an obligation and that treat no subject as undiscussable."

Clearly, for members who are appointed to the board to be in a position to best perform their fiduciary responsibilities to shareholders, at a minimum a majority of the members must be independent of management. However, global best practice now recommends that *at least three-quarters* of the board members should be independent.

Some experts in corporate governance have argued that all members of the board should be independent, eliminating the possibility of any senior executives serving on the board. Those who hold this position argue that the presence of managers in board deliberations may work to the detriment of the best interests of investors and other shareholders by intimidating the board or otherwise limiting debate and full discussion of important matters. Others argue that with appropriate additional safeguards, such potential problems can be overcome to the benefit of all stakeholders.

---

[11] *Amendments to Rules Governing the Investment Company Act of 1940*, 17 CFR Part 270, July 2004, p. 3.

[12] *Corporate Governance Handbook*, New York Society of Securities Analysts, September 2003, p. 3.

Independence is difficult to evaluate. Factors that often indicate a lack of independence include:

▶ former employment with the company, including founders, executives, or other employees;

▶ business relationships, for example, prior or current service as outside counsel, auditors, or consultants, or business interests involving contractual commitments and obligations;

▶ personal relationships, whether familial, friendship, or other affiliations;

▶ inter-locking directorships, a director of another company whose independence might be impaired by the relationship with the other board or company, particularly if the director serves on inter-locking compensation committees; and

▶ ongoing banking or other creditor relationships.

Information on the business and other relationships of board members as well as nominees for the board may be obtained from regulatory filings in most jurisdictions. For example, in the United States, such information is required to be provided in the Proxy Statement, SEC Form DEF 14A, sent to shareholders and filed with the SEC prior to shareholder meetings.

5.1.2 Independent Chairman of the Board

Many, if not most, corporate boards now permit a senior executive of a corporation to serve as the chairman of the board of directors. However, corporate governance experts do not regard such an arrangement to be in the best interests of the shareholders of the company. As the U.S. SEC observes:

> This practice may contribute to the [company's] ability to dominate the actions of the board of directors. The chairman of a . . . board can largely control the board's agenda, which may include matters not welcomed by the [company's manage-ment] . . . Perhaps more important, the chairman of the board can have a substan-tial influence on the . . . boardroom's culture. The boardroom culture can foster (or suppress) the type of meaningful dialogue between . . . management and independent directors that is critical for healthy . . . governance. It can support (or diminish) the role of the independent directors in the continuous, active engage-ment of . . . management necessary for them to fulfill their duties. A boardroom culture conducive to decisions favoring the long-term interest of . . . shareholders may be more likely to prevail when the chairman does not have the conflicts of interest inherent in his role as an executive of the [company]. Moreover, a . . . board may be more effective when negotiating with the [company] over matters such as the [compensation] if it were not at the same time led by an executive of the [company] with whom it is negotiating.[13]

Not all market participants agree with this view. Many corporate managers argue that it is essential for efficient and effective board functioning that the chair-man be the senior executive in the company. They base their arguments on the proposition that only such an executive has the knowledge and experience neces-sary to provide needed information to the board on questions on strategy, policy, and the operational functioning of the company. Critics of this position counter

---

[13] *Amendments to Rules Governing the Investment Company Act of 1940*, 17 CFR Part 270, July 2004, p. 4.

that it is incumbent upon corporate management to provide all such necessary information to the board. Indeed, many argue that this obligation is the sole reason that one or more corporate managers serve as members of the board.

Whether the company has separate positions for the chief executive and chairman of the board can be determined readily from regulatory filings of the company. If the positions are not separate, an investor may doubt that the board is operating efficiently and effectively in its monitoring and oversight of corporate operations, and that decisions made are necessarily in the best interests of investors and other stakeholders.

Tradition and practice in many countries prescribe a so-called "unitary" board system, a single board of directors. However, some countries, notably Germany, have developed a formal system whose intent is to overcome such difficulties as lack of independence of board members and lack of independence of the chairman of the board from company management. The latter approach requires a tiered hierarchy of boards, a management board responsible for overseeing management's strategy, planning, and similar functions, and an independent supervisory board charged with monitoring and reviewing decisions of the management board, and making decisions in which conflicts of interest in the management board may impair their independence, for example, in determining managerial compensation.

Clearly, independence of the chairman of the board does not guarantee that the board will function properly. However, independence should be regarded as a necessary condition, even if it is not a sufficient one.

5.1.3 Qualifications of Directors

In addition to independence, directors need to bring sufficient skill and experience to the position to ensure that they will be able to fulfill their fiduciary responsibilities to investors and other stakeholders. Information on directors' prior business experience and other biographical material, including current and past business affiliations, can generally be found in regulatory filings.

Boards of directors require a variety of skills and experience in order to function properly. These skills will vary by industry although such core skills as knowledge of finance, accounting, and legal matters are required by all boards. Evaluation of the members should include an assessment of whether needed skills are available among the board members. Among the qualifications and core competencies that an investor should look for in the board as a group, and in individual members or candidates for the board, are:

▶ independence (see factors to consider in Section 5.1.1);

▶ relevant expertise in the industry, including the principal technologies used in the business and in financial operations, legal matters, accounting and auditing; and managerial considerations such as the success of companies with which the director has been associated in the past;

▶ indications of ethical soundness, including public statements or writings of the director, problems in companies with which the director has been associated in the past such as legal or other regulatory violations involving ethical lapses;

▶ experience in strategic planning and risk management;

▶ other board experience with companies regarded as having sound governance practices and that are effective stewards of investors' capital as compared to serving management's interests;

► dedication and commitment to serving the board and investors' interests. Board members with such qualities will not serve on more than a few boards, have an excellent record of attendance at board meetings, and will limit other business commitments that require large amounts of time; and

► commitment to the needs of investors as shown, for example, by significant personal investments in this or other companies for which he or she serves as a director, and by an absence of conflicts of interest.

Such attributes are essential to the sound functioning of a board of directors and should be carefully considered in any investment decision. Board members may be selected as much for their general stature and name recognition as for the specialized expertise they bring to their responsibilities. However, the skills, knowledge, and experience we have described are essential to effective corporate governance, oversight, and monitoring on behalf of shareholders.

5.1.4 Annual Election of Directors

Members of boards of directors may be elected either on an annual or a staggered basis. In annual votes, every member of the board stands for re-election every year. Such an approach ensures that shareholders are able to express their views on individual members' performance during the year, and to exercise their right to control who will represent them in corporate governance and oversight of the company. Opponents argue that subjecting members to annual re-election is disruptive to effective board oversight over the company.

Those who support election of board members on a staggered basis with re-election of only a portion of the board each year, argue that such a scheme is necessary to ensure continuity of the knowledge and experience in the company essential for good corporate governance. Critics express the view that such a practice diminishes the limited power that shareholders have to control who will serve on the board and ensure the responsiveness of board members to investor concerns, such as poor management performance and practices. They also argue that **staggered boards** better serve the interests of entrenched managers by making the board less responsive to the needs of shareholders, more likely to align their interests with those of managers, and more likely to resist takeover attempts that would benefit shareholders to the detriment of managers.

Corporate governance best practice generally supports the annual election of directors as being in the best interests of investors. When shareholders can express their views annually, either by casting a positive vote or by withholding their votes for poorly performing directors, directors are thought to be more likely to weigh their decisions carefully, to be better prepared and more attentive to the needs of investors, and to be more effective in their oversight of management.

Information on directors' terms and the frequency of elections may be obtained by examining the term structure of the board members in regulatory filings.

5.1.5 Annual Board Self-Assessment

Board members have a fiduciary duty to shareholders to oversee management's use of assets, to monitor and review strategies, policies and practices, and to take those actions necessary to fulfill their responsibilities to stakeholders. It is essential that a process be in place for periodically reviewing and evaluating their performance and making recommendations for improvement. Generally, this evaluation should occur at least once annually. The review should include:

▶ an assessment of the board's effectiveness as a whole;

▶ evaluations of the performance of individual board members, including assessments of the participation of each member, with regard to both attendance and the number and relevance of contributions made, and an assessment of the member's willingness to think independently of management and address challenging or controversial issues;

▶ a review of board committee activities;

▶ an assessment of the board's effectiveness in monitoring and overseeing their specific functions;

▶ an evaluation of the qualities the company will need in its board in the future, along with a comparison of the qualities current board members currently have; and

▶ a report of the board self-assessment, typically prepared by the nominations committee, and included in the proxy in the U.S. and in the corporate governance report in Europe.

The process of periodic self-assessment by directors can improve board and company performance by reminding directors of their role and responsibilities, improving their understanding of the role, improving communications between board members, and enhancing the cohesiveness of the board. Self-assessment allows directors to improve not only their own performance but to make needed changes in corporate governance structures. All of these will lead to greater efficiency and effectiveness in serving investors' and other stakeholders' interests.

The process of self-assessment should focus on board responsibilities and individual members' accountability for fulfilling these responsibilities. It should consider both substantive matters and procedural issues, for example, evaluations of the adequacy and effectiveness of the committee structure. The committees regarded as essential by corporate governance experts include the auditing, nominations, and compensation committees, all of which should be staffed by independent directors who are experts in the relevant areas. (The specific functions of these committees will be considered in later sections.)

The company, however, may need to establish additional committees. For example, for a mutual fund company, these might include a securities valuation committee responsible for setting policies for the pricing of securities, and monitoring the application of the policies by management. For a high technology company, the committees might include one tasked with the valuation of intellectual property, or perhaps, management's success in creating new intellectual property through its investments in research and development.

In evaluating the effectiveness of the corporate governance system and specifically, the board of directors, an investment professional should consider the critical functions specific to a particular company and evaluate whether or not the board's structure and membership provides adequate oversight and control over management's strategic business decision-making and policy-making.

5.1.6 Separate Sessions of Independent Directors

Corporate governance best practice requires that independent directors of the board meet at least annually, and preferably quarterly, in separate sessions—that is, meetings without the presence of the management, other representatives, or interested persons (for example, retired founders of the company). The purpose of these sessions is to provide an opportunity for those entrusted with the best interests of the shareholders to engage in candid and frank discussions and debate regarding the management of the company, their strategies and policies, strengths and weaknesses, and other matters of concern. Such regular sessions would avoid the suggestion that directors are concerned with specific problems or threats to the company's well-being. Separate sessions could also enhance the board's effectiveness by improving the cooperation among board members, and their cohesiveness as a board, attributes that can strengthen the board in the fulfillment of its responsibilities to shareholders.

Regulatory filings should indicate how often boards have met, and which meetings were separate sessions of the independent directors. The investment professional should be concerned if such meetings appeared to be nonexistent, infrequent or irregular in occurrence. These could suggest a variety of negative conclusions, including the presence of a "captive," that is, non-independent board, inattention or disinterest among board members, lack of cohesion and sense of purpose, or other conditions that can be detrimental to the interests of investors.

5.1.7 Audit Committee and Audit Oversight

The audit committee of the board is established to provide independent oversight of the company's financial reporting, non-financial corporate disclosure, and internal control systems. This function is essential for effective corporate governance and for seeing that their responsibilities to shareholders are fulfilled.

The primary responsibility for overseeing the design, maintenance, and continuing development of the control and compliance systems rests with this committee. At a minimum the audit committee must:

▶ include only independent directors;

▶ have sufficient expertise in financial, accounting, auditing, and legal matters to be able to adequately oversee and evaluate the control, risk management, and compliance systems, and the quality of the company's financial disclosure to shareholders and others. It is advisable for at least two members of the committee to have relevant accounting and auditing expertise;

▶ oversee the internal audit function; the internal audit staff should report directly and routinely to this committee of the board, and, when necessary report any concerns regarding the quality of controls or compliance issues;

▶ have sufficient resources to be able to properly fulfill their responsibilities;

▶ have full access to and the cooperation of management;

▶ have authority to investigate fully any matters within its purview;

▶ have the authority for the hiring of auditors, including the setting of contractual provisions, review of the cost-effectiveness of the audit, approving of non-audit services provided by the auditor, and assessing the auditors' independence;

▶ meet with auditors independently of management or other company interest parties periodically but at least once annually; and

▶ have the full authority to review the audit and financial statements, question auditors regarding audit findings, including the review of the system of internal controls, and to determine the quality and transparency of financial reporting choices.

Strong internal controls, risk management, and compliance systems are critical to a company's long-term success, the meeting of its business objectives, and enhancing the best interests of shareholders. Nearly all of the major corporate collapses have involved an absence of effective control systems, or the overriding of the systems by management to achieve their own interests and objectives to the detriment of those of investors.

The internal audit function should be entirely independent and separate from any of the activities being audited. Internal auditors should report directly to the chairman of the audit committee of the board of directors. The board should regularly meet with the internal audit supervisor and review the activities and address any concerns.

In evaluating the effectiveness of the board of directors, an investor should review the qualifications of the members of the audit committee, being alert to any conflicts of interest that individual members might have, for example, having previously been employed or otherwise associated with the current auditor or the company, determine the number of meetings held by the committee during the year and whether these meetings were held independent of management. A report on the activities of the audit committee, including a statement on whether the committee met independently and without the presence of management, should be included in the proxy in the U.S. and in the corporate governance report in Europe.

The audit committee should discuss in the regulatory filings the responsibilities and authority it has to evaluate and assess these functions, any findings or concerns the committee has with regard to the audit, internal control and compliance systems, and corrective action taken.

5.1.8 Nominating Committee

In most corporations, currently, nominations of members of the board of directors and for executive officers of the company are made by members of the board, most often at the recommendation of, or in consultation with, the management of the company. In such circumstances, the criteria for selection of nominees may favor management's best interests at the expense of the interests of shareholders. This is all the more important because in the usual case, shareholders have no authority to nominate slates of directors who might best represent them. Consequently, corporate governance best practice requires that nominees to the board be selected by a nominating committee comprising only independent directors. The responsibilities of the nominating committee are to:

▶ establish criteria for evaluating candidates for the board of directors;

▶ identify candidates for the general board and for all committees of the board;

▶ review the qualifications of the nominees to the board and for members of individual committees;

▶ establish criteria for evaluating nominees for senior management positions in the company;

▶ identify candidates for management positions;

▶ review the qualifications of the nominees for management positions; and

▶ document the reasons for the selection of candidates recommended to the board as a whole for consideration.

Given the pivotal role that the members of the nominating committee have in representing and protecting the interests of investors and other stakeholders, it is essential that the qualifications of these members be carefully reviewed in assessing the long-term investment prospects of a company. Particular attention should be paid to evaluating their independence, the qualities of those selected for senior management positions, and the success of businesses with which they've been associated. This information is available in the regulatory filings of the company.

5.1.9 Compensation Committee

Ideally, compensation should be a tool used by directors, acting on behalf of shareholders, to attract, retain, and motivate the highest quality and most experienced managers for the company. The compensation should include incentives to meet and exceed corporate *long-term* goals, rather than short-term performance targets.

Decisions regarding the amounts and types of compensation to be awarded to senior executives and directors of a company are thought by many corporate governance experts to be the most important decisions to be made by those in a position of trust. Reports abound of compensation that is excessive relative to corporate performance, awarded to executives by compliant boards. The problem has been particularly acute in the United States, but examples are found worldwide.

In recent years, a practice has developed of gauging levels of compensation awards based not upon company objectives and goals but rather by comparison to the highest levels of compensation awarded in other companies. This occurs whether the reference companies are relevant benchmarks or not, and has caused compensation packages in many cases to be unrelated to the performance of the company. Needless to say, such excessive compensation is highly detrimental to the interests of shareholders.

In one well-known case, that of the New York Stock Exchange, the compensation of the chief executive was a substantial proportion of the net earnings of the Exchange and considerably higher than the compensation awarded to senior executives of comparable companies. The facts that have come to light in the case suggest that the compensation committee of the board was not independent as measured by the usual criteria, was not expert in compensation matters and did not seek outside counsel, was not well-informed on the details of the compensation package, and acquiesced in management's proposal of its own compensation.[14] This case is currently the subject of extensive legal and regulatory action.

Several different types of compensation awards are in common use today:

► salary, generally set by contractual commitments between the company and the executive or director;

► perquisites, additional compensation in the form of benefits, such as insurance, use of company planes, cars, and apartments, services, ranging from investment advice, tax assistance, and financial planning advice to household services;

► bonus awards, normally based on performance as compared to company goals and objectives;

---

[14] Landon Thomas Jr., "Saying Grasso Duped Big Board, Suit Seeks Return of $100 Million," *The New York Times*, May 25, 2004; and "Regulators Said To Be Focusing On Board's Vote For Grasso Pay," *The New York Times*, March 26, 2004.

► stock options, options on future awards of company stock; and

► stock awards or restricted stock.

In general, shareholders would prefer that salary and perquisite awards constitute a relatively small portion of the total compensation award. That is, the fixed, non-performance-based portion of the award should be adequate, but not excessive. Because these fixed costs must be borne by shareholders regardless of corporate performance, executives should not be automatically rewarded by poor performance. Information on salaries and some perquisites can be found in regulatory filings of companies. For example, in the United States, this information is found in the Proxy Statement in tables and accompanying text. The investor should be alert to the fact that significant amounts of perquisites may not be fully disclosed, as has been shown to be the case in a number of corporate scandals recently in Europe and the United States.

Bonuses should be awarded based solely on exceeding expected performance. They should provide an incentive to motivate managers to achieve the highest and most stable long-term performance, rather than to reward short-term non-sustainable "growth" at the expense of the best interests of shareholders. To the extent that management controls the operations of the company as well as corporate disclosure, incentive-based awards require the most diligent monitoring by the members of the compensation committee. Directors must ascertain that management is not manipulating variables within its control, for example, accounting disclosure choices, to artificially achieve performance targets. The investor should examine the bonus awards carefully, evaluating the performance targets for reasonableness, and to make certain that the awards are consistent with the investor's best interests.

Stock options and stock awards have been argued to better align the interests of managers with those of shareholders by making a portion of the manager's compensation dependent on the value of the stock. Unfortunately, as recent events have made clear, stock options do not always result in such an alignment of interests. Indeed, until recently, the lack of appropriate accounting recognition of the expense of stock option awards has led to widespread abuse of this form of compensation. Large grants of stock options dilute shareholders' positions in the company and diminish the value of their holdings.

Appropriate accounting for stock options, that is, expensing in the income statement with assumed conversion to stock in the earnings-per-share calculation, has come to be seen as a litmus test for high quality financial reporting and transparency.[15] Nevertheless, abusive practices involving information manipulation related to stock option grants and option exercise still occur.

In theory, grants of stock options to executives and other employees should be subject to shareholder approval. As a practical matter, however, there are loopholes that permit managers and directors to by pass such approval, although some jurisdictions have closed some of these loopholes recently.

Stock options' potential dilutive effect on shareholders can be assessed by a measure known as the "share overhang." The overhang is simply the number of shares represented by the options, relative to the total amount of stock outstanding. Both of these numbers are readily available in company regulatory filings in most jurisdictions.

---

[15] In 2003, the International Accounting Standards Board (IASB) issued a standard requiring the fair value expensing of stock options for all companies that use IASB standards. Some ninety countries worldwide adhere to IASB standards.

In addition, investors should be alert to any provisions permitting the so-called "repricing" of stock options. Repricing means that the company can, with approval of the board of directors, adjust the exercise price of outstanding option grants downward to the current price of the stock. This is done by some companies when the price of the stock has declined significantly and the options are out-of-the-money. As is readily apparent, such repricing is inconsistent with the argument that options should serve the interests of managers and shareholders and provide an incentive for managers to strive for excellent long-term corporate performance. The managers may have at-the-money options following repricing, but investors cannot recoup their losses so easily. Abuse in this area has been stemmed somewhat by accounting rule changes that now require that such repriced options be expensed in the income statement, although companies can still cancel the options and reissue them later at a time consistent with the rules, usually six months.

Stock grants by companies to executives can be an effective means of motivating them to achieve sustainable, long-term performance objectives. Restricted stock grants, that is, stock awards that cannot be sold or otherwise disposed of for a period of time, or that are contingent upon reaching certain performance goals, can be subject to the same abusive practices as stock option awards, depending upon the terms of the awards. Well-designed restricted stock awards are increasingly used by companies to reward executives for their performance as well as to remunerate lower-level employees. Most jurisdictions require companies to disclose such grants in regulatory filings.

5.1.10 Board's Independent Legal and Expert Counsel

The board of directors should have the ability and sufficient resources to hire such legal and other expert counsel as they require to fulfill their fiduciary duties. In most companies, for example, the corporate counsel also has the responsibility to advise the board of directors. Because the board of directors is charged with overseeing management on behalf of the shareholders, this represents a direct conflict of interest. That is, the corporate counsel cannot be wholly independent with regard to the advice provided to the directors if it also serves, and is paid by, corporate management.

Legal counsel will be needed to help the board assess the company's compliance with legal and regulatory requirements. Outside counsel becomes increasingly important for companies with global operations. Similarly, for example, in high technology companies, the members of the board will likely require the assistance of experts in the particular specialized technologies employed or developed by the company. However, all boards, regardless of the industry, are likely to require additional counsel and should be able to obtain such services when they require it.

The investor should review regulatory filings carefully to determine if the board makes use of independent outside counsel. If the filings are silent on the issue, the analyst or investor should specifically inquire about the board's use of independent counsel. If satisfactory answers are not forthcoming, this should reflect negatively on the board's independence as well as its ability to perform its fiduciary duties.

5.1.11 Statement of Governance Policies

Companies that have a strong commitment to corporate governance frequently supply a statement of their corporate governance policies, variously in their regulatory filings, on their websites, or as part other investor information packets.

Investors and investment analysts should assess the following elements of a statement of corporate governance policies:

▶ codes of ethics;

▶ statements of the oversight, monitoring, and review responsibilities of directors, including internal control, risk management, audit and accounting and disclosure policy, compliance assessment, nominations, compensation awards, and other responsibilities;

▶ statements of management's responsibilities to provide complete and timely information to the board members prior to board meetings, and to provide directors with free and unfettered access to control and compliance functions within the company;

▶ reports of directors' examinations, evaluations, and findings in their oversight and review function;

▶ board and committee performance self-assessments;

▶ management performance assessments; and

▶ training provided to directors prior to joining the board and periodically thereafter.

Obviously, one cannot rely solely on the corporate governance statement for assurance that the company has a sound corporate governance structure. Nevertheless, such disclosures provide investors with a comparison for evaluating company and director performance over time. For example, such disclosures should not be "boilerplate" statements that do not change over time and that provide no real content or information.

5.1.12 Disclosure and Transparency

The purpose of accounting and disclosure is to tell the company's economic story as it is, not as some might want it to be in order to achieve some personal objective. Investors depend critically on the quality, clarity, timeliness, and completeness of financial information in valuing securities and assessing risk. Attempts to hide or otherwise obfuscate essential information can result in the mispricing of securities and the misallocation of capital, reducing the efficiency and effectiveness of markets.

It is worth observing that nearly all of the major corporate collapses in recent years have involved equally massive attempts to hide, obfuscate, or falsify information that could have alerted investors to the seriousness of the financial problems and the impending implosions. Enron attempted to hide its massive and growing debt by moving it off the balance sheet and into "partnerships," run by insiders, for which no information was available. Tyco failed to report billions in "loans" to insiders. WorldCom not only hid $11 billion in operating expenses by recording them as assets in the balance sheet, but also failed to disclose hundreds of billions of dollars in loans to the chief executive. Parmalat staved off collapse for some time by reporting falsely that the company had nearly $5 billion in a corporate account with a major international financial institution.

The crisis of the loss of confidence and trust in the broad financial markets globally, rather than just the companies involved, signals the depths of the concern that investors have had about the quality and completeness of the disclosure they are receiving. Not surprisingly, the response has been a major overhaul of legislative, regulatory, and related criminal code provisions in countries in North America and Europe, as well as elsewhere. Such provisions as the requirements in the United States that the chief executive officer and chief financial officer certify the accuracy of financial statements and develop rigorous new systems of internal controls, backed up by new audit attestation requirements and stiffer criminal penalties, make clear the seriousness of the offenses and the public's response to such malfeasance.

However, such changes do not guarantee that those in a position of trust will not again willingly mislead and misinform their investors and others, particularly when they are faced with serious financial difficulties. Consequently, an evaluation of the quality and extent of financial information provided to investors is a crucial element in evaluating the corporate governance structure of a company and the risk borne by an investor in the company's securities. In assessing the quality of disclosure, some indicators of good quality financial reporting are:[16]

► conservative assumptions used for employee benefit plans;

► adequate provisions for lawsuits and other loss contingencies;

► minimal use of off-balance-sheet financing techniques and full disclosure of assets, liabilities, revenues, and expenses associated with such activities;

► absence of nonrecurring gains;

► absence of noncash earnings;

► clear and adequate disclosure;

► conservative revenue and expense recognition methods;

► use of LIFO inventory accounting (during periods of generally rising prices);

► bad-debt reserves that are high relative to receivables and past credit losses;

► use of accelerated depreciation methods and short lives;

► rapid write-off of acquisition-related intangible assets;

► minimal capitalization of interest and overhead;

► minimal capitalization of computer software costs;

► expensing of startup costs of new operations; and

► use of the completed contract method of accounting for contracts.

One area of concern in recent years is the reporting by companies of so-called "pro forma" earnings numbers, earnings before non-cash or "non-recurring" charges. Pro forma earnings have occasionally been dubbed "earnings-before-the-bad-stuff." Such misleading disclosures have been widely used by companies with poor performance and poor prospects. Unfortunately, some analysts and investors have been willing to accept the deception as reflective of economic reality, frequently to their regret. To survive and flourish long-term, companies must be able to cover all of their costs.

In addition to high quality financial disclosure, the company should make readily available in its regulatory filings clear and complete information on such items as:

► governance policies and procedures;

► reporting lines and organizational structure;

► corporate strategy, goals, and objectives;

---

[16] White, Gerald I., Ashwinpaul C. Sondhi, and Dov Fried, *The Analysis and Use of Financial Statements*, Third Edition, 2003, Wiley, p. 637 ff.

- ▶ competitive threats and other risks and contingencies faced by the company and the potential effect of these on the company's operations;

- ▶ insider transactions involving executives or other senior employees, and directors;

- ▶ compensation policies and amounts of compensation awarded, including perquisites, for key executives and directors; and

- ▶ changes to governance structures, including the corporate charter and by-laws.

The investor should be alert particularly to references to off-balance-sheet or insider transactions that are not accompanied by full disclosure of the effects of the items on the company. The investor should also consider the implications of a lack of disclosure. For example, many large companies maintain fleets of corporate jets for the use of executives and other employees. They routinely make such planes available to executives for their private use on holidays. A failure to mention such perquisites should raise questions, not only about this item but about other possible compensation that has not been disclosed.

5.1.13 Insider or Related-Party Transactions

The corporate collapse cases cited above involve egregious insider transactions by senior executives, frequently with the acquiescence of a compliant board of directors. The executives' objective was self-aggrandizement at the expense of shareholders and other stakeholders in the company. This is not a new problem. Indeed, audit standards have required for decades that auditors investigate such items and flag them for users of the statements. However, both the frequency and extent of the theft and fraud, and the losses incurred by investors, employees, and others recently have dismayed even the most seasoned professionals in the financial markets.

The analyst should assess the company's policies concerning related-party transactions, whether the company has entered into any such transactions, and, if so, what the effects are on the company's financial statements. Any related-party transaction should require the prior approval of the board of directors and a statement that such transactions are consistent with company policy. Financial disclosures and related notes in regulatory filings are a source for analysts in researching such transactions.

5.1.14 Responsiveness of Board of Directors to Shareholder Proxy Votes

A clear indicator of the extent to which directors and executives take seriously their fiduciary responsibility to shareholders is the response of the company to shareholder votes on proxy matters. A recent example involves the issue of expensing stock options, which has been put to **proxy vote** in a sizable number of companies. Shareholders in many of the companies have voted in the majority that the company begin expensing stock options. Very few company managers and directors have responded positively to the votes.

Directors cannot be expected to respond to trivial or frivolous shareholder initiatives, but few such issues carry a large portion of the vote of shareholders. However, when matters related to governance, executive compensation, mergers and acquisitions, or other matters of great importance to investors are put to a vote of the shareholders, and the results of the vote are ignored, the implications are abundantly clear: management and the board are not concerned for or motivated by the best interests of the company's shareholders. An analyst should review all such proxies put to the shareholders, determine the shareholders' consensus as reflected in the relative size of the affirmative vote, and determine the directors' response to the vote as reflected in the actions taken by the board and management. The responsiveness is a clear signal of the board's willingness to act in the best interests of the owners of the company.

5.2 Examples of Codes of Corporate Governance

We provide examples of three codes of corporate governance, one from General Electric, one from the Monetary Authority of Singapore, and a third from an international organization, the Organization for Economic Co-Operation and Development. The first code provides an example for one of the largest globally-diversified corporations. The second addresses corporate governance issues for financial institutions, specifically commercial banks and insurers operating in Singapore. The third has a much broader scope, addressing corporate governance issues in any type of firm in any industry, operating in a variety of countries that are members of the organization. Taken together, these three codes indicate the varying approaches to corporate governance worldwide while also illustrating how the core conflicts of interest between managers and owners are addressed.

5.2.1 General Electric: Governance Principles

General Electric's *Governance Principles* are a particularly good example of a company code of corporate governance. GE established the code to guide not only its managers and board of directors in their activities and decision-making, but to serve as a benchmark by which their performance may be evaluated. The company publishes their *Principles* in a prominent place on their website. A review of these principles will show that many of the major governance concerns discussed above are reflected here. The principles also explicitly address issues such as the company's policy on the adoption of "poison pills" and director education.

EXAMPLE 5

General Electric's *Governance Principles*

1. Role of Board and Management

GE's business is conducted by its employees, managers and officers, under the direction of the chief executive officer (CEO) and the oversight of the board, to enhance the long-term value of the company for its shareowners. The board of directors is elected by the shareowners to oversee management and to assure that the long-term interests of the shareowners are being served. Both the board of directors and management recognize that the long-term interests of shareowners are advanced by responsibly addressing the concerns of other stakeholders and interested parties including employees, recruits, customers, suppliers, GE communities, government officials and the public at large.

2. Functions of Board

The board of directors has eight scheduled meetings a year at which it reviews and discusses reports by management on the performance of the company, its plans and prospects, as well as immediate issues facing the company. Directors are expected to attend all scheduled board and committee meetings. In addition to its general oversight of management, the board also performs a number of specific functions, including:

▶ selecting, evaluating and compensating the CEO and overseeing CEO succession planning;

▶ providing counsel and oversight on the selection, evaluation, development and compensation of senior management;

▶ reviewing, monitoring and, where appropriate, approving fundamental financial and business strategies and major corporate actions;

▶ assessing major risks facing the company—and reviewing options for their mitigation; and

▶ ensuring processes are in place for maintaining the integrity of the company—the integrity of the financial statements, the integrity of compliance with law and ethics, the integrity of relationships with customers and suppliers, and the integrity of relationships with other stakeholders.

3. Qualifications

Directors should possess the highest personal and professional ethics, integrity and values, and be committed to representing the long-term interests of the shareowners. They must also have an inquisitive and objective perspective, practical wisdom and mature judgment. We endeavor to have a board representing diverse experience at policy-making levels in business, government, education and technology, and in areas that are relevant to the company's global activities. Directors must be willing to devote sufficient time to carrying out their duties and responsibilities effectively, and should be committed to serve on the board for an extended period of time. Directors should offer their resignation in the event of any significant change in their personal circumstances, including a change in their principal job responsibilities.

Directors who also serve as CEOs or in equivalent positions should not serve on more than two boards of public companies in addition to the GE board, and other directors should not serve on more than four other boards of public companies in addition to the GE board. Current positions in excess of these limits may be maintained unless the board determines that doing so would impair the director's service on the GE board.

The board does not believe that arbitrary term limits on directors' service are appropriate, nor does it believe that directors should expect to be renominated annually until they reach the mandatory retirement age. The board self-evaluation process described below will be an important determinant for board tenure. Directors will not be nominated for election to the board after their 73rd birthday, although the full board may nominate candidates over 73 for special circumstances.

4. Independence of Directors

A majority of the directors will be independent directors, as independence is determined by the board, based on the guidelines set forth below.

All future non-employee directors will be independent. GE seeks to have a minimum of ten independent directors at all times, and it is the board's goal that at least two-thirds of the directors will be independent. Directors who do not satisfy GE's independence guidelines also make valuable contributions to the board and to the company by reason of their experience and wisdom.

For a director to be considered independent, the board must determine that the director does not have any direct or indirect material relationship with GE. The board has established guidelines to assist it in determining director independence, which conform to or are more exacting than the independence requirements in the New York Stock Exchange listing requirements (NYSE rules). In addition to applying these guidelines, the board will consider all relevant facts and circumstances in making an independence determination, and not merely from the standpoint of the director, but also from that of persons or organizations with which the director has an affiliation.

The board will make and publicly disclose its independence determination for each director when the director is first elected to the board and annually thereafter for all nominees for election as directors. If the board determines that a director who satisfies the NYSE rules is independent even though he or she does not satisfy all of GE's independence guidelines, this determination will be disclosed and explained in the next proxy statement.

In accordance with the revised NYSE rules, independence determinations under the guidelines in section (a) below will be based upon a director's relationships with GE during the 36 months preceding the determination. Similarly, independence determinations under the guidelines in section (b) below will be based upon the extent of commercial relationships during the three completed fiscal years preceding the determination.

a. A director will not be independent if:

▶ the director is employed by GE, or an immediate family member is an executive officer of GE;

▶ the director receives any direct compensation from GE, other than director and committee fees and pension or other forms of deferred compensation for prior service (provided such compensation is not contingent in any way on continued service);

▶ an immediate family member who is a GE executive officer receives more than $100,000 per year in direct compensation from GE;

▶ the director is affiliated with or employed by GE's independent auditor, or an immediate family member is affiliated with or employed in a professional capacity by GE's independent auditor; or

▶ a GE executive officer is on the compensation committee of the board of directors of a company which employs the GE director or an immediate family member as an executive officer.

b. A director will not be independent if, at the time of the independence determination, the director is an executive officer or employee, or if an immediate family member is an executive officer, of another company that does business with GE and the sales by that company to GE or purchases by that company from GE, in any single fiscal year during the evaluation period, are more than the greater of one percent of the annual revenues of that company or $1 million.

c. A director will not be independent if, at the time of the independence determination, the director is an executive officer or employee, or an immediate family member is an executive officer, of another company which is indebted to GE, or to which GE is indebted, and the total amount of either company's indebtedness to the other at the end of the last completed fiscal year is more than one percent of the other company's total consolidated assets.

d. A director will not be independent if, at the time of the independence determination, the director serves as an officer, director or trustee of a charitable organization, and GE's discretionary charitable contributions to the organization are more than one percent of that organization's total annual charitable receipts during its last completed fiscal year. (GE's automatic matching of employee charitable contributions will not be included in the amount of GE's contributions for this purpose.)

5. Size of Board and Selection Process

The directors are elected each year by the shareowners at the annual meeting of shareowners. Shareowners may propose nominees for consideration by the nominating and corporate governance committee by submitting the names and supporting information to: Secretary, General Electric Company, 3135 Easton Turnpike, Fairfield, CT 06828. The board proposes a slate of nominees to the shareowners for election to the board. The board also determines the number of directors on the board provided that there are at least 10. Between annual shareowner meetings, the board may elect directors to serve until the next annual meeting. The board believes that, given the size and breadth of GE and the need for diversity of board views, the size of the board should be in the range of 13 to 17 directors.

6. Board Committees

The board has established the following committees to assist the board in discharging its responsibilities: (i) audit; (ii) management development and compensation; (iii) nominating and corporate governance; and (iv) public responsibilities. The current charters and key practices of these committees are published on the GE website, and will be mailed to shareowners on written request. The committee chairs report the highlights of their meetings to the full board following each meeting of the respective committees. The committees occasionally hold meetings in conjunction with the full board. For example, it is the practice of the audit committee to meet in conjunction with the full board in February so that all directors may participate in the review of the annual financial statements and Management's Discussion and Analysis of Financial Condition and Results of Operations for the prior year and financial plans for the current year.

7. Independence of Committee Members

In addition to the requirement that a majority of the board satisfy the independence standards discussed in section 4 above, members of the audit committee must also satisfy an additional NYSE independence requirement. Specifically, they may not accept directly or indirectly any consulting, advisory or other compensatory fee from GE or any of its subsidiaries other than their directors' compensation. As a matter of policy, the board will also apply a separate and heightened independence standard to members of both the management development and compensation committee and the nominating and corporate governance committee. No member of either committee may be a partner, member or principal of a law firm, accounting firm or investment banking firm that accepts consulting or advisory fees from GE or any of its subsidiaries.

8. Meetings of Non-Employee Directors

The board will have at least three regularly scheduled meetings a year for the non-employee directors without management present. The directors have determined that the chairman of the management development and compensation committee will preside at such meetings, and will serve as the presiding director in performing such other functions as the board may direct, including advising on the selection of committee chairs and advising management on the agenda for board meetings. The non-employee directors may meet without management present at such other times as determined by the presiding director.

9. Self-Evaluation

As described more fully in the key practices of the nominating and corporate governance committee, the board and each of the committees will perform an annual self-evaluation. Each November, each director will provide to an independent governance expert his or her assessment of the effectiveness of the board and its committees, as well as director performance and board dynamics. The individual assessments will be organized and summarized by this independent governance expert for discussion with the board and the committees in December.

10. Setting Board Agenda

The board shall be responsible for its agenda. At the December board meeting, the CEO and the presiding director will propose for the board's approval key issues of strategy, risk and integrity to be scheduled and discussed during the course of the next calendar year. Before that meeting, the board will be invited to offer its suggestions. As a result of this process, a schedule of major discussion items for the following year will be established. Prior to each board meeting, the CEO will discuss the other specific agenda items for the meeting with the presiding director, who shall have authority to approve the agenda for the meeting. The CEO and the presiding director, or committee chair as appropriate, shall determine the nature and extent of information that shall be provided regularly to the directors before each scheduled board or committee meeting. Directors are urged to make suggestions for agenda items, or additional pre-meeting materials, to the CEO, the presiding director, or appropriate committee chair at any time.

11. Ethics and Conflicts of Interest

The board expects GE directors, as well as officers and employees, to act ethically at all times and to acknowledge their adherence to the policies comprising GE's code of conduct set forth in the company's integrity manual, "Integrity: The Spirit and the Letter of Our Commitment." GE will not make any personal loans or extensions of credit to directors or executive officers, other than consumer loans or credit card services on terms offered to the general public. No non-employee director may provide personal services for compensation to GE, other than in connection with serving as a GE director. The board will not permit any waiver of any ethics policy for any director or executive officer. If an actual or potential conflict of interest arises for a director, the director shall promptly inform the CEO and the presiding director. If a significant conflict exists and cannot be resolved, the director should resign. All directors will recuse themselves from any discussion or decision affecting their personal, business or professional interests. The board shall resolve any conflict of interest question involving the CEO, a vice chairman or a senior vice president, and the CEO shall resolve any conflict of interest issue involving any other officer of the company.

12. Reporting of Concerns to Non-Employee Directors or the Audit Committee

The audit committee and the non-employee directors have established the following procedures to enable anyone who has a concern about GE's conduct, or any employee who has a complaint about the company's accounting, internal accounting controls or auditing matters, to communicate that concern directly to the presiding director, to the non-employee directors or to the audit committee. Such communications may be confidential or anonymous, and may be e-mailed, submitted in writing or reported by phone to special addresses and a toll-free phone number that are published on the company's website. All such communications shall be promptly reviewed by GE's ombudsman, and any concerns relating to accounting, internal controls, auditing or officer conduct shall be sent immediately to the presiding director and to the chair of the audit committee. All concerns will be reviewed and addressed by GE's ombudsman in the same way that other concerns are addressed by the company. The status of all outstanding concerns addressed to the non-employee directors, the presiding director or the audit committee will be reported to the presiding director and the chair of the audit committee on a quarterly basis. The presiding director or the audit committee chair may direct that certain matters be presented to the audit committee or the full board and may direct special treatment, including the retention of outside advisors or counsel, for any concern addressed to them. The company's integrity manual prohibits any employee from retaliating or taking any adverse action against anyone for raising or helping to resolve an integrity concern.

13. Compensation of the Board

The nominating and corporate governance committee shall have the responsibility for recommending to the board compensation and benefits for non-employee directors. In discharging this duty, the committee shall be guided by three goals: compensation should fairly pay directors for work required in a company of GE's size and scope; compensation should align directors' interests with the long-term interests of shareowners; and the structure of the compensation should be simple, transparent and easy for shareowners to understand. As discussed more fully in the key practices of the nominating and corporate governance committee, the committee believes these goals will be served by providing 40% of non-employee director compensation in cash and 60% in deferred stock units. At the end of each year, the nominating and corporate governance committee shall review non-employee director compensation and benefits.

14. Succession Plan

The board shall approve and maintain a succession plan for the CEO and senior executives, based upon recommendations from the management development and compensation committee.

15. Annual Compensation Review of Senior Management

The management development and compensation committee shall annually approve the goals and objectives for compensating the CEO. That committee shall evaluate the CEO's performance in light of these goals before setting the CEO's salary, bonus and other incentive and equity compensation. The committee shall also annually approve the compensation structure for the company's officers, and shall evaluate the performance of the company's senior executive officers before approving their salary, bonus and other incentive and equity compensation.

16. Access to Senior Management

Non-employee directors are encouraged to contact senior managers of the company without senior corporate management present. To facilitate such contact, non-employee directors are expected to make two regularly scheduled visits to GE businesses a year without corporate management being present.

17. Access to Independent Advisors

The board and its committees shall have the right at any time to retain independent outside auditors and financial, legal or other advisors, and the company shall provide appropriate funding, as determined by the board or any committee, to compensate such independent outside auditors or advisors, as well as to cover the ordinary administrative expenses incurred by the board and its committees in carrying out their duties.

18. Director Education

The general counsel and the chief financial officer shall be responsible for providing an orientation for new directors. Each new director shall, within three months of election to the board, spend a day at corporate headquarters for personal briefing by senior management on the company's strategic plans, its financial statements, and its key policies and practices. In addition, directors shall be provided with continuing education on subjects that would assist them in discharging their duties, including regular programs on GE's financial planning and analysis, compliance and corporate governance developments; business-specific learning opportunities through site visits and Board meetings; and briefing sessions on topics that present special risks and opportunities to the company.

19. Policy on Poison Pills

The term "poison pill" refers to the type of shareowner rights plan that some companies adopt to make a hostile takeover of the company more difficult. GE does not have a poison pill and has no intention of adopting a poison pill because a hostile takeover of a company of our size is impractical and unrealistic. However, if GE were ever to adopt a poison pill, the board would seek prior shareowner approval unless, due to timing constraints or other reasons, a committee consisting solely of independent directors determines that it would be in the best interests of shareowners to adopt a poison pill before obtaining shareowner approval. If the GE board of directors were ever to adopt a poison pill without prior shareowner approval, the board would either submit the poison pill to shareowners for ratification, or would cause the poison pill to expire, without being renewed or replaced, within one year.

5.2.2 Monetary Authority of Singapore: Guidelines and Regulations on Corporate Governance

In February 2003, the Monetary Authority of Singapore (MAS) established principles of corporate governance for the banks and insurers that fall within its regulatory purview. The code, *Guidelines and Regulations on Corporate Governance*,[17] defines and explains corporate governance as:

> . . . The processes and structures by which the business and affairs of an Institution are directed, managed and controlled. [p. 6]

The MAS makes clear that the key element in an effective system of corporate governance rests with the board of directors, and that its primary duties are to shareholders and depositors, or, in the case of an insurer, the policyholders:

> The board of directors is responsible for directing the management of the Institution. Besides its obligations to the shareholders, the board of directors of an Institution has a duty to act in the best interest of the Institution and to ensure that the Institution has sufficient resources to meet its obligations to other stakeholders, in particular a bank's depositors or an insurer's policyholders.

The Monetary Authority of Singapore has the following thirteen principles to guide the banks and insurers within its regulatory authority in compliance with the corporate governance standards in its *Guidelines and Regulations on Corporate Governance:*

Principle 1:   Every Institution should be headed by an effective Board.

Principle 2:   There should be a strong and independent element on the Board which is able to exercise objective judgment on corporate

---

[17] These guidelines expand and build upon the *Code of Corporate Governance,* issued in 2001 by the Corporate Governance Committee, established by the Ministry of Finance, the Authority and the Attorney-General's Chambers.

affairs independently from management and substantial shareholders.

Principle 3:   The Board should set and enforce clear lines of responsibility and accountability throughout the Institution.

Principle 4:   There should be a formal and transparent process for the appointment of new directors to the Board.

Principle 5:   There should be a formal assessment of the effectiveness of the Board as a whole and the contribution by each director to the effectiveness of the Board.

Principle 6:   In order to fulfill their responsibilities, Board members should be provided with complete, adequate and timely information prior to board meetings and on an on-going basis by the management.

Principle 7:   There should be a formal and transparent procedure for fixing the remuneration packages of individual directors. No director should be involved in deciding his own remuneration.

Principle 8:   The level and composition of remuneration should be appropriate to attract, retain and motivate the directors to perform their roles and carry out their responsibilities.

Principle 9:   The Board should establish an Audit Committee with a set of written terms of reference that clearly sets out its authority and duties.

Principle 10:   The Board should ensure that there is an adequate risk management system and sound internal controls.

Principle 11:   The Board should ensure that an internal audit function that is independent of the activities audited is established.

Principle 12:   The Board should ensure that management formulates policies to ensure dealings with the public, the Institution's policyholders and claimants, depositors and other customers are conducted fairly, responsibly and professionally.

Principle 13:   The Board should ensure that related party transactions with the Institution are made on an arm's length basis.

These principles are supported by requirements for extensive disclosures regarding companies' implementation and of the standards and their procedures for continuous monitoring of compliance. It is notable that the Monetary Authority does not require that a majority of the board members be independent, but only that one-third meet such a test.

5.2.3 Organisation for Economic Co-Operation and Development: OECD Principles of Corporate Governance

The Organisation for Economic Co-Operation and Development ("OECD")[18] issued its code, *OECD Principles of Corporate Governance* ("OECD Principles"), which applies to all Member countries. These countries comprise a number of different legislative, regulatory and market systems.

---

[18] Issued in 1999, and subsequently revised, the OECD Principles are intended to be adopted by each of the OECD Member countries, which include: Australia, Austria, Belgium, Canada, the Czech Republic, Denmark, Finland, France, Germany, Greece, Hungary, Iceland, Ireland, Italy, Japan, Korea, Luxembourg, Mexico, the Netherlands, New Zealand, Norway, Poland, Portugal, Spain, Sweden, Switzerland, Turkey, the United Kingdom, and the United States.

The OECD observes that its Principles "represent the first initiative by an inter-governmental organisation to develop the core elements of a good corporate governance regime. As such, the Principles can be used as a benchmark by governments as they evaluate and improve their laws and regulations." The Preface to the OECD Principles states:

> A good corporate governance regime helps to assure that corporations use their capital efficiently. Good corporate governance helps, too, to ensure that corporations take into account the interests of a wide range of constituencies as well as of the communities within which they operate, and that their boards are accountable to the company and the shareholders. This, in turn, helps to assure that corporations operate for the benefit of society as a whole. It helps to maintain the confidence of investors—both foreign and domestic—and to attract more "patient", long-term capital . . . . **Common to all good corporate governance regimes, however, is a high degree of priority placed on the interests of shareholders, who place their trust in corporations to use their investment funds wisely and effectively.** [Emphasis added]

Despite the application of the OECD Principles to a wide variety of regimes, the OECD provides a special emphasis on the rights and fair treatment of shareholders. This characteristic, although considered to be a fundamental requirement for good systems of corporate governance, is not frequently found in either corporate codes or those of other business organizations. For example, the General Electric code is silent on shareholder rights although it acknowledges in the first principle that managers and the directors have an obligation to attend to the interests of shareholders. The Monetary Authority of Singapore's code takes a similar approach.

EXAMPLE 6

OECD Principles of Corporate Governance

I. The Rights of Shareholders

The corporate governance framework should protect shareholders' rights.

A. Basic shareholder rights include the right to: 1) secure methods of ownership registration; 2) convey or transfer shares; 3) obtain relevant information on the corporation on a timely and regular basis; 4) participate and vote in general shareholder meetings; 5) elect members of the board; and 6) share in the profits of the corporation.

B. Shareholders have the right to participate in, and to be sufficiently informed on, decisions concerning fundamental corporate changes such as:

1. Amendments to the statutes, or articles of incorporation or similar governing documents of the company;

2. The authorisation of additional shares; and

3. Extraordinary transactions that in effect result in the sale of the company.

C. Shareholders should have the opportunity to participate effectively and vote in general shareholder meetings and should be informed of the rules, including voting procedures, that govern general shareholder meetings:

1. Shareholders should be furnished with sufficient and timely information concerning the date, location and agenda of general meetings, as well as full and timely information regarding the issues to be decided at the meeting.

2. Opportunity should be provided for shareholders to ask questions of the board and to place items on the agenda at general meetings, subject to reasonable limitations.

3. Shareholders should be able to vote in person or in absentia, and equal effect should be given to votes whether cast in person or in absentia.

D. Capital structures and arrangements that enable certain shareholders to obtain a degree of control disproportionate to their equity ownership should be disclosed.

E. Markets for corporate control should be allowed to function in an efficient and transparent manner.

1. The rules and procedures governing the acquisition of corporate control in the capital markets, and extraordinary transactions such as mergers, and sales of substantial portions of corporate assets, should be clearly articulated and disclosed so that investors understand their rights and recourse. Transactions should occur at transparent prices and under fair conditions that protect the rights of all shareholders according to their class.

2. Anti-take-over devices should not be used to shield management from accountability.

F. Shareholders, including institutional investors, should consider the costs and benefits of exercising their voting rights.

II. The Equitable Treatment of Shareholders

The corporate governance framework should ensure the equitable treatment of all shareholders, including minority and foreign shareholders. All shareholders should have the opportunity to obtain effective redress for violation of their rights.

A. All shareholders of the same class should be treated equally.

1. Within any class, all shareholders should have the same voting rights. All investors should be able to obtain information about the voting rights attached to all classes of shares before they purchase. Any changes in voting rights should be subject to shareholder vote.

2. Votes should be cast by custodians or nominees in a manner agreed upon with the beneficial owner of the shares.

3. Processes and procedures for general shareholder meetings should allow for equitable treatment of all shareholders. Company procedures should not make it unduly difficult or expensive to cast votes.

B. **Insider trading** and abusive self-dealing should be prohibited.

C. Members of the board and managers should be required to disclose any material interests in transactions or matters affecting the corporation.

III. The Role of Stakeholders in Corporate Governance

The corporate governance framework should recognise the rights of stakeholders as established by law and encourage active co-operation between corporations and stakeholders in creating wealth, jobs, and the sustainability of financially sound enterprises.

A. The corporate governance framework should assure that the rights of stakeholders that are protected by law are respected.

B. Where stakeholder interests are protected by law, stakeholders should have the opportunity to obtain effective redress for violation of their rights.

C. The corporate governance framework should permit performance-enhancing mechanisms for stakeholder participation.

D. Where stakeholders participate in the corporate governance process, they should have access to relevant information.

IV. Disclosure and Transparency

The corporate governance framework should ensure that timely and accurate disclosure is made on all material matters regarding the corporation, including the financial situation, performance, ownership, and governance of the company.

A. Disclosure should include, but not be limited to, material information on:

1. The financial and operating results of the company.
2. Company objectives.
3. Major share ownership and voting rights.
4. Members of the board and key executives, and their remuneration.
5. Material foreseeable risk factors.
6. Material issues regarding employees and other stakeholders.
7. Governance structures and policies.

B. Information should be prepared, audited, and disclosed in accordance with high quality standards of accounting, financial and non-financial disclosure, and audit.

C. An annual audit should be conducted by an independent auditor in order to provide an external and objective assurance on the way in which financial statements have been prepared and presented.

D. Channels for disseminating information should provide for fair, timely and cost-efficient access to relevant information by users.

V. The Responsibilities of the Board

The corporate governance framework should ensure the strategic guidance of the company, the effective monitoring of management by the board, and the board's accountability to the company and the shareholders.

A. Board members should act on a fully informed basis, in good faith, with due diligence and care, and in the best interest of the company and the shareholders.

B. Where board decisions may affect different shareholder groups differently, the board should treat all shareholders fairly.

C. The board should ensure compliance with applicable law and take into account the interests of stakeholders.

D. The board should fulfill certain key functions, including:

  1. Reviewing and guiding corporate strategy, major plans of action, risk policy, annual budgets and business plans; setting performance objectives; monitoring implementation and corporate performance; and overseeing major capital expenditures, acquisitions and divestitures.

  2. Selecting, compensating, monitoring and, when necessary, replacing key executives and overseeing succession planning.

  3. Reviewing key executive and board remuneration, and ensuring a formal and transparent board nomination process.

  4. Monitoring and managing potential conflicts of interest of management, board members and shareholders, including misuse of corporate assets and abuse in related party transactions.

  5. Ensuring the integrity of the corporation's accounting and financial reporting systems, including the independent audit, and that appropriate systems of control are in place, in particular, systems for monitoring risk, financial control, and compliance with the law.

  6. Monitoring the effectiveness of the governance practices under which it operates and making changes as needed.

  7. Overseeing the process of disclosure and communications.

E. The board should be able to exercise objective judgement on corporate affairs independent, in particular, from management.

  1. Boards should consider assigning a sufficient number of non-executive board members capable of exercising independent judgement to tasks where there is a potential for conflict of interest. Examples of such key responsibilities are financial reporting, nomination and executive and board remuneration.

  2. Board members should devote sufficient time to their responsibilities.

F. In order to fulfill their responsibilities, board members should have access to accurate, relevant and timely information.

This code, and its predecessor variants, is not only among the earliest efforts to establish guidelines for good governance, but with its global reach has had wide influence on the development of other codes and regulatory frameworks.

ENVIRONMENTAL, SOCIAL, AND GOVERNANCE FACTORS

Investors now understand that nontraditional business factors—specifically, a company's environmental, social, and governance (ESG) risk exposures—may be as critical to the company's long-term sustainability as more traditional concerns. Indeed, many major financial institutions and portfolio managers routinely integrate ESG analyses into their equity valuations and other investment decisions.[19] Those analysts who fail to consider ESG factors in their valuations may well be assuming far greater long-term risks than they or their clients realize.[20]

ESG factors range from those associated with climate change (for example, carbon-based greenhouse gas emissions resulting from a company's operations) to labor rights, public and occupational health issues, and the soundness of the company's governance structures.[21]

The risks resulting from exposure to these various issues include the following:

▶ *Legislative and regulatory risk.* The risk that governmental laws and regulations directly or indirectly affecting a company's operations will change with potentially severe adverse effects on the company's continued profitability and even its long-term sustainability.

For example, in the United States, a law enacted in California in 2004 requires a 30 percent reduction in carbon dioxide emissions by 2016 for all new automobiles sold in the state. Other states, including Connecticut, Maine, Massachusetts, New Jersey, New York, Oregon, Pennsylvania, Rhode Island, Vermont, and Washington, are following California's example.[22] These states currently represent more than half of all U.S. automobile sales. Consequently, manufacturers that fail to meet the standards can expect to suffer a reduction in revenues and earnings as well as market power. Given strong industry competition, the effects of the changes in the laws on companies operating in the industry could be severe.

Other national and global efforts have brought rapid changes in operations for companies in affected countries. For example, the Kyoto Protocol is a 1997 amendment to the United Nations Framework Convention on Climate Change (UNFCCC). The Protocol now covers more than 160 countries, not including the United States and Australia, and over 60 percent of greenhouse gas emissions. The agreement calls for staged reductions in emissions of carbon dioxide and five other greenhouse gases for those countries that have ratified the agreement. The Protocol also provides for emissions credit trading for those signatories, principally in emerging countries, that could not otherwise afford the investment.

Companies in most industries are likely to be affected to at least some degree by these mandated changes, although the effects will vary widely across industries. Even within industries with the greatest exposures, companies that have invested in newer, more up-to-date technologies are

---

[19] See, for example, Miranda Anderson and David Gardiner, *Climate Risk and Energy in the Auto Sector: Guidance for Investors and Analysts on Key Off-balance Sheet Drivers*, Ceres, Inc., 2006.

[20] *The Materiality of Social, Environmental and Corporate Governance Issues to Equity Pricing: 11 Sector Studies by Brokerage House Analysts*, United Nations Environmental Programme Finance Initiative (UNEP FI), Asset Management Working Group. 2004.

[21] Ibid.

[22] Anderson et al., p. 7.

likely to be affected less by the changes than their competitors. Thus, investors who consider ESG factors and who monitor regulatory and legislative developments for the companies they follow will be better equipped to make sound investment decisions.

▶ *Legal risk.* The risk that failures by company managers to effectively manage ESG factors will lead to lawsuits and other judicial remedies, resulting in potentially catastrophic losses for the company.

All areas of ESG can, and sometimes do, lead to such lawsuits. The actions can be brought by employees for workplace issues and contractual defaults, by shareholders for management or director governance or other lapses that impair shareholder value, or by government attorneys for abridgement of federal or state laws.

An investor can begin to analyze the potential for such risks in a particular company by reviewing regulatory filings for the particular jurisdictions in which the company operates. Many such filings, such as the U.S. SEC required disclosures in the Form 10-K Business, Risks, and Legal Proceedings sections, as well as the Management Discussion and Analysis of Financial Condition and Results of Operations, require substantial discussion of possible legal risk exposures. For those companies that provide them, the GRI reports may include useful insights.[23] However, an analyst should make an independent assessment of the company and carefully consider the nature of a company's operations to evaluate the possible scope of such exposures and their potential effects. The business press may also be a good source of information regarding such risks on both the company of immediate interest as well as other companies in the same industry.

▶ *Reputational risk.* This particular source of risk has risen in importance as ESG factors are increasingly recognized as a potentially major source of risk. Specifically, companies whose managers have demonstrated a lack of concern for managing ESG factors in the past, so as to eliminate or otherwise mitigate risk exposures, will suffer a diminution in market value relative to other companies in the same industry that may persist for a long period of time.

▶ *Operating risk.* The risk that a company's operations may be severely affected by ESG factors, even to the requirement that one or more product lines or possibly all operations might be shut down.

An example of such a risk is that deriving from the industrial use of benzene, a powerful carcinogen and one of the most toxic chemicals known. Because of its use as both a building block in the plastics and rubber industry, as well as its more general use as an industrial solvent, benzene was widely used in industry and was dispersed into the air, drinking water, and soil. Billions of pounds of the chemical were produced and used annually.

Once studies confirmed the harmful effects of the chemical, the U.S. Environmental Protection Agency (EPA) moved, for example, under the 1974 Safe Drinking Water Act to set targets for acceptable levels in water. The EPA Maximum Contaminant Level for benzene in drinking water was set at five parts per billion. Thus, companies that had previously relied on extensive use of benzene in their operations had either to modify their operations to ensure that no benzene escaped into the environment, or to cease those operations that used benzene altogether.

---

[23] The Global Reporting Initiative (GRI) promotes systematic reporting of economic, environmental, and social performance. The website for the GRI is www.globalreporting.org.

▶ *Financial risk.* The risk that ESG factors will result in significant costs or other losses to the company and its shareholders. Any of the above sources of risk can affect a company and its financial health, sometimes severely.

In summary, investors are well advised to consider the potential effects of ESG factors on companies in which they invest and to carefully analyze all sources of information relevant to such risk exposures. These analyses may alert the analyst to risk factors that should be incorporated into company valuations.

VALUATION IMPLICATIONS OF CORPORATE GOVERNANCE

7

The relative quality, strength and reliability of a company's corporate governance system have direct and profound implications for investors' assessments of investments and their valuations. As we have seen in the massive corporate collapses in recent years, most or all of an investor's capital can be lost suddenly if a company fails to establish an effective corporate governance system with the appropriate checks and balances.

Weak corporate governance systems pose the following risks to the value of investments in the company:

▶ *Accounting risk.* The risk that a company's financial statement recognition and related disclosures, upon which investors base their financial decisions, are incomplete, misleading, or materially misstated.

▶ *Asset risk.* The risk that the firm's assets, which belong to investors, will be misappropriated by managers or directors in the form of excessive compensation or other perquisites.

▶ *Liability risk.* The risk that management will enter into excessive obligations, committed to on behalf of shareholders, that effectively destroy the value of shareholders' equity; these frequently take the form of off-balance-sheet obligations.

▶ *Strategic policy risk.* The risk that managers may enter into transactions, such as mergers and acquisitions, or incur other business risks, that may not be in the best long-term interest of shareholders, but which may result in large payoffs for management or directors.

Not surprisingly, a growing body of evidence indicates that companies with sound corporate governance systems show higher profitability and investment performance measures, including returns, relative to those assessed to have weaker structures. For example, a joint study of Institutional Shareholder Services (ISS) and Georgia State University[24] found that the best-governed companies, as measured by the ISS Corporate Governance Quotient, generated returns on investment and equity over the period under study that were 18.7 percent and 23.8 percent, respectively, better than those of companies with poor governance. Similarly, a study of U.S. markets, conducted by researchers at

---

[24] Brown, Lawrence D., and Caylor, Marcus, "Corporate Governance Study: The Correlation between Corporate Governance and Company Performance," Institutional Shareholder Services (2004).

Harvard University and the University of Pennsylvania[25] found that portfolios of companies with strong shareholder-rights protections outperformed portfolios of companies with weaker protections by 8.5 percent per year. A study of European firms found annual mean return differences of 3.0 percent.[26]

This phenomenon is not limited to developed markets. Even before the collapse of Enron, a Malaysia-based analyst found that investors in emerging markets overwhelmingly preferred companies with good governance.[27] Of the 100 largest emerging markets companies his firm followed, those with the best governance, based on management discipline, transparency, independence, accountability, responsibility, fairness and social responsibility, generated three-year U.S. dollar returns of 267 percent, compared with average returns of 127 percent. The disparity in five-year returns was even greater, at 930 percent versus an average of 388 percent.

The conclusion from these and other studies is that good corporate governance leads to better results, both for companies and for investors. Therefore, investors and analysts should carefully evaluate the corporate governance structures of companies they are considering as investments and should continue to monitor the systems once the investments are made.

---

[25] Gompers, Paul A., Joy L. Ishii, and Andrew Metrick, "Corporate Governance and Equity Prices," *Quarterly Journal of Economics*, 118(1) (February 2003), 107–155. The authors compared the investment performance of some 1,500 U.S.-listed companies against a corporate governance index the authors constructed from 24 distinct governance rules.

[26] Bauer, Rod, and Nadja Guenster, "Good Corporate Governance Pays Off!: Well-governed companies perform better on the stock market," (2003). This study used Deminor Ratings as the basis for determining companies' relative corporate governance quality (www.deminor.org).

[27] Gill, Amar, "Corporate Governance in Emerging Markets – Saints and Sinners: Who's Got Religion?", CLSA Emerging Markets, April 2001; Gill points out that CLSA assigned corporate governance ratings to 495 companies in 25 markets.

SUMMARY

Corporate governance is an essential concern for investors and investment analysts. This reading has presented the attributes of an effective corporate governance system and the types of practices that should raise investors' concerns. This reading has made the following points:

▶ Corporate governance is the system of principles, policies, procedures, and clearly defined responsibilities and accountabilities, used by stakeholders to eliminate or minimize conflicts of interest.

▶ The objectives of a corporate governance system are (1) to eliminate or mitigate conflicts of interest among stakeholders, particularly between managers and shareholders, and (2) to ensure that the assets of the company are used efficiently and productively and in the best interests of the investors and other stakeholders.

▶ The failure of a company to establish an effective system of corporate governance represents a major operational risk to the company and its investors. To understand the risks inherent in an investment in a company, it is essential to understand the quality of the company's corporate governance practices.

▶ The core attributes of an effective corporate governance system are:

   a. delineation of the rights of shareholders and other core stakeholders;

   b. clearly defined manager and director governance responsibilities to the stakeholders;

   c. identifiable and measurable accountabilities for the performance of the responsibilities;

   d. fairness and equitable treatment in all dealings between managers, directors and shareholders; and

   e. complete transparency and accuracy in disclosures regarding operations, performance, risk and financial position.

▶ The specific sources of conflict in corporate agency relationships are:

   a. Manager-shareholder conflicts. Managers may, for example:
      ▶ use funds to try to expand the size of a business even when this is not in the best interests of shareholders; and
      ▶ grant themselves numerous expensive perquisites which are treated as ordinary business expenses.

   b. Director-shareholder conflicts. Directors may, for example, identify with the managers' interests rather than those of the shareholders as a result of personal or business relationships with the manager.

▶ The responsibilities of board members, both individually and as a group, are to:

   a. establish corporate values and governance structures for the company to ensure that the business is conducted in an ethical, competent, fair, and professional manner;

   b. ensure that all legal and regulatory requirements are met and complied with fully and in a timely fashion;

    c. establish long-term strategic objectives for the company with a goal of ensuring that the best interests of shareholders come first and that the company's obligations to others are met in a timely and complete manner;

    d. establish clear lines of responsibility and a strong system of accountability and performance measurement in all phases of a company's operations;

    e. hire the chief executive officer, determine the compensation package, and periodically evaluate the officer's performance;

    f. ensure that management has supplied the board with sufficient information for it to be fully informed and prepared to make the decisions that are its responsibility, and to be able to adequately monitor and oversee the company's management;

    g. meet regularly to perform its duties and in extraordinary session as required by events; and

    h. acquire adequate training so that members are able to adequately perform their duties.

▶ An investor or investment analyst must assess:

    a. board composition and independence;

    b. whether the chairman of the board is independent;

    c. the qualifications of the directors;

    d. whether the board is elected on an annual or staggered basis;

    e. board self-assessment practices;

    f. the frequency of separate sessions of independent directors;

    g. the audit committee and audit oversight;

    h. the nominating committee;

    i. the compensation committee and compensation awards to management; and

    j. the use (or not) of independent legal and expert counsel.

▶ Companies committed to corporate governance often provide a statement of corporate governance policies. Analysts should assess: the code of ethics; statements of the oversight, monitoring, and review responsibilities of directors; statements of management's responsibilities with respect to information and access of directors to internal company functions; reports of directors' examinations, evaluations, and findings; board and committee self-assessments; management self-assessments; and training policies for directors.

▶ Weak corporate governance systems give rise to risks including accounting risk, asset risk, liability risk, and strategic policy risk. Such risks may compromise the value of investments in the company.

PRACTICE PROBLEMS FOR READING 34

1. Which of the following *best* defines the concept of corporate governance?

   A. A system for monitoring managers' activities, rewarding performance, and disciplining misbehavior.

   B. Identifiable and measurable accountabilities for all stakeholders.

   C. Corporate values and governance structures that ensure the business is conducted in an ethical, competent, fair, and professional manner.

   D. A system of principles, policies, and procedures used to manage and control the activities of a corporation so as to overcome conflicts of interest inherent in the corporate form.

2. Which of the following is an example of a conflict of interest that an effective corporate governance system would mitigate or eliminate?

   A. A majority of the board is independent of management.

   B. Directors who have come to identify with the managers' interests rather than those of the shareholders.

   C. Directors have board experience with companies regarded as having sound governance practices.

   D. The process of performing a periodic self-assessment by directors.

3. Which of the following *best* describes the corporate governance responsibilities of members of the board of directors?

   A. Establish long-term strategic objectives for the company.

   B. Establish global best practice standards for proxy voting.

   C. Ensure that at board meetings no subject is undiscussable and dissent is regarded as an obligation.

   D. Ensure that the board negotiates with the company over all matters such as compensation.

4. Which of the following is *least likely* to be useful in evaluating a company's corporate governance system for investment analysis purposes?

   A. Assess issues related to the board, managers, and shareholders.

   B. Review the company's regulatory filings and financial information provided to shareholders.

   C. Identify any off-balance sheet or insider transactions and determine the company's policies with regard to related party transactions.

   D. Flag items such as egregious use of insider transactions for users of the financial statements.

5. The objectives of an effective system of corporate governance include all of the following *except:*

   A. ensure that the assets of the company are used efficiently and productively.

   B. eliminate or mitigate conflicts of interest among stakeholders.

   C. ensure that the assets of the company are used in the best interests of investors and other stakeholders.

   D. ensure complete transparency in disclosures regarding operations, performance, risk, and financial position.

6. All of the following are core attributes of an effective corporate governance system *except:*

   A. fairness and accuracy in identifying inherent conflicts of interest.

   B. clearly defined governance responsibilities for managers and directors.

   C. identifiable and measurable accountabilities for the performance of responsibilities.

   D. delineation of shareholders and other core stakeholders' rights.

7. All of the following are examples of conflicts of interest that an effective corporate governance system should address *except* relationships between:

   A. managers and shareholders.

   B. directors and shareholders.

   C. managers and directors.

   D. managers and institutional analysts.

8. All of the following are true of an effective system of corporate governance *except:*

   A. the system must be continually monitored especially with changes in management and the board.

   B. a single system of effective corporate governance applies to all firms worldwide.

   C. the failure to establish an effective system of corporate governance to overcome inherent conflicts of interest represents a major operational risk.

   D. there are a number of common characteristics of all sound corporate governance structures.

The following information relates to Questions 9–14

Jane Smith, CFA, has recently joined Zero Asset Management, Inc. (Zero) as a board member. Since Smith is also outside council for Zero Asset Management, she is already very familiar with Zero's operations and expects to begin contributing good ideas right away. Zero is a publicly traded investment management firm that historically focused on mutual fund management. Although there is current market opportunity to add a new type of mutual fund, the board recently decided against adding the fund. Instead, the board decided to expand its business to include a hedge fund operation within the existing corporation.

Bill Week, CEO of Zero, has publicly stated that he is willing to bet the company's future on hedge fund management. Week is the founder of Zero, as well as Chairman of the board, and maintains a controlling interest in the company.

Like the rest of Zero, the firm's new hedge fund is quantitatively driven and index based. The fund has been set up in a separate office with new systems so that the analysts and managers can create a unique hedge fund culture. Trading and execution are the only operations that remain with Zero. The fund is run by one of Zero's most successful portfolio managers.

Smith learns that although none of the board members sit on other companies' boards, most have at one point or another worked at Zero and so they are very familiar with Zero's operations. A board member has attempted to make the health insurance and retirement concerns of the board members an agenda item, without success to date. Smith eagerly anticipates the next board meeting as they are always in a luxurious setting.

The board becomes concerned by Smith's questions and decides to hire an independent consultant to review their corporate governance responsibilities. The consultant starts his analysis by stating that a corporate governance system relies upon checks and balances among managers, directors, and investors. Smith asks if Zero has the proper systems in place. The consultant says that he has looked at conflicts of interest and has one more area to review in order to verify that the board is meeting its major objectives. Concerned about the company's stock price, Smith asks the consultant what work he has done concerning Zero's corporate disclosures for investment professionals. The consultant indicates that he has reviewed Zero's regulatory filings for clear and complete information, as well as the company's policies regarding related party transactions.

9. All of the following indicate Zero's board's lack of independence *except*:
   A. former employment with the company.
   B. personal relationships.
   C. service of the outside counsel as a board member.
   D. lack of inter-locking directorships.

10. Which of the following is the most effective action for the board to take to address their oversight responsibilities concerning the hedge fund's proxy voting?
   A. Establish corporate values and governance structure for the company.
   B. Establish long-term strategic objectives that are met and fully complied with.
   C. Perform adequate training so that employees are able to perform their duties.
   D. Monitor and oversee the company's operations on a daily basis to ensure that all legal and regulatory requirements are met and complied with in a timely manner.

11. Which of the following omissions best describes a corporate governance shortcoming of Zero's board of directors? The board's failure to

   A. address the potential conflicts of interest between managing the firm's hedge fund and its mutual fund business.

   B. make the health insurance and retirement concerns of board members an agenda item.

   C. meet the market opportunity for a new kind of mutual fund.

   D. establish the hedge fund operation in a separate corporation.

12. Given that Zero's directors all previously worked at the company, which of the following would you recommend for a more effective system of corporate governance?

   A. Ensure that assets are used efficiently and productively and in the best interests of investors and stakeholders.

   B. Eliminate or mitigate conflicts of interest among stakeholders, particularly between managers and shareholders.

   C. Identify and measure accountabilities for the performance of the board's responsibilities.

   D. Provide complete transparency and accuracy regarding operations, performance, and financial position.

13. Which of the following best describes the objectives of Zero's board that the consultant has not yet reviewed?

   A. Where board decisions may affect shareholder groups differently, the board should treat all shareholders fairly.

   B. Ensure that the assets of the company are used efficiently and productively and in the best interests of the investors and other stakeholders.

   C. Ensure that material foreseeable risk factors are addressed and considered.

   D. The board should ensure compliance with applicable laws and take into account the interest of stakeholders.

14. Which of the following is the most critical activity that an analyst can engage in to assess the quality of the corporate governance system at Zero, among those that the consultant did not review?

   A. Look for vague references to off balance sheet or insider information.

   B. Identify the responsiveness of the board to shareholder proxy votes.

   C. Clearly identified reporting lines and organizational structure.

   D. Evaluate the quality and extent of financial information provided to investors.

The following information relates to Questions 15–19

Shelley Newcome is the new CEO for a publicly traded financial services company, Asset Management Co. (AMC). Newcome is new to the corporate governance requirements of a publicly traded company, as she previously worked for a family office that invested in private equity.

AMC's board meets irregularly, but has decided to convene to give board members an opportunity to meet Newcome. At the board meeting, the company's first in six months, she asks a director what the objectives of corporate governance should be. The director tells her that the most important objective he can think of is to eliminate or mitigate conflicts of interest among stakeholders.

One of Newcome's first steps as CEO is to fly to New York City in order to address a group of Wall Street analysts. Newcome is happy to discover that AMC provides her, and other senior management, with a company jet to attend such meetings.

At the opening of the meeting, Newcome is surprised to hear that most of the analysts are extremely interested in learning about AMC's corporate governance system. One analyst indicates that he has studied several of AMC's competitors and found that they share a set of critical and core attributes. The analyst goes on to note that like its competitors, AMC has included in its corporate governance system the following attributes: the rights of shareholders and other core stakeholders are clearly delineated; there is complete transparency and accuracy in disclosures regarding operations, performance, risk, and financial position; and identifiable and measurable accountabilities for the performance of responsibilities. The analyst also says that in order to verify that the board is meeting its major objectives he has looked at AMC's conflicts of interest and has one more area to review.

Newcome then asks the analyst why his corporate governance evaluation of AMC is so important. The analyst responds by saying that his decision whether or not to invest in AMC, and ultimately the long-term performance of the company, is dependent upon the quality of AMC's managers' decisions and the skill they use in applying sound management practices.

Closing the meeting, Newcome is delayed by one analyst who complains about the difficulties of flying these days and how he has to get to the airport hours ahead of time. The analyst goes on to say that he reviewed AMC's regulatory filings and was happy to see that the company does not spend its money on frivolous perquisites like executive jets.

---

15. Which of the following would *best* complete the objectives of corporate governance for the CEO?

A. Ensure that assets of the company are used efficiently and productively and in the best interests of investors and other stakeholders.

B. Clearly define governance responsibilities for both managers and directors.

C. Evaluate the quality of corporate governance of a company prior to investing or working for that company.

D. Establish clear lines of responsibility and a strong system of accountability and performance measurement in all phases of a company's operations.

16. On the basis of the Wall Street analyst's comments about AMC's corporate governance system, which of the following would be most effective for AMC to attract investors' interest?

   A. Implement a corporate governance system in which business activity is encouraged and rewarded, and that leads to innovation.

   B. Establish a corporate governance system that overcomes inherent conflicts of interest since they represent a major operational risk to investors and the continued existence of the company.

   C. Provide full transparency of all material information on a timely basis to all investment analysts.

   D. Deal fairly with all stakeholders, including investors and creditors.

17. Which of the following is a core attribute that the Wall Street analyst left out of his analysis of AMC?

   A. Corporate governance systems rely on checks and balances among managers, directors, and investors.

   B. Fairness in all dealings between managers, directors, and shareholders.

   C. Clearly defined governance responsibilities for the managers and directors.

   D. Both B and C.

18. Based on the information provided in the case, which of the following corporate disclosures could investment professionals use to evaluate the quality of the corporate governance system at AMC?

   A. Inclusion of all vague references to off-balance sheet or insider transactions in board minutes.

   B. Failure to disclose executive perquisites such as the use of corporate jets by senior management.

   C. Provide other compensation that has not been disclosed to investment analysts.

   D. Prior approval by the board of directors of all transactions and a statement that such transactions are consistent with company policy.

19. Which of the following is an example of a corporate governance responsibility that AMC's board of directors has failed to meet?

   A. Ensure that the board adequately monitors and oversees the company's management.

   B. Ensure that management has supplied the board with sufficient information for it to be fully informed.

   C. Meet regularly to perform its duties.

   D. Require adequate training so that members will be able to perform their duties.

Questions 20–25 relate to Bobby Lee and are based on Readings 32 and 34

Bobby Lee is an equity analyst for the U.S. investment management firm Larocque & Frères. Larocque & Frères has a substantial ownership stake in Skylark Industries, a U.S.-based company that operates in several business segments related to defense.

Lee is reviewing the corporate governance standards at Skylark and how they may affect the firm's valuation. After extensive conversations with Skylark's chief financial officer, Doreen Miller, he summarizes the attributes of Skylark's governance system as:

1. Defining the rights of shareholders relative to bondholders, suppliers, customers, and employees.

2. Outlining specific responsibilities toward stakeholders that managers and directors must fulfill.

3. Specifying how managers and directors will be held accountable for meeting their responsibilities.

4. Separating the roles of chairman and chief executive officer.

Lee is aware that weak corporate governance systems pose risks to the value of investments in the form of accounting risk, asset risk, liability risk, and strategic policy risk. He is considering whether Skylark's frequent acquisitions and extensive use of operating leases, respectively, represent examples of these risks.

Lee is also interested in determining whether Skylark's capital structure is optimal. He asks the director of research, "Does the 'optimal capital structure' result in the lowest beta, the lowest cost of equity, the highest earnings per share, or the lowest weighted average cost of capital?"

Using various sources, Lee estimates Skylark's costs of debt and equity for various capital structures, shown in Exhibit 1. Currently, Skylark has a market capitalization of $2 billion of debt and $8 billion of equity. The income tax rate is 36 percent.

EXHIBIT 1	Skylark Industries Estimated Costs of Capital for Various Capital Structures			
Weight of Debt at Market Value (%)	Weight of Equity at Market Value (%)	Pretax Cost of Debt (%)	Cost of Equity (%)	Weighted Average Cost of Capital (%)
10	90	5.3	9.7	—
20	80	5.5	10.0	—
30	70	6.0	10.5	—
40	60	6.7	11.2	8.44
50	50	7.5	12.0	8.40
60	40	8.6	13.2	8.58
70	30	10.0	15.0	8.98

Note: Current capital structure (indicated in italics) is $2 billion of debt, $8 billion of equity.

During a shareholder conference call, Miller states that the company's objective is to minimize the weighted average cost of capital. She describes four possible corporate actions. Use an amount equal to half of its net income to:

1. initiate a dividend;

2. repurchase shares; or

3. reduce existing debt.

Alternatively,

4. implement a stock split.

After the conference call, Lee decides that Skylark should raise an additional $1 billion of debt and use the proceeds to repurchase common shares.

Lee also thinks that distributing an amount equal to half of its net income as a dividend may change Skylark's leading P/E. Miller responds, "Skylark's competitors that pay a dividend appear to benefit from a 100 basis point reduction in cost of equity, regardless of capital structure. I assume Skylark's cost of equity would decline by the same amount if it initiates a dividend." Lee estimates that Skylark's long-term earnings and dividend growth rate is 7.0 percent.

20. Of the four attributes summarized by Lee, which is *not* a requirement of an effective corporate governance system?

    A. Attribute #1.

    B. Attribute #2.

    C. Attribute #3.

    D. Attribute #4.

21. Skylark's frequent acquisitions and extensive use of operating leases *best* represent which of the following risks?

	Frequent Acquisitions	Extensive Use of Operating Leases
A.	Asset	Asset
B.	Asset	Liability
C.	Strategic Policy	Asset
D.	Strategic Policy	Liability

22. The director of research's *best* response to Lee's question about the optimal capital structure is

    A. lowest beta.

    B. lowest cost of equity.

    C. highest earnings per share.

    D. lowest weighted average cost of capital.

23. Given its objective and the four possible corporate actions, Skylark is *least likely* to select

   A. corporate action #1.

   B. corporate action #2.

   C. corporate action #3.

   D. corporate action #4.

24. If Skylark implements Lee's proposal to issue $1 billion of debt and use the proceeds to repurchase common shares, its weighted average cost of capital following the buyback will *most likely*

   A. increase to 8.50%.

   B. increase to 8.70%.

   C. decrease to 8.50%.

   D. decrease to 8.70%.

25. Given Skylark's current capital structure and Miller's assumption about the dividend's effect on the cost of equity, initiating a dividend will result in a price-to-earnings multiple *closest* to

   A. 16.7.

   B. 20.0.

   C. 25.0.

   D. 29.4.

$4\frac{5}{8}$

$5\frac{1}{2}$ $5\frac{1}{2}$ $- \frac{3}{8}$

$5\frac{1}{2}$ $2^{13}\!/_{16}$ $- \frac{1}{16}$

$20\frac{5}{8}$ $21^{3}\!/_{16}$ $+ \frac{7}{8}$

$17\frac{3}{8}$ $18\frac{1}{8}$ $+$

$18\frac{1}{2}$ $6\frac{1}{2}$ $6\frac{1}{2}$ $- \frac{1}{2}$

$7\frac{1}{4}$ $6\frac{1}{2}$ $3^{1}\!/_{32}$ $- \frac{1}{8}$

$^{15}\!/_{16}$ $^{9}\!/_{16}$

$^{9}\!/_{16}$ $^{9}\!/_{16}$

$^{9}\!/_{32}$ $7^{13}\!/_{16}$ $7^{15}\!/_{16}$

$7^{15}\!/_{16}$ $2^{11}\!/_{32}$ $2\frac{1}{2}$ $+$

$2\frac{5}{8}$ $2\frac{1}{4}$ $2\frac{1}{4}$

$2\frac{3}{4}$ $11\frac{3}{8}$ $11\frac{3}{4}$ $+$

$6\frac{1}{8}$ $12^{1}\!/_{16}$ 33 $33^{1}\!/_{16}$ $-$

87 $33\frac{3}{4}$

$25\frac{5}{8}$ $24^{9}\!/_{16}$ $25\frac{3}{8}$ $+$

$6\frac{1}{2}$ 12 $11\frac{5}{8}$ $11\frac{7}{8}$ $+$

833 16 $10\frac{1}{2}$ $10\frac{1}{2}$ $10\frac{1}{2}$ $-$

78 $15\frac{5}{8}$ $15^{13}\!/_{16}$ $15\frac{3}{4}$ $-$

4508 $9^{1}\!/_{16}$ $8\frac{1}{4}$ $8\frac{1}{4}$

430 $11\frac{1}{4}$ $10\frac{1}{8}$ $10\frac{1}{8}$

5 $4\frac{1}{8}$

MERGERS AND ACQUISITIONS

by Rosita P. Chang and Keith M. Moore

LEARNING OUTCOMES

The candidate should be able to:

a. categorize merger and acquisition (M&A) activities based on forms of integration and types of mergers;

b. explain the common motivations behind M&A activity;

c. illustrate how earnings per share (EPS) bootstrapping works and calculate a company's post-merger EPS;

d. discuss the relation between merger motivations and types of mergers based on industry lifecycles;

e. contrast merger transaction characteristics by form of acquisition, method of payment, and attitude of target management;

f. distinguish and describe pre-offer and post-offer takeover defense mechanisms;

g. summarize U.S. antitrust legislation;

h. calculate the Hirfendahl-Hirschman Index (HHI) and evaluate the likelihood of an antitrust challenge for a given business combination;

i. compare and contrast the three major methods for valuing a target company including the advantages and disadvantages of each;

j. calculate free cash flows for a target company and estimate the company's intrinsic value based upon discounted cash flow analysis;

k. estimate the intrinsic value of a company using comparable company analysis;

l. estimate the intrinsic value of a company using comparable transaction analysis;

m. evaluate a merger bid, calculate the estimated post-merger value of an acquirer, and calculate the gains accrued to the target shareholders versus the acquirer shareholders;

n. explain the effects of price and payment method on the distribution of risks and benefits in a merger transaction;

o. describe the empirical evidence related to the distribution of benefits in a merger;

p. define, compare, and contrast divestitures, equity carve-outs, spin-offs, split-offs, and liquidation;

q. discuss the major reasons for divestitures.

245

1

INTRODUCTION

Companies enter into merger and acquisition activities for a variety of reasons. Many companies use mergers as a means to achieve growth. Others seek to diversify their businesses. In all cases, it is important for corporate executives and analysts to understand both the motives for mergers and their financial and operational consequences.

Merger and acquisition (M&A) activities involve a variety of complexities and risks. For the case described in Example 1, corporate managers, investors, regulators, and a bevy of advisers—including investment bankers, financial analysts, lawyers, and accountants—each evaluated the various offers from a variety of perspectives.

EXAMPLE 1

Guidant–Boston Scientific Merger

On 15 December 2004, Guidant Corporation (GDT), a manufacturer of heart defibrillators and other specialized medical equipment, agreed to merge with Johnson & Johnson (JNJ), a large, multinational producer of medical products and equipment. Guidant shareholders were to receive $30.40 in cash and $45.60 in JNJ stock (subject to conditions) per share of Guidant stock held. Although a merger such as the combination between GDT and JNJ normally would take about fours months to complete, unanticipated events caused the planned merger transaction to become a year-long saga.

While the companies worked to obtain the required regulatory clearances, a number of investigative articles exposing problems with GDT's defibrillators appeared in the *New York Times* in the spring of 2005. The company issued notices to physicians who prescribed the company's products warning them of potential problems with various defibrillator models. During the summer of 2005, GDT removed some defibrillators from the market as it tried to correct the technical problems. Meanwhile, numerous liability suits were filed against the company, and GDT subsequently lost a significant portion of its sales. Because of these negative developments, JNJ sought to renegotiate the terms of the transaction claiming that the "material adverse change" clause in the merger agreement had been violated.[1]

GDT held that the loss of business did not violate the "material adverse change" clause. After initially filing a lawsuit in the U.S. District Court in an attempt to force JNJ to adhere to the original agreement, GDT later decided to enter into negotiations with JNJ to see if the two companies could agree on an acceptable modified agreement. In November 2005, the two companies agreed to modify the consideration

---

[1] Many merger and acquisition agreements include provisions for renegotiation or cancellation following events that have a significant negative effect on the company's value or business operations.

that JNJ would pay GDT shareholders. In the new agreement, GDT shareholders were to receive $33.25 in cash and 0.493 shares of JNJ stock for each share of GDT held. With JNJ stock trading at a price of about $62.00 in November 2005, the total value of the deal to GDT shareholders was about $63.82 per share of GDT held, which was a significantly lower merger price than in the original agreement.

Shortly after the modified merger agreement was announced, the chairman of another medical device manufacturer, Boston Scientific Corporation (BSX), contacted the chairman of GDT and indicated an interest in pursuing a business combination as an alternative to the JNJ merger. Because of the existing GDT–JNJ merger agreement, Guidant's legal advisers reminded the company's managers that they were prevented from entering into any competing merger discussions unless there was a merger proposal that could be deemed "superior" to the JNJ offer. As a result, on 5 December 2005, BSX communicated an offer to acquire GDT for $36 in cash and $36 in BSX common stock (subject to various conditions).

Although JNJ had fought for many months to acquire GDT at a reduced price, within a month, it improved the price it was willing to pay for GDT. A bidding war was under way. On 11 January 2006, JNJ's offer was for $37.25 in cash and 0.493 shares of JNJ stock—an increase of $4 in cash. The following day, BSX responded by increasing its offer to a total of $73—$36.50 in cash and $36.50 in stock plus $0.012 interest per day for every day after 1 April that the merger was not completed. By offering compensation for any delay past 1 April, BSX sought to reassure any shareholders who might otherwise decline the offer out of concerns that antitrust objections might delay completion of the merger.

JNJ responded the next day, on 13 January, by increasing its offer to $40.52 in cash and 0.493 shares of JNJ stock. Although some believed that the auction was over, BSX was not done. On 15 January 2006, BSX increased its offer to $42 in cash and $38 in BSX stock for a total of $80. The two companies entered into a definitive merger agreement, the agreement with JNJ was terminated, and the GDT–BSX merger was ultimately completed in April 2006.

Despite all the legal issues and product liability problems, a competitive bidding war resulted in a more lucrative merger consideration for Guidant shareholders, who ultimately received $4.00 more than the original JNJ merger proposal.

This reading will discuss many of the issues brought forth in Example 1, such as the forms of payment in a merger, legal and contractual issues, and the necessity for regulatory approval. More importantly, this reading aims to equip you with the basic tools for analyzing M&A deals and the companies behind them. In subsequent sections, we will discuss the motives behind business combinations, various transaction characteristics of M&A deals, the regulations governing M&A activity, and how to evaluate a target company and a proposed merger. Section 2 discusses the basic types of mergers. Section 3 examines the common motives that drive merger activities. In Section 4, we consider various transaction characteristics and their impact on different facets of M&A deals. Section 5 focuses on takeovers and the common defenses used to defeat unwelcome takeover attempts. In Section 6, we outline the various regulations that apply to M&A activity. Section 7 explores methods for analyzing a target company and provides a framework for analyzing merger bids. In Section 8, we review the empirical evidence related to the distribution of gains in mergers. Section 9 provides a brief introduction to corporate restructuring activities, and we conclude the reading with a summary.

2   MERGERS AND ACQUISITIONS: DEFINITIONS AND CLASSIFICATIONS

Business combinations come in different forms. A distinction can be made between acquisitions and mergers. In the context of M&A, an **acquisition** is the purchase of some portion of one company by another. An acquisition might refer to the purchase of assets from another company, the purchase of a definable segment of another entity, such as a subsidiary, or the purchase of an entire company, in which case the acquisition would be known as a merger. A **merger** represents the absorption of one company by another. That is, one of the companies remains and the other ceases to exist as a separate entity. Typically, the smaller of the two entities is merged into the larger, but that is not always the case.

Mergers can be classified by the form of integration. In a **statutory merger**, one of the companies ceases to exist as an identifiable entity and all its assets and liabilities become part of the purchasing company. In a **subsidiary merger**, the company being purchased becomes a subsidiary of the purchaser, which is often done in cases where the company being purchased has a strong brand or good image among consumers that the acquiring company wants to retain. A **consolidation** is similar to a statutory merger except that in a consolidation, *both* companies terminate their previous legal existence and become part of a newly formed company. A consolidation is common in mergers where both companies are approximately the same size.

The parties to a merger are often identified as the target company and the acquiring company. The company that is being acquired is the **target company**, or simply the **target**. The company acquiring the target is called the **acquiring company**, or the **acquirer**. We will use this terminology throughout the reading.

In practice, many of the terms used to describe various types of transactions are used loosely such that the distinctions between them are blurred. For example, the term "consolidation" is often applied to transactions where the entities are about the same size, even if the transaction is technically a statutory merger. Similarly, mergers are often described more generally as **takeovers**, although that term is often reserved to describe **hostile transactions**, which are attempts to acquire a company against the wishes of its managers and board of directors. A **friendly transaction**, in contrast, describes a potential business combination that is endorsed by the managers of both companies, although that is certainly no guarantee that the merger will ultimately occur.

An additional way that mergers are classified is based on the relatedness of the merging companies' business activities. Considered this way, there are three basic types of mergers: horizontal, vertical, and conglomerate.

A **horizontal merger** is one in which the merging companies are in the same kind of business, usually as competitors. The Vodafone AirTouch acquisition of telecommunications competitor Mannesmann AG in 2000 is one example of a horizontal merger. Another example is the merger of Mobil and Exxon in 1999. One of the great motivators behind horizontal mergers is the pursuit of economies of scale, which are savings achieved through the consolidation of operations and elimination of duplicate resources. Another common reason for horizontal mergers is to increase market power, because the merger results in a reduction of the number of industry competitors and an increase in the size of the acquiring company.

In a **vertical merger**, the acquirer buys another company in the same production chain, for example, a supplier or a distributor. In addition to cost savings, a vertical merger may provide greater control over the production process in terms of quality or procurement of resources or greater control over the distribution of the acquirer's finished goods. If the acquirer purchases a target that is ahead of it in the value chain (a supplier), it is called **backward integration**. An example of backward integration is if a steel manufacturer purchases an iron ore mining company. When an acquirer purchases a company that is further down the **value chain** (a distributor), it is called **forward integration**. An example of forward integration is Merck & Co.'s 1993 acquisition of Medco Containment Services, a marketer of discount prescription medicines. The merger brought together the production and distribution of pharmaceuticals into one integrated company.

When an acquirer purchases another company that is unrelated to its core business, it may be called a **conglomerate merger**. General Electric is an example of a conglomerate, having purchased companies in a wide range of industries, including media, finance, home appliances, aircraft parts, and medical equipment. Conglomerate mergers were particularly popular from the 1960s through the 1980s. The concept of company-level diversification was commonly used as a rationale for inter-industry mergers during this period. By investing in companies from a variety of industries, companies hoped to reduce the volatility of the conglomerate's total cash flows. As we will discuss in the section on merger motivations, company-level diversification is not necessarily in the shareholders' best interests.

EXAMPLE 2

History of U.S. Merger Activity

The history of merger activity in the United States illustrates the various types of M&A combinations. Merger and acquisition activities have historically been clustered in waves. The predominant types of mergers and the structures of merger deals have varied with each wave, typically as a result of differences in the regulatory environment. Similarly, the industries involved tend to vary by wave. Merger activity is apt to be concentrated in a relatively small number of industries, usually those going through dramatic changes, such as deregulation or rapid technological advancement.

First Wave (1897–1904)

At the close of the 1800s, growth in the railroads linked regional markets and created an environment conducive to larger companies that could capitalize on the emerging national U.S. economy, particularly within the mining and manufacturing industries. A relatively lax regulatory environment contributed to the situation, and many horizontal mergers resulted in near monopolistic conditions in several industries. The wave ended in 1904 as a result of a landmark decision by the U.S. Supreme Court limiting horizontal mergers among large competitors.

Second Wave (1916–1929)

In the 1920s, motor vehicles and radio coupled with improved railroad infrastructure further bolstered the U.S. economy. Like the previous wave, the second wave was accompanied by a sharp increase in stock prices. This time, however, the regulatory environment was less friendly to horizontal combinations and more sensitive to market power. Because market power was already concentrated among a few companies and further horizontal integration was difficult, companies sought to integrate backward into supply and forward into distribution through vertical mergers. Consequently, business combinations in this wave tended to create oligopolies. This second wave came to a conclusion with the 1929 stock market crash.

Third Wave (1965–1969)

The third wave occurred in a regulatory environment that strongly discouraged any merger—horizontal or vertical—that would reduce competition within an industry. Companies seeking to expand thus looked outside their own industries and began forming conglomerates. Many of the conglomerates created during this period subsequently underperformed the market. The third merger wave ended in 1969 as antitrust enforcement curtailed the rise of conglomerates.

Fourth Wave (1981–1989)

The regulatory environment in the 1980s was friendlier to both horizontal and vertical mergers than it had been in the 1960s, but what really fueled business combinations during this period was the development of the high-yield bond market, which benefited as falling interest rates and rising stock prices created an environment conducive to the greater use of leverage.

Although hostile takeovers were nothing new, increased ability to tap the high-yield bond market put the capacity to finance a takeover in the hands of people and companies that otherwise might not have had access to the necessary capital. This period was marked by the rise of the corporate raider and increasingly sophisticated takeover attempts (and defenses). A **corporate raider** is a person or organization seeking to profit by acquiring a company and reselling it.[2] As the 1980s came to a close, the stock market and economy softened, bringing the fourth wave to its conclusion.

Fifth Wave (1992–2001)

Following the 1990–91 recession, merger activity increased in 1992 and intensified throughout the decade. A strong and long-running bull market created many companies with high market valuations, which were then more easily able to use their equity to purchase other

---

[2] As we will point out later in the section on takeover defenses, in some circumstances a corporate raider can profit from an unsuccessful takeover attempt. It was common during this merger wave for companies to pay raiders a premium in exchange for the raider terminating the attempted takeover, a tactic commonly referred to as "greenmail." Indeed, many raiders initiated takeover attempts without expecting to complete the acquisition.

companies; thus, stock-swap mergers became more common during this wave. Additionally, during the latter half of the 1990s, U.S. regulators were more open to industry consolidation as merger waves in Europe and Asia created larger international competitors. Deregulation and technological advancement further fueled merger activity, particularly in banking, health care, defense, and telecommunications. The fifth wave ended with a dramatic decline in transactions in 2001 as the market and the economy waned following the end of the internet bubble of the late 1990s.

Sixth Wave (2003–Present)

Based on M&A industry statistics, such as M&A deal volume, it appears that we are in the midst of a sixth wave that began in 2003. After a sharp decline in the number of M&A deals directly following the conclusion of the fifth wave in 2001, the market began to pick up again in 2003 and strengthened rapidly through 2004. The number of transactions increased again in 2005 and surpassed the transaction volume records set at the height of the internet bubble to reach a new all-time high. As in the fifth wave, there has been much industry consolidation in the sixth wave, which is producing larger companies that are better able to compete globally.

MOTIVES FOR MERGER   3

In the previous section, we mentioned some of the basic motives behind mergers, such as the search for economies of scale (in a horizontal merger) or cost savings through integration (in a vertical merger). In this section, we will expand on this topic and survey some of the reasons companies merge—the motives or rationales for merger.

The topic is important because in assessing a proposed combination, investors and analysts need to carefully evaluate the rationale behind the merger. Does the stated rationale make sense? Is the merger likely to create value? What is the probability that each of the stated goals for the merger will be attained? Keep in mind that many motives are interrelated and that there are typically several motives, both acknowledged and tacit, behind any given merger.

3.1 Synergy

Among the most common motivations for a merger is the creation of **synergy**, in which the whole of the combined company will be worth more than the sum of its parts. Generally speaking, synergies created through a merger will either reduce costs or enhance revenues. Cost synergies are typically achieved through economies of scale in research and development, procurement, manufacturing, sales and marketing, distribution, and administration. Revenue synergies are created through the cross-selling of products, expanded market share, or higher prices arising from reduced competition. For example, a bank that acquires its competitors can both increase its market share and realize operating efficiencies by closing duplicate branches and integrating back-office operations.

3.2 Growth

Corporate managers are under constant pressure to grow their companies' revenues, and they often turn to M&A activity to achieve that growth. Companies can grow either by making investments internally (i.e., **organic growth**) or by buying the necessary resources externally (i.e., **external growth**). It is typically faster for companies to grow externally. Growth through M&A activity is common when a company is in a mature industry. For example, the global oil industry is a mature industry, and BP, Exxon Mobil, and Chevron Corporation have increased their reserves and output by acquiring smaller competitors.

External growth can also mitigate risk. It is considered less risky to merge with an existing company than to enter an unfamiliar market and establish the resources internally. The last several years of the fifth merger wave in the 1990s were characterized by a surge in cross-border M&A transactions, many of which were motivated by the desire to establish footholds in international markets.

3.3 Increasing Market Power

In industries where there are few competitors or where market share is sufficiently concentrated, horizontal integration may be a means by which to increase market power. When a company increases its market power through horizontal mergers, it may have a greater ability to influence market prices. Taken to an extreme, horizontal integration results in a monopoly.

Vertical integration may also result in increased market power. Vertical mergers can lock in a company's sources of critical supplies or create captive markets for its products. Imagine, for example, an industry in which one company supplies raw materials to two separate manufacturing companies. If one of the manufacturers were to acquire the raw materials provider, the acquirer would be in a position to influence industry output and ultimately prices. As we will discuss further in the section on antitrust regulation, government regulators routinely block both horizontal and vertical mergers that sufficiently reduce competition in an industry and concentrate market power in the hands of too few companies.

3.4 Acquiring Unique Capabilities and Resources

Many companies undertake a merger or an acquisition either to pursue competitive advantages or to shore up lacking resources. When a company cannot cost-effectively create internally the capabilities needed to sustain its future success, it may seek to acquire them elsewhere. For example, a company may engage in M&A activity in order to acquire specific competencies or resources it lacks, such as a strong research department, nimble sales force, intellectual capital, or creative talent.

3.5 Diversification

Companies sometimes cite diversification as one of the motives behind a merger. Indeed, this was an especially popular motive for conglomerates during the third merger wave. The idea behind company-level diversification is that the company can be treated as a portfolio of investments in other companies. If a conglomerate invests in companies from a variety of industries, then the variability of the conglomerate's total cash flows should be reduced, at least to the extent that the industries are uncorrelated.

Although this may seem like a rational motive, typically, it is not in the best interests of the conglomerate's shareholders. In a well-functioning capital market, investors can diversify their own portfolios more easily and at less expense. Additionally, the desire to diversify has led some companies to lose sight of their major competitive strengths and to expand into businesses where they lack comparative advantages.

3.6 Bootstrapping Earnings

Even when there are no reasons to believe that synergies or growth would result from a merger, it is possible to create the illusion of synergies or growth. When a company's earnings increase as a consequence of the merger transaction itself (rather than because of resulting economic benefits of the combination), it is referred to as the "bootstrap effect" or "**bootstrapping earnings**." The bootstrap effect occurs when the shares of the acquirer trade at a higher **price–earnings ratio** (P/E) than those of the target and the acquirer's P/E does not decline following the merger.

EXAMPLE 3

Bootstrapping Earnings

Assume two companies are planning a merger. Company A is the acquirer, Company T is the target, and Company A* is the post-merger combination of the two companies. The companies' stock prices and earnings per share are as shown below. Note that the acquirer has a P/E of 25.0 and the target has a P/E of 20.0:

	A	T	A*
Stock price	$100.00	$50.00	
EPS	$4.00	$2.50	$4.20
P/E	25.0	20.0	
Total shares outstanding	100,000	50,000	125,000
Total earnings	$400,000	$125,000	$525,000
Market value of equity	$10,000,000	$2,500,000	

Given its stock price, the acquirer can issue 25,000 of its own shares and use the proceeds to buy the target company. This amount is determined by dividing the target's market value by the acquirer's stock price ($2,500,000/$100 = 25,000). The total shares outstanding of the merged company will be 125,000—the acquirer's initial 100,000 shares plus the 25,000 shares that the acquirer issued to purchase the target. After the merger, the company's combined earnings are divided by the number of shares outstanding to determine the new EPS ($525,000/125,000 = $4.20), which is $0.20 higher per share than the acquirer would have reported without the merger.

> If the acquirer's pre-merger stock price had been $80 instead of $100, then A's pre-merger P/E would have been 20.0 ($80/$4.00). Under that scenario, the acquirer would have issued 31,250 shares to purchase the target. The EPS of the merged company would then have been $525,000/131,250 = $4.00, thus illustrating that for bootstrapping to work, the acquirer's P/E must be higher than the target's P/E.

If the market is efficient, the post-merger P/E should adjust to the weighted average of the two companies' contributions to the merged company's earnings. In the previous example, the P/E of the merged company would be about 23.8, which implies that the acquirer's stock price would remain at $100. If, however, the acquiring company's P/E is higher than the target's and management can convince investors to value the merged company using the acquirer's pre-merger P/E, then the stock price of the new company should rise. If the acquirer bootstraps earnings to $4.20 per share as shown in the example above, then the share price should increase to $105 if investors apply the pre-merger P/E of 25.0 times earnings ($4.20 × 25.0 = $105). When there are no expected gains from synergy or other factors, such share price increases are not expected.

The market usually recognizes the bootstrapping effect, and post-merger P/Es adjust accordingly. But there have been periods when bootstrapping seemed to pay off for managers, at least in the short run. During the third merger wave, many conglomerates benefited from bootstrapping as investors grappled with how to value these diversified corporate behemoths. Likewise, during the internet bubble of the late 1990s, many high P/E companies bootstrapped their earnings and showed continuous EPS growth through a constant string of mergers with lower P/E companies.

3.7 Managers' Personal Incentives

Various managerial-related theories for mergers have been developed over the years based on evidence of agency problems. **Managerialism theories** posit that because executive compensation is highly correlated with company size, corporate executives are motivated to engage in mergers to maximize the size of their company rather than shareholder value. Additionally, corporate executives may be motivated by self-aggrandizement. For example, being the senior executive of a large company conveys greater power and more prestige.

3.8 Tax Considerations

It is possible for a profitable acquirer to benefit from merging with a target that has accumulated a large amount of tax losses. Instead of carrying the tax losses forward, the merged company would use the tax losses to immediately lower its tax liability. In many countries, the taxing authority disallows an offset in cases where the primary reason for the merger is tax avoidance. Mergers are typically conducted for a variety of reasons, however, and it is difficult for regulatory authorities to prove that tax considerations are a primary motivator.

3.9 Unlocking Hidden Value

A potential target company may be uncompetitive over a sustained period for a host of reasons, including poor management, lack of resources, high legacy costs, or poor organizational structure. In those instances, when a potential target is underperforming, an acquirer may believe it can acquire the company cheaply and then unlock hidden value through reorganization, better management, or synergy. If the target has been underperforming significantly, the acquirer may even believe it can obtain the company for less than its breakup value. A company's **breakup value** is the value that can be achieved if a company's assets are divided and sold separately.

Sometimes mergers are conducted because the acquirer believes that it is purchasing assets for below their **replacement cost**. For example, a pharmaceutical company may believe it can acquire another company's research more cheaply than to undergo a lengthy development process of its own. Or, an oil company may believe it will be less expensive to acquire another oil company's assets than to find and develop additional reserves of its own.

3.10 Cross-Border Motivations

The growth of cross-border deals was high during the 1990s, and foreign M&A became a popular strategic tool for multinational companies seeking to extend their market reach, acquire new manufacturing facilities, develop new sources of raw materials, and tap into the capital markets. Given the increasing international privatization trends, reduction in cumbersome industry regulations and bureaucracy, and development of uniform accounting standards, cross-border mergers and acquisitions will likely intensify in the future. In addition to the various factors that drive domestic mergers, cross-border mergers can provide an efficient way of achieving other international business goals.

3.10.1 Exploiting Market Imperfections

Cross-border transactions can enable companies to more fully exploit market imperfections. For example, to take advantage of differences in the relative cost of labor, a manufacturer may purchase a company in a country where the relative cost of labor is lower.

3.10.2 Overcoming Adverse Government Policy

Cross-border mergers can be a means by which to overcome disadvantageous government policy, for example, to circumvent protective tariffs, quotas, or other barriers to free trade.

3.10.3 Technology Transfer

Companies that possess a new or superior technology may make acquisitions abroad in order to open new markets or otherwise more fully exploit their business advantage. Conversely, it is common for a company to purchase a foreign company that possesses a new or superior technology in order to enhance the acquirer's competitive position both at home and abroad.

3.10.4 Product Differentiation

Companies often purchase foreign companies to exploit the advantages of having a highly differentiated line of products. Similarly, buying certain intangibles, such as a good reputation, helps to ensure success in the global market. Lenovo's (China) acquisition of IBM's (United States) personal computer line is one example of this strategy.

3.10.5 Following Clients

Companies may engage in a cross-border merger to follow and support domestic clients more effectively. As an example, many German banks have established cross-border presences to provide services abroad to their domestic clients.

EXAMPLE 4

Mergers and the Industry Life Cycle

The types of mergers (e.g., horizontal, vertical, or conglomerate) occurring in an industry and the motivations behind those mergers will vary over time as an industry proceeds through its life cycle. The stages in an industry life cycle are normally categorized by their rates of growth in sales; growth stages can vary in length.

Mergers and Industry Life Cycles

Industry Life Cycle Stage	Industry Description	Motives for Merger	Types of Mergers
Pioneering development	► Industry exhibits substantial development costs and has low, but slowly increasing, sales growth.	► Younger, smaller companies may sell themselves to larger companies in mature or declining industries and look for ways to enter into a new growth industry. ► Young companies may look to merge with companies that allow them to pool management and capital resources.	► Conglomerate ► Horizontal
Rapid accelerating growth	► Industry exhibits high profit margins caused by few participants in the market.	► Explosive growth in sales may require large capital requirements to expand existing capacity.	► Conglomerate ► Horizontal
Mature growth	► Industry experiences a drop in the entry of new competitors, but growth potential remains.	► Mergers may be undertaken to achieve economies of scale, savings, and operational efficiencies.	► Horizontal ► Vertical

Industry Life Cycle Stage	Industry Description	Motives for Merger	Types of Mergers
Stabilization and market maturity	▶ Industry faces increasing competition and capacity constraints.	▶ Mergers may be undertaken to achieve economies of scale in research, production, and marketing to match the low cost and price performance of other companies (domestic and foreign). ▶ Large companies may acquire smaller companies to improve management and provide a broader financial base.	▶ Horizontal
Deceleration of growth and decline	▶ Industry faces overcapacity and eroding profit margins.	▶ Horizontal mergers may be undertaken to ensure survival. ▶ Vertical mergers may be carried out to increase efficiency and profit margins. ▶ Companies in related industries may merge to exploit synergy. ▶ Companies in this industry may acquire companies in young industries.	▶ Horizontal ▶ Vertical ▶ Conglomerate

Adapted from J. Fred Weston, Kwang S. Chung, and Susan E. Hoag, *Mergers, Restructuring, and Corporate Control* (New York: Prentice Hall, 1990, p. 102) and Bruno Solnik and Dennis McLeavey, *International Investments*, 5th edition (Boston: Addison Wesley, 2004, p. 264–265).

TRANSACTION CHARACTERISTICS   4

The specifics of M&A transactions can vary along many dimensions, including the form of acquisition, financing, timing, control and governance, accounting choices, and numerous details ranging from the post-merger board composition to the location of the new headquarters. In this section, we will focus on the form of acquisition, method of payment, and mind-set of target management. These three characteristics play a large role in determining how the transaction will occur, which regulatory rules might apply, how the transaction will be valued, and how it will be taxed.

4.1 Form of Acquisition

There are two basic forms of acquisition: An acquirer can purchase the target's stock or its assets. The decision will have several consequences, as summarized in Exhibit 1.

Stock purchases are the most common form of acquisition. A **stock purchase** occurs when the acquirer gives the target company's shareholders some combination of cash and securities in exchange for shares of the target company's stock. For a stock purchase to proceed, it must be approved by at least 50 percent of the target company's shareholders and sometimes more depending on the legal jurisdiction. Although it can be difficult and time consuming to win shareholder approval, it also stands as an opportunity to circumvent the target company's management in cases where management opposes the merger.

In an **asset purchase**, the acquirer purchases the target company's assets and payment is made directly to the target company. One advantage of this type of transaction is that it can be conducted more quickly and easily than a stock purchase because shareholder approval is not normally required unless a substantial proportion of the assets are being sold, usually more than 50 percent. Another advantage is that an acquirer can focus on buying the parts of a company of particular interest, such as a specific division, rather than the entire company.

EXHIBIT 1	Major Differences of Stock versus Asset Purchases	
	Stock Purchase	**Asset Purchase**
Payment	Target shareholders receive compensation in exchange for their shares.	Payment is made to the selling company rather than directly to the shareholders.
Approval	Shareholder approval required.	Shareholder approval might not be required.
Tax: Corporate	No corporate-level taxes.	Target company pays taxes on any capital gains.
Tax: Shareholder	Target company's shareholders are taxed on their capital gain.	No direct tax consequence for target company's shareholders.
Liabilities	Acquirer assumes the target's liabilities.	Acquirer generally avoids the assumption of liabilities.

Some of the more dramatic consequences of the decision to pursue one form of acquisition versus another concern taxation. In a stock purchase, the target company's shareholders exchange their shares for compensation and must pay tax on their gains, but there are no tax consequences at the corporate level.[3] For an asset purchase, in contrast, there are no direct tax consequences for the target company's shareholders but the target company itself may be subject to corporate taxes.

In addition to shifting the basic tax burden, the form-of-acquisition decision plays a role in determining how tax rules are applied in accounting for the merger. For example, use of a target's accumulated tax losses is allowable in the United States for stock purchases, but not for asset purchases.

---

[3] Keep in mind throughout this discussion of taxation that we are speaking in generalities and that the complexity of M&A deals, coupled with the complexity and variability of tax laws in different jurisdictions, can generate a host of exceptions.

Another key difference between stock and asset purchases relates to the assumption of liabilities. In stock purchases, the acquiring company assumes the target company's liabilities. Acquiring companies must thus be on guard to avoid assuming unexpected or undisclosed liabilities. With asset purchases, acquiring companies generally avoid assuming the target's liabilities. However, purchasing substantially all of a company's assets instead of conducting a stock purchase so as to specifically avoid assuming liabilities is fraught with legal risk because courts have tended to hold acquirers responsible for the liabilities in these cases.

4.2 Method of Payment

The acquirer can pay for the merger with cash, securities, or some combination of the two in what is called a **mixed offering**. In a **cash offering**, the cash might come from the acquiring company's existing assets or from a debt issue. In the most general case of a **securities offering**, the target shareholders receive shares of the acquirer's common stock as compensation.[4] Instead of common stock, however, the acquirer might offer other securities, such as preferred shares or even debt securities.

In a stock offering, the **exchange ratio** determines the number of shares that stockholders in the target company receive in exchange for each of their shares in the target company. Because share prices are constantly fluctuating, exchange ratios are typically negotiated in advance for a range of stock prices. The acquirer's cost is the product of the exchange ratio, the number of outstanding shares of the target company, and the value of the stock given to target shareholders. Each shareholder of the target company receives new shares based on the number of target shares he or she owns multiplied by the exchange ratio.

EXAMPLE 5

Stock Offering

Discount Books, a Canadian bookseller, has announced its intended acquisition of Premier Marketing Corporation, a small marketing company specializing in print media. In a press release, Discount Books outlines the terms of the merger, which specify that Premier Marketing's shareholders will each receive 0.90 shares of Discount Books for every share of Premier Marketing owned. Premier Marketing has 1 million shares outstanding. On the day of the merger announcement, Discount Books' stock closed at C$20.00 and Premier Marketing's stock closed at C$15.00. Catherine Willis is an individual investor who owns 500 shares of Premier Marketing, currently worth C$7,500 (500 × C$15.00).

1. Based on the current share prices, what is the cost of the acquisition for Discount Books?

2. How many shares of Discount Books will Catherine Willis receive, and what is the value of those shares (based on current share prices)?

---

[4] In the case of a consolidation, the target company's shareholders may receive new shares in the surviving entity.

Solution to 1: Because there are 1 million shares of Premier Marketing outstanding and the exchange ratio is 0.90 shares, Discount Books will need to issue 0.90 × 1 million = 900,000 shares of Discount Books stock to complete the transaction. Because the cost per share of Discount Books stock is currently C$20.00, the cost of the transaction to Discount Books will be C$20.00 × 900,000 = C$18 million.

Solution to 2: Catherine Willis will turn over her 500 shares of Premier Marketing stock. As compensation, she will receive 0.90 × 500 = 450 shares of stock in Discount Books. With each share of Discount Books being worth C$20.00, the value of those shares to Catherine is C$9,000.

Note that the value of Willis's Premier Marketing shares was C$7,500. The C$1,500 difference in value is a premium paid by Discount Books for control of Premier Marketing. The pre-merger value of Premier Marketing was C$15 million, but Discount Books' total cost to purchase the company was C$18 million. The 20 percent or C$3 million difference is the total-control premium paid by Discount Books.

A variety of factors influence a company's decision to negotiate for one method of payment versus another. As we shall explore in more detail later, the form of payment has an impact on the distribution of risk and reward between acquirer and target shareholders. In a stock offering, target company shareholders assume a portion of the reward as well as a portion of the risk related to the estimated synergies and the target company's value. Consequently, when an acquiring company's management is highly confident both in their ability to complete the merger and in the value to be created by the merger, they are more inclined to negotiate for a cash offering rather than a stock offering.

Another factor in the decision relates to the relative valuations of the companies involved in the transaction. When an acquirer's shares are considered overvalued by the market relative to the target company's shares, stock financing is more appropriate. In effect, the shares are more valuable as a currency. In fact, investors sometimes interpret an acquirer's stock offering as a signal that the company's shares may be overvalued. This effect is similar to the negative market reaction observed in seasoned equity offerings. Indeed, during the stock market bubble in the late 1990s, stock financing of mergers was quite popular.

Another important consideration when deciding on the payment method is the accompanying change in capital structure. The costs and benefits of different payment structures reflect how the offer will affect the acquirer's capital structure. For instance, on the one hand, borrowing to raise funds for a cash offering increases the acquirer's financial leverage and risk. On the other hand, issuing a significant number of new common shares for a stock offering can dilute the ownership interests of existing shareholders.

Preferences in the use of cash versus stock vary over time, but the proportions in 2005 are characteristic of the past several years. According to *Mergerstat Review 2006*, cash payment accounted for 54 percent of merger transactions in 2005, pure stock exchanges accounted for about 19 percent, and mixed offerings represented 25 percent.[5] A very small portion of deals, about 2 percent, were completed with other securities, such as debt, options, or warrants.

---

[5] *Mergerstat Review 2006*. FactSet Mergerstat, LLC (www.mergerstat.com).

4.3 Mind-Set of Target Management

Mergers are referred to as either friendly or hostile depending on how the target company's senior managers and board of directors view the offer. The distinction is not trivial because an enormous amount of time and resources can be expended by both acquirer and target when the takeover is hostile. Whether a merger is friendly or hostile has an impact on how it is completed, what regulations must be followed, how long the transaction takes, and possibly how much value is created (or destroyed) as a result of the combination.

4.3.1 Friendly Mergers

Unless there is cause to think the target will be hostile to a merger, the acquirer will generally start the process by approaching target management directly. The target could approach the acquirer, although this method is much less common. If both management teams are amenable to a potential deal, then the two companies enter into merger discussions. The negotiations revolve around the consideration to be received by the target company's shareholders and the terms of the transaction as well as other aspects, such as the post-merger management structure.

Before negotiations can culminate in a formal deal, each of the parties examines the others' books and records in a process called due diligence. The purpose of due diligence is to protect the companies' respective shareholders by attempting to confirm the accuracy of representations made during negotiations. For example, an acquirer would want to ensure that the target's assets exist and are worth approximately what was claimed by the target. Likewise, a target might want to examine an acquirer's financial records to gauge the likelihood that the acquirer has the capacity to pay for the acquisition as outlined in negotiations. Any deficiencies or problems uncovered during the due diligence process could have an impact on negotiations, resulting in adjustments to the terms or price of the deal. If the issue is large enough, the business combination might be called off entirely.

Once due diligence and negotiations have been completed, the companies enter into a definitive merger agreement. The **definitive merger agreement** is a contract written by both companies' attorneys and is ultimately signed by each party to the transaction. The agreement contains the details of the transaction, including the terms, warranties, conditions, termination details, and the rights of all parties.

Common industry practice has evolved such that companies typically discuss potential transactions in private and maintain secrecy until the definitive merger agreement is reached. This trend may have been influenced by shifts in securities laws toward more stringent rules related to the disclosure of material developments to the public. Additionally, news of a merger can cause dramatic changes in the stock prices of the parties to the transaction. Premature announcement of a deal can cause volatile swings in the stock prices of the companies as they proceed through negotiations.

After the definitive merger agreement has been signed, the transaction is generally announced to the public through a joint press release by the companies. In a friendly merger, the target company's management endorses the merger and recommends that its stockholders approve the transaction. In cases where a shareholder vote is needed, whether it is the target shareholders approving the stock purchase or the acquirer shareholders approving the issuance of a significant number of new shares, the material facts are provided to the appropriate shareholders in a public document called a **proxy statement**, which is given to shareholders in anticipation of their vote.

After all the necessary approvals have been obtained—from shareholders as well as any other parties, such as regulatory bodies—the attorneys file the required documentation with securities regulators and the merger is officially completed. Target shareholders receive the consideration agreed upon under the terms of the transaction, and the companies are officially and legally combined.

4.3.2 Hostile Mergers

In a hostile merger, which is a merger that is opposed by the target company's management, the acquirer may decide to circumvent the target management's objections by submitting a merger proposal directly to the target company's board of directors and bypassing the CEO. This tactic is known as a **bear hug**.

Because bear hugs are not formal offers and have not been mutually agreed upon, there are no standard procedures in these cases. If the offer is high enough to warrant serious consideration, then the board may appoint a special committee to negotiate a sale of the target.

Although unlikely in practice, it is possible that target management will capitulate after a bear hug and enter into negotiations, which may ultimately lead to a friendly merger. If the bear hug is not successful, then the hopeful acquirer will attempt to appeal more directly to the target company's shareholders.

One method for taking a merger appeal directly to shareholders is through a **tender offer**, whereby the acquirer invites target shareholders to submit ("tender") their shares in return for the proposed payment.[6] It is up to the individual shareholders to physically tender shares to the acquiring company's agent in order to receive payment. A tender offer can be made with cash, shares of the acquirer's own stock, other securities, or some combination of securities and cash. Because a cash tender offer can be completed in less time than a cash merger, some acquiring companies use this type of transaction to gain control of a target company quickly.

Another method of taking over a target company involves the use of a proxy fight. In a **proxy fight**, a company or individual seeks to take control of a company through a shareholder vote. Proxy solicitation is approved by regulators and then mailed directly to target company shareholders. The shareholders are asked to vote for the acquirer's proposed slate of directors. If the acquirer's slate is elected to the target's board, then it is able to replace the target company's management. At this point, the transaction may evolve into a friendly merger.

Regardless of how an acquirer seeks to establish control, target managers have a variety of alternatives available for defending the company against unwanted overtures. In these cases, the target usually retains the services of law firms and investment bankers to design a defense against the unwanted takeover attempt. As we will discuss in the next section, target company managers may use a variety of legal and financial defensive maneuvers to ward off a takeover attempt.

5   TAKEOVERS

When a target company is faced with a hostile tender offer (takeover) attempt, the target managers and board of directors face a basic choice. They can decide

---

[6] Tender offers are often associated with hostile mergers, but they also occur in a friendly context. Tender offers are considered hostile only when the offer is opposed by the target company's management and board of directors.

to negotiate and sell the company, either to the hostile **bidder** or a third party, or they can attempt to remain independent. Aside from the strength of the company's defenses and target management's resolve to stay independent, the premium over the market price offered by the acquirer for the target company's shares is the major driving factor in the decision to support or resist any given takeover.

If the target management decides to resist the unwanted overture, they have a variety of takeover defense mechanisms at their disposal. Once the decision has been reached, the target company generally seeks the counsel of investment bankers and lawyers to explore the fairness of the hostile offer and to advise the board of the alternatives.

A target might use defensive measures to delay, negotiate a better deal for shareholders, or attempt to keep the company independent. Defensive measures can be implemented either before or after a takeover attempt has begun. Most law firms specializing in takeovers recommend that defenses be set up before a company receives or expects any takeover activity.

5.1 Pre-Offer Takeover Defense Mechanisms

In the United States, most hostile takeover attempts result in litigation. The courts generally bless legal pre-offer defense mechanisms but tend to scrutinize post-offer defenses very closely. The target usually assumes the burden of proof in showing that the recently enacted defenses are not simply intended to perpetuate management's tenure at the target company. It is for this reason that most attorneys recommend that target companies put defenses in place prior to any takeover action. Following this policy gives the target more flexibility when defending against a takeover bid.

With different twists in takeover strategy come new innovations and variations in takeover defenses. Given the many possible variations, the following is not an exhaustive list but an overview of the more well known anti-takeover strategies. The two broad varieties of pre-offer defenses are rights-based defenses, such as poison pills and poison puts, and a variety of changes to the corporate charter (e.g., staggered boards of directors and **supermajority** provisions) that are sometimes collectively referred to as **shark repellents**.

5.1.1 Poison Pills

The **poison pill** is a legal device that makes it prohibitively costly for an acquirer to take control of a target without the prior approval of the target's board of directors. Most poison pills make the target company less attractive by creating rights that allow for the issuance of shares of the target company's stock at a substantial discount to market value.

There are two basic types of poison pills: the **flip-in pill** and the **flip-over pill**. When the common shareholder of the target company has the right to buy its shares at a discount, the pill is known as a flip-in. The pill is triggered when a specific level of ownership is exceeded. Because the acquiring company is generally prohibited from participating in the purchase through the pill, the acquirer is subject to a significant level of dilution. Most plans give the target's board of directors the right to redeem the pill prior to any triggering event. If the takeover becomes friendly, the board generally exercises this waiver.

In the case of a flip-over pill, the target company's common shareholders receive the right to purchase shares of the acquiring company at a significant discount from the market price, which has the effect of causing dilution to all existing acquiring company shareholders. Again, the board of the target generally retains the right to redeem the pill should the transaction become friendly.

Another possible aspect of the poison pill is the **"dead-hand" provision**. This provision allows the board of the target to redeem or cancel the poison pill only by a vote of the continuing directors. Because continuing directors are generally defined as directors who were on the target company's board prior to the takeover attempt, this provision has the effect of making it much more difficult to take over a target without prior board approval.

5.1.2 Poison Puts

Whereas poison pills grant common shareholders certain rights in a hostile takeover attempt, **poison puts** give rights to the target company's bondholders. In the event of a takeover, poison puts allow bondholders to put the bonds to the company. In other words, if the provision is triggered by a hostile takeover attempt, then bondholders have the right to sell their bonds back to the target at a redemption price that is pre-specified in the **bond indenture**, typically at or above par value. The effect of a poison put defense is to require that an acquirer be prepared to refinance the target's debt immediately after the takeover. This defense increases the need for cash and raises the cost of the acquisition.

5.1.3 Incorporation in a State with Restrictive Takeover Laws (United States)

In the United States, many states have adopted laws that specifically address unfriendly takeover attempts. These laws are designed to provide target companies with flexibility in dealing with unwanted suitors. Some states have designed their laws to give the company maximum protection and leeway in defending against an offer. As a result, companies that anticipate the possibility of a hostile takeover attempt may find it attractive to reincorporate in a jurisdiction that has enacted strict anti-takeover laws. Ohio and Pennsylvania are examples of two U.S. states that have been regarded historically as "target friendly" states; their state laws tend to give target companies the most power in defending against hostile takeover attempts.[7]

5.1.4 Staggered Board of Directors

Instead of electing the entire board of directors each year at the company's annual meeting, a company may arrange to stagger the terms for board members so that only a portion of the board seats are due for election each year. For example, if the company has a board consisting of nine directors, members could be elected for three-year terms with only three directors coming up for election each year. The effect of this staggered board is that it would take at least two years to elect enough directors to take control of the board.

---

[7] Delaware has historically been the most popular state for corporations to domicile their legal entities. To protect this status, the state has found it necessary to toughen its laws regarding takeover attempts. In the past, as some states adopted strict takeover laws, some corporations left Delaware and reincorporated in these "friendly" states. In order to compete, Delaware has changed its own laws to make it more difficult to take over a Delaware corporation on a hostile basis.

5.1.5 Restricted Voting Rights

Some target companies adopt a mechanism that restricts stockholders who have recently acquired large blocks of stock from voting their shares. Usually, there is a trigger stockholding level, such as 15 or 20 percent. Shareholders who meet or exceed this trigger point are no longer able to exercise their voting rights without the target company's board releasing the shareholder from the constraint. The possibility of owning a controlling position in the target without being able to vote the shares serves as a deterrent.

5.1.6 Supermajority Voting Provisions

Many target companies change their charter and bylaws to provide for a higher percentage approval by shareholders for mergers than normally is required. A typical provision might require a vote of 80 percent of the outstanding shares of the target company (as opposed to a simple 51 percent majority). This supermajority requirement is triggered by a hostile takeover attempt and is frequently accompanied by a provision that prevents the hostile acquirer from voting its shares. Thus, even if an acquirer is able to accumulate a substantial portion of the target's shares, it may have great difficulty accumulating enough votes to approve a merger.

5.1.7 Fair Price Amendments

Fair price amendments are changes to the corporate charter and bylaws that disallow mergers for which the offer is below some threshold. For example, a fair price amendment might require an acquirer to pay at least as much as the highest stock price at which the target has traded in the public market over a specified period. Fair price amendments protect targets against temporary declines in their share prices by setting a floor value bid. Additionally, fair price amendments protect against two-tiered tender offers where the acquirer offers a higher bid in a first step tender offer with the threat of a lower bid in a second step tender offer for those who do not tender right away.

5.1.8 Golden Parachutes

Golden parachutes are compensation agreements between the target company and its senior managers. These employment contracts allow the executives to receive lucrative payouts, usually several years worth of salary, if they leave the target company following a change in corporate control. In practice, golden parachutes do not offer much deterrent, especially for large deals where the managers' compensation is small relative to the overall takeover price. One reason they persist is that they help alleviate target management's concerns about job loss. Golden parachutes may encourage key executives to stay with the target as the takeover progresses and the target explores all options to generate shareholder value. Without a golden parachute, some contend that target company executives might be quicker to seek employment offers from other companies to secure their financial future. Whether this is actually the case and whether golden parachutes are fair and in the best interest of shareholders is the subject of considerable debate among shareholder rights activists and senior managers.

5.2 Post-Offer Takeover Defense Mechanisms

A target also has several defensive mechanisms that can be used once a takeover has already been initiated. Because they may not be as successful when used in isolation and because they have historically been subject to greater scrutiny by the courts, post-offer defenses are typically used in conjunction with pre-offer defenses.

5.2.1 "Just Say No" Defense

Probably the simplest place for a target company to start when confronted with a hostile takeover bid is to rely on pre-takeover defenses and to decline the offer. If the acquirer attempts a bear hug or tender offer, then target management typically lobbies the board of directors and shareholders to decline and build a case for why the offering price is inadequate or why the offer is otherwise not in the shareholders' best interests. This strategy forces the hopeful acquirer to adjust its bid or further reveal its own strategy in order to advance the takeover attempt.

5.2.2 Litigation

A popular technique used by many target companies is to file a lawsuit against the acquiring company based on alleged violations of securities or antitrust laws. In the United States, these suits may be filed in either state or federal courts. Unless there is a serious antitrust violation, these suits rarely stop a takeover bid. Instead, lawsuits often serve as a delaying tactic to create additional time for target management to develop other responses to the unwanted offer. Generally, any securities law violations, even if upheld, can be corrected with additional public disclosures. In the United States, most antitrust claims that eventually prevent takeover attempts are initiated by either antitrust or securities regulators rather than by the target company.

5.2.3 Greenmail

This technique involves an agreement allowing the target to repurchase its own shares back from the acquiring company, usually at a premium to the market price. Greenmail is usually accompanied by an agreement that the acquirer will not pursue another hostile takeover attempt of the target for a set period. In effect, greenmail is the termination of a hostile takeover through a payoff to the acquirer. The shareholders of the target company do not receive any compensation for their shares. Greenmail was popular in the United States during the 1980s, but its use has been extremely restricted since 1986 when the U.S. Internal Revenue Code was amended to add a 50 percent tax on profits realized by acquirers through greenmail.

5.2.4 Share Repurchase

Rather than repurchasing only the shares held by the acquiring company, as in greenmail, a target might use a share repurchase to acquire shares from any shareholder. For example, a target may initiate a cash tender offer for its own outstanding shares. An effective repurchase can increase the potential cost for an acquirer by either increasing the stock's price outright or by causing the acquirer to increase its bid to remain competitive with the target company's tender offer for its own shares. Additionally, a share repurchase often has the effect of increasing the target company's use of leverage because borrowing is typically required to purchase the shares. This additional debt makes the target less attractive as a takeover candidate.

In some cases, a target company buys all of its shares and converts to a privately held company in a transaction called a leveraged buyout. In a **leveraged buyout (LBO)**, the management team generally partners with a private equity firm that specializes in buyouts. The new entity borrows a high proportion of the overall purchase price; the financial firm contributes a certain amount of capital; and the management team provides the management expertise to run the business. In exchange for their expertise, management generally receives a payout percentage based on the profitability and success of the company after the LBO is completed. This strategy may allow the target to defend against a hostile bid provided that the LBO provides target shareholders with a level of value that exceeds the would-be acquirer's offer.

5.2.5 Leveraged Recapitalization

A technique somewhat related to the leveraged buyout is the leveraged recapitalization. A **leveraged recapitalization** involves the assumption of a large amount of debt that is then used to finance share repurchases (but in contrast to a leveraged buyout, in a recapitalization, some shares remain in public hands). The effect is to dramatically change the company's capital structure while attempting to deliver a value to target shareholders in excess of the hostile bid.

5.2.6 "Crown Jewel" Defense

After a hostile takeover is announced, a target may decide to sell off a subsidiary or asset to a third party. If the acquisition of this subsidiary or asset was one of the acquirer's major motivations for the proposed merger, then this strategy could cause the acquirer to abandon its takeover effort. When a target initiates such a sale after a hostile takeover bid is announced, there is a good chance that the courts will declare this strategy illegal.

5.2.7 "Pac-Man" Defense

The target can defend itself by making a counteroffer to acquire the hostile bidder. This technique is rarely used because, in most cases, it means that a smaller company (the target) is making a bid for a larger entity. Additionally, once a target uses a Pac-Man defense, it forgoes the ability to use a number of other defensive strategies. For instance, after making a counteroffer, a target cannot very well take the acquirer to court claiming an antitrust violation.

5.2.8 White Knight Defense

Often the best outcome for target shareholders is for the target company's board to seek a third party to purchase the company in lieu of the hostile bidder. This third party is called a **white knight** because it is coming to the aid of the target. A target usually initiates this technique by seeking out another company that has a strategic fit with the target. Based on a good strategic fit, the third party can often justify a higher price for the target than what the hostile bidder is offering.

Once a white knight bid is made public, it may elicit an additional higher bid from the hostile bidder. This can help kick off a competitive bidding situation. In some cases, because of the competitive nature of the bidders, the winner's curse can prevail and the target company shareholders may receive a very good deal. **Winner's curse** is the tendency for the winner in certain competitive bidding situations to overpay, whether because of overestimation of intrinsic value, emotion, or information asymmetries.[8]

5.2.9 White Squire Defense

In the **white squire** defense, the target seeks a friendly party to buy a substantial minority stake in the target—enough to block the hostile takeover without selling the entire company. Although the white squire may pay a significant premium for a substantial number of the target's shares, these shares may be purchased directly from the target company and the target shareholders may not receive any of the proceeds.[9]

The use of the white squire defense may carry a high litigation risk depending on the details of the transaction and local regulations. Additionally, stock exchange listing requirements sometimes require that target shareholders vote to approve these types of transactions, and shareholders may not endorse any transaction that does not provide an adequate premium to them directly.

EXAMPLE 6

Engelhard Takeover Defenses

On 14 December 2005, BASF, a worldwide producer of chemicals and high-performance products, offered to acquire Engelhard Corporation for $37 cash per share. Engelhard, a manufacturer and developer of value-added technologies, determined that the $37 offer was inadequate and decided to defend itself against the unwanted takeover attempt.

Prior to the BASF takeover offer, Engelhard had participating preferred stock purchase rights in place.[10] These rights acted as a poison pill by allowing Engelhard to issue shares at a discount if triggered by a takeover that was unsupported by Engelhard's board of directors. Additionally, in advance of the takeover attempt, Engelhard restated its certificate of incorporation to include a supermajority provision. It stated that business combinations with a holder of more than 5 percent of Engelhard's outstanding shares would require an affirmative vote of both the holders of 80 percent of the outstanding shares and at least 50 percent of the outstanding shares not held by the acquirer unless the board of directors approved the business combination.

After the tender offer was commenced by BASF, Engelhard also pursued a recapitalization plan that involved the repurchase of approximately 20 percent of Engelhard's outstanding shares through a tender offer at $45 per share, a price superior to BASF's tender offer. Together these pre- and post-offer defenses made it very difficult for BASF to succeed with its $37 cash tender offer.

---

[8] The winner's curse is most likely to occur when the target company has roughly the same value to all bidders but the target's true value is hard to ascertain. The average bid in such cases may represent the best estimate of the target's intrinsic value, and the high (winning), an overestimate of its intrinsic value.

[9] For example, the white squire may purchase shares of convertible preferred stock instead of common stock.

[10] Shares of participating preferred stock offer the possibility of a higher dividend when the dividend on common shares reaches a pre-specified threshold.

Although Engelhard did not complete the tender for its own shares, the recapitalization plan was incentive enough for BASF to increase its offer. Takeover targets frequently use their takeover defenses to negotiate a better deal for their shareholders. After much negotiation, BASF increased its tender offer and Engelhard withdrew all takeover defenses. On 30 May 2006, the companies announced a definitive merger agreement under which BASF would acquire all outstanding shares of Engelhard for $39 per share in cash.

REGULATION   6

Even when a merger has been accepted by the target company's senior managers, the board of directors, and shareholders, the combination must still be approved by regulatory authorities. Additionally, there are a variety of rules that companies must follow when initiating and completing the merger transaction itself. This section provides an overview of the key rules and issues that arise from M&A activity.

The two major bodies of jurisprudence relating to mergers are antitrust law and securities law. Antitrust laws are intended to ensure that markets remain competitive; the securities laws we will discuss are concerned largely with maintaining both fairness in merger activities and confidence in the financial markets.

6.1 Antitrust

Most countries have antitrust laws, which prohibit mergers and acquisitions that impede competition. Antitrust legislation began in the United States with the Sherman Antitrust Act of 1890, which made contracts, combinations, and conspiracies in restraint of trade or attempts to monopolize an industry illegal. The Sherman Antitrust Act was not effective at deterring antitrust activity partly because the U.S. Department of Justice at the time lacked the resources necessary to enforce the law rigorously. Within a few years of its passage, the law was challenged in the courts and rendered unenforceable because of ambiguous aspects of its wording.

To resurrect antitrust law, the U.S. Congress passed the Clayton Antitrust Act in 1914, which clarified and strengthened the Sherman Antitrust Act by detailing the specific business practices that the U.S. Congress wished to outlaw. In order to ensure that the law could be effectively enforced, the legislature also passed the Federal Trade Commission Act of 1914, which established the Federal Trade Commission (FTC) as a regulatory agency to work in tandem with the Department of Justice to enforce antitrust law.

During the ensuing years, additional weaknesses and loopholes in antitrust legislation became apparent. For instance, the Clayton Act regulated only the acquisition of shares of stock, not the acquisition of assets. The Celler–Kefauver Act was passed in 1950 to close this loophole; the law also addressed vertical and conglomerate mergers, whereas previous legislation had focused primarily on horizontal combinations.

The last major piece of U.S. antitrust legislation was the Hart–Scott–Rodino Antitrust Improvements Act of 1976, which required that the FTC and Department of Justice have the opportunity to review and approve mergers in advance. A key benefit of the Hart–Scott–Rodino Act is that it gives regulators an opportunity to halt a merger prior to its completion rather than having to disassemble a company after a merger is later deemed to be anticompetitive.

Just as U.S. transactions are reviewed by the FTC and the Department of Justice, the European Commission (EC) has the authority to review the antitrust implications of transactions among companies that generate significant revenues within the European Union. Although the European Commission's member states have jurisdiction on mergers within their respective national borders, mergers with significant cross-border effects are subject to EC review. Similar to the requirements in the United States, pre-merger notification is required.

In addition to regulatory watchdogs, such as the FTC and the European Commission, approval may be needed from other regulatory agencies. For example, in the United States, a merger involving banks requires approvals from state banking authorities as well as the Federal Reserve Bank and possibly the Federal Deposit Insurance Corporation (FDIC). Insurance mergers require the approval of state insurance commissioners. In some cases where one of the company's businesses is deemed to be of strategic national interest, additional government approvals may be necessary. Each merger must be analyzed by legal experts to determine the specific regulatory approvals required to comply with the relevant rules and laws. This is a very specialized area and can cause significant delays in the closing of some transactions.

The situation can become further complicated when the merging companies have a global presence that falls within multiple jurisdictions of regulatory control. For example, a large trans-Atlantic merger would require approval of both the United States regulatory bodies and the European Commission. Global companies often face dozens of regulatory agencies with different standards and filing requirements. For example, Coca-Cola Company's 1999 acquisition of the Cadbury Schweppes beverage brands involved sales and production in more than 160 countries, requiring antitrust approval in more than 40 jurisdictions around the world.

Prior to 1982, the FTC and Department of Justice used market share as a measure of market power when determining potential antitrust violations among peer competitors in an industry. Using a simple measure of industry concentration and the market shares of the acquirer and the target, companies contemplating a horizontal merger could determine in advance whether the combination would likely be challenged. The transparency and predictability of the measure was advantageous, but the approach proved to be too simplistic and rigid in practice.

In 1982, the agencies shifted toward using a new measure of market power called the **Herfindahl–Hirschman Index (HHI)**. By summing the squares of the market shares for each company in an industry, the HHI does a better job of modeling market concentration while remaining relatively easy to calculate and interpret. To calculate the HHI, the market shares for competing companies are squared and then summed:

$$\text{HHI} = \sum_{i}^{n} \left(\frac{\text{Sales or output of firm } i}{\text{Total sales or output of market}} \times 100 \right)^2 \qquad \textbf{(35-1)}$$

Regulators initially calculate the HHI based on *post-merger* market shares. If post-merger market shares results in an HHI of less than 1,000, the market is not considered to be concentrated and a challenge is unlikely unless other anti-competitive issues arise. A moderately concentrated HHI measure of between 1,000 and 1,800, or a highly concentrated measure of more than 1,800, requires a comparison of post-merger and pre-merger HHI. A merger resulting in an increase of 100 points in a moderately concentrated market or 50 points in a highly concentrated market is likely to evoke antitrust concerns; smaller increases are less likely to pose a problem.[11] Exhibit 2 summarizes HHI ranges and the corresponding probability for regulatory action:

EXHIBIT 2	HHI Concentration Level and Possible Government Action

HHI Concentration Level

Post-Merger HHI	Concentration	Change in HHI	Government Action
Less than 1,000	Not concentrated	Any amount	No action
Between 1,000 and 1,800	Moderately concentrated	100 or more	Possible challenge
More than 1,800	Highly concentrated	50 or more	Challenge

EXAMPLE 7

Herfindahl–Hirschman Index

Given an industry with 10 competitors and the following market shares, calculate the pre-merger HHI. How would the HHI change if Companies 2 and 3 merged? How would it change if Companies 9 and 10 merged instead? Would either set of mergers be likely to evoke an antitrust challenge?

Company	1	2	3	4	5	6	7	8	9	10
Market Share (%)	25	20	10	10	10	5	5	5	5	5

Solution: To calculate the pre-merger HHI, first square the market share for each company. Then add together the squared market shares to obtain an HHI of 1,450, which indicates that this is a moderately concentrated industry. If Companies 2 and 3 were to merge, the HHI would jump 400 points to 1,850. The large change in the HHI combined with the high post-merger HHI value indicates that this merger would likely evoke antitrust objections. If Companies 9 and 10 were to merge instead of Companies 2 and 3, the HHI would climb only 50 points to 1,500. Although the post-merger HHI indicates a moderately concentrated industry, the combination is unlikely to raise antitrust concerns because the post-merger HHI is only 50 points higher than the pre-merger HHI.

---

[11] See the U.S. Department of Justice and the Federal Trade Commission's Horizontal Merger Guidelines, issued 2 April 1992 and revised 8 April 1997.

Pre-Merger			Post-Merger: Companies 2 and 3			Post-Merger: Companies 9 and 10		
Company	Market Share (%)	Market Share Squared	Company	Market Share (%)	Market Share Squared	Company	Market Share (%)	Market Share Squared
1	25	625	1	25	625	1	25	625
2	20	400	2+3	30	900	2	20	400
3	10	100	4	10	100	3	10	100
4	10	100	5	10	100	4	10	100
5	10	100	6	5	25	5	10	100
6	5	25	7	5	25	6	5	25
7	5	25	8	5	25	7	5	25
8	5	25	9	5	25	8	5	25
9	5	25	10	5	25	9+10	10	100
10	5	25						
HHI:	1,450			HHI:	1,850		HHI:	1,500
				HHI Change:	400		HHI Change:	50

Although the introduction of the Herfindahl–Hirschman Index was an improvement, regulators still found it to be too mechanical and inflexible. Thus, by 1984, the Department of Justice sought to increase the flexibility of its policies through the inclusion of additional information, such as market power measured by the responsiveness of consumers to price changes, as well as qualitative information, such as the efficiency of companies in the industry, the financial viability of potential merger candidates, and the ability of U.S. companies to compete in foreign markets.[12]

When reviewing quantitative and qualitative data, one should note that merger guidelines are just that—guidelines. It is possible that under unusual circumstances the government may not challenge one merger that does violate the guidelines and may challenge another merger that does not. Each transaction must be analyzed carefully to fully explore all potential antitrust issues.

When conflicts between companies and regulators arise, it is often because of disagreements about how the markets are defined. Regulators must consider the market in terms of both geography and product. When considering the industry's geography, regulators must decide whether the relevant competitors are global, national, regional, or local. When considering product offerings, there may be one or multiple relevant product market overlaps. In some cases the overlap may be clear, and in other transactions it may not be obvious.

---

[12] Patrick A. Gaughan, *Mergers, Acquisitions, and Corporate Restructurings*, 3rd ed. (New York: John Wiley & Sons, 2002), p. 95.

Parties to the transaction are usually counseled by attorneys who have relevant experience in the antitrust area. Most companies try to complete their analyses prior to signing a merger agreement in order to avoid entering into a long period of uncertainty while the government decides whether to challenge the transaction. Not only do delays increase costs, but they may also cause the companies to lose other important strategic opportunities.

6.2 Securities Laws

As we discussed in the section covering pre-offer takeover defense mechanisms, in the United States individual states regulate M&A activities to varying degrees. But companies must also comply with federal U.S. securities regulations. In the United States, the cornerstone of securities legislation regulating merger and acquisition activities is the Williams Amendment to the Securities Exchange Act of 1934 (also known as the Williams Act), which was passed in 1968 near the end of the third merger wave.

During the 1960s, tender offers became a popular means to execute hostile takeovers. Acquirers often announced tender offers that expired in short time frames or threatened lower bids and less desirable terms for those shareholders who waited to tender. In addition to giving shareholders little time to evaluate the fairness of an offer, it gave target management little time to respond. The Williams Act sought to remedy these problems in two keys ways: disclosure requirements and a formal process for tender offers.

Section 13(d) of the Williams Act requires public disclosure whenever a party acquires 5 percent or more of a target's outstanding common stock. As part of this disclosure, the company acquiring the stake must provide a variety of details, including self-identification, the purpose of the transaction, and the source of the funds used to finance the stock purchases. This disclosure requirement calls target managers' and shareholders' attention to large share purchases, which keeps acquirers from gaining too large a toehold before the target is aware of the acquirer's interest.

Section 14 of the Williams Act creates a tender offer process by setting forth various rules and restrictions that companies must observe. For example, as part of initiating a tender offer, an acquirer must file a public statement that contains the details of the offer and information about the acquirer. Target management must then respond through a formal statement containing their opinion and advice to accept or reject the offer; target management can abstain from offering an opinion as long as they provide the reasons for doing so.

Other important provisions of Section 14 are that the tender offer period be at least 20 business days, that the acquirer must accept all shares tendered, that all tendered shares must receive the same price, and that target shareholders can withdraw tendered shares during the offer period. These provisions ensure that target shareholders receive equitable treatment and that they have adequate time to investigate and evaluate a tender offer without the risk of receiving a lower price. Section 14 also gives target management the time and opportunity to adequately respond to a hostile tender offer.

MERGER ANALYSIS   7

In this section, we will examine the analysis of merger activity from two perspectives. First, we will discuss valuation of the target company, something of key importance for analysts on both sides of the deal as well as for shareholders as they all grapple to determine the fairness and adequacy of an offer. Then, we will discuss the analysis of the bid. Analysts can estimate the distribution of benefits in a merger based on expected synergies relative to the premium paid for the target in excess of its intrinsic value.

7.1 Target Company Valuation

The three basic valuation techniques that companies and their advisers use to value companies in an M&A context are discounted cash flow analysis, comparable company analysis, and comparable transaction analysis. An analyst is likely to use some combination of these primary techniques, and possibly others, when gauging a company's fair value.

7.1.1 Discounted Cash Flow Analysis

Discounted cash flow (DCF) analysis, as it is generally applied in this context, discounts the company's expected future free cash flows to the present in order to derive an estimate for the value of the company. **Free cash flow** (FCF) is the relevant measure in this context because it represents the actual cash that would be available to the company's investors after making all investments necessary to maintain the company as an ongoing enterprise.[13] Free cash flows are the internally generated funds that can be distributed to the company's investors (e.g., shareholders and bondholders) without impairing the value of the company.

There are several variations to the models an analyst might use to estimate and discount free cash flows. In the following, we will develop an approximation to free cash flow and illustrate its use in valuation using a two-stage model.[14] Estimating a company's free cash flows begins with the creation of pro forma financial statements. The first step is to select an appropriate time horizon for the first stage. The first stage should include only those years over which the analyst feels capable of generating reasonably accurate estimates of the company's free cash flows. These free cash flow estimates are then discounted to their present value.

To incorporate value deriving from years beyond the first stage, the analyst estimates the value of expected second-stage free cash flows as of the end of the first stage. The result is the so-called terminal value (or continuing value) of the company. The analyst then discounts the terminal value back to the present. The sum of the two pieces (the present value of first-stage expected free cash flows plus the present value of the company's terminal value) is the estimated value of the company.

There is no standard approach for creating pro forma financial statements. The art of financial analysis involves an ability to use the appropriate tools and to exercise good judgment in order to produce the best possible estimates for each financial statement item. In the process, analysts make adjustments to their prior projections based on proposed synergies and the announced plans for the merged company. For example, duplicated resources might result in the sale of one of the target's divisions. Or, the operating costs might be adjusted downward in anticipa-

---

[13] Free cash flow as used here is also called **free cash flow to the firm**, particularly when a distinction is being made between free cash flows accruing to all providers of capital and those accruing only to equityholders (**free cash flow to equity**).

[14] See Stowe, Robinson, Pinto, and McLeavey (2002) for details of estimating free cash flow (free cash flow to the firm) more precisely.

tion of economies of scale. These adjustments are easier to estimate in friendly mergers where the analyst has access to detailed financial data about the target than in hostile mergers. But even in a hostile merger scenario, an analyst with experience in the appropriate industry can still make reasonably good estimates.

Once pro forma financial statements have been generated, the analyst can begin the conversion from pro forma net income to pro forma free cash flow for each year of the first stage. To demonstrate this process, we will use the pro forma financial statements and FCF calculations provided in Exhibit 3. The perspective is that of a valuation being done at the beginning of 2007.

EXHIBIT 3	**Sample Pro Forma Financial Statements and FCF Calculations**					
	Historical	**Pro Forma**				
	2006	**2007**	**2008**	**2009**	**2010**	**2011**
Income Statement (*thousands of dollars*)						
Revenues	$ 14,451	$ 15,752	$ 17,327	$ 19,060	$ 20,966	$ 23,063
Cost of goods sold	7,948	8,664	9,530	10,483	11,531	12,685
Gross profit	$ 6,503	$ 7,088	$ 7,797	$ 8,577	$ 9,435	$ 10,378
Selling, general, and administrative expenses	2,168	2,363	2,599	2,859	3,145	3,459
Depreciation	506	551	606	667	734	807
Earnings before interest and taxes	$ 3,829	$ 4,174	$ 4,592	$ 5,051	$ 5,556	$ 6,112
Net interest expense	674	642	616	583	543	495
Earnings before taxes	$ 3,155	$ 3,532	$ 3,976	$ 4,468	$ 5,013	$ 5,617
Income tax	1,104	1,236	1,392	1,564	1,755	1,966
Net income	$ 2,051	$ 2,296	$ 2,584	$ 2,904	$ 3,258	$ 3,651
Balance Sheet (*thousands of dollars*)						
Current assets	$ 8,671	$ 9,451	$ 10,396	$ 11,436	$ 12,580	$ 13,838
Net property, plant, and equipment	10,116	11,026	12,129	13,342	14,676	16,144
Total assets	$ 18,787	$ 20,477	$ 22,525	$ 24,778	$ 27,256	$ 29,982
Current liabilities	$ 3,613	$ 3,938	$ 4,332	$ 4,765	$ 5,242	$ 5,766
Deferred income taxes	92	111	132	155	181	209
Long-term debt	7,924	7,548	7,243	6,862	6,394	5,830
Total liabilities	$ 11,629	$ 11,597	$ 11,707	$ 11,782	$ 11,817	$ 11,805
Common stock and paid-in capital	1,200	1,200	1,200	1,200	1,200	1,200
Retained earnings	5,958	7,680	9,618	11,796	14,239	16,977
Shareholders' equity	$ 7,158	$ 8,880	$ 10,818	$ 12,996	$ 15,439	$ 18,177
Total liabilities and shareholders' equity	$ 18,787	$ 20,477	$ 22,525	$ 24,778	$ 27,256	$ 29,982
Selected Pro Forma Cash Flow Data (*thousands of dollars*)						
Change in net working capital		$ 455	$ 551	$ 607	$ 667	$ 734
Capital expenditures		$ 1,461	$ 1,709	$ 1,880	$ 2,068	$ 2,275

(Exhibit continued on next page . . .)

EXHIBIT 3	(continued)

	Pro Forma				
	2007	**2008**	**2009**	**2010**	**2011**
FCF Calculations					
Net income	$ 2,296	$ 2,584	$ 2,904	$ 3,258	$ 3,651
Plus: Net interest after tax	417	400	379	353	322
Unlevered net income	$ 2,713	$ 2,984	$ 3,283	$ 3,611	$ 3,973
Plus: Change in deferred taxes	19	21	23	26	28
Net op. profit less adj. taxes (NOPLAT)	$ 2,732	$ 3,005	$ 3,306	$ 3,637	$ 4,001
Plus: Depreciation	551	606	667	734	807
Less: Change in net working capital	455	551	607	667	734
Less: Capital expenditures	1,461	1,709	1,880	2,068	2,275
Free cash flow	$ 1,367	$ 1,351	$ 1,486	$ 1,636	$ 1,799
Valuation Calculations					
WACC	9.41%				
PV of FCF		$ 5,802			
Terminal growth rate	6.0%				
Terminal value, 2011	$ 55,922				
Terminal value, 2006		$ 35,670			
Enterprise Value, 2006		$ 41,471			

The calculation of FCF involves first making adjustments to net income to convert it to **net operating profit less adjusted taxes (NOPLAT)**. This adjustment is made so that the resulting estimate of FCF represents the after-tax cash flows available to all providers of capital to the company. The first step in this process is to add net interest after tax to net income. This step removes the tax shield from interest payments and puts the cash flows on common footing with other cash flows that are available to all capital providers of the company.[15] This is referred to as unlevered net income.[16] For the year 2007 in Exhibit 3, pro forma net income for the year is $2.296 million. There is no reported interest income, so net interest expense is simply $642,000. The company's estimated tax rate is 35 percent, found by dividing the previous year's income tax by the company's earnings before tax.

Step 1:
Unlevered net income = Net income + Net interest after tax
Net interest after tax = (Interest expense − Interest income)
$$\times (1 - \text{tax rate}) \tag{35-2}$$

For 2007,
Unlevered net income = $2,296 + 642(1 − 0.35) = $2,713
= $2.713 million

---

[15] The tax deductibility of interest will be accounted for later in the calculation when we discount free cash flows by the weighted average cost of capital (WACC).

[16] It is also possible to calculate unlevered net income as earnings before interest and taxes (EBIT) × (1 − tax rate).

To convert unlevered net income to NOPLAT, we must account for differences in depreciation for financial reporting purposes versus depreciation for tax purposes, which has an impact on cash flows. Companies typically report depreciation for property, plant, and equipment at a faster rate for tax purposes (higher depreciation shields more income from taxes) than for financial reporting purposes (lower depreciation results in higher net income). The differences in depreciation result in different taxes. This difference is accounted for as a liability on the balance sheet—deferred income taxes. To account for this impact on cash flow, we add the change in deferred taxes to unlevered net income (an increase in deferred taxes increases cash flow; a decrease in deferred taxes reduces cash flow).[17]

Step 2:

$$\text{NOPLAT} = \text{Unlevered net income} + \text{Change in deferred taxes} \quad \text{(35-3)}$$

For 2007,

$$\text{NOPLAT} = \$2{,}713 + (111 - 92) = \$2{,}732$$
$$= \$2.732 \text{ million}$$

At this point, NOPLAT is adjusted to add back net noncash charges (NCC), which prominently include depreciation (of tangible assets) and amortization and impairment (of intangible assets); noncash charges affect net income but do not represent cash expenditures. To estimate free cash flow, we then subtract the value of necessary or otherwise planned investments in working capital and property, plant, and equipment.[18] They are recorded as the change in net working capital and capital expenditures (capex), respectively.

Step 3:

$$\text{FCF} = \text{NOPLAT} + \text{NCC} - \text{Change in net working capital} - \text{Capex} \quad \text{(35-4)}$$

For 2007,

$$\text{FCF} = \$2{,}732 + 551 - 455 - 1{,}461 = \$1{,}367 = \$1.367 \text{ million}$$
(The only NCC in this example is depreciation)

Summarizing, FCF is approximated by:

Net income
+ <u>Net interest after tax</u>
Unlevered net income
+ <u>Change in deferred taxes</u>
Net operating profit less adjusted taxes (NOPLAT)
+ Net noncash charges
− Change in net working capital
− <u>Capital expenditures (capex)</u>
Free cash flow (FCF)

Once free cash flow has been estimated for each year in the first stage (2007–2011 in Exhibit 3), the free cash flows are discounted back to present at the company's weighted average cost of capital (WACC).[19] When evaluating the target from a noncontrol perspective, we would use the target's WACC, which reflects that company's existing business risk and operating environment. In

[17] Some analysts also estimate and subtract the value of after-tax nonoperating income to obtain an estimate more closely reflecting operating results only. See Copeland, Koller, Murrin (2000), Chapter 9, for more details on NOPLAT.

[18] Working capital is defined in this use as current assets (excluding cash and equivalents) minus current liabilities (excluding short-term debt).

[19] For details on the estimation of WACC, see the reading on cost of capital.

anticipation of a merger, however, we would adjust that WACC to reflect any anticipated changes in the target's risk from such actions as a redeployment of assets or change in capital structure.

For the company in Exhibit 3, we will assume that the appropriate discount rate is 9.41 percent. Discounting free cash flow for the years 2007 through 2011 at 9.41 percent results in a present value of $5.802 million. That is the portion of the company's current value that can be attributed to the free cash flows that occur over the first stage. Next, we must determine the portion of the present value attributable to the company's terminal value, which arises from those cash flows occurring from the end of the first stage to perpetuity.

There are two standard methods for calculating a terminal value. The first method makes use of the constant growth formula. To apply the constant growth formula, an analyst must select a terminal growth rate, which is the long-term equilibrium growth rate that the company can expect to achieve in perpetuity, accounting for both inflation and real growth. The terminal growth rate is often lower than the growth rate applied during the first stage because any advantages from synergies, new opportunities, or cost reductions are transitory as competitors adjust and the industry evolves over time. The constant growth formula can be applied whenever the terminal growth rate is less than the WACC.

$$\text{Terminal value}_T = \frac{\text{FCF}_T(1 + g)}{(\text{WACC} - g)} \qquad \textbf{(35-5)}$$

where

FCF_T = free cash flow produced during the final year of the first stage
g = terminal growth rate

For the company in Exhibit 3, we will assume a terminal growth rate of 6.0 percent:

$$\text{Terminal value}_{2011} = \frac{\$1,799(1 + 0.06)}{(0.0941 - 0.06)} = \$55,922 = \$55.922 \text{ million}$$

A second method for estimating the terminal value involves applying a multiple at which the analyst expects the average company to sell at the end of the first stage. The analyst might use a free cash flow or other multiple that reflects the expected risk, growth, and economic conditions in the terminal year. Market multiples are rules of thumb applied by analysts, investment bankers, and venture capitalists to produce rough estimates of a company's value. Multiples tend to vary by industry. They can be based on anything applicable to the industry and correlated with market prices. Some service industries tend to be priced as multiples of EBITDA (earnings before interest, taxes, depreciation, and amortization). In contrast, retail stores in some industries might be priced based on multiples applied to floor space. In these cases, the respective multiples can be used directly to produce a terminal value, or they can be incorporated into a pro forma analysis to convert the multiple into a consistent value for free cash flow.

If the company in Exhibit 3 is in an industry where the typical company sells for about 20 times its free cash flow, then the company's terminal value estimate would be:

$$\text{Terminal value}_{2011} = 20 \times \$1,799 = \$35,980 = \$36.0 \text{ million}$$

Having established an estimate for the terminal value, the analyst must discount it back from the end of the estimate horizon to present. The discount rate used is the same WACC estimate that was previously applied to discount the free cash flows. If we decide that the terminal value found using the constant growth method is more accurate than a market multiple, we would discount that value back five years (2011 back to the present):

$$\text{Terminal value}_{2006} = \frac{\$55,922}{(1 + 0.0941)^5} = \$35,670 = \$35.670 \text{ million}$$

Adding the present value of the free cash flows (\$5.802 million) to the present value of the terminal value (\$35.670 million), we can estimate the value of the company to be \$41.471 million.[20] Note that a large proportion of the company's value is attributable to its terminal value (more than 85 percent in our example). The assumed terminal growth rate and WACC estimate can have a dramatic impact on the terminal value calculation: The final estimate of the company's value will only be as accurate as the estimates used in the model.

Advantages of Using Discounted Cash Flow Analysis

▶ Expected changes in the target company's cash flows (e.g., from operating synergies and cost structure changes) can be readily modeled.

▶ An estimate of intrinsic value based on forecast fundamentals is provided by the model.

▶ Changes in assumptions and estimates can be incorporated by customizing and modifying the model.

Disadvantages of Using Discounted Cash Flow Analysis

▶ It is difficult to apply when free cash flows do not align with profitability within the first stage. For example, a rapidly expanding company may be profitable but have negative free cash flows because of heavy capital expenditures to the horizon that can be forecast with confidence. The free cash flow value of the company will then derive from a later and harder to estimate period when free cash flow turns positive.

▶ Estimating cash flows and earnings far into the future is not an exact science. There is a great deal of uncertainty in estimates even for the following year, much less in perpetuity.

▶ Estimates of discount rates can change over time because of capital market developments or changes that specifically affect the companies in question. These changes can also significantly affect acquisition estimates.

▶ Terminal value estimates often subject the acquisition value calculations to a disproportionate degree of estimate error. The estimate of terminal value can differ depending on the specific technique used. Additionally, the range of estimates can be affected dramatically by small changes in the assumed growth and WACC estimates.

7.1.2 Comparable Company Analysis

A second approach that investment bankers use to estimate acquisition values is called "comparable company analysis." In this approach, the analyst first defines a set of other companies that are similar to the target company under review. This set may include companies within the target's primary industry as well as companies in similar industries. The sample should be formed to include as many companies as possible that have similar size and capital structure to the target.

---

[20] The estimate differs slightly from the sum due to rounding.

Once a set of comparable companies is defined, the next step is to calculate various relative value measures based on the current market prices of the comparable companies in the sample. Such valuation is often based on enterprise multiples. A company's enterprise value is the market value of its debt and equity minus the value of its cash and investments. Examples include enterprise value to free cash flow, enterprise value to EBITDA, enterprise value to EBIT, and enterprise value to sales. Because the denominator in such ratios is pre-interest, they may be preferred when the companies being compared have differences in leverage. The equity can also be valued directly using equity multiples, such as price to cash flow per share (P/CF), price to sales per share (P/S), price to earnings per share (P/E), and price to book value per share (P/BV).

The specific ratios that the analyst selects are determined by the industry under observation. Often, in addition to common market multiples, analysts will include industry-specific multiples. For instance, in the oil and gas industry, in addition to looking at price paid to earnings and cash flow ratios, many analysts evaluate the price paid per barrel of oil or per thousand cubic feet of natural gas reserves.

Analysts typically review the mean, median, and range for whichever metrics are chosen, and then they apply those values to corresponding estimates for the target to develop an estimated company value. This is quite similar to the approach we discussed earlier for using multiples to produce a terminal value estimate. In this case, however, we are calculating various relative value metrics rather than using an industry rule of thumb.

Each metric (P/E, P/CF, etc.) is likely to produce a different estimate for the target's value. Analysts hope that these values converge because that increases confidence in the overall estimate. To the extent that they diverge, analysts must apply judgment and experience to decide which estimates are producing the most accurate market values.

It should be noted that the value determined up to this point in the process yields an estimate of where the target company should trade as a stock in the marketplace relative to the companies in the sample. In order to calculate an acquisition value, the analyst must also estimate a takeover premium. The **takeover premium** is the amount by which the takeover price for each share of stock must exceed the current stock price in order to entice shareholders to relinquish control of the company to an acquirer. This premium is usually expressed as a percentage of the stock price and is calculated as:

$$\text{PRM} = \frac{(\text{DP} - \text{SP})}{\text{SP}} \tag{35-6}$$

where

$\quad$ PRM = takeover premium (as a percentage of stock price)
$\quad\quad$ DP = deal price per share of the target company
$\quad\quad$ SP = stock price of the target company[21]

To calculate the relevant takeover premium for a transaction, analysts usually compile a list of the takeover premiums paid for companies similar to the target. Preferably, the calculations will be from the recent past because acquisition values and premiums tend to vary over time and economic cycles.

---

[21] The analyst must be careful to note any pre-deal jump in the price that may have occurred because of takeover speculation in the market. In these cases, the analyst should apply the takeover premium to a selected representative price from before any speculative influences on the stock price.

EXAMPLE 8

Comparable Company Analysis

Sam Jones, an investment banker, has been retained by the Big Box Company to estimate the price that should be paid to acquire New Life Books Inc. Jones decides to use comparable company analysis to find a fair value for New Life, and has gathered the following information about three comparable companies:

Valuation Variables	Company 1	Company 2	Company 3
Current stock price ($)	20.00	32.00	16.00
Earnings per share ($)	1.00	1.82	0.93
Cash flow per share ($)	2.55	3.90	2.25
Book value per share ($)	6.87	12.80	5.35
Sales per share ($)	12.62	18.82	7.62

First, Jones calculates valuation metrics using the data he gathered. For each metric, he also calculates the mean.

Relative Valuation Ratio	Company 1	Company 2	Company 3	Mean
P/E	20.00	17.58	17.20	18.26
P/CF	7.84	8.21	7.11	7.72
P/BV	2.91	2.50	2.99	2.80
P/S	1.58	1.70	2.10	1.79

Jones then applies the mean relative valuation ratios to the corresponding data for New Life Books to estimate the comparable *stock* price. Because the four valuation metrics produce estimates that are all relatively close, he decides he is comfortable using an average of the four estimates to produce the estimated stock value.

Target Company Valuation Variables	Target Company (a)	Comparable Companies' Valuation Variables	Mean Multiples for Comparable Companies (b)	Estimated Stock Value Based on Comparables (a × b)
Earnings per share	1.95	P/E	18.26	$35.61
Cash flow per share	4.12	P/CF	7.72	$31.81
Book value per share	12.15	P/BV	2.80	$34.02
Sales per share	18.11	P/S	1.79	$32.42
Estimated stock value				Mean: $33.47

To determine the proper acquisition or takeover value, Jones must now estimate the relevant takeover premium. Using five of the most recent takeovers of companies that are similar to the target, he has compiled the following estimates:

Target Company	Stock Price Prior to Takeover	Takeover Price	Takeover Premium
Target 1	$23.00	$28.50	23.9%
Target 2	$17.25	$22.65	31.3%
Target 3	$86.75	$102.00	17.6%
Target 4	$45.00	$53.75	19.4%
Target 5	$36.75	$45.00	22.4%
Mean premium			22.9%

After examining the data, Jones decides that the mean estimated premium is reasonable. His next step is to apply the takeover premium to his mean estimate of the stock price for New Life Books:

Target's estimated stock value	$33.47
Estimated takeover premium	22.9%
Estimated takeover price of target	($33.47)(1.229) = $41.14

From all the calculations and estimates above, Jones concludes that a fair takeover price for the Big Box Company to pay for each share of New Life Books would be $41.14.[22]

Advantages of Using Comparable Company Analysis

► This method provides a reasonable approximation of a target company's value relative to similar companies in the market. This assumes that "like" assets should be valued on a similar basis in the market.

► With this method, most of the required data are readily available.

► The estimates of value are derived directly from the market. This is unlike the discounted cash flow method where the takeover value is determined based on many assumptions and estimates.

Disadvantages of Using Comparable Company Analysis

► The method is sensitive to market mispricing. To illustrate the issue, suppose that the comparable companies are overvalued. A valuation relative to those companies may suggest a value that is too high in the sense that values would be revised downward when the market corrects.

---

[22] As we shall discuss in Section 7.2 (covering bid evaluation) the analysis in Example 8 is not quite complete because the acquirer must evaluate the estimated takeover price relative to any expected synergies.

▶ Using this approach yields a market-estimated fair *stock* price for the target company. In order to estimate a fair *takeover* price, analysts must additionally estimate a fair takeover premium and use that information to adjust the estimated stock price.

▶ The analysis may be inaccurate because it is difficult for the analyst to incorporate any specific plans for the target (e.g., changing capital structure or eliminating duplicate resources) in the analysis.

▶ The data available for past premiums may not be timely or accurate for the particular target company under consideration.

7.1.3 Comparable Transaction Analysis

A third common approach to value target companies is known as "comparable transaction analysis." This approach is closely related to comparable company analysis except that the analyst uses details from recent takeover transactions for comparable companies to make direct estimates of the target company's takeover value.

The first step in comparable transaction analysis is to collect a relevant sample of recent takeover transactions. The sample should be as broad as possible but limited to companies in the same industry as the target, or at least closely related. Once the transactions are identified, the analyst can look at the same types of relative value multiples that were used in comparable company analysis (P/E, P/CF, other industry-specific multiples, etc.). In this case, however, we are not comparing the target against market multiples. For this approach we compare the multiples actually paid for similar companies in other M&A deals. As before, analysts typically look at descriptive statistics, such as the mean, median, and range for the multiples, and apply judgment and experience when applying that information to estimate the target's value.

EXAMPLE 9

Comparable Transaction Analysis

Joel Hofer, an analyst with an investment banking firm, has been asked to estimate a fair price for the General Health Company's proposed acquisition of Medical Services, Inc. He has already taken the initial step and assembled a sample containing companies involved in acquisitions within the same industry in which Medical Services operates. These companies have all been acquired in the past two years. Details on the acquisition prices and relevant pricing variables are shown below.

Valuation Variables	Acquired Company 1	Acquired Company 2	Acquired Company 3
Acquisition share price ($)	35.00	16.50	87.00
Earnings per share ($)	2.12	0.89	4.37
Cash flow per share ($)	3.06	1.98	7.95
Book value per share ($)	9.62	4.90	21.62
Sales per share ($)	15.26	7.61	32.66

The next step in the process is for Hofer to calculate the multiples at which each company was acquired:

Relative Valuation Ratio	Comparable Company 1	Comparable Company 2	Comparable Company 3	Mean
P/E	16.5	18.5	19.9	18.3
P/CF	11.4	8.3	10.9	10.2
P/BV	3.6	3.4	4.0	3.7
P/S	2.3	2.2	2.7	2.4

After reviewing the distribution of the various values around their respective means, Hofer is confident about using the mean value for each ratio because the range in values above and below the mean is reasonably small. Based on his experience with this particular industry, Hofer believes that cash flows are a particularly important predictor of value for these types of companies. Consequently, instead of finding an equally weighted average, Hofer has decided to apply the weights shown below for calculating a weighted average estimated price.

Target Company Valuation Variables	Target Company (a)	Comparable Companies' Valuation Multiples	Mean Multiple Paid for Comparable Companies (b)	Estimated Takeover Value Based on Comparables (c = a × b)	Weight (d)	Weighted Estimates (e = c × d)
Earnings per share	$ 2.62	P/E	18.3	$47.95	20%	$ 9.59
Cash flow per share	$ 4.33	P/CF	10.2	$44.17	40%	$17.67
Book value per share	$12.65	P/BV	3.7	$46.81	20%	$ 9.36
Sales per share	$22.98	P/S	2.4	$55.15	20%	$11.03
Weighted average estimate						$47.65

In sum, Hofer multiplied each valuation multiple by the corresponding variable for the target company to produce an estimated takeover value based on each comparable. He then decided to overweight cash flow per share and calculated a weighted average to determine an overall takeover value estimate of $47.65 per share for Medical Services, Inc. The same procedure could be repeated using the median, high, and low valuations for each of the valuation variables. This would generate a range of takeover values for Medical Services, Inc.

Advantages of Comparable Transaction Approach

▶ It is not necessary to separately estimate a takeover premium. The takeover premium is derived directly from the comparable transactions.

▶ The takeover value estimates come directly from values that were recently established in the market. This is unlike the discounted cash flow method where the takeover value is determined based on many assumptions and estimates.

▶ The use of prices established through other recent transactions reduces litigation risk for both companies' board of directors and managers regarding the merger transaction's pricing.

Disadvantages of Comparable Transaction Approach

▶ Because the value estimates assume that the M&A market has properly determined the intrinsic value of the target companies, there is a risk that the real takeover values in past transactions were not accurate. If true, these inaccurate takeover values are imputed in the estimates based on them.

▶ There may not be any, or an adequate number of, comparable transactions to use for calculating the takeover value. In these cases, analysts may try to use data from related industries. These derived values may not be accurate for the specific industry under study.

▶ The analysis may be inaccurate because it is difficult for the analyst to incorporate any specific plans for the target (e.g., changing capital structure or eliminating duplicate resources) in the analysis.

7.2 Bid Evaluation

Assessing the target's value is important, but it is insufficient for an assessment of the deal. Even if both the acquirer and the target separately agree on the target company's underlying value, the acquirer will obviously want to pay the lowest price possible while the target will negotiate for the highest price possible. Both the price and form of payment in a merger will determine the distribution of risks and benefits between the counterparties to the deal.

Acquirers must typically pay a premium to induce the owners of the target company to relinquish control. In an M&A transaction, the premium is the portion of the compensation received by the target company's shareholders that is in excess of the pre-merger market value of their shares. The target company's managers will attempt to negotiate the highest possible premium relative to the value of the target company.[23]

$$\text{Target shareholders' gain} = \text{Premium} = P_T - V_T \qquad \textbf{(35-7)}$$

where

P_T = price paid for the target company
V_T = pre-merger value of the target company

The acquirer is willing to pay in excess of the target company's value in anticipation of reaping its own gains. The acquirer's gains are derived from the synergies generated by the transaction—usually from some combination of cost reductions and revenue enhancements. All else constant, synergies increase the

---

[23] A burst of speculative stock activity typically accompanies merger negotiations. This activity typically results in a higher share price for the target company in anticipation of a takeover premium. When conducting a bid evaluation, the analyst should use some combination of an assessment of the company's intrinsic value and a representative stock price from before any merger speculation.

value of the acquiring company by the value of the synergies minus the premium paid to target shareholders:

$$\text{Acquirer's gain} = \text{Synergies} - \text{Premium} = S - (P_T - V_T) \qquad \textbf{(35-8)}$$

where

S = synergies created by the business combination

The post-merger value of the combined company is a function of the pre-merger values of the two companies, the synergies created by the merger, and any cash paid to the target shareholders as part of the transaction:

$$V_{A*} = V_A + V_T + S - C \qquad \textbf{(35-9)}$$

where

V_{A*} = post-merger value of the combined companies
V_A = pre-merger value of the acquirer
C = cash paid to target shareholders

When evaluating a bid, the pre-merger value of the target company is the absolute minimum bid that target shareholders should accept. Individual shareholders could sell their shares in the open market for that much instead of tendering their shares for a lower bid. At the other extreme, unless there are mitigating circumstances or other economic justifications, the acquirer's shareholders would not want to pay more than the pre-merger value of the target company plus the value of any expected synergies. If the acquirer were to pay more than that, then the acquirer's post-merger value would be lower than its pre-merger value—therefore, a reduction in shareholder value.

Bidding should thus generally be confined to a range dictated by the synergies expected from the transaction, with each side of the transaction negotiating to capture as much of the synergies as possible. Consequently, analysis of a merger depends not only on an assessment of the target company's value but also on estimates of the value of any synergies that the merged company is expected to attain.

Confidence in synergy estimates will have implications not only for the bid price but also for the method of payment. The reason for this is that different methods of payment for the merger—cash offer, stock offer, or mixed offer—inherently provide varying degrees of risk shifting with respect to misestimating the value of merger synergies. To see why this is the case, we will first walk through the evaluation of an offer for each method of payment.

EXAMPLE 10

Adagio Software Offer

Adagio Software, Inc., and Tantalus Software Solutions, Inc., are negotiating a friendly acquisition of Tantalus by Adagio. The management teams at both companies have informally agreed upon a transaction value of about €12.00 per share of Tantalus Software Solutions stock but are presently negotiating alternative forms of payment. Sunil

Agrawal, CFA, works for Tantalus Software Solutions' investment banking team and is evaluating three alternative offers presented by Adagio Software:

1. Cash Offer: Adagio will pay €12.00 per share of Tantalus stock.
2. Stock Offer: Adagio will give Tantalus shareholders 0.80 shares of Adagio stock per share of Tantalus stock.
3. Mixed offer: Adagio will pay €6.00 plus 0.40 shares of Adagio stock per share of Tantalus stock.

Agrawal estimates that the merger of the two companies will result in economies of scale with a net present value of €90 million. To aid in the analysis, Agrawal has also compiled the following data:

	Adagio	Tantalus
Pre-merger stock price	€ 15.00	€ 10.00
Number of shares outstanding (millions)	75	30
Pre-merger market value (millions)	€ 1,125	€ 300

Based only on the information given, which of the three offers should Agrawal recommend to the Tantalus Software Solutions management team?

Solution:

▶ **Alternative 1:** *Cash offer of €12.00 per share of Tantalus stock.* A cash offer is the most straightforward and easiest to evaluate. The price paid for the target company, P_T, is equal to cash price per share times the number of target shares: €12.00 × 30 million = €360 million. Because Tantalus' value, V_T, is €300 million, the premium is the difference between the two: €360 million − €300 million = €60 million.

Adagio's gain in this transaction is €30 million, which equals the value of the synergies minus the premium paid to Tantalus shareholders. A longer way to get to the same conclusion is to remember that the value of the post-merger combined company equals the pre-merger values of both companies plus the value of created synergies less the cash paid to target shareholders: $V_{A*} = V_A + V_T + S − C = $ €1,125 + 300 + 90 − 360 = €1,155 million. Adagio's pre-merger market value was €1,125 million, and Adagio's gain from the transaction is thus €1,155 − 1,125 = €30 million. Agrawal can divide the post-merger market value of €1,155 by the number of shares outstanding to determine Adagio's post-merger stock price. Under a cash offer, Adagio will not issue additional shares of stock, so Agrawal divides €1,155 by 75 million shares to see that, all else constant, Adagio's stock price after the merger should rise to €15.40.

In an all cash offer, Tantalus shareholders receive €60 million—the premium. Adagio's gain from the transaction equals the expected synergies (€90 million) less the premium paid to Tantalus shareholders (€60 million), which equals €30 million.

▶ **Alternative 2:** *Stock offer of 0.80 shares of Adagio stock per share of Tantalus stock.* A stock offer of 0.80 shares might seem at first glance to be equivalent to a cash offer of €12.00 because Adagio's share price is €15.00 (0.80 × €15 = €12). The results are actually slightly different, however, because Agrawal must account for the dilution that occurs when Adagio issues new shares to Tantalus stockholders. Because there are 30 million shares of the target outstanding, Adagio must issue: 30 million × 0.80 = 24 million shares.

To calculate the price paid for Tantalus, Agrawal starts by ascertaining the post-merger value of the combined company. Agrawal uses the same formula as before while using a value of zero for C because this is a stock offer and no cash is changing hands: $V_{A*} = V_A + V_T + S - C = €1,125 + 300 + 90 - 0 = €1,515$ million. Next, Agrawal divides Adagio's post-merger value by the post-merger number of shares outstanding. Because Adagio issued 24 million shares to complete the transaction, Agrawal adds 24 million to the original 75 million shares outstanding and arrives at 99 million. Dividing the post-merger market value by the post-merger number of shares outstanding, Agrawal determines that the value of each share given to Tantalus shareholders is actually worth €1,515 million/99 million = €15.30 and that the total value paid to Tantalus shareholders is €15.30 × 24 million = €367 million.

The premium is thus €367 − 300 = €67 million, which is €7 million higher than it was for the cash offer. Because the target shareholders receive €7 million more than in the cash offer, the acquirer's gain is correspondingly less. Because the synergies are valued at €90 million and the premium is €67 million, the acquirer's gain under a stock transaction with these terms is €23 million.

▶ **Alternative 3:** *Mixed offer of €6.00 plus 0.40 shares of Adagio stock per share of Tantalus stock.* A mixed offer will still result in some dilution, although not as much as a pure stock offer. Agrawal begins by calculating Adagio's post-merger value. Agrawal inserts €180 million for C because the company is paying €6 per share for 30 million shares: $V_{A*} = V_A + V_T + S - C = €1,125 + 300 + 90 - 180 = €1,335$ million.

Next, Agrawal determines that Adagio must issue 12 million shares to complete the transaction: 0.40 × 30 million = 12 million. Combined with the original 75 million shares outstanding, Adagio's post-merger number of shares outstanding will be 87 million. Agrawal divides €1,335 million by 87 million and find that each share given to the Tantalus shareholders is worth €15.35.

The total value paid to Tantalus shareholders includes a cash component, €6.00 × 30 million = €180 million, and a stock component, 12 million shares issued with a value of €15.35 each equaling €184 million. Added together, the total value is €180 + 184 = €364 million, and the premium is therefore €364 million − 300 million = €64 million. The acquirer's gain is $26 million.

▶ **Conclusion:** Agrawal should recommend that the Tantalus Software Solutions management team opt for the all stock offer because that alternative provides Tantalus shareholders the most value (the highest premium).

In Example 10, Adagio's gain ranged from €30 million in the pure cash offer to €26 million in the mixed offer and €23 million in the pure stock offer. If the dilution of a stock offer reduces the acquirer's gains from the transaction, why would an acquirer ever pay stock in a merger? The answer brings us back to the beginning of the section where we pointed out that the price and form of payment in a merger determine the distribution of risks and benefits. The choice of payment method is influenced by both parties' confidence in the estimated synergies and the relative value of the acquirer's shares.

The more confident the managers are that the estimated synergies will be realized, the more the acquiring managers will prefer to pay with cash and the more the target managers will prefer to receive stock. And the more the merger is paid for with the acquirer's stock, the more that the risks and benefits of realizing synergies will be passed on to the target shareholders. For example, in the cash offer we analyzed in Example 10, if the synergies later turned out to be worth €60 million rather than the originally estimated €90 million, then the Tantalus shareholders' premium would be unaffected but Adagio's gain would completely evaporate. In contrast, if the synergies were greater than estimated, then Tantalus shareholders' premium would still be unchanged but Adagio's gain would increase.

When stock is used as payment, the target shareholders become part owners of the acquiring company. In the Adagio stock offer, Tantalus shareholders would receive 24 million shares and thus own 24/99 (24.2 percent) of the post-merger acquirer. Thus, Tantalus shareholders would participate by that proportion in any deviation of synergies from pre-merger estimates. If synergies were worth only €60 million, Adagio would lose its €23 million gain and Tantalus shareholders' gain from the transaction would fall by €7 million.

The other factor affecting the method of payment decision relates to the counterparties' confidence in the companies' relative values. The more confident managers are in estimates of the target company's value, the more the acquirer would prefer cash and the more the target would prefer stock. For example, what if Adagio estimates that Tantalus is worth more than €10 per share and consequently offers €12.50 per share in cash instead of €12.00? In that case, Tantalus shareholders would receive a premium that is €15 million higher and Adagio's gain from the transaction would be reduced by €15 million to €15 million.

If Adagio and Tantalus had agreed on a stock offer, then Adagio would have shifted some of the cost of its error to Tantalus shareholders. Suppose Adagio still overestimates the value of Tantalus, but instead of a cash offer the company makes a stock offer of 0.83 shares (instead of the 0.80 shares that was offered in Example 10). In that case, Tantalus shareholders' gain increases by nearly €12 million to €78.8 million. Conversely, Adagio's gain falls by the same amount to €11.3 million, making the company slightly better off than it would have been in the cash offer where its gain was reduced by €15 million.

WHO BENEFITS FROM MERGERS?   8

What does the empirical evidence say about who actually gains in business combinations? Studies on the performance of mergers fall into two categories: short-term performance studies, which examine stock returns surrounding merger announcement dates, and long-term performance studies of post-merger companies. The empirical evidence suggests that merger transactions create value for target company shareholders in the short run. On average, target shareholders reap 30 percent premiums over the stock's pre-announcement market price, and the acquirer's stock price falls, on average, between 1 and 3 percent.[24] Moreover, on average, both the acquirer and target tend to see higher stock returns surrounding cash acquisition offers than around share offers.[25]

The high average premiums paid to target shareholders may be attributed, at least partly, to the winner's curse—the tendency for competitive bidding to result in overpayment. Even if the average bidding company accurately estimates the target company's value, some bidders will overestimate the target's value and other potential buyers will underestimate its value. Unless the winner can exploit some strong synergies that are not available to other bidders, the winning bidder is likely to be the one who most overestimates the value.

Roll argues that high takeover bids may stem from hubris, from "the overbearing presumption of bidders that their valuations are correct."[26] Implied in this behavior is that these executives are somehow smarter than everyone else and can see value where others cannot. Even if there were no synergies from a merger, managerial hubris would still lead to higher-than-market bids and a transfer of wealth from the acquiring company's shareholders to the target's shareholders. The empirical evidence is consistent with Roll's hubris hypothesis.

When examining a longer period, empirical evidence shows that acquirers tend to underperform comparable companies during the three years following an acquisition. This implies a general post-merger operational failure to capture synergies. Average returns to acquiring companies subsequent to merger transactions are negative 4.3 percent with about 61 percent of acquirers lagging their industry peers.[27] This finding suggests that financial analysts would be well served to thoroughly scrutinize estimates of synergy and post-merger value creation.

Analysts must attempt to distinguish those deals that create value and those that do not. Too often, companies with surplus cash but few new investment opportunities are prone to make acquisitions rather than distribute excess cash to shareholders. When distinguishing value-creating deals, analysts must examine the operational strengths possessed by the acquirer and the target to discern the likelihood that post-merger synergies will be achieved.

Based on past empirical results, the following are characteristics of M&A deals that create value:[28]

▶ **The buyer is strong**. Acquirers whose earnings and share prices grow at a rate above the industry average for three years before the acquisition earn statistically significant positive returns on announcement.

▶ **The transaction premiums are relatively low**. Acquirers earn negative returns on announcement when paying a high premium.

▶ **The number of bidders is low**. Acquirer stock returns are negatively related to the number of bidders.

▶ **The initial market reaction is favorable**. Initial market reaction is an important barometer for the value investors place on the gains from merging as well as an indication of future returns. If the acquiring company's stock

[24] J. Fred Weston and Samuel C. Weaver, *Mergers & Acquisitions* (New York: McGraw-Hill, 2001), pp. 93–116.

[25] Robert F. Bruner, *Deals from Hell: M&A Lessons That Rise above the Ashes* (New York: John Wiley & Sons, 2005), p. 33.

[26] Richard Roll, "The Hubris Hypothesis on Corporate Takeovers," *Journal of Business*, vol. 59 (April 1986), pp. 176–216.

[27] T. Koller, M. Goedhart, and D. Wessels, *Valuation: Measuring and Managing the Value of Companies*, 4th ed. (Hoboken, NJ: John Wiley & Sons, 2005), p. 439, footnotes 3 and 4.

[28] J. Fred Weston and Samuel C. Weaver, *Mergers & Acquisitions* (New York: McGraw-Hill, 2001), Chapter 5.

price falls when the deal is announced, investors are sending a message that the merger benefits are doubtful or that the acquirer is paying too much.

CORPORATE RESTRUCTURING   9

Just as mergers and acquisitions are a means by which companies get bigger, a corporate restructuring is usually used in reference to ways that companies get smaller—by selling, splitting off, or otherwise shedding operating assets. When a company decides to sell, liquidate, or spin off a division or a subsidiary, it is referred to as a **divestiture**.

Given, as we have discussed, that many companies have great difficulty actually achieving the planned synergies of a business combination, it is not surprising that many companies seek to undo previous mergers. Indeed, periods of intense merger activity are often followed by periods of heightened restructuring activity. Of course, previous mergers that did not work out as planned are not the only reason companies may choose to divest assets. Some of the common reasons for restructuring follow:

- ▶ **Change in strategic focus**. Either through acquisitions or other investments over time, companies often become engaged in multiple markets. Management may hope to improve performance by eliminating divisions or subsidiaries that are outside the company's core strategic focus.

- ▶ **Poor fit**. Sometimes a company will decide that a particular division is a poor fit within the overall company. For example, the company many not have the expertise or resources to fully exploit opportunities pursued by the division and may decide to sell the segment to another company that does have the necessary resources. Or, the division might simply not be profitable enough to justify continued investment based on the company's cost of capital.

- ▶ **Reverse synergy**. Managers may feel that a segment of the company is undervalued by the market, sometimes because of poor performance of the overall company or because the division is not a good strategic fit. In these cases, it is possible that the division and the company will be worth more separately than combined.

- ▶ **Financial or cash flow needs**. If times are tough, managers may decide to sell off portions of the company as a means by which to raise cash or cut expenses.

Restructuring can take many forms, but the three basic ways that a company divests assets are a sale to another company, a spin-off to shareholders, or liquidation. As part of a sale to another company, a company might offer to sell the assets of a division or may offer an equity carve-out. An **equity carve-out** involves the creation of a new legal entity and sales of equity in it to outsiders.

In a **spin-off**, shareholders of the parent company receive a proportional number of shares in a new, separate entity. Whereas the sale of a division results in an inflow of cash to the parent company, a spin-off does not. A spin-off simply results in shareholders owning stock in two different companies where there used to be one. A similar type of transaction is called a **split-off**, where some of the parent company's shareholders are given shares in a newly created entity in exchange for their shares of the parent company. **Liquidation** involves breaking up a company, division, or subsidiary and selling off its assets piecemeal. For a company, liquidation is typically associated with bankruptcy.

SUMMARY

Mergers and acquisitions are complex transactions. The process often involves not only the acquiring and target companies but also a variety of other stakeholders, including securities antitrust regulatory agencies. To fully evaluate a merger, analysts must ask two fundamental questions: First, will the transaction create value; and second, does the acquisition price outweigh the potential benefit? This reading has made the following important points.

▶ An acquisition is the purchase of some portion of one company by another. A merger represents the absorption of one company by another such that only one entity survives following the transaction.

▶ Mergers can be categorized by the form of integration. In a statutory merger, one company is merged into another; in a subsidiary merger, the target becomes a subsidiary of the acquirer; and in a consolidation, both the acquirer and target become part of a newly formed company.

▶ Horizontal mergers occur among peer companies engaged in the same kind of business. Vertical mergers occur among companies along a given value chain. Conglomerates are formed by companies in unrelated businesses.

▶ Merger activity has historically occurred in waves. These waves have typically coincided with a strong economy and buoyant stock market activity. Merger activity tends to be concentrated in a few industries, usually those undergoing changes, such as deregulation or technological advancement.

▶ The motives for M&A activity include synergy, growth, market power, the acquisition of unique capabilities and resources, diversification, increased earnings, management's personal incentives, tax considerations, and the possibilities of uncovering hidden value. Cross-border motivations may involve technology transfer, **product differentiation**, government policy, and the opportunities to serve existing clients abroad.

▶ A merger transaction may take the form of a stock purchase (when the acquirer gives the target company's shareholders some combination of cash or securities in exchange for shares of the target company's stock) or an asset purchase (when the acquirer purchases the target company's assets and payment is made directly to the target company). The decision of which approach to take will affect other aspects of the transaction, such as how approval is obtained, which laws apply, how the liabilities are treated, and how the shareholders and the company are taxed.

▶ The method of payment for a merger can be cash, securities, or a mixed offering with some of both. The exchange ratio in a stock or mixed offering determines the number of shares that stockholders in the target company will receive in exchange for each of their shares in the target company.

▶ Hostile transactions are those opposed by target managers, whereas friendly transactions are endorsed by the target company's managers. There are a variety of both pre- and post-offer defenses a target can use to ward off an unwanted takeover bid.

▶ Examples of pre-offer defense mechanisms include poison pills and puts, incorporation in a jurisdiction with restrictive takeover laws, staggered boards of directors, restricted voting rights, supermajority voting provisions, fair price amendments, and golden parachutes.

▶ Examples of post-offer defenses include "just say no" defense, litigation, greenmail, share repurchases, leveraged recapitalization, "crown jewel" defense, "Pac-Man" defense, or finding a white knight or a white squire.

▶ Antitrust legislation prohibits mergers and acquisitions that impede competition. Major U.S. antitrust legislation includes the Sherman Antitrust Act, the Clayton Act, the Celler–Kefauver Act, and the Hart–Scott–Rodino Act.

▶ The Federal Trade Commission and Department of Justice review mergers for antitrust concerns in the United States. The European Commission reviews transactions in the European Union.

▶ The Herfindahl–Hirschman Index (HHI) is a measure of market power based on the sum of the squared market shares for each company in an industry. Higher index values or combinations that result in a large jump in the index are more likely to meet regulatory challenges.

▶ The Williams Act is the cornerstone of securities legislation for M&A activities in the United States. The Williams Act ensures a fair tender offer process through the establishment of disclosure requirements and formal tender offer procedures.

▶ Three major tools for valuing a target company are discounted cash flow analysis (which involves discounting free cash flows estimated with pro forma financial statements), comparable company analysis (which estimates a company's intrinsic value based on relative valuation metrics for similar companies), and comparable transaction analysis (which derives valuation from details of recent takeover transactions for comparable companies).

▶ In a merger bid, the gain to target shareholders is measured as the **control premium**, which equals the price paid for the target company in excess of its value. The acquirer gains equal the value of any synergies created by the merger minus the premium paid to target shareholders. Together, the bid and the method of payment determine the distribution of risks and returns among acquirer and target shareholders with regard to realization of synergies as well as correct estimation of the target company's value.

▶ The empirical evidence suggests that merger transactions create value for target company shareholders. Acquirers, in contrast, tend to accrue value in the years following a merger. This finding suggests that synergies are often overestimated or difficult to achieve.

▶ When a company decides to sell, liquidate, or spin off a division or a subsidiary, it is referred to as a divestiture. Companies may divest assets for a variety of reasons, including a change in strategic focus, poor fit of the asset within the corporation, reverse synergy, or cash flow needs.

▶ The three basic ways that a company divests assets are a sale to another company, a spin-off to shareholders, and liquidation.

PRACTICE PROBLEMS FOR READING 35

The following information relates to Questions 1–6

Modern Auto, an automobile parts supplier, has made an offer to acquire Sky Systems, creator of software for the airline industry. The offer is to pay Sky Systems' shareholders the current market value of their stock in Modern Auto's stock. The relevant information it used in those calculations is given below:

	Modern Auto	Sky Systems
Share price	$40	$25
Number of outstanding shares (millions)	40	15
Earnings (millions)	$100	$30

Although the total earnings of the combined company will not increase and are estimated to be $130 million, Charles Wilhelm (treasurer of Modern Auto) argues that there are two attractive reasons to merge. First, Wilhelm says, "The merger of Modern Auto and Sky Systems will result in lower risk for our shareholders because of the diversification effect." Second, Wilhelm also says, "If our EPS increases, our stock price will increase in line with the EPS increase because our P/E will stay the same."

Sky Systems managers are not interested in the offer by Modern Auto. The managers, instead, approach HiFly, Inc., which is in the same industry as Sky Systems, to see if it would be interested in acquiring Sky Systems. HiFly is interested, and both companies believe there will be synergies from this acquisition. If HiFly were to acquire Sky Systems, it would do so by paying $400 million in cash.

HiFly is somewhat concerned whether antitrust regulators would consider the acquisition of Sky Systems an antitrust violation. The market in which the two companies operate consists of eight competitors. The largest company has a 25 percent market share. HiFly has the second largest market share of 20 percent. Five companies, including Sky Systems, each have a market share of 10 percent. The smallest company has a 5 percent market share.

1. The acquisition of Sky Systems by Modern Auto and the acquisition of Sky Systems by HiFly, respectively, would be examples of a

   A. horizontal merger and a vertical merger.

   B. vertical merger and a horizontal merger.

   C. conglomerate merger and a vertical merger.

   D. conglomerate merger and a horizontal merger.

2. If Sky Systems were to be acquired by Modern Auto under the terms of the original offer, the post-merger EPS of the new company would be *closest* to

   A. $2.00.

   B. $2.32.

   C. $2.63.

   D. $3.25.

3. Are Wilhelm's two statements about his shareholders benefiting from the diversification effect of the merger and about the increase in the stock price, respectively, correct?

	The Merger Will Result in Lower Risk for Shareholders	Stock Price Will Increase in Line with the EPS Increase
A.	No	No
B.	No	Yes
C.	Yes	No
D.	Yes	Yes

4. Which of the following defenses *best* describes the role of HiFly in the acquisition scenario?

   A. Crown jewel.

   B. Pac-Man.

   C. White knight.

   D. White squire.

5. Suppose HiFly acquires Sky Systems for the stated terms. The gain to Sky Systems shareholders resulting from the merger transaction would be *closest* to

   A. $25 million.

   B. $160 million.

   C. $375 million.

   D. $400 million.

6. If HiFly and Sky Systems attempt to merge, what would be the increase in the Herfindahl–Hirschman Index (HHI) and the probable action by the Department of Justice and the FTC, respectively, in response to the merger announcement?

	Increase in the HHI	Probable Response of Department of Justice and FTC
A.	290	To challenge the merger
B.	290	To investigate the merger
C.	400	To challenge the merger
D.	400	To investigate the merger

The following information relates to Questions 7–12

Kinetic Corporation is considering acquiring High Tech Systems. Jim Smith, the vice president of finance at Kinetic, has been assigned the task of estimating a fair acquisition price for High Tech. Smith is aware of several approaches that could be used for this purpose. He plans to estimate the acquisition price based on each of these approaches, and has collected or estimated the necessary financial data.

High Tech has 10 million shares outstanding. Smith has estimated that the post-merger free cash flows from High Tech, in millions of dollars, would be 15, 17, 20, and 23 at the end of the following four years. After Year 4, he projects the free cash flow to grow at a constant rate of 6.5 percent a year. He determines that the appropriate rate for discounting these estimated cash flows is 11 percent. He also estimates that after four years High Tech would be worth 23 times its free cash flow at the end of the fourth year.

Smith has determined that three companies—Alpha, Neutron, and Techno—are comparable to High Tech. He has also identified three recent takeover transactions—Quadrant, ProTech, and Automator—that are similar to the takeover of High Tech under consideration. He believes that price-to-earnings, price-to-sales, and price-to-book value per share of these companies could be used to estimate the value of High Tech. The relevant data for the three comparable companies and for High Tech are as follows:

Valuation Variables	Alpha	Neutron	Techno	High Tech
Current stock price ($)	44.00	23.00	51.00	31.00
Earnings/share ($)	3.01	1.68	2.52	1.98
Sales/share ($)	20.16	14.22	18.15	17.23
Book value/share ($)	15.16	7.18	11.15	10.02

The relevant data for the three recently acquired companies are given below:

Valuation Variables	Quadrant	ProTech	Automator
Stock price pre-takeover ($)	24.90	43.20	29.00
Acquisition stock price ($)	28.00	52.00	34.50
Earnings/share ($)	1.40	2.10	2.35
Sales/share ($)	10.58	20.41	15.93
Book value/share ($)	8.29	10.14	9.17

While discussing his analysis with a colleague, Smith makes two comments. Smith's first comment is: "If there were a pre-announcement run-up in Quadrant's price because of speculation, the takeover premium should be computed based on the price prior to the run-up." His second comment is: "Because the comparable transaction approach is based on the acquisition price, the takeover premium is implicitly recognized in this approach."

7. What is the present value per share of High Tech stock using the discounted cash flow approach if the terminal value of High Tech is based on using the **constant growth model** to determine terminal value?

    A. $35.22.

    B. $39.38.

    C. $40.56.

    D. $41.57.

8. What is the value per share of High Tech stock using the discounted cash flow approach if the terminal value of High Tech is based on using the cash flow multiple method to determine terminal value?

    A. $35.22.

    B. $40.56.

    C. $41.57.

    D. $58.61.

9. The average stock price of High Tech for the three relative valuation ratios (if it is traded at the mean of the three valuations) is *closest* to

    A. $35.21.

    B. $39.38.

    C. $40.56.

    D. $41.57.

10. Taking into account the mean takeover premium on recent comparable takeovers, what would be the estimate of the fair acquisition price of High Tech based on the comparable company approach?

    A. $35.22.

    B. $40.83.

    C. $41.29.

    D. $52.48.

11. The fair acquisition price of High Tech using the comparable transaction approach is *closest* to

    A. $35.22.

    B. $40.86.

    C. $41.31.

    D. $52.48.

12. Are Smith's two comments about his analysis correct?

    A. Both of his comments are correct.

    B. Both of his comments are incorrect.

    C. His first comment is correct, and his second comment is incorrect.

    D. His first comment is incorrect, and his second comment is correct.

4⅝ 4...
5½ 5½ — ⅝
5½ 21³/₁₆ — ⅛
20⅝ 21³/₁₆
17⅜ 18⅛ + ⅞
13½ 6½ — ½
6½ 6½
7¼ 3¹/₃₂ —
15/16
9/16 9/16
⅛/₃₂ 7¹³/₁₆ 7¹⁵/₁₆
7¹³/₁₆
2⅝ 2¹¹/₃₂ 2½ +
2¾ 2¼ 2¼
12¹/₁₆ 11⅜ 11¾ +
33¾ 33 33¹/₁₆ —
25⅝ 24⁹/₁₆ 25⅜ +
12 11⅝ 11⅞ +
16 10½ 10½ 10½ —
78 15⅞ 15¹³/₁₆ 15⅞ —
9¹/₁₆ 8¼ 8⅛ +
430 11¼ 10⅛

APPENDIX

Appendix A Solutions to End-of-Reading Problems

SOLUTIONS FOR READING 31

1. D is correct.

$$\text{Outlay} = \text{FCInv} + \text{NWCInv} - \text{Sal}_0 + T(\text{Sal}_0 - B_0)$$
$$\text{Outlay} = (350,000 + 110,000) + 73,000 - 0 + 0 = \$533,000$$

The installed cost is $350,000 + $110,000 = $460,000, so the annual depreciation is $460,000/5 = $92,000. The annual after-tax operating cash flow for Years 1–5 is

$$\begin{aligned}
\text{CF} &= (S - C - D)(1 - T) + D \\
&= (265,000 - 83,000 - 92,000)(1 - 0.40) + 92,000 \\
\text{CF} &= \$146,000
\end{aligned}$$

The terminal year after-tax non-operating cash flow in Year 5 is

$$\begin{aligned}
\text{TNOCF} &= \text{Sal}_5 + \text{NWCInv} - T(\text{Sal}_5 - B_5) \\
&= 85,000 + 73,000 - 0.40(85,000 - 0) \\
\text{TNOCF} &= \$124,000
\end{aligned}$$

The NPV is

$$\text{NPV} = -533,000 + \sum_{t=1}^{5} \frac{146,000}{1.10^t} + \frac{124,000}{1.10^5} = \$97,449$$

2. B is correct. The additional annual depreciation is $100,000/8 = $12,500. The depreciation tax savings is 0.40 ($12,500) = $5,000. The change in project NPV is

$$-100,000 + \sum_{t=1}^{8} \frac{5,000}{(1.10)^t} = -100,000 + 26,675 = -\$73,325$$

3. D is correct. Financing costs are not subtracted from the cash flows for either the NPV or the IRR. The effects of financing costs are captured in the discount rate used.

4. C is correct. The annual depreciation charge is $400,000/10 = $40,000. The after-tax operating cash flow in Year 1 should be

$$\begin{aligned}
\text{CF} &= (S - C - D)(1 - T) + D \\
&= (240,000 - 110,000 - 40,000)(1 - 0.30) + 40,000 \\
&= 63,000 + 40,000 = \$103,000
\end{aligned}$$

5. C is correct. The terminal year after-tax non-operating cash flow is

$$\begin{aligned}
\text{TNOCF} &= \text{Sal}_5 + \text{NWCInv} - T(\text{Sal}_5 - B_5) \\
&= 21 + 8 - 0.40(21 - 15) = £26.6 \text{ million}
\end{aligned}$$

6. D is correct. The investment outlay is

$$\begin{aligned}
\text{Outlay} &= \text{FCInv} + \text{NWCInv} - \text{Sal}_0 + T(\text{Sal}_0 - B_0) \\
&= (360,000 + 40,000) + 60,000 - 0 + 0 = \$460,000
\end{aligned}$$

7. A is correct. Depreciation will be $400,000/5 = $80,000 per year. The annual after-tax operating cash flow is

$$CF = (S - C - D)(1 - T) + D$$
$$= [0 - (-140,000) - 80,000](1 - 0.40) + 80,000 = \$116,000$$

8. C is correct. The terminal year non-operating cash flow is

$$TNOCF = Sal_5 + NWCInv - T(Sal_5 - B_5)$$
$$= 120,000 + 60,000 - 0.40(120,000 - 0) = \$132,000$$

9. D is correct. The value of the depreciation tax savings is increased, and the real after-tax interest expense is also increased.

10. A is correct. The statement is correct for sensitivity analysis, but not for scenario analysis (in which several input variables are changed for each scenario).

11. B is correct. Either the least-common multiple of lives or the equivalent annual annuity approach should be used (both using the NPV, not the IRR). Concept 4 is correct as given.

12. D is correct.

$$CF = (S - C - D)(1 - T) + D = 50(1 - 0.3) + 50 = €85 \text{ each year}$$

13. B is correct. Economic income is the cash flow plus the change in value, or economic income is the cash flow minus the economic depreciation (we will use the second expression):

$$V_0 = \frac{85}{1.12} + \frac{85}{1.12^2} = 143.65 \qquad V_1 = \frac{85}{1.12} = 75.89 \quad V_2 = 0$$

$$\begin{aligned}
\text{Economic income (Year 1)} &= CF_1 - (V_0 - V_1) \\
&= 85 - (143.65 - 75.89) \\
&= 85 - 67.76 = €17.24
\end{aligned}$$

$$\begin{aligned}
\text{Economic income (Year 2)} &= CF_2 - (V_1 - V_2) \\
&= 85 - (75.89 - 0) \\
&= 85 - 75.89 = €9.11
\end{aligned}$$

14. C is correct.

$$EP = NOPAT - \$WACC = EBIT(1 - T) - WACC \times Capital$$
$$EP \text{ (Year 1)} = 50(1 - 0.30) - 0.12(100) = 35 - 12 = €23$$
$$EP \text{ (Year 2)} = 50(1 - 0.30) - 0.12(50) = 35 - 6 = €29$$

$$MVA = \frac{EP\,(\text{Year 1})}{1 + WACC} + \frac{EP\,(\text{Year 2})}{(1 + WACC)^2} = \frac{23}{1.12} + \frac{29}{1.12^2} = €43.65$$

(An alternative way to get MVA is simply to find the NPV of the investment project.)

15. B is correct. The way to solve the problem is to calculate the equivalent annual annuity and choose the service life with the lowest annual cost.

For a two-year service life, the NPV is

$$NPV = -40,000 + \frac{-12,000}{1.10^1} + \frac{-15,000}{1.10^2} + \frac{20,000}{1.10^2} = -46,776.86$$

The EAA (PV = −46,776.86, $N = 2$, and $i = 10\%$) is −26,952.38.

For a three-year service life, the NPV is

$$\text{NPV} = -40,000 + \frac{-12,000}{1.10^1} + \frac{-15,000}{1.10^2} + \frac{-20,000}{1.10^3} + \frac{17,000}{1.10^3}$$
$$= -65,559.73$$

The EAA (PV = −65,559.73, $N = 3$, and $i = 10\%$) is −26,362.54.

For a four-year service life, the NPV is

$$\text{NPV} = -40,000 + \frac{-12,000}{1.10^1} + \frac{-15,000}{1.10^2} + \frac{-20,000}{1.10^3} + \frac{-25,000}{1.10^4} + \frac{12,000}{1.10^4}$$
$$= -87,211.26$$

The EAA (PV = −87,211.26, $N = 4$, and $i = 10\%$) is −27,512.61.

The three-year service life has the lowest annual cost. Laroche should replace the vans every three years.

16. A is correct. To help the selection process, use the profitability index for each project, which shows the total present value per dollar invested.

Project	Outlay	PV of Future Cash Flows	NPV	PI	PI Rank
1	31	44	13	1.419	1
2	15	21	6	1.400	2
3	12	16.5	4.5	1.375	(tie) 3
4	10	13	3	1.300	6
5	8	11	3	1.375	(tie) 3
6	6	8	2	1.333	5

Try to incorporate the high PI projects into the budget using trial and error. These trials include the following:

Set of Projects	Total Outlay	Total NPV
1 and 5	39	16
2, 3, and 4	37	13.5
2, 3, and 5	35	13.5
2, 4, 5, and 6	39	14

Among the sets of projects suggested, the optimal set is the one with the highest NPV, provided its total outlay does not exceed C$40 million. The set consisting of Projects 1 and 5 produces the highest NPV.

17. B is correct. If demand is "high," the NPV is

$$\text{NPV} = -190 + \sum_{t=1}^{10} \frac{40}{1.10^t} = \text{C\$55.783 million}$$

If demand is "low," the NPV is

$$\text{NPV} = -190 + \sum_{t=1}^{10} \frac{20}{1.10^t} = -\text{C\$67.109 million}$$

The expected NPV is $0.50(55.783) + 0.50(-67.109) = -\text{C\$5.663 million}$.

18. D is correct. Assume we are at time = 1. The NPV of the expansion (at time 1) if demand is "high" is

$$\text{NPV} = -190 + \sum_{t=1}^{9} \frac{40}{1.10^t} = \text{C\$40.361 million}$$

The NPV of the expansion (at time 1) if demand is "low" is

$$\text{NPV} = -190 + \sum_{t=1}^{9} \frac{20}{1.10^t} = -\text{C\$74.820 million}$$

The optimal decision is to expand if demand is "high" and not expand if "low."

Because the expansion option is exercised only when its value is positive, which happens 50 percent of the time, the expected value of the expansion project, at time zero, is

$$\text{NPV} = \frac{1}{1.10} \, 0.50(40.361) = \text{C\$18.346 million}$$

The total NPV of the initial project and the expansion project is

$$\text{NPV} = -\text{C\$5.663 million} + \text{C\$18.346 million} = \text{C\$12.683 million}$$

The optional expansion project, handled optimally, adds sufficient value to make this a positive NPV project.

19. A is correct. Both suggestions are bad. In valuing projects, expected cash flows should be discounted at required rates of return that reflect their risk, not at a risk-free rate that ignores risk; moreover, when comparing the projects, the NPVs may not have the same ranking when using the risk-free rate as when using the required rate of return. Even though both options cannot be exercised, they can both add value. If demand is high, you can exercise the growth option, and if demand is low, you can exercise the abandonment option.

20. D is correct. Both suggestions are good. Choosing projects with high IRRs might cause the company to concentrate on short-term projects that reduce the NPV of the company. Whenever the project risk differs from the company risk, a project-specific required rate of return should be used.

21. D is correct. The after-tax operating cash flow for each of the next three years is $\$20,000 + \$40,000 = \$60,000$. The book value in three years will be $\$380,000$ (the original cost less three years' depreciation). So the terminal year after-tax non-operating cash flow will be $\text{Sal}_3 - 0.30(\text{Sal}_3 - \$380,000)$, where Sal_3 is the selling price. For a 15 percent return, the PV of future cash flows must equal the investment:

$$500,000 = \frac{60,000}{1.15} + \frac{60,000}{1.15^2} + \frac{60,000}{1.15^3} + \frac{\text{Sal}_3 - 0.30(\text{Sal}_3 - 380,000)}{1.15^3}$$

There are several paths to follow to solve for Sal_3.

$$363,006.5 = \frac{Sal_3 - 0.30(Sal_3 - 380,000)}{1.15^3}$$

$$Sal_3 - 0.30(Sal_3 - 380,000) = 552,087.5$$
$$0.70\ Sal_3 = 438,087.5$$
$$Sal_3 = \$625,839$$

22. A is correct. The cash flows (in $ million) for the 5-year gas project are as follows:

Time	Outlays	After-Tax Operating Cash Flows	Total After-Tax Cash Flows
0	6.0	0.0	−6.0
1	1.0	0.5	−0.5
2	0.0	4.0	4.0
3	0.0	4.0	4.0
4	0.0	4.0	4.0
5	5.0	4.0	−1.0

Given the required rate of return of 18 percent, the NPV can be calculated with Equation 31–2:

$$NPV = -6.0 + \frac{-0.5}{1.18} + \frac{4.0}{1.18^2} + \frac{4.0}{1.18^3} + \frac{4.0}{1.18^4} + \frac{-1.0}{1.18^5}$$

$$NPV = \$509,579$$

Similarly, the IRR can be calculated from Equation 31-3:

$$-6.0 + \frac{-0.5}{1+r} + \frac{4.0}{(1+r)^2} + \frac{4.0}{(1+r)^3} + \frac{4.0}{(1+r)^4} + \frac{-1.0}{(1+r)^5} = 0$$

Solving for r with a financial calculator or spreadsheet software will yield 21.4 percent for the internal rate of return. Note that in spite of the fact that we are dealing with a nonconventional cash flow pattern, the IRR has a unique solution. The NPV profile declines as the required rate of return increases, and the NPV value crosses the x-axis (required rate of return) only one time, at 21.4 percent.

23. D is correct. Because this is a replacement chain, the EAA should be used instead of the NPV. The NPV and EAA for the Pinto grinder are correct. For the Bolten grinder, the NPV is

$$NPV = -125,000 + \sum_{t=1}^{4} \frac{47,000}{1.10^t} + \frac{20,000}{1.10^4} = 37,644$$

To find the Bolten EAA, take the NPV for Bolten and annualize it for four years ($N = 4$, $PV = 37,644$, and $i = 10\%$). The Bolten EAA is $11,876. Consequently, the Pinto grinder has the better EAA of $12,341.

24. B is correct. Goldberg's first comment is wrong. A project should be abandoned in the future only when its abandonment value is more than the

discounted value of the remaining cash flows. Goldberg's second comment is correct.

25. A is correct. The $10 million original cost is a sunk cost and not relevant. The correct investment is today's opportunity cost, the market value today. The correct discount rate is the project required rate of return. The after-tax cost of debt is too low, even if the project is all debt financed.

26. B is correct. Even if they are the same size, a short-term project with a high IRR can have a lower NPV than a longer-term project. The immediate impact on EPS does not capture the full effect of the cash flows over the project's entire life.

27. A is correct. The annual depreciation charge for Years 1–6 is $1.5/6 = 0.25$. Annual after-tax operating cash flows for Years 1–6 are:

$$CF = (S - C - D)(1 - T) + D$$
$$CF = [0.10 - (-0.25) - 0.25](1 - 0.40) + 0.25$$
$$CF = 0.06 + 0.25 = €0.31 \text{ billion}$$

Annual after-tax operating cash flows for Years 7–12 are:

$$CF = (S - C - D)(1 - T) + D$$
$$CF = [0.10 - (-0.25) - 0](1 - 0.40) + 0$$
$$CF = €0.21 \text{ billion}$$

28. C is correct. Outlay at time zero is:

$$\text{Outlay} = FCInv + NWCInv - Sal_0 + T(Sal_0 - B_0)$$
$$\text{Outlay} = 1.50 + 0.40 - 0 + 0 = €1.90 \text{ billion.}$$

Terminal year after-tax non-operating cash flow is

$$TNOCF = Sal_{12} + NWCInv - T(Sal_{12} - B_{12})$$
$$TNOCF = 0.50 + 0.40 - 0.40(0.50 - 0) = €0.70 \text{ billion}$$

29. B is correct. The cash flows, computed in the first two questions, are as follows:

Time 0	−€1.90 billion
Time 1–6	€0.31 billion
Time 7–12	€0.21 billion
Time 12	€0.70 billion

The NPV is

$$NPV = -1.90 + \sum_{t=1}^{6} \frac{0.31}{1.12^t} + \sum_{t=7}^{12} \frac{0.21}{1.12^t} + \frac{0.70}{1.12^{12}}$$

$$NPV = -1.90 + 1.2745 + 0.4374 + 0.1797 = -€0.0084 \text{ billion}$$
$$\approx -€0.01 \text{ billion}$$

30. A is correct. Accelerated depreciation shifts depreciation expense toward the earlier years so that first-year operating income after taxes will be lower. However, because depreciation is a noncash expense, it must be added back to operating income after taxes in order to obtain after-tax operating cash flow. This process shifts cash flows from later years to earlier years, increasing the NPV.

31. C is correct. The outlay is lower by €0.24, which will decrease the annual depreciation by €0.04 for the first six years. The annual additional taxes from the loss of the depreciation tax shelter are €0.04(0.40) = €0.016. The after-tax cash flows are higher by €0.24 at time zero (because of the smaller investment) and lower by €0.016 for the first six years. The NPV increases by

$$\text{NPV} = +0.24 - \sum_{t=1}^{6} \frac{0.016}{1.12^t} = 0.24 - 0.0658 = 0.1742 = €0.17 \text{ billion}$$

32. D is correct. Both of the supervisor's comments are incorrect. Because the Bayonne Pharma project is a conventional project (an outflow followed by inflows), the multiple IRR problem cannot occur. The EAA is preferred over the NPV when dealing with mutually exclusive projects with differing lives, a scenario which is not relevant for this decision. The Bayonne Pharma project is free-standing, so the NPV approach is appropriate.

33. B is correct.

Economic income = Cash flow − Economic depreciation.

Economic income (Year 1) = $CF_1 - (V_0 - V_1)$

After-tax operating cash flow (CF) = (S − C − D)(1 − T) + D + After-tax salvage = EBIT(1 − T) + D + After-tax salvage

Year	1	2	3	4	5
EBIT	30,000	40,000	50,000	60,000	40,000
EBIT(1 − 0.40)	18,000	24,000	30,000	36,000	24,000
D	40,000	40,000	40,000	40,000	40,000
After-tax salvage					12,000
CF	58,000	64,000	70,000	76,000	76,000

$CF_1 = 58,000$

$$V_0 = \frac{58,000}{1.12} + \frac{64,000}{1.12^2} + \frac{70,000}{1.12^3} + \frac{76,000}{1.12^4} + \frac{76,000}{1.12^5} = 244,054.55$$

$$V_1 = \frac{64,000}{1.12} + \frac{70,000}{1.12^2} + \frac{76,000}{1.12^3} + \frac{76,000}{1.12^4} = 215,341.10$$

Economic income (Year 1) = 58,000 − (244,054.55 − 215,341.10)
Economic income (Year 1) = 58,000 − 28,713.45 = 29,286.55

34. B is correct.

EP = NOPAT − $WACC
NOPAT = EBIT(1 − Tax rate) = 30,000(1 − 0.40) = 18,000
$WACC = WACC × Capital = 0.12(200,000) = 24,000
EP = 18,000 − 24,000 = −6,000

35. A is correct.

$RI_t = NI_t - r_e B_{t-1}$
$RI_1 = 11,899 - 0.19(77,973) = 11,899 - 14,815 = -2,916$

36. D is correct. The value of equity is the PV of cash distributions to equity:

$$PV = \frac{37{,}542}{1.19} + \frac{39{,}536}{1.19^2} + \frac{41{,}201}{1.19^3} + \frac{42{,}496}{1.19^4} + \frac{40{,}375}{1.19^5} = 122{,}027$$

37. B is correct. Robinson's first statement is wrong. The value of an asset is the present value of its future cash flows. Economic income each year is the cash flow minus economic depreciation, $EI = CF - ED$. For this company, which is declining in value each year, the economic depreciation is positive and EI is less than CF each year. Consequently, the present value of economic income (EI) will be less than the present value of future cash flows (CF). Robinson's second statement is actually correct.

38. C is correct. Market value added is equal to the present value of EP. Its value, however, is not equal to the book value of equity. The calculation of MVA is shown below:

Year	1	2	3	4	5[a]
EBIT	30,000	40,000	50,000	60,000	60,000
NOPAT = EBIT(1 − 0.40)	18,000	24,000	30,000	36,000	36,000
Capital (beginning)	200,000	160,000	120,000	80,000	40,000
\$WACC = 0.12 × Capital	24,000	19,200	14,400	9,600	4,800
EP = NOPAT − \$WACC	−6,000	4,800	15,600	26,400	31,200

[a] The fifth year figures include the effects of salvage. Before-tax salvage of 20,000 (= 12,000/(1 − 0.40)) is added to EBIT. The after-tax salvage of 12,000 is included in NOPAT.

$$MVA = \frac{-6{,}000}{1.12} + \frac{4{,}800}{1.12^2} + \frac{15{,}600}{1.12^3} + \frac{26{,}400}{1.12^4} + \frac{26{,}400}{1.12^5} = 44{,}054.55$$

39. B is correct. The weighted average cost of capital for Embelesado is calculated as:

$$WACC = (\text{market weight of debt} \times \text{after-tax cost of debt})$$
$$+ (\text{market weight of equity} \times \text{cost of equity})$$
$$WACC = w_d k_d (1 - T) + w_{cs} k_{cs} = 0.231(8.0\%)(1 - 0.35) + 0.769(13.0\%)$$
$$= 1.201\% + 9.997\%$$
$$WACC = 11.198\% = 11.20\%$$

40. C is correct. The terminal year cash flow is:

Revenues	€60.00
Less operating costs	25.00
Less depreciation expenses	20.00
= Taxable Income	15.00
Less taxes @ 35%	(5.25)
= Net Income	9.75
Plus depreciation expenses	20.00
= After-tax operating CF	29.75
+ Recover WC	10.00
+ Ending market value	5.00
Less taxes on sale proceeds @ 35%	(1.75)*
= Terminal Year CF	€43.00

* The tax on the sale proceeds is 35% times the gain of €5.00 = €1.75

41. C is correct. This is the IRR for a project with the following cash flows: (€70,000) in Time 0, €29,750 at Times 1 and 2, and €43,000 at Time 3.

	Years 1 & 2	Year 3
Revenues	€60,000	€60,000
Less operating costs	25,000	25,000
Less depreciation expense	20,000	20,000
= Taxable income	15,000	15,000
Less taxes @ 35%	5,250	5,250
= Net income	9,750	9,750
Plus depreciation expense	20,000	20,000
= After-tax operating CF	€29,750	29,750
+ Recover WC		10,000
+ Salvage value		5,000
− Less taxes on sal. value @ 35%		1,750
= Terminal year CF		€43,000

The IRR of 20.29% is readily found with a financial calculator:

$$70,000 = \frac{29,750}{(1 + IRR)^1} + \frac{29,750}{(1 + IRR)^2} + \frac{43,000}{(1 + IRR)^3}$$

You can also "reverse-engineer" the answer using the choices given in the question.

42. A is correct. Projects with shorter paybacks do not necessarily have a positive NPV. For mutually exclusive projects, the NPV and IRR criteria will not necessarily provide the same project ranking.

43. B is correct. Additional depreciation in earlier time periods will shield Embelesado from additional taxes, thus increasing the net cash flows in earlier years of the project and increasing the project's NPV. However, this also means that there will be less depreciation expense in the terminal year of the project, thus shielding less income and increasing taxes. Terminal-year net cash flow will likely decrease.

44. A is correct. The entire €10 million will be subject to taxes, resulting in an additional €6.5 million after taxes. As indicated below, when discounted at 13 percent for three years, this has a present value of €4.5048 (rounded to €4.50 millions):

$$PV = \frac{10.0(1 - 0.35)}{(1.13)^3} = \frac{6.50}{(1.13)^3} = 4.50$$

SOLUTIONS FOR READING 32

1. D is correct. *Operating risk* is the sensitivity of operating earnings to changes in the number of units produced and sold. *Sales risk* refers to the uncertainty of the number of units produced and sold and the price at which units are sold. *Business risk* is the joint effect of sales risk and operating risk. *Total leverage* is the joint effect of operating leverage and financial leverage.

2. D is correct. Operating leverage is the sensitivity of earnings before interest and taxes to changes in the number of units produced and sold. The *degree of operating leverage* is the elasticity of operating earnings with respect to the number of units produced and sold.

3. C is correct. *Calculations:*

$$DOL = \frac{40 \text{ million}(\$100 - \$65)}{[40 \text{ million}(\$100 - \$65)] - \$1.05 \text{ billion}}$$

$$= \frac{\$1.400 \text{ billion}}{\$1.400 \text{ billion} - \$1.05 \text{ billion}}$$

$$= \frac{\$1.4}{\$0.35}$$

$$= 4$$

$$\text{Operating breakeven} = \frac{\$1.05 \text{ billion}}{\$35} = 30 \text{ million units}$$

- ▶ Fulcrum produces positive operating income if it produces more than 30 million units. If it produces and sells fewer than 30 million, it will generate a loss.
- ▶ The DOL is 4.
- ▶ If unit sales increase by 5 percent, Fulcrum's operating earnings are expected to increase by $4 \times 5\% = 20\%$.
- ▶ Increasing fixed production costs will *increase* the sensitivity of Fulcrum's operating earnings to changes in sales.

4. C is correct. Business risk results from economic factors and operating leverage.

5. C is correct. The degree of total leverage of the Grundlegend Company exceeds that of the Basic Company, but the extent of the difference depends on the amount of interest expense, not the amount of debt. In the case of financial leverage, it is the interest that acts as a fulcrum.

6. B is correct.

$$\text{Operating breakeven units} = \frac{¥1290 \text{ million}}{(¥3529 - ¥1500)} = 635{,}781.173 \text{ units}$$

$$\text{Operating breakeven sales} = ¥3529 \times 635{,}781.173 \text{ units}$$

$$= ¥2{,}243{,}671{,}760$$

or

$$\text{Operating breakeven sales} = \frac{¥1290 \text{ million}}{1 - (¥1500/¥3529)} = ¥2{,}243{,}671{,}760$$

$$\text{Total breakeven} = \frac{\text{¥1290 million} + \text{¥410 million}}{(\text{¥3529} - \text{¥1500})}$$

$$= \frac{\text{¥1700 million}}{\text{¥2029}} = 837{,}851.1582 \text{ units}$$

$$\text{Breakeven sales} = \text{¥3529} \times 837{,}851.1582 \text{ units} = \text{¥2,956,776,737}$$

or

$$\text{Breakeven sales} = \frac{\text{¥1700 million}}{1 - (\text{¥1500}/\text{¥3529})} = \text{¥2,956,776,737}$$

7. A is correct.

$$\text{Total breakeven}_{\text{Gearing}} = \frac{(\$40{,}000{,}000 + \$20{,}000{,}000)}{(\$200 - \$120)} = 750{,}000 \text{ units}$$

$$\text{Total breakeven}_{\text{Hebelkraft}} = \frac{(\$90{,}000{,}000 + \$20{,}000{,}000)}{(\$200 - \$100)} = 1{,}100{,}000 \text{ units}$$

8. B is correct. Proposition I, or the capital structure irrelevance theory, states that the level of debt versus equity has no effect on company value in the absence of taxes and imperfect markets.

9. D is correct. The cost of equity rises with the level of debt because equity capital providers demand more potential return for the added financial risk.

10. C is correct.

$r_e = r_a + (r_a - r_d)(D/E)$
Note: If $D/(D + E) = 0.50$, then $D/E = 1.0$
$r_e = 0.10 + (0.10 - 0.05)(1.0)(1 - 0.2)$
$r_e = 0.10 + [0.05(0.90)] = 0.10 + 0.04 = 0.14$, or 14%

11. C is correct. If the company's cost of capital increases as a result of taking on additional debt, the company has moved beyond the optimal capital structure and therefore is signaling its difficulty in raising capital.

12. B is correct. North American companies are found to use long-term debt more intensively, whereas the proportion of long-term debt financing is typically low in the case of Japanese companies.

13. C is correct. Low inflation has a beneficial impact on long-term debt usage, but researchers would expect lower debt maturity in the three other cases.

14. A is correct. If the legal system is inefficient, researchers expect to see higher leverage, because debt contracts define the rights of creditors and make them easier to enforce than the rights of shareholders.

15. A is correct. According to pecking order theory, internally generated funds are preferable to both new equity and new debt.

16. D is correct. The static trade-off theory indicates that there is a trade-off between the tax shield from interest on debt and the costs of financial distress, leading to an optimal range of debt for a company.

17. B is correct.

$r_d^{*} = r_d(1 - t)$
$0.08(1 - 0.35) = 0.052 = 5.20\%$

18. D is correct.

$$r_e = r_a + (r_a - r_d^*)\left(\frac{D}{E}\right)$$

$$0.1082 + (0.1082 - 0.0520)\left(\frac{100 \text{ million}}{300 \text{ million}}\right) = 0.1269 = 12.69\%$$

19. B is correct.

$$r_a = \left(\frac{D}{V}\right)r_d(1 - t) + \left(\frac{E}{V}\right)r_e$$

At D/V = 20%, r_a = (0.2)(0.077)(1 − 0.35) + (0.8)(0.125) = 0.1100
= 11.00%

At D/V = 30%, r_a = (0.3)(0.084)(1 − 0.35) + (0.7)(0.130) = 0.1074
= 10.74%

At D/V = 40%, r_a = (0.4)(0.093)(1 − 0.35) + (0.6)(0.140) = 0.1082
= 10.82%

At D/V = 50%, r_a = (0.5)(0.104)(1 − 0.35) + (0.5)(0.160) = 0.1138
= 11.38%

20. A is correct. The after-tax cost of debt decreases as the marginal tax rate increases.

21. D is correct. Depending on the value of the tax shield provided by the interest on debt relative to the costs of financial distress, the market value could increase or decrease.

22. C is correct. According to the pecking order theory, internally generated financing provides the most positive signals and external equity financing provides the most negative signals.

SOLUTIONS FOR READING 33

1. C is correct. A cash dividend would decrease stockholders' equity, increasing the debt/equity ratio. A cash dividend would reduce cash, resulting in a lower current ratio. A stock dividend would leave both of these ratios unchanged.

2. D is correct. A stock dividend will decrease the price per share, all other things being equal. A stock split will reduce the price and earnings per share proportionately, leaving the price-to-earnings ratio the same.

3. B is correct. If the P/E is 32x, the earnings/price ratio is $1/32 = 3.125\%$. When the cost of capital is greater than the earnings yield (E/P), earnings dilution will result from the buyback.

4. Dividend chronology:

Friday, 10 June	B
Thursday, 23 June	F
Friday, 24 June	E
Sunday, 26 June	D
Tues, 28 June	A
Sunday, 10 July	C

   ▶ B. The declaration date is the day that the corporation issues a statement declaring a dividend.

   ▶ E. The ex-date is the first day that the stock trades "ex" (i.e. without) the dividend. If the stock is bought on the ex-date, the seller (not the buyer) will receive the dividend.

   ▶ A. The holder-of-record date is the date that the company uses to document which shareholders will receive the dividend.

   ▶ C. The payment date is the date that the company sends out its dividend checks.

5. C is correct.

6. A is correct. To receive the dividend, one must purchase before the ex-date.

7. C is correct. For each dollar of WL pretax income: [$1.00 × 0.40 = $0.40 in corporate taxes] plus $0.60 in net income paid in dividends × 0.30 = $0.18 in personal income taxes. Total tax = $0.40 + $0.18 = $0.58.

8. C is correct.

9. D is correct.

10. C is correct. Decreases send negative signals regarding future prospects.

11. A is correct.

> Last year's DPS = \$0.60
> Expected increase in EPS = \$4 − \$3 = \$1
> Target payout ratio = 0.25
> 5-year adjustment factor = 1/5 = 0.2
> Expected DPS = last year's DPS + (increase in EPS) × target payout × adjustment factor
> = \$0.60 + (\$1.00 × 0.25 × 0.2)
> = \$0.65

12. B is correct.

13. D is correct. The ex-dividend stock price declines to €40 − €1.50 = €38.50. She will purchase €150,000/ €38.50 = 3,896 additional shares. This increases her total shares owned to 103,896.

14. A is correct. To receive the dividend, one must purchase before the ex-date.

15. A is correct. 40 percent or \$16 million of the \$40 million in capital expenditures will be financed with debt, leaving \$24 million to be financed with retained earnings. \$30 million net income − \$24 million retained earnings = \$6 million for dividends.

16. C is correct.

17. 1 = a

2 = b

3 = a

4 = b

18. D is correct.

19. B is correct. Old Book Value = \$750 million − \$70 million buyback = \$680 million; \$680 million/23 million shares = \$29.56.

20. C is correct. When a company has more cash than it can profitably reinvest internally, it might repurchase its shares.

21. B is correct. Earnings = \$25 million − \$15 million in capital spending = \$10 million available for dividends. \$10 million/\$25 million = 40% dividend payout ratio.

22. B is correct. \$70 million × 0.07 = \$4.9 million after-tax cost of borrowing; Earnings \$25 million − \$4.9 million = \$20.1 million/23 million shares = \$0.87 EPS.

23. B is correct. If the cost of capital is 7 percent and the earnings yield is \$1/\$35 = 2.86%, there will be earnings dilution.

24. B is correct. Share repurchase using borrowed funds will rearrange the company's value between debt and equity; but the value of the company remains unchanged.

25. D is correct. Shareholders would prefer the company repurchase its shares instead of paying dividends when the tax rate on capital gains is lower than the tax rate on dividends.

SOLUTIONS FOR READING 34

1. D is correct.

2. B is correct.

3. A is correct.

4. D is correct.

5. D is correct.

6. A is correct.

7. D is correct.

8. B is correct.

9. D is correct.

10. A is correct.

11. A is correct.

12. B is correct.

13. B is correct.

14. D is correct.

15. A is correct.

16. B is correct.

17. D is correct.

18. B is correct.

19. C is correct.

20. D is correct. Separating the roles of chairman and chief executive officer is not a *required* attribute of an effective corporate governance policy. There is disagreement as to whether separating the roles of chairman and chief executive officer is an effective corporate governance attribute. The other attributes listed are part of an effective governance system.

21. D is correct. Transactions such as mergers and acquisitions that may not be in the best long-term interest of shareholders represent a strategic policy risk. Excessive obligations (frequently off-balance-sheet) that may reduce the value of shareholder equity are classified as a liability risk.

22. D is correct. The capital structure that maximizes the company's stock value is also the capital structure that minimizes its WACC.

23. C is correct. At the current debt weight of 20%, the WACC is declining with increases in debt. If you calculate the WACC, it is currently 8.7% and would decline to 8.5% if the debt weight is 30%. Repurchasing debt or paying a dividend would reduce the debt weight, which would increase the WACC. The stock split would have no effect. Reducing debt would increase the WACC, so this is the corporate action that Skylark should be least likely to select.

24. C is correct. The WACC is the weight of debt times the after-tax cost of debt plus the weight of equity times the cost of equity. Skylark currently has a market value of $8 billion of equity and $2 billion of debt, for an 80/20 ratio. Using Exhibit 1, we find that this capital structure has a 5.5% pretax and 3.52% [5.5 × (1− 0.36)] after-tax cost of debt and a 10.0% cost of

equity. Thus the WACC equals $(0.2 \times 3.52) + (0.8 \times 10.0) = 0.70 + 8.0 = 8.7\%$. After the buyback, Skylark's capital structure will be 70/30, which results in a 6.0% pretax cost of debt (3.84% after tax) and a 10.5% cost of equity. Thus, the new WACC will be $(0.3 \times 3.84) + (0.7 \times 10.5) = 1.15 + 7.35 = 8.5\%$, which is a decrease.

25. C is correct. The Gordon growth model can be used to calculate the P/E as the payout ratio divided by the difference between cost of equity and growth. In this case, the payout ratio would be 50%, cost of equity would drop from the current 10% (see table) to 9%, and the growth rate is 7%. The leading P/E is $0.5/(0.09 - 0.07) = 25\times$.

SOLUTIONS FOR READING 35

1. D is correct. These are conglomerate and horizontal mergers, respectively.

2. C is correct. EPS is $2.63. Because Modern Auto's stock price is $40 and Sky Systems' stock price is $25, Modern Auto will acquire Sky Systems by exchanging 1 of its shares for $40/25 = 1.60$ shares of Sky Systems. There are 15 million shares of Sky Systems. Their acquisition will take $15/1.60 = 9.375$ million shares of Modern Auto. The total number of shares after the merger = 49.375 million. The EPS after the merger = $130/49.375 = 2.63.

3. A is correct. Both of the statements by Wilhelm are wrong. The first statement is wrong because diversification by itself does not lower risk for shareholders. Investors can diversify very cheaply on their own by purchasing stocks of different companies (for example, a Modern Auto shareholder could purchase stocks of Sky Systems).

The second statement is also wrong. The P/E ratio will not necessarily remain the same following the merger and is more likely to decline. The pre-merger P/E for Modern Auto is $40/2.50 = 16$. After the merger, the EPS would be $130 million/49.375 million shares, or 2.6329. The post-merger P/E will probably fall to $40/2.6329 = 15.19$.

4. C is correct. HiFly is a white knight.

5. A is correct.

> Target shareholders' gain = Premium = $P_T - V_T$
> P_T = price paid for the target company = $400 million as provided in the vignette
> V_T = pre-merger value of the target = $25 share price $\times$ 15 million shares = $375 million
> $400 million $-$ $375 million = $25 million

6. C is correct. The pre- and post-merger HHI measures are 1,550 and 1,950, respectively. Not only is the HHI increasing by 400 points, but the industry concentration level also moves from moderately to highly concentrated. The probable action by the regulatory authorities is thus a challenge.

	Pre-Merger			**Post-Merger**	
Company	Market Share	Market Share Squared	Company	Market Share	Market Share Squared
1	25%	625	1	25%	625
2 (HiFly)	20%	400	2 & 3 (Combined)	30%	900
3 (Sky)	10%	100	4	10%	100
4	10%	100	5	10%	100
5	10%	100	6	10%	100
6	10%	100	7	10%	100
7	10%	100	8	5%	25
8	5%	25			
	HHI =	**1,550**		**HHI =**	**1,950**

7. D is correct. The estimated stock value is $41.57.

The value of High Tech = Total PV (present value) of free cash flows during the first four years + PV of the terminal value of High Tech at the end of the fourth year using the constant growth model.

Total PV of free cash flows during the first four years = $15/1.11 + 17/1.11^2 + 20/1.11^3 + 23/1.11^4 = \$57.09$ million.

Based on the constant growth model, the terminal value (TV) of High Tech at the end of the fourth year is TV = FCF at the end of the fifth year/ $(k - g) = (23 \times 1.065)/(0.11 - 0.065) = \$544.33$ million.

PV of the terminal value = $544.33/1.11^4 = \$358.57$ million.

Estimated value of High Tech = 57.09 + 358.57 = $415.66 million.

Estimated stock price = 415.66 million/10 million shares = $41.57.

8. B is correct. The estimated stock price is $40.56.

Total PV of free cash flows during the first four years = $15/1.11 + 17/1.11^2 + 20/1.11^3 + 23/1.11^4 = \$57.09$ million.

Based on the cash flow multiple method, the terminal value of High Tech four years later = $23 \times 23 = \$529$ million.

PV of the terminal value = $529/1.11^4 = \$348.47$ million.

Estimated value of High Tech = Total PV of free cash flows during the first four years + PV of the terminal value at the end of the fourth year = 57.09 + 348.47 = $405.55 million.

Estimated stock price = 405.55 million/10 million shares = $40.56.

9. A is correct. The estimated value is $35.21. First, calculate the relative valuation ratios for the three comparable companies and their means.

Relative Valuation Ratio	Alpha	Neutron	Techno	Mean
P/E	14.62	13.69	20.24	16.18
P/S	2.18	1.62	2.81	2.20
P/BV	2.90	3.20	4.57	3.56

Then apply the means to the valuation variables for High Tech to get the estimated stock price for High Tech based on the comparable companies.

Valuation Variables	High Tech	Mean Multiple for Comparables	Estimated Stock Price
Current stock price	31.00		
Earnings/share	1.98	16.18	32.04
Sales/share	17.23	2.20	37.91
Book value/share	10.02	3.56	35.67

The mean estimated stock price is (32.04 + 37.91 + 35.67)/3 = $35.21.

10. C is correct. The price is $41.29. The takeover premiums on three recent comparable takeovers are:

$(28.00 - 24.90)/24.90 = 12.45\%$
$(52.00 - 43.20)/43.20 = 20.37\%$
$(34.50 - 29.00)/29.00 = 18.97\%$
Mean takeover premium $= 17.26\%$

Using the comparable company approach, the stock price of High Tech if it is traded at the mean of the comparable company valuations is $35.21. Considering the mean takeover premium, the estimated fair acquisition price for High Tech is $35.21 \times 1.1726 = \$41.29$.

11. B is correct. The fair acquisition price is $40.86. First, calculate the relative valuation ratios based on the acquisition price for the three comparable transactions and their means.

Relative Valuation Ratio	Quadrant	ProTech	Automator	Mean
P/E	20.00	24.76	14.68	19.81
P/S	2.65	2.55	2.17	2.46
P/BV	3.38	5.13	3.76	4.09

Then apply the means to the valuation variables for High Tech to get the estimated acquisition price for High Tech based on the comparable transactions.

Valuation Variables	High Tech	Mean Multiple Paid for Comparables	Estimated Acquisition Price
Earnings/share	1.98	19.81	39.22
Sales/share	17.23	2.46	42.39
Book value/share	10.02	4.09	40.98

The mean estimated acquisition stock price is $(39.22 + 42.39 + 40.98)/3 = \$40.86$.

12. A is correct. Both of Smith's statements are correct. If there was a pre-announcement run-up in Quadrant's price because of speculation, the takeover premium should be computed based on the price prior to the run-up. Because the comparable transaction approach is based on the acquisition price, the takeover premium is implicitly recognized in this approach.

Abandonment option The ability to terminate a project at some future time if the financial results are disappointing.

Abnormal earnings See *Residual income.*

Abnormal rate of return The amount by which a security's actual return differs from its expected rate of return which is based on the market's rate of return and the security's relationship with the market.

Abnormal return Return on a stock beyond what would be predicted by market movements alone. Cumulative abnormal return (CAR) is the total abnormal return for the period surrounding an announcement or the release of information.

Absolute dispersion The amount of variability present without comparison to any reference point or benchmark.

Absolute frequency The number of observations in a given interval (for grouped data).

Absolute priority rule The hierarchy whereby claims are satisfied in corporate liquidation.

Absolute valuation model A model that specifies an asset's intrinsic value.

Accounting A detailed report to the trust beneficiaries by a trustee of his stewardship, also used to discharge the trustee.

Accounting earnings Earnings of a firm as reported on its income statement.

Accounting estimates Estimates of items such as the useful lives of assets, warranty costs, and the amount of uncollectible receivables.

Accounting profit Total revenues minus total explicit costs.

Accounting risk The risk associated with accounting standards that vary from country to country or with any uncertainty about how certain transactions should be recorded.

Accounting Standards Board (ASB) The Accounting Standards Board issues Financial Reporting Standards (FRSs) for the United Kingdom. It took over the task of setting accounting standards from the Accounting Standards Committee in 1990.

Accounts payable A liability that results from the purchase of goods or services on open account, that is, without a signed note payable.

Accounts receivable Amounts owed to a company by customers as a result of delivering goods or services and extending credit in the ordinary course of business. Also referred to as *trade receivables.*

Accrual accounting The system of recording financial transactions as they come into existence as a legally enforceable claim, rather than when they settle.

Accrued interest Interest earned but not yet paid.

Accumulate Wall Street expression for buying on a large scale over time, typically by an institution. "Accumulation" of a stock is said to occur if a number of institutions are gradually adding to their holdings.

Accumulated other comprehensive income Cumulative gains or losses reported in shareholders' equity that arise from changes in the fair value of available-for-sale securities, from the effects of changes in foreign-currency exchange rates on consolidated foreign-currency financial statements, from certain gains and losses on financial derivatives and from adjustments for underfunded pension plans.

Acquiring company or acquirer The company in a merger or acquisition that is acquiring the target.

Acquisition The purchase of some portion of one company by another; the purchase may be for assets, a definable segment of another entity, or the purchase of an entire company.

Active factor risk The contribution to active risk squared resulting from the portfolio's different-than-benchmark exposures relative to factors specified in the risk model.

Active investment managers Managers who hold portfolios that differ from their benchmark portfolio in an attempt to produce positive risk-adjusted returns.

Active management Attempts to achieve portfolio returns more than commensurate with risk, either by forecasting broad market trends or by identifying particular mispriced sectors of a market or securities in a market.

Active portfolio In the context of the Treynor-Black model, the portfolio formed by mixing analyzed stocks of perceived nonzero alpha values. This portfolio is ultimately mixed with the passive market index portfolio.

Active return The return on a portfolio minus the return on the portfolio's benchmark.

Active risk The standard deviation of active returns.

Active risk squared The variance of active returns; active risk raised to the second power.

Active specific risk or asset selection risk The contribution to active risk squared resulting from the portfolio's active weights on individual assets as those weights interact with assets' residual risk.

Addition rule for probabilities A principle stating that the probability that *A* or *B* occurs (both occur) equals the probability that *A* occurs, plus the probability that *B* occurs, minus the probability that both *A* and *B* occur.

Additional information Information that is required or recommended under the GIPS standards and is not considered as "supplemental information" for the purposes of compliance.

Additions Assets transferred to a trust after the initial funding.

Add-on interest A procedure for determining the interest on a bond or loan in which the interest is added onto the face value of a contract.

Adjustable-rate mortgage A mortgage whose interest rate varies according to some specified measure of the current market interest rate.

Adjusted beta Historical beta adjusted to reflect the tendency of beta to be mean reverting.

Adjusted present value (APV) As an approach to valuing a company, the sum of the value of the company, assuming no use of debt, and the net present value of any effects of debt on company value.

Adjusted R^2 A measure of goodness-of-fit of a regression that is adjusted for degrees of freedom and hence does not automatically increase when another independent variable is added to a regression.

Administrative fees All fees other than the trading expenses and the investment management fee. Administrative fees include custody fees, accounting fees, consulting fees, legal fees, performance measurement fees, or other related fees. These administrative fees are typically outside the control of the investment management firm and are not included in either the gross-of-fees return or the net-of-fees return. However, there are some markets and investment vehicles where administrative fees are controlled by the firm.

After-tax cash flow (ATCF) Net operating income less debt service and less taxes payable on income from operations.

Agency costs Agency costs are the incremental costs arising from conflicts of interest when an agent makes decisions for a principal. In the context of a corporation, agency costs arise from conflicts of interest between managers, shareholders, and bondholders.

Agency problem or principal-agent problem or agency conflict A conflict of interest that arises when the agent in an agency relationship has goals and incentives that differ from those of the principal.

Agency relationships An arrangement whereby someone, an agent, acts on behalf of another person, the principal.

Agency trade A trade in which a broker acts as an agent only, not taking a position on the opposite side of the trade.

Aggregate demand (1) The relationship between the quantity of real GDP demanded and the price level. (2) The total of all planned expenditures for the entire economy.

Aggregate production function The relationship between the quantity of real GDP supplied and the quantities of labor and capital and the state of technology.

Aggressive With respect to equity valuation, the term implies a concentrated portfolio holding smaller capitalization stocks than the general market, often with higher price/earnings and lower yields, together with low reserves. Often implies unusual volatility.

AICPA The American Institute of Certified Public Accountants. The AICPA is the national association of CPAs in the United States.

AIMR Performance presentation standards (AIMR-PPS®) A comprehensive set of reporting guidelines created by the Association for Investment Management and Research (AIMR) (now CFA Institute) in 1993 that converged to the Global Investment Performance Standards on 1 January 2006.

Allocative efficiency A situation in which we cannot produce more of any good without giving up some of another good that we value more highly.

Alpha (or abnormal return) The return on an asset in excess of the asset's required rate of return; the risk-adjusted excess return.

Alternative hypothesis The hypothesis accepted when the null hypothesis is rejected.

Alternative investments Hedge funds, venture capital pools, options and other derivatives, real estate, and other non-stock or -bond market assets.

American Depositary Receipt (ADR) A certificate of ownership issued by a U.S. bank to promote local trading in a foreign stock. The U.S. bank holds the foreign shares and issues ADRs against them.

American option An option contract that can be exercised at any time until its expiration date.

American terms With reference to U.S. dollar exchange rate quotations, the U.S. dollar price of a unit of another currency.

Amortizing or accreting swaps A swap in which the notional principal changes according to a formula related to changes in the underlying.

Analysis of variance (ANOVA) The analysis of the total variability of a dataset (such as observations on the dependent variable in a regression) into components representing different sources of variation; with reference to regression, ANOVA provides the inputs for an *F*-test of the significance of the regression as a whole.

Annual percentage rate The cost of borrowing expressed as a yearly rate.

Annuity A finite set of level sequential cash flows.

Annuity due An annuity having a first cash flow that is paid immediately.

Anomalies (1) Security price relationships that appear to contradict a well-regarded hypothesis; in this case, the efficient market hypothesis. (2) Patterns of returns that seem to contradict the efficient market hypothesis.

Antitrust legislation or antitrust laws Laws that restrict the formation of monopolies and regulate certain anticompetitive business practices.

A priori probability A probability based on logical analysis rather than on observation or personal judgment.

Appraisal ratio The ratio of alpha to residual standard deviation.

Appreciation An increase in the exchange value of one nation's currency in terms of the currency of another nation.

Arbitrage The simultaneous purchase of an undervalued asset or portfolio and sale of an overvalued but equivalent asset or portfolio, in order to obtain a riskless profit on the price differential.

Arbitrage opportunity An opportunity to conduct an arbitrage; an opportunity to earn an expected positive net profit without risk and with no net investment of money.

Arbitrage portfolio The portfolio that exploits an arbitrage opportunity.

Arbitrage pricing theory (APT) An asset pricing theory that is derived from a factor model, using diversification and arbitrage arguments. The theory describes the relationship between expected returns on securities, given that there are no opportunities to create wealth through risk-free arbitrage investments.

Arithmetic mean The sum of the observations divided by the number of observations.

Arrears swap A type of interest rate swap in which the floating payment is set at the end of the period and the interest is paid at that same time.

Asian call option A European-style option with a value at maturity equal to the difference between the stock price at maturity and the average stock price during the life of the option, or $0, whichever is greater.

Ask price The price at which a market maker is willing to sell a security (also called *offer price*).

Asset allocation Dividing of investment funds among several asset classes to achieve diversification.

Asset allocation decision Choosing among broad asset classes such as stocks versus bonds.

Asset beta The unlevered beta; reflects the business risk of the assets; the asset's systematic risk.

Asset class Securities that have similar characteristics, attributes, and risk/return relationships.

Asset purchase An acquisition in which the acquirer purchases the target company's assets and payment is made directly to the target company.

Asset turnover (ATO) The annual sales generated by each dollar of assets (sales/assets).

Asset-based valuation An approach to valuing natural resource companies that estimates company value on the basis of the market value of the natural resources the company controls.

Assets under management (AUM) The total market value of the assets managed by an investment firm.

Assets Amounts owned; all items to which a business or household holds legal claim.

Asymmetric information Possession of information by one party in a financial transaction but not by the other party.

At the money option An option for which the underlying's market price equals the option's exercise price.

Auction market A market in which the orders of multiple buyers compete for execution.

Autocorrelation The correlation of a time series with its own past values.

Autoregressive (AR) model A time series regressed on its own past values, in which the independent variable is a lagged value of the dependent variable.

Available-for-sale security A default classification for an investment in a debt or equity security that is not classified as either a held-to-maturity security or a trading security.

Average tax rate The total tax payment divided by total income. It is the proportion of total income paid in taxes.

Backward integration A merger involving the purchase of a target ahead of the acquirer in the value or production chain; for example, to acquire a supplier.

Backwardation Condition in which spot price of commodity exceeds the futures price (cf. *contango*).

Balance of payments A system of accounts that measures transactions of goods, services, income, and financial assets between domestic households, businesses, and governments and residents of the rest of the world during a specific time period.

Balance of payments accounts A country's record of international trading, borrowing, and lending.

Balance sheet A financial statement that shows what assets the firm controls at a fixed point in time and how it has financed these assets.

Balanced budget A government budget in which tax revenues and expenditures are equal.

Balanced fund A mutual fund with, generally, a three-part investment objective: (1) to conserve the investor's principal, (2) to pay current income, and (3) to increase both principal and income. The fund aims to achieve this by owning a mixture of bonds, preferred stocks, and common stocks.

Balloon payment Large final payment (e.g., when a loan is repaid in installments).

Band-of-investment method A widely used approach to estimate an overall capitalization rate. It is based on the premise that debt and equity financing is typically involved in a real estate transaction.

Bank discount basis A quoting convention that annualizes, on a 360-day year, the discount as a percentage of face value.

Barriers to entry Legal or natural constraints that protect a firm from potential competitors.

Barter The direct exchange of goods and services for other goods and services without the use of money.

Base year The year that is chosen as the point of reference for comparison of prices in other years.

Basic earnings per share Total earnings divided by the weighted average number of shares actually outstanding during the period.

Basis point A hundredth of a percent; thus 75 basis points equals three-quarters of 1 percentage point.

Basis point value (BPV) Also called *present value of a basis point* or *price value of a basis point* (PVBP), the change in the bond price for a 1 basis point change in yield.

Basis swap A swap in which both parties pay a floating rate.

Bayes' formula A method for updating probabilities based on new information.

Bear hug A tactic used by acquirers to circumvent target management's objections to a proposed merger by submitting the proposal directly to the target company's board of directors.

Bear market Widespread decline in security prices (cf. *bull market*).

Bear spread An option strategy that involves selling a put with a lower exercise price and buying a put with a higher exercise price. It can also be executed with calls.

Before-tax cash flow A measure of the expected annual cash flow from the operation of a real estate investment after all expenses but before taxes.

Behavioral finance (1) The analysis of various psychological traits of individuals and how these traits affect how they act as investors, analysts, and portfolio managers. (2) Branch of finance that stresses aspects of investor irrationality.

Benchmark A comparison portfolio used to evaluate performance; a point of reference or comparison.

Benchmark bond A bond representative of current market conditions and used for performance comparison.

Benchmark value of the multiple In using the method of comparables, the value of a price multiple for the comparison asset; when we have comparison assets (a group), the mean or median value of the multiple for the group of assets.

Bernoulli random variable A random variable having the outcomes 0 and 1.

Bernoulli trial An experiment that can produce one of two outcomes.

Beta A measure of an asset's systematic risk based upon an asset's covariance with the market portfolio.

Bid price The price at which a dealer is willing to purchase a security.

Bid-ask spread (or bid-asked spread) The difference between the quoted ask and the bid prices.

Bidder The acquiring firm.

Bilateral arbitrage With reference to currencies, an arbitrage involving two currencies only.

Bill-and-hold basis Sales on a bill-and-hold basis involve selling products but not delivering those products until a later date.

Binomial model A model for pricing options in which the underlying price can move to only one of two possible new prices in each specified time interval.

Binomial random variable The number of successes in n Bernoulli trials for which the probability of success is constant for all trials and the trials are independent.

Binomial tree The graphical representation of a model of asset price dynamics in which, at each period, the asset moves up with probability p or down with probability $(1 - p)$.

Black-Scholes or Black-Scholes-Merton option pricing model (formula) An equation to value a call option based on five variables: the price of the underlying, the exercise price, the risk-free interest rate, the time to maturity, and the standard deviation of the underlying's return.

Block   Orders to buy or sell that are too large for the liquidity ordinarily available in dealer networks or stock exchanges.

Blue chip   A large, stable, well-known, widely held, seasoned company with a strong financial position, usually paying a reasonable dividend.

Boilerplate   Standard terms and conditions, e.g., in a debt contract.

Bond   A security issued by a borrower that obligates the issuer to make specified payments to the holder over a specific period. A *coupon bond* obligates the issuer to make interest payments called coupon payments over the life of the bond, then to repay the *face value* at maturity.

Bond-equivalent yield   The yield to maturity on a basis that ignores compounding.

Bond indenture   A legal contract specifying the terms of a bond issue.

Bond option   An option in which the underlying is a bond; primarily traded in over-the-counter markets.

Bond rating   Rating of the likelihood of bond's default.

Bond yield plus risk premium method   A method of determining the required rate of return on equity (cost of equity) for a company as the sum of the yield to maturity on the company's long-term debt plus a risk premium.

Bonding costs   Costs borne by management to assure owners that they are working in the owners' best interest (e.g., implicit cost of non-compete agreements).

Book entry   Registered ownership of stock without issue of stock certificate.

Book value of equity (or book value)   Shareholders' equity (total assets minus total liabilities) minus the value of preferred stock; common shareholders' equity; book value per share is book value of equity divided by the number of common shares outstanding.

Books   In accounting, a shorthand reference to shareholder as opposed to income tax financial information.

Bootstrapping earnings   An increase in a company's earnings that results as a consequence of the idiosyncrasies of a merger transaction itself rather than because of resulting economic benefits of the combination.

Bottom-up forecasting approach   A forecasting approach that involves aggregating the individual company forecasts of analysts into industry forecasts, and finally into macroeconomic forecasts.

Bottom-up or bottom-up investing   An approach to investing that focuses on the individual characteristics of securities rather than on macroeconomic or overall market forecasts.

Bourse   A French term often used to refer to a stock market.

Box spread   An option strategy that combines a bull spread and a bear spread having two different exercise prices, which produces a risk-free payoff of the difference in the exercise prices.

Breakeven point   The number of units produced and sold at which the company's net income is zero (revenues = total costs).

Breakup value (or private market value)   The value that can be achieved if a company's assets are divided and sold separately.

Breusch–Pagan test   A test for conditional heteroskedasticity in the error term of a regression.

Broker   An agent who executes orders to buy or sell securities on behalf of a client in exchange for a commission.

Brokerage   The business of acting as agents for buyers or sellers, usually in return for commissions.

Brokered market   A market where an intermediary (a broker) offers search services to buyers and sellers.

Budget constraint   All of the possible combinations of goods that can be purchased (at fixed prices) with a specific budget.

Budget deficit   The amount by which government spending exceeds government revenues.

Build-up method   A method for determining the required rate of return on equity as the sum of risk premiums, in which one or more of the risk premiums is typically subjective rather than grounded in a formal equilibrium model.

Bull market   Widespread rise in security prices (cf. *bear market*).

Bull spread   An option strategy that involves buying a call with a lower exercise price and selling a call with a higher exercise price. It can also be executed with puts.

Bullet payment   Single final payment, e.g., of a loan (in contrast to payment in installments).

Bund   Long-term German government *bond*.

Business cycle   The periodic but irregular up-and-down movement in production.

Business risk   The risk associated with operating earnings; risk that is related to the uncertainty of revenues.

Butterfly spread   An option strategy that combines two bull or bear spreads and has three exercise prices.

Buy-and-hold strategy   A passive portfolio management strategy in which securities (bonds or stocks) are bought and held to maturity.

Buyback   Repurchase agreement.

Buy-side analysts   Analysts who work for investment management firms, trusts, and bank trust departments, and similar institutions.

Call   An option that gives the holder the right to buy an underlying asset from another party at a fixed price over a specific period of time.

Callable bond   A bond that the issuer may repurchase at a given price in some specified period.

Call auction   See *fixing*.

Call option   A contract that gives its holder the right to buy an asset, typically a financial instrument, at a specified price through a specified date.

Call provision   Provision that allows an issuer to buy back the *bond* issue at a stated price.

Cannibalization   Cannibalization occurs when an investment takes customers and sales away from another part of the company.

Cap agreement (or cap)   A contract that on each settlement date pays the holder the greater of the difference between the reference rate and the cap rate or zero; it is equivalent to a series of call options at the reference rate.

Capital   The tools, equipment, buildings, and other constructions that businesses now use to produce goods and services.

Capital account   Foreign investment in a country minus its investment abroad.

Capital accumulation   The growth of capital resources.

Capital allocation decision   Allocation of invested funds between risk-free assets versus the risky portfolio.

Capital allocation line (CAL)   A graph line that describes the combinations of expected return and standard deviation of return available to an investor from combining the optimal portfolio of risky assets with the risk-free asset.

Capital appreciation   A return objective in which the investor seeks to increase the portfolio value, primarily through capital gains, over time to meet a future need rather than dividend yield.

Capital asset pricing model (CAPM)   An equation describing the expected return on any asset (or portfolio) as a linear function of its beta.

Capital budget   List of planned investment projects, usually prepared annually.

Capital budgeting   The allocation of funds to relatively long-range projects or investments.

Capital charge   The company's total cost of capital in money terms.

Capital consumption   The decrease in the capital stock that results from wear and tear and obsolescence.

Capital Employed (Real Estate)   The denominator of the return expressions, defined as the "weighted-average equity" (weighted-average capital) during the measurement period. Capital employed should not include any income or capital return accrued *during* the measurement period. Beginning capital is adjusted by weighting the cash flows (contributions and distributions) that occurred during the period. Cash flows are typically weighted based on the actual days the flows are in or out of the portfolio. Other weighting methods are acceptable; however, once a methodology is chosen, it should be consistently applied.

Capital expenditures   Expenditures made in the purchase of long-term productive assets, such as property, plant, and equipment, whose cost is amortized against income in future periods.

Capital gain   The amount by which the sale price of an asset exceeds the purchase price. If a share of stock is bought for $5 and then sold for $15, the capital gain is $10.

Capital goods   Producer durables; nonconsumable goods that firms use to make other goods.

Capital lease   A lease that transfers, in an economic sense, the risks and rewards of ownership to the lessee without transferring title. Lease payments made are comprised of interest and principal. Property held under a capital-lease agreement is accounted for as an asset. This cost is amortized over the relevant useful life.

Capital loss   The amount by which the sale price of an asset is less than the purchase price. If a share of stock is bought for $15 and then sold for $5, the capital loss is $10.

Capital market   Financial market (particularly the market for long-term securities).

Capital market instruments   Fixed-income or equity investments that trade in the secondary market.

Capital market line (CML)   The line with an intercept point equal to the risk-free rate that is tangent to the efficient frontier of risky assets; represents the efficient frontier when a risk-free asset is available for investment.

Capital rationing   Shortage of funds that forces a company to choose between worthwhile projects.

Capital stock   The total quantity of plant, equipment, buildings, and inventories.

Capital structure   The mix of debt and equity that a company uses to finance its business.

Capitalization   Long-term debt plus preferred stock plus net worth.

Capitalization rate   The divisor in the expression for the value of a perpetuity.

Capitalized interest   Interest incurred during the construction period on monies invested in assets under construction that is added to the cost of the assets.

Caplet Each component call option in a cap.

CAPM Capital asset pricing model.

Capped swap A swap in which the floating payments have an upper limit.

Capture hypothesis A theory of regulatory behavior that predicts that the regulators will eventually be captured by the special interests of the industry being regulated.

Capture theory A theory of regulation that states that the regulations are supplied to satisfy the demand of producers to maximize producer surplus.

Cash Currency, coin, and funds on deposit that are available for immediate withdrawal without restriction. Money orders, certified checks, cashier's checks, personal checks, and bank drafts are also considered cash.

Cash and carry Purchase of a security and simultaneous sale of a *future*, with the balance being financed with a loan or *repo*.

Cash earnings Cash revenue minus cash expenses.

Cash equivalents Short-term and highly liquid investments readily convertible into known amounts of cash and close enough to maturity that there is insignificant risk of changes in value from interest rate movements.

Cash flow A flow based on cash receipts and cash disbursements; may refer to either total cash flow or, more commonly, operating cash flow.

Cash flow additivity principle The principle that dollar amounts indexed at the same point in time are additive.

Cash flow analysis The search for the fundamental drivers that underlie a company's cash flow stream and affect its sustainability.

Cash flow at risk (CFAR) A variation of VAR that reflects the risk of a company's cash flow instead of its market value.

Cash flow from operations A term used on the cash flow analysis statement that consists of cash flow available for debt service less total interest paid. The term also is used to refer to cash provided or used by operating activities and operating cash flow as those terms are defined by generally accepted accounting principles.

Cash offering A merger or acquisition that is to be paid for with cash; the cash for the merger might come from the acquiring company's existing assets or from a debt issue.

Cash operating expense A Uniform Credit Analysis®– defined cash flow amount that consists of cash paid for sales and marketing, general and administrative, and research and development expenditures. The term is defined the same way on the cash flow analysis statement.

Cash price or spot price The price for immediate purchase of the underlying asset.

Cash settlement A procedure used in certain derivative transactions that specifies that the long and short parties engage in the equivalent cash value of a delivery transaction.

Catalyst An event or piece of information that causes the marketplace to re-evaluate the prospects of a company.

Caution One of the three components of the standard of prudence governing trustees; avoidance of undue risk and attentiveness to the protection of trust property.

Central bank A bank's bank and a public authority that regulates a nation's depository institutions and controls the quantity of money.

Central limit theorem A result in statistics that states that the sample mean computed from large samples of size n from a population with finite variance will follow an approximate normal distribution with a mean equal to the population mean and a variance equal to the population variance divided by n.

Centralized risk management or companywide risk management When a company has a single risk management group that monitors and controls all of the risk-taking activities of the organization. Centralization permits economies of scale and allows a company to use some of its risks to offset other risks. See also *enterprise risk management*.

CEO Chief executive officer.

Certificate of deposit (CD) An unsecured evidence of indebtedness of a bank, which may be sold to others. Usually with a face value of $100,000 or more and bearing interest below the prime rate.

Ceteris paribus Other things being equal—all other relevant things remaining the same.

CFO Chief financial officer.

CFTC Commodity Futures Trading Commission.

Chaebol A Korean conglomerate.

Chain rule of forecasting A forecasting process in which the next period's value as predicted by the forecasting equation is substituted into the right-hand side of the equation to give a predicted value two periods ahead.

Chapter 11 A U.S. bankruptcy procedure designed to reorganize and rehabilitate defaulting firm.

Chapter 7 A U.S. bankruptcy procedure whereby a debtor's assets are sold and the proceeds are used to repay creditors.

Cheapest to deliver A bond in which the amount received for delivering the bond is largest compared with the amount paid in the market for the bond.

Cherry-picking   When a bankrupt company is allowed to enforce contracts that are favorable to it while walking away from contracts that are unfavorable to it.

CHIPS   Clearinghouse Interbank Payments System.

Classical growth theory   A theory of economic growth based on the view that real GDP growth is temporary and that when real GDP per person increases above subsistence level, a population explosion brings real GDP back to subsistence level.

Clayton Act   A federal antitrust law passed in 1914. Section 7, which is most relevant to mergers and acquisitions, prohibits the acquisition of stock and assets of a company when the effect is to lessen competition.

Clean surplus accounting   Accounting that satisfies the condition that all changes in the book value of equity other than transactions with owners are reflected in income.

Clean surplus relation   The relationship between earnings, dividends, and book value in which ending book value is equal to the beginning book value plus earnings less dividends, apart from ownership transactions.

Clearinghouse   An entity associated with a futures market that acts as middleman between the contracting parties and guarantees to each party the performance of the other.

Clientele effect   The preference some investors have for shares that exhibit certain characteristics.

Closed-end fund   An investment company with a fixed number of shares. New shares cannot be issued and the old shares cannot be redeemed. Shares are traded in the marketplace, and their value may differ from the underlying net asset value of the fund.

Closeout netting   Netting the market values of *all* derivative contracts between two parties to determine one overall value owed by one party to another in the event of bankruptcy.

CMOs   Collateralized mortgage obligations.

Coefficient of variation (CV)   The ratio of a set of observations' standard deviation to the observations' mean value.

Cointegrated   Describes two time series that have a long-term financial or economic relationship such that they do not diverge from each other without bound in the long run.

Collar   An option strategy involving the purchase of a put and sale of a call in which the holder of an asset gains protection below a certain level, the exercise price of the put, and pays for it by giving up gains above a certain level, the exercise price of the call. Collars also can be used to provide protection against rising interest rates on a floating-rate loan by giving up gains from lower interest rates.

Collateral   A specific asset pledged against possible default on a bond. Mortgage bonds are backed by claims on property. Collateral trust bonds are backed by claims on other securities. Equipment obligation bonds are backed by claims on equipment.

Collateralized mortgage obligation (CMO)   A mortgage pass-through security that partitions cash flows from underlying mortgages into classes called tranches that receive principal payments according to stipulated rules.

Combination   A listing in which the order of the listed items does not matter.

Commercial bank   A firm that is licensed by the Comptroller of the Currency in the U.S. Treasury or by a state agency to receive deposits and make loans.

Commercial paper   Unsecured short-term corporate debt that is characterized by a single payment at maturity.

Commingled fund   Typically, an investment pool run by a bank, in which participation is represented by accounting units rather than shares.

Commission recapture   Credit for brokerage generated is then applied to such services as custody and appraisal.

Commodity forward   A contract in which the underlying asset is oil, a precious metal, or some other commodity.

Commodity futures   Futures contracts in which the underlying is a traditional agricultural, metal, or petroleum product.

Commodity option   An option in which the asset underlying the futures is a commodity, such as oil, gold, wheat, or soybeans.

Commodity swap   A swap in which the underlying is a commodity such as oil, gold, or an agricultural product.

Common size statements   Financial statements in which all elements (accounts) are stated as a percentage of a key figure such as revenue for an income statement or total assets for a balance sheet.

Common stock   Equities, or equity securities, issued as ownership shares in a publicly held corporation. Shareholders have voting rights and may receive dividends based on their proportionate ownership.

Company fundamental factors   Factors related to the company's internal performance, such as factors relating to earnings growth, earnings variability, earnings momentum, and financial leverage.

Company share-related factors Valuation measures and other factors related to share price or the trading characteristics of the shares, such as earnings yield, dividend yield, and book-to-market value.

Comparative advantage A person or country has a comparative advantage in an activity if that person or country can perform the activity at a lower opportunity cost than anyone else or any other country.

Competitive environment The level of intensity of competition among firms in an industry, determined by an examination of five competitive forces.

Competitive market A market that has many buyers and many sellers, so no single buyer or seller can influence the price.

Competitive strategy The search by a firm for a favorable competitive position within an industry within the known competitive environment.

Complement With reference to an event S, the event that S does not occur.

Complete portfolio The entire portfolio, including risky and risk-free assets.

Composite A universe of portfolios with similar investment objectives.

Composition Voluntary agreement to reduce payments on a firm's debt.

Compound interest Reinvestment of each interest payment on money invested to earn more interest (cf. *simple interest*).

Compounding The process of accumulating interest on interest.

Comprehensive income All changes in equity other than contributions by, and distributions to, owners; income under clean surplus accounting.

Concentration ratio The percentage of all sales contributed by the leading four or leading eight firms in an industry; sometimes called the *industry concentration ratio*.

Conditional expected value The expected value of a stated event given that another event has occurred.

Conditional heteroskedasticity Heteroskedasticity in the error variance that is correlated with the values of the independent variable(s) in the regression.

Conditional probability The probability of an event given (conditioned on) another event.

Conditional variances The variance of one variable, given the outcome of another.

Confidence interval A range that has a given probability that it will contain the population parameter it is intended to estimate.

Conglomerate A combination of unrelated firms.

Conglomerate merger A merger involving companies that are in unrelated businesses.

Consistency A desirable property of estimators; a consistent estimator is one for which the probability of estimates close to the value of the population parameter increases as sample size increases.

Consistent With reference to estimators, describes an estimator for which the probability of estimates close to the value of the population parameter increases as sample size increases.

Consolidation A merger in which both companies terminate their previous legal existence and become part of a newly formed company.

Constant growth model A form of the dividend discount model that assumes dividends will grow at a constant rate.

Constant maturity swap or CMT swap A swap in which the floating rate is the rate on a security known as a constant maturity treasury or CMT security.

Constant maturity treasury or CMT A hypothetical U.S. Treasury note with a constant maturity. A CMT exists for various years in the range of 2 to 10.

Consumer Price Index (CPI) An index that measures the average of the prices paid by urban consumers for a fixed "basket" of the consumer goods and services.

Consumption The use of goods and services for personal satisfaction. Can also be viewed as spending on new goods and services out of a household's current income. Whatever is not consumed is saved. Consumption includes such things as buying food and going to a concert.

Consumption expenditure The total payment for consumer goods and services.

Consumption goods Goods bought by households to use up, such as food and movies.

Contango A situation in a futures market where the current futures price is greater than the current spot price for the underlying asset.

Contestable market A market in which firms can enter and leave so easily that firms in the market face competition from potential entrants.

Contingent claims Derivatives in which the payoffs occur if a specific event occurs; generally referred to as options.

Continuing residual income Residual income after the forecast horizon.

Continuous compounding Interest compounded continuously rather than at fixed intervals.

Continuous random variable A random variable for which the range of possible outcomes is the real line (all real numbers between $-\infty$ and $+\infty$) or some subset of the real line.

Continuous time Time thought of as advancing in extremely small increments.

Continuously compounded return The natural logarithm of 1 plus the holding period return, or equivalently, the natural logarithm of the ending price over the beginning price.

Contract price The transaction price specified in a forward or futures contract.

Contraction A business fluctuation during which the pace of national economic activity is slowing down.

Contribution margin The amount available for fixed costs and profit after paying variable costs; revenue minus variable costs.

Control premium An increment or premium to value associated with a controlling ownership interest in a company.

Controller Officer responsible for budgeting, accounting, and auditing in a firm (cf. *treasurer*).

Convenience yield The nonmonetary return offered by an asset when the asset is in short supply, often associated with assets with seasonal production processes.

Conventional cash flow A conventional cash flow pattern is one with an initial outflow followed by a series of inflows.

Conversion factor An adjustment used to facilitate delivery on bond futures contracts in which any of a number of bonds with different characteristics are eligible for delivery.

Conversion parity price The price at which common stock can be obtained by surrendering the convertible instrument at par value.

Conversion premium The excess of the market value of the convertible security over its equity value if immediately converted into common stock. Typically expressed as a percentage of the equity value.

Conversion ratio The number of shares of common stock for which a convertible security may be exchanged.

Conversion value The value of the convertible security if converted into common stock at the stock's current market price.

Convertible A bond or preferred stock that offers the investor the right to convert his holding into common stock under set terms.

Convertible bond A bond with an option allowing the bondholder to exchange the bond for a specified number of shares of common stock in the firm. A *conversion ratio* specifies the number of shares. The *market conversion price* is the current value of the shares for which the bond may be exchanged. The *conversion premium* is the excess of the bond's value over the conversion price.

Convexity A measure of the degree to which a bond's price-yield curve departs from a straight line. This characteristic affects estimates of a bond's price volatility for a given change in yields.

Corporate bonds Long-term debt issued by private corporations typically paying semiannual coupons and returning the face value of the bond at maturity.

Corporate governance The system of principles, policies, procedures, and clearly defined responsibilities and accountabilities used by stakeholders to overcome the conflicts of interest inherent in the corporate form.

Corporate raider A person or organization seeking to profit by acquiring a company and reselling it, or seeking to profit from the takeover attempt itself (e.g. greenmail).

Corporate trustee A bank or trust company having federal or state authority to serve as a trustee.

Corporation A legal entity that may conduct business in its own name just as an individual does; the owners of a corporation, called shareholders, own shares of the firm's profits and enjoy the protection of limited liability.

Correlation analysis The analysis of the strength of the linear relationship between two data series.

Correlation or correlation coefficient A number between -1 and $+1$ that measures the co-movement (linear association) between two random variables.

Cost averaging The periodic investment of a fixed amount of money.

Cost leadership The competitive strategy of being the lowest cost producer while offering products comparable to those of other firms, so that products can be priced at or near the industry average.

Cost of capital Opportunity cost of capital.

Cost of carry The cost associated with holding some asset, including financing, storage, and insurance costs. Any yield received on the asset is treated as a negative carrying cost.

Cost of carry model A model for pricing futures contracts in which the futures price is determined by adding the cost of carry to the spot price.

Cost of equity The required rate of return on common stock.

Cost-of-service regulation Regulation based on allowing prices to reflect only the actual cost of production and no monopoly profits.

Cost structure The mix of a company's variable costs and fixed costs.

Counterparty Party on the other side of a *derivative* contract.

Coupon The interest rate on a bond, expressed as a percentage of its face (not market) value. At one time bonds (and indeed stocks) contained coupons resembling postage stamps, which one "clipped" or cut periodically and presented for payment of interest (or dividends).

Coupon rate A bond's interest payments per dollar of par value.

Covariance A measure of the co-movement (linear association) between two random variables.

Covariance matrix A matrix or square array whose entries are covariances; also known as a variance-covariance matrix.

Covariance stationary Describes a time series when its expected value and variance are constant and finite in all periods and when its covariance with itself for a fixed number of periods in the past or future is constant and finite in all periods.

Covenant Clause in a loan agreement.

Covered call An option strategy involving the holding of an asset and sale of a call on the asset.

Covered interest arbitrage A transaction executed in the foreign exchange market in which a currency is purchased (sold) and a forward contract is sold (purchased) to lock in the exchange rate for future delivery of the currency. This transaction should earn the risk-free rate of the investor's home country.

Covered option *Option* position with an offsetting position in the underlying asset.

Creative response Behavior on the part of a firm that allows it to comply with the letter of the law but violates the spirit, significantly lessening the law's effects.

Credit analysis An active bond portfolio management strategy designed to identify bonds that are expected to experience changes in rating. This strategy is critical when investing in high-yield bonds.

Credit derivatives A contract in which one party has the right to claim a payment from another party in the event that a specific credit event occurs over the life of the contract.

Credit enhancement Contract for *hedging* against loan default or changes in credit risk (see *default swap*).

Credit-linked notes Fixed-income securities in which the holder of the security has the right to withhold payment of the full amount due at maturity if a credit event occurs.

Credit risk or default risk The risk of loss due to nonpayment by a counterparty.

Credit scoring A procedure for assigning scores to borrowers on the basis of the risk of default.

Credit spread option An option on the yield spread on a bond.

Credit swap A type of swap transaction used as a credit derivative in which one party makes periodic payments to the other and receives the promise of a payoff if a third party defaults.

Credit VAR, Default VAR, or Credit at Risk A variation of VAR that reflects credit risk.

Creditor nation A country that during its entire history has invested more in the rest of the world than other countries have invested in it.

Cross-product netting Netting the market values of all contracts, not just derivatives, between parties.

Cross-rate The exchange rate between two currencies, derived from their exchange rates with a third currency.

Cross-sectional data Observations over individual units at a point in time, as opposed to time-series data.

Cum dividend With dividend.

Cumulative distribution function A function giving the probability that a random variable is less than or equal to a specified value.

Cumulative relative frequency For data grouped into intervals, the fraction of total observations that are less than the value of the upper limit of a stated interval.

Currency The bills and coins that we use today.

Currency appreciation The rise in the value of one currency in terms of another currency.

Currency depreciation The fall in the value of one currency in terms of another currency.

Currency exposure The sensitivity of the asset return, measured in the investor's domestic currency, to a movement in the exchange rate.

Currency forward A forward contract in which the underlying is a foreign currency.

Currency option An option that allows the holder to buy (if a call) or sell (if a put) an underlying currency at a fixed exercise rate, expressed as an exchange rate.

Currency swap A contract to exchange streams of fixed cash flows denominated in two different currencies.

Current account A record of the payments for imports of goods and services, receipts from exports of goods and services, the interest income, and net transfers.

Current asset Asset that will normally be turned into cash within a year.

Current credit risk The risk associated with the possibility that a payment currently due will not be made.

Current income A return objective in which the investor seeks to generate income rather than capital gains; generally a goal of an investor who wants to supplement earnings with income to meet living expenses.

Current liability Liability that will normally be repaid within a year.

Current ratio A ratio representing the ability of the firm to pay off its current liabilities by liquidating current assets (current assets/current liabilities).

Current yield A bond's annual coupon payment divided by its price. Differs from yield to maturity.

Custodians Agents who hold property in safekeeping for others, usually without inherent investment management responsibility.

Customer acquisition costs Initial direct costs incurred in adding to a company's customer base, including direct-response advertising, commissions, and related administrative costs. When capitalized, prospective customer-related revenues must be expected to exceed amounts capitalized. Depending on the industry, such costs may have other names, including subscriber acquisition costs and policy acquisition costs.

Cyclical businesses or cyclical companies Businesses with high sensitivity to business- or industry-cycle influences.

Cyclical industries Industries with above-average sensitivity to the state of the economy.

Cyclical stock A stock with a high beta; its gains typically exceed those of a rising market and its losses typically exceed those of a falling market.

Cyclicals Some industries are perennially subject to the vagaries of the business cycle: mining, steel, construction, automobiles, chemicals, machine tools, and the like. It is impossible to get away from the cyclical effect in business, just as there is always alternation between good and bad weather, so a cyclical company will have an irregular earnings pattern, and usually an irregular stock price pattern too.

Daily settlement See *marking to market*.

Data mining The practice of determining a model by extensive searching through a dataset for statistically significant patterns.

Day trader A trader holding a position open somewhat longer than a scalper but closing all positions at the end of the day.

DCF Discounted cash flow.

DDM Dividend discount model.

Dead-hand provision A poison pill provision that allows for the redemption or cancellation of a poison pill provision only by a vote of continuing directors (generally directors who were on the target company's board prior to the takeover attempt).

Dealer An agent that buys and sells securities as a principal (for its own account) rather than as a broker for clients. A dealer may function, at different times, as a broker or as a dealer. Sometimes called a *market maker*.

Debenture Unsecured bond.

Debt ratings An objective measure of the quality and safety of a company's debt based upon an analysis of the company's ability to pay the promised cash flows, as well as an analysis of any indentures.

Debtor nation A country that during its entire history has borrowed more from the rest of the world than it has lent to it.

Decentralized risk management A system that allows individual units within an organization to manage risk. Decentralization results in duplication of effort but has the advantage of having people closer to the risk be more directly involved in its management.

Deciles Quantiles that divide a distribution into 10 equal parts.

Decision rule With respect to hypothesis testing, the rule according to which the null hypothesis will be rejected or not rejected; involves the comparison of the test statistic to rejection point(s).

Decision tree Method of representing alternative sequential decisions and the possible outcomes from these decisions.

Declaration date The day that the corporation issues a statement declaring a specific dividend.

Deep in the money Said of call options for which the market price of the underlying is far above the exercise price or of put options for which the market price of the underlying is far below the exercise price.

Deep out of the money Said of call options for which the market price of the underlying is far below the exercise price or of put options for which the market price of the underlying is far above the exercise price.

Default risk The risk that an issuer will be unable to make interest and principal payments on time.

Default risk premium A differential in promised return relative to default-free debt that compensates investors for the possibility that the borrower will fail to make a promised payment at the contracted time and in the contracted amount.

Default swap *Credit derivative* in which one party makes fixed payments while the payments by the other party depend on the occurrence of a loan default.

Defeasance Practice whereby the borrower sets aside cash or *bonds* sufficient to service the borrower's debt. Both the borrower's debt and the offsetting cash or bonds are removed from the balance sheet.

Defensive industries Industries with little sensitivity to the state of the economy.

Deferred tax assets Future tax benefits that result from (1) the origination of a deductible temporary difference, that is, a tax deduction that can be used in a future period, or (2) a loss or tax-credit carryover. These future tax benefits are realized upon the reversal of deductible temporary differences. In addition, realization can occur by the offsetting of a loss carryforward against taxable income or a tax credit carryforward against taxes currently payable.

Deferred tax liabilities Future tax obligations that result from the origination of taxable temporary differences. Upon origination, these temporary difference cause pretax financial income to exceed taxable income. These future tax obligations are paid later when temporary differences reverse, now causing taxable income to exceed pretax book income.

Defined benefit pension plan or defined benefit plan A pension plan to which the company contributes a certain amount each year and promises to pay employees a specified income after they retire. The benefit size is based on factors such as workers' salary and time of employment.

Defined contribution pension plan or defined contribution plan A pension plan in which worker benefits are determined by the size of employees' contributions to the plan and the returns earned on the fund's investments.

Definitive merger agreement A contract signed by both parties to a merger that clarifies the details of the transaction, including the terms, warranties, conditions, termination details, and the rights of all parties.

Deflation The situation in which the average of all prices of goods and services in an economy is falling.

Degree of confidence The probability that a confidence interval includes the unknown population parameter.

Degree of financial leverage (DFL) The ratio of the percentage change in net income to the percentage change in operating income; the sensitivity of the cash flows available to owners when operating income changes.

Degree of operating leverage (DOL) The ratio of the percentage change in operating income to the percentage change in units sold; the sensitivity of operating income to changes in units sold.

Degree of total leverage The ratio of the percentage change in net income to the percentage change in units sold; the sensitivity of the cash flows to owners to changes in the number of units produced and sold.

Degrees of freedom (df) The number of independent observations used.

Delivery A process used in a deliverable forward contract in which the long pays the agreed-upon price to the short, which in turn delivers the underlying asset to the long.

Delivery option The feature of a futures contract giving the short the right to make decisions about what, when, and where to deliver.

Delta The relationship between the option price and the underlying price, which reflects the sensitivity of the price of the option to changes in the price of the underlying.

Delta hedge An option strategy in which a position in an asset is converted to a risk-free position with a position in a specific number of options. The number of options per unit of the underlying changes through time, and the position must be revised to maintain the hedge.

Delta-normal method A measure of VAR equivalent to the analytical method but that refers to the use of delta to estimate the option's price sensitivity.

Demand The relationship between the quantity of a good that consumers plan to buy and the price of the good when all other influences on buyers' plans remain the same. It is described by a demand schedule and illustrated by a demand curve.

Demand curve A curve that shows the relationship between the quantity demanded of a good and its price when all other influences on consumers' planned purchases remain the same.

Demand for labor The relationship between the quantity of labor demanded and the real wage rate when all other influences on a firm's hiring plans remain the same.

Dependent With reference to events, the property that the probability of one event occurring depends on (is related to) the occurrence of another event.

Dependent variable The variable whose variation about its mean is to be explained by the regression; the left-hand-side variable in a regression equation.

Depreciation Reduction in the value of capital goods over a one-year period due to physical wear and tear and also to obsolescence; also called *capital consumption allowance*. Can also be viewed as a decrease in the exchange value of one nation's currency in terms of the currency of another nation.

Depression An extremely severe recession.

Deregulation   The elimination or phasing out of regulations on economic activity.

Derivative   A financial instrument that offers a return based on the return of an underlying asset.

Derivatives dealers   The commercial and investment banks that make markets in derivatives. Also referred to as market makers.

Descriptive statistics   The study of how data can be summarized effectively.

Devaluation   Deliberate downward adjustment of a currency against its fixed parity.

Differential expectations   Expectations that differ from consensus expectations.

Differential swap or diff swap or diff   A swap in which the payments are based on the difference between interest rates in two countries but payments are made in only a single currency.

Differentiation   The competitive strategy of offering unique products or services along some dimensions that are widely valued by buyers so that the firm can command premium prices.

Diffuse prior   The assumption of equal prior probabilities.

Diluted earnings per share   Total earnings divided by the number of shares that would be outstanding if holders of securities such as executive stock options and convertible bonds exercised their options to obtain common stock.

Dilution   Reduction in shareholders' equity per share or earnings per share that arises from some changes among shareholders' proportionate interests.

Diminishing marginal returns   The tendency for the marginal product of an additional unit of a factor of production to be less than the marginal product of the previous unit of the factor.

Direct exchange rate   The amount of local or domestic currency required to purchase one unit of foreign currency.

Direct income capitalization approach   Division of net operating income by an overall capitalization rate to arrive at market value.

Direct Investments (Private Equity)   An investment made directly in venture capital or private equity assets (i.e., not via a partnership or fund).

Direct quote   For foreign exchange, the number of U.S. dollars needed to buy one unit of a foreign currency (cf. *indirect quote*).

Directed brokerage   A manager is asked to direct business to a specified broker, usually to pay for services.

Dirty surplus items   Items that affect comprehensive income but which bypass the income statement.

Discontinued operations   Net income and the gain or loss on disposal of a discontinued business segment or separately measured business unit.

Discount   To reduce the value of a future payment in allowance for how far away it is in time; to calculate the present value of some future amount. Also, the amount by which an instrument is priced below its face value.

Discount factor   *Present value* of $1 received at a stated future date.

Discount interest   A procedure for determining the interest on a loan or bond in which the interest is deducted from the face value in advance.

Discount rate   (1) Rate used to calculate the present value of future cash flows. (2) The interest rate at which the U.S. Federal Reserve System stands ready to lend reserves to depository institutions.

Discounted cash flow (DCF)   Future cash flows multiplied by discount factors to obtain present value.

Discounted cash flow analysis   Analysis of value in terms of the present value of expected future cash flows.

Discounting   The conversion of a future amount of money to its present value.

Discrete random variable   A random variable that can take on at most a countable number of possible values.

Discrete time   Time thought of as advancing in distinct finite increments.

Discretionary account   An account of a customer who gives a broker the authority to make buy and sell decisions on the customer's behalf.

Discriminant analysis   A multivariate classification technique used to discriminate between groups, such as companies that either will or will not become bankrupt during some time frame.

Dispersion   The variability around the central tendency.

Diversifiable risk   Risk attributable to firm-specific risk, or nonmarket risk. *Nondiversifiable* risk refers to systematic or market risk.

Diversification   (1) Spreading a portfolio over many investments to avoid excessive exposure to any one source of risk. (2) In mergers and acquisitions, a term that refers to buying companies or assets outside the companies' current lines of business.

Divestiture   The sale, liquidation, or spin-off of some major component of a business.

Dividend   Payment by a company to its stockholders.

Dividend discount model (DDM)   A present value model of stock value that views the intrinsic value of a stock as present value of the stock's expected future dividends.

Dividend displacement of earnings The concept that dividends paid now displace earnings in all future periods.

Dividend payout policy The strategy a company follows with regard to the amount and timing of dividend payments.

Dividend payout ratio Percentage of earnings paid out as dividends.

Dividend rate The most recent quarterly dividend multiplied by four.

Dividend reinvestment plan (DRIP) Plan that allows shareholders to reinvest dividends automatically.

Dividend yield Annual dividend divided by share price.

Dividends paid A term used on the cash flow analysis statement that refers to cash disbursements for dividends on common and preferred stock.

Double taxation With reference to certain tax jurisdictions, the practice of taxing corporate earnings twice. First, corporate earnings are taxed regardless of whether they will be distributed as dividends or retained at the corporate level, and second, dividends are taxed again at the individual shareholder level.

Dow Jones Industrial Average (DJI or DJIA) A price-weighted average of thirty industrial companies.

Down transition probability The probability that an asset's value moves down in a model of asset price dynamics.

Due diligence Investigation and analysis in support of a recommendation; the failure to exercise due diligence may sometimes result in liability according to various securities laws.

Dummy variable A type of qualitative variable that takes on a value of 1 if a particular condition is true and 0 if that condition is false.

Dumping The sale by a foreign firm of exports at a lower price that the cost of production.

Duration A measure of an option-free bond's average maturity. Specifically, the weighted average maturity of all future cash flows paid by a security, in which the weights are the present value of these cash flows as a fraction of the bond's price. A measure of a bond's price sensitivity to interest rate movements.

Dutch Book Theorem A result in probability theory stating that inconsistent probabilities create profit opportunities.

Dynamic hedging Hedging that involves making frequent adjustments to the quantity of the instrument used for hedging in relation to the instrument being hedged.

Early stage With reference to venture capital financing, the stage associated with moving into operation and before commercial manufacturing and sales have occurred. Includes the start-up and first stages.

Earnings at risk (EAR) A variation of VAR that reflects the risk of a company's earnings instead of its market value.

Earnings before interest and taxes (EBIT) Net income measured before interest expense and before income tax expense. EBIT has a long history of being used as a basis for measuring fixed-charge coverage.

Earnings before interest, taxes, depreciation, and amortization (EBITDA) An earnings-based measure that often serves as a surrogate for cash flow. The measure actually represents working capital provided by operations before interest and taxes.

Earnings management The practice of using flexibility in accounting rules to improve the apparent profitability of the firm.

Earnings momentum A strategy in which portfolios are constructed of stocks of firms with rising earnings.

Earnings retention ratio Plowback ratio.

Earnings surprise A company announcement of earnings that differs from analysts' prevailing expectations.

Earnings yield Earnings per share divided by price; the reciprocal of the P/E ratio.

EBIT Earnings before interest and taxes.

EBITDA Earnings before interest, taxes, depreciation, and amortization.

Economic depreciation The change in the market value of capital over a given period.

Economic efficiency A situation that occurs when the firm produces a given output at the least cost.

Economic exposure Risk that arises from changes in real exchange rates (cf. *transaction exposure, translation exposure*).

Economic growth (1) Increases in per capita real GDP measured by its rate of change per year. (2) The expansion of production possibilities that results from capital accumulation and technological change.

Economic growth rate The percentage change in the quantity of goods and services produced from one year to the next.

Economic income Cash flow plus change in *present value.*

Economic model A description of some aspect of the economic world that includes only those features of the world that are needed for the purpose at hand.

Economic profit Total revenue minus total opportunity costs of all inputs used, or the total of all implicit and explicit costs; a firm's after-tax net operating profit minus its opportunity cost of capital.

Economic rent A payment for the use of any resource over and above its opportunity cost.

Economic risk As used in currency risk management, the risk that arises when the foreign currency value of a foreign investment reacts systematically to an exchange rate movement.

Economic sectors Large industry groupings.

Economic theory A generalization that summarizes what we think we understand about the economic choices that people make and the performance of industries and entire economies.

Economic value added (EVA®) The spread between ROA and cost of capital multiplied by the capital invested in the firm. It measures the dollar value of the firm's return in excess of its opportunity cost.

Economic welfare A comprehensive measure of the general state of economic well-being.

Economics The social science that studies the choices that individuals, businesses, governments, and entire societies make and how they cope with scarcity and the incentives that influence and reconcile those choices.

Economies of scale The reduction of a company's average costs due to increasing output and spreading out fixed costs over higher output levels; the savings achieved through the consolidation of operations and elimination of duplicate resources.

Economies of scope The ability of a firm to utilize one set of inputs to provide a broader range of outputs or services.

Effective annual rate The amount by which a unit of currency will grow in a year with interest on interest included.

Effective annual yield (EAY) An annualized return that accounts for the effect of interest on interest; EAY is computed by compounding 1 plus the holding period yield forward to one year, then subtracting 1.

Effective tax rate The income tax provision divided by income before the income tax provision.

Efficiency In statistics, a desirable property of estimators; an efficient estimator is the unbiased estimator with the smallest variance among unbiased estimators of the same parameter.

Efficient capital market A market in which security prices rapidly reflect all information about securities.

Efficient diversification The organizing principle of modern portfolio theory, which maintains that any risk-averse investor will search for the highest expected return for any level of portfolio risk.

Efficient frontier The portion of the minimum-variance frontier beginning with the global minimum-variance portfolio and continuing above it; the graph of the set of portfolios offering the maximum expected return for their level of variance of return.

Efficient market A market in which any relevant information is immediately impounded in asset prices.

Efficient portfolio A portfolio offering the highest expected return for a given level of risk as measured by variance or standard deviation of return.

Elasticity A measure of sensitivity; the incremental change in one variable with respect to an incremental change in another variable.

Electronic crossing networks Order-driven trading systems in which market orders are anonymously matched at prespecified times at prices determined in the primary market for the system.

Emerging Issues Task Force (EITF) The EITF assists the Financial Accounting Standards Board through the timely identification, discussion, and resolution of financial accounting issues based on existing authoritative literature.

Emerging markets Often, countries so defined by the International Finance Corporation (IFC), based on their per capita income.

Empirical Relying on real-world data in evaluating the usefulness of a model.

Empirical duration Measures directly the interest rate sensitivity of an asset by examining the percentage price change for an asset in response to a change in yield during a specified period of time.

Employee Retirement Income Security Act (ERISA) Governs most private pension and benefit plans.

Endogenous growth theory A theory of economic growth that does not assume that the marginal productivity of capital declines as capital is added.

Endowment funds Organizations chartered to invest money for specific purposes.

Endowments The various resources in an economy, including both physical resources and such human resources as ingenuity and management skills.

Enhanced derivatives products companies (EDPC) or special purpose vehicles (SPVs) A type of subsidiary engaged in derivatives transactions that is separated from the parent company in order to have a higher credit rating than the parent company.

Enterprise risk management A form of *centralized risk management* that typically encompasses the management of a broad variety of risks, including insurance risk.

Enterprise value (EV) Total company value (the market value of debt, common equity, and preferred equity) minus the value of cash and investments.

EPS Earnings per share.

Equilibrium The condition in which supply equals demand.

Equilibrium price The price at which the quantity demanded equals the quantity supplied.

Equities Another name for shares. The capitalization of a company consists of "equity"—or ownership—represented by common or preferred shares (stock), and debt, represented by bonds, notes, and the like. (In England, "corporation stock" means municipal bonds, incidentally.)

Equitizing cash A strategy used to replicate an index. It is also used to take a given amount of cash and turn it into an equity position while maintaining the liquidity provided by the cash.

Equity (1) *Common stock* and *preferred stock*. Often used to refer to common stock only. (2) *Net worth*.

Equity carve-out A form of restructuring that involves the creation of a new legal entity and the sale of equity in it to outsiders.

Equity charge The estimated cost of equity capital in money terms.

Equity dividend rate Income rate that reflects the relationship between equity income and equity capital.

Equity forward A contract calling for the purchase of an individual stock, a stock portfolio, or a stock index at a later date at an agreed-upon price.

Equity options Options on individual stocks; also known as stock options.

Equity risk premium The expected return on equities minus the risk-free rate.

Equity security An ownership interest in an enterprise, including preferred and common stock.

Equity swap A swap transaction in which at least one cash flow is tied to the return to an equity portfolio position, often an index.

Error autocorrelation The autocorrelation of the error term.

Error term The portion of the dependent variable that is not explained by the independent variable(s) in the regression.

Estimate The particular value calculated from sample observations using an estimator.

Estimated (or fitted) parameters With reference to regression analysis, the estimated values of the population intercept and population slope coefficient(s) in a regression.

Estimated rate of return The rate of return an investor anticipates earning from a specific investment over a particular future holding period.

Estimation With reference to statistical inference, the subdivision dealing with estimating the value of a population parameter.

Estimator An estimation formula; the formula used to compute the sample mean and other sample statistics are examples of estimators.

Euribor Interbank offer rate for short-term deposits in euros. Euribor is determined by an association of European banks.

Eurobond A bond underwritten by a multinational syndicate of banks and placed mainly in countries other than the country of the issuer; sometimes called an *international bond*.

Eurodollar A dollar deposited outside the United States.

Eurodollar deposit Dollar deposit with a bank outside the United States.

Eurodollar market The U.S. dollar segment of the Eurocurrency market.

European option An option that can be exercised only at expiration.

European terms With reference to U.S. dollar exchange rate quotations, the price of a U.S. dollar in terms of another currency.

European Union (EU) A formal association of European countries founded by the Treaty of Rome in 1957. Formerly known as the EEC.

EVA Economic value added.

Event Any outcome or specified set of outcomes of a random variable.

Excess kurtosis Degree of peakedness (fatness of tails) in excess of the peakedness of the normal distribution.

Excess return Rate of return in excess of the risk-free rate.

Exchange for physicals (EFP) A permissible delivery procedure used by futures market participants, in which the long and short arrange a delivery procedure other than the normal procedures stipulated by the futures exchange.

Exchange of assets Acquisition of another company by purchase of its assets in exchange for cash or shares.

Exchange rate Price of a unit of one country's currency in terms of another country's currency.

Exchange rate risk Uncertainty due to the denomination of an investment in a currency other than that of the investor's own country.

Exchange ratio The number of shares that target stockholders are to receive in exchange for each of their shares in the target company.

Exchanges National or regional auction markets providing a facility for members to trade securities. A seat is a membership on an exchange.

Exchange-traded funds (ETFs) A type of mutual fund traded like other shares on a stock market, having special characteristics particularly related to redemption, and generally designed to closely track the performance of a specified stock market index.

Ex-dividend date The first date that a share trades without (i.e. "ex") the right to a declared dividend.

Executor The legal representative of a person who dies with a will.

Exercise or exercising the option The process of using an option to buy or sell the underlying.

Exercise price (striking price) Price at which a call option or put option may be exercised.

Exercise rate or strike rate The fixed rate at which the holder of an interest rate option can buy or sell the underlying.

Exhaustive Covering or containing all possible outcomes.

Expansion A business cycle phase between a trough and a peak—phase in which real GDP increases.

Expectational arbitrage Investing on the basis of differential expectations.

Expectations theory Theory that forward interest rate (forward exchange rate) equals expected spot rate.

Expected holding-period return The expected total return on an asset over a stated holding period; for stocks, the sum of the expected dividend yield and the expected price appreciation over the holding period.

Expected return or expected rate of return Average of possible returns weighted by their probabilities.

Expected return–beta relationship Implication of the CAPM that security risk premiums (expected excess returns) will be proportional to beta.

Expected utility The average utility arising from all possible outcomes.

Expected value The probability-weighted average of the possible outcomes of a random variable.

Expiration date The date on which a derivative contract expires.

Exports The goods and services that we sell to people in other countries.

Ex-Post After the fact.

External financing A term used on the cash flow analysis statement that consists of net debt and equity capital raised from external sources.

External growth Company growth in output or sales that is achieved by buying the necessary resources externally (i.e., achieved through mergers and acquisitions).

Externality A consequence of an economic activity that spills over to affect third parties; a situation in which the costs (or benefits) of an action are not fully borne (or gained) by the two parties engaged in exchange or by an individual engaging in a scarce-resource-using activity.

Extra dividend *Dividend* that may or may not be repeated (cf. *regular dividend*).

Extraordinary item Gain or loss that is unusual and infrequent in occurrence.

Face value The promised payment at maturity separate from any coupon payment. Sometimes referred to as *par value*.

Factor A common or underlying element with which several variables are correlated.

Factor beta Sensitivity of security returns to changes in a systematic factor. Alternatively, factor loading; factor sensitivity.

Factor loading See *factor beta*.

Factor model A way of decomposing the factors that influence a security's rate of return into common and firm-specific influences.

Factor portfolio A well-diversified portfolio constructed to have a beta of 1.0 on one factor and a beta of zero on any other factor.

Factor risk premium (or factor price) The expected return in excess of the risk-free rate for a portfolio with a sensitivity of 1 to one factor and a sensitivity of 0 to all other factors.

Factor sensitivity (also factor betas or factor loadings) An asset's sensitivity to a particular factor (holding all other factors constant).

Factors of production The productive resources that businesses use to produce goods and services.

Fair value (1) The amount at which an asset could be acquired or sold in a current transaction between willing parties in which the parties each acted knowledgeably, prudently, and without compulsion. (2) The theoretical value of a security based on current market conditions. The fair value is the value such that no arbitrage opportunities exist.

FASB Financial Accounting Standards Board.

Federal Deposit Insurance Corporation (FDIC) A government agency that insures the deposits held in banks and most other depository institutions; all U.S. banks are insured this way.

Federal funds Non-interest-bearing deposits by banks at the Federal Reserve. Excess reserves are lent by banks to each other.

Federal funds rate The interest rate that depository institutions pay to borrow reserves in the interbank federal funds market.

Fictitious revenue Revenue recognized on a nonexistent sale or service transaction.

Fiduciary A person who supervises or oversees the investment portfolio of a third party, such as in a trust account, and makes investment decisions in accordance with the owner's wishes.

Fiduciary call A combination of a European call and a risk-free bond that matures on the option expiration day and has a face value equal to the exercise price of the call.

Fiduciary relationship An arrangement under which a person (the fiduciary) has a duty to act for another's benefit (the beneficiary).

FIFO The first-in first-out accounting method of inventory valuation.

Financial account A component of the balance of payments covering investments by residents abroad and investments by nonresidents in the home country. Examples include direct investment made by companies, portfolio investments in equity and bonds, and other investments and liabilities.

Financial Accounting Standards Board (FASB) The principal standard-setting body in the United States. Its primary standards are Statements of Financial Accounting Standards (SFASs).

Financial assets Financial assets such as stocks and bonds are claims to the income generated by real assets or claims on income from the government.

Financial capital Funds used to purchase physical capital goods such as buildings and equipment.

Financial distress Heightened uncertainty regarding a company's ability to meet its various obligations because of lower or negative earnings.

Financial engineering Combining or dividing existing instruments to create new financial products.

Financial futures Futures contracts in which the underlying is a stock, bond, or currency.

Financial innovation The development of new financial products—new ways of borrowing and lending.

Financial intermediaries Institutions that transfer funds between ultimate lenders (savers) and ultimate borrowers.

Financial lease (capital lease, full-payout lease) Long-term, noncancelable lease (cf. *operating lease*).

Financial risk The variability of future income arising from the firm's fixed financing costs, for example, interest payments. The effect of fixed financial costs is to magnify the effect of changes in operating profit on net income or earnings per share.

Firm (1) An economic unit that hires factors of production and organizes those factors to produce and sell goods and services. (2) For purposes of the GIPS standards, the term "firm" refers to the entity defined for compliance with the GIPS standards.

Firm-specific risk See *diversifiable risk*.

First-differencing A transformation that subtracts the value of the time series in period $t - 1$ from its value in period t.

First-order serial correlation Correlation between adjacent observations in a time series.

Fiscal policy The government's attempt to achieve macroeconomic objectives such as full employment, sustained economic growth, and price level stability by setting and changing taxes, making transfer payments, and purchasing goods and services.

Fixed costs Costs that remain at the same level regardless of a company's level of production and sales.

Fixed investment Purchases by businesses of newly produced producer durables, or capital goods, such as production machinery and office equipment.

Fixed-income forward A forward contract in which the underlying is a bond.

Fixed-income security A security such as a bond that pays a specified cash flow over a specific period.

Fixed-rate perpetual preferred stock Stock with a specified dividend rate that has a claim on earnings senior to the claim of common stock, and no maturity date.

Fixing A method for determining the market price of a security by finding the price that balances buyers and sellers. A fixing takes place periodically each day at defined times. Sometimes called a *call auction*.

Flexible exchange rates Exchange rates that are allowed to fluctuate in the open market in response to changes in supply and demand. Sometimes called *floating exchange rates*.

Flexible exchange rate system A system in which exchange rates are determined by supply and demand.

Flip-in pill A poison pill takeover defense that dilutes an acquirer's ownership in a target by giving other existing target company shareholders the right to buy additional target company shares at a discount.

Flip-over pill A poison pill takeover defense that gives target company shareholders the right to purchase shares of the acquirer at a significant discount to the market price, which has the effect of causing dilution to all existing acquiring company shareholders.

Floating-rate bond A bond whose interest rate is reset periodically according to a specified market rate.

Floating-rate loan A loan in which the interest rate is reset at least once after the starting date.

Floating-rate note (FRN) Short- to intermediate-term bonds with regularly scheduled coupon payments linked to a variable interest rate, most often LIBOR.

Floor A combination of interest rate put options designed to hedge a lender against lower rates on a floating-rate loan.

Floor agreement A contract that on each settlement date pays the holder the greater of the difference between the floor rate and the reference rate or zero; it is equivalent to a series of put options on the reference rate.

Floor traders or locals Market makers that buy and sell by quoting a bid and an ask price. They are the primary providers of liquidity to the market.

Floored swap A swap in which the floating payments have a lower limit.

Floorlet Each component put option in a floor.

Flotation cost Fees charged to companies by investment bankers and other costs associated with raising new capital.

Flow A quantity measured per unit of time; something that occurs over time, such as the income you make per week or per year or the number of individuals who are fired every month.

Focus The competitive strategy of seeking a competitive advantage within a target segment or segments of the industry, either on the basis of cost leadership (cost focus) or differentiation (differentiation focus).

Foreign bond A bond issued on the domestic capital market of another country.

Foreign currency risk premium The expected movement in the (direct) exchange rate minus the interest rate differential (domestic risk-free rate minus foreign risk-free rate).

Foreign direct investment The acquisition of more than 10 percent of the shares of ownership in a company in another nation.

Foreign exchange The purchase (sale) of a currency against the sale (purchase) of another.

Foreign exchange expectation A relation that states that the forward exchange rate, quoted at time 0 for delivery at time 1, is equal to the expected value of the spot exchange rate at time 1. When stated relative to the current spot exchange rate, the relation states that the forward discount (premium) is equal to the expected exchange rate movement.

Foreign exchange market The market in which the currency of one country is exchanged for the currency of another.

Foreign exchange rate The price at which one currency exchanges for another.

Forex Foreign exchange.

Forward contract An agreement between two parties in which one party, the buyer, agrees to buy from the other party, the seller, an underlying asset at a later date for a price established at the start of the contract.

Forward discount or premium Refers to the percentage difference between the forward exchange rate and the spot exchange rate (premium if positive, discount if negative).

Forward exchange rate Exchange rate fixed today for exchanging currency at some future date (cf. *spot exchange rate*).

Forward integration A merger involving the purchase of a target that is farther along the value or production chain; for example, to acquire a distributor.

Forward interest rate (1) Interest rate fixed today on a loan to be made at some future date (cf. *spot interest rate*). (2) Rate of interest for a future period that would equate the total return of a long-term bond with that of a strategy of rolling over shorter-term bonds. The forward rate is inferred from the term structure.

Forward premium A situation where, from the perspective of the domestic country, the spot exchange rate is larger than the forward exchange rate with a foreign country.

Forward price or forward rate The fixed price or rate at which the transaction scheduled to occur at the expiration of a forward contract will take place. This price is agreed on at the initiation date of the contract. With respect to the yield curve, a short-term yield for a future holding period implied by the spot rates of two securities with different maturities.

Forward rate agreement (FRA) A forward contract calling for one party to make a fixed interest payment and the other to make an interest payment at a rate to be determined at the contract expiration.

Forward swap A forward contract to enter into a swap.

Franchise factor A firm's unique competitive advantage that makes it possible for a firm to earn excess returns (rates of return above a firm's cost of capital) on its capital projects. In turn, these excess returns and the franchise factor cause the firm's stock price to have a *P/E* ratio above its base *P/E* ratio that is equal to $1/k$.

Franchise value In P/E ratio analysis, the present value of growth opportunities divided by next year's expected earnings.

Free cash flow The actual cash that would be available to the company's investors after making all investments necessary to maintain the company as an ongoing enterprise (also referred to as free cash flow to the firm); the internally generated funds that can be distributed to the company's investors (e.g., shareholders and bondholders) without impairing the value of the company.

Free cash flow hypothesis The hypothesis that higher debt levels discipline managers by forcing them to make fixed debt service payments and by reducing the company's free cash flow.

Free cash flow to equity The cash flow available to a company's common shareholders after all operating expenses, interest, and principal payments have been made, and necessary investments in working and fixed capital have been made.

Free cash flow to equity model A model of stock valuation that views a stock's intrinsic value as the present value of expected future free cash flows to equity.

Free cash flow to the firm The cash flow available to the company's suppliers of capital after all operating expenses (including taxes) have been paid and necessary investments in working and fixed capital have been made.

Free cash flow to the firm model A model of stock valuation that views the value of a firm as the present value of expected future free cash flows to the firm.

Frequency distribution A tabular display of data summarized into a relatively small number of intervals.

Frequency polygon A graph of a frequency distribution obtained by drawing straight lines joining successive points representing the class frequencies.

Friendly transaction A potential business combination that is endorsed by the managers of both companies.

Full price (or dirty price) The total price of a bond, including accrued interest.

Fundamental beta A beta that is based at least in part on fundamental data for a company.

Fundamental factor models A multifactor model in which the factors are attributes of stocks or companies that are important in explaining cross-sectional differences in stock prices.

Fundamentals Economic characteristics of a business such as profitability, financial strength, and risk.

Funded debt Debt maturing after more than one year (cf. *unfunded debt*).

Funds Traditionally defined as working capital, that is, the excess of current assets over current liabilities.

Funds from operations (FFO) A term used by real estate investment trusts (REITs) and defined as net income or loss excluding gains or losses from debt restructuring and sales of property, plus depreciation and amortization of real estate assets.

Future value (FV) The amount to which a payment or series of payments will grow by a stated future date.

Futures commission merchants (FCMs) Individuals or companies that execute futures transactions for other parties off the exchange.

Futures contract A standardized contract to buy (sell) an asset at a specified date and a specified price (futures price). The contract is traded on an organized exchange, and the potential gain/loss is realized each day (marking to market).

Futures exchange An exchange on which futures contracts are traded.

Futures option The right to enter a specified futures contract at a futures price equal to the stipulated exercise price.

Futures price The price at which a futures trader commits to make or take delivery of the underlying asset.

GAAP See generally accepted accounting principles.

Game theory A tool that economists use to analyze strategic behavior—behavior that takes into account the expected behavior of others and the mutual recognition of independence.

Gamma A numerical measure of how sensitive an option's delta is to a change in the underlying.

GDP deflator One measure of the price level, which is the average of current-year prices as a percentage of base-year prices.

Gearing Financial leverage.

General Agreement on Tariffs and Trade An international agreement signed in 1947 to reduce tariffs on international trade.

General Partner (Private Equity) (GP) A class of partner in a partnership. The GP retains liability for the actions of the partnership. In the PRIVATE EQUITY world, the GP is the fund manager and the LIMITED PARTNERS (LPs) are the institutional and high-net-worth investors in the partnership. The GP earns a management fee and a percentage of profits.

Generalized least squares A regression estimation technique that addresses heteroskedasticity of the error term.

Generally accepted accounting principles (GAAP) A common set of standards and procedures for the preparation of general-purpose financial statements that either have been established by an authoritative accounting rule-making body, such as the Financial Accounting Standards Board (FASB), or have over time become common accepted practice.

Generic See *plain-vanilla*.

Geometric mean A measure of central tendency computed by taking the *n*th root of the product of *n* non-negative values.

Global Of a fund or portfolio, invested both in the United States and abroad.

Global Investment Performance Standards™ (GIPS®) A global industry standard for the ethical presentation of investment performance results promulgated by CFA Institute.

Globalization Tendency toward a worldwide investment environment, and the integration of national capital markets.

Going-concern assumption The assumption that the business will maintain its business activities into the foreseeable future.

Going-concern value A business's value under a going-concern assumption.

Gold standard An international monetary system in which the parity of a currency is fixed in terms of its gold content.

Golden parachute Employment contract of upper management that provides a larger payout upon the occurrence of certain control transactions, such as a certain percentage share purchase by an outside entity or when there is a tender offer for a certain percentage of the company's shares.

Goods All things from which individuals derive satisfaction or happiness.

Goods and services The objects that people value and produce to satisfy their wants.

Goodwill An intangible asset that represents the excess of the purchase price of an acquisition over the value of the net assets acquired.

Governance The oversight of a firm's management.

Government debt The total amount of borrowing that the government has borrowed. It equals the sum of past budget deficits minus budget surpluses.

Government sector surplus or deficit An amount equal to net taxes minus government purchases of goods and services.

Great Depression A decade (1929-1939) of high unemployment and stagnant production throughout the world economy.

Greenmail The purchase of the accumulated shares of a hostile investor by a company that is targeted for takeover by that investor, usually at a substantial premium over market price.

Gross domestic product A money measure of the goods and services produced within a country's borders over a stated time period.

Gross investment The total amount spent on purchases of new capital and on replacing depreciated capital.

Gross margin Revenue minus cost of goods sold. Also referred to as *gross profit*.

Gross national product (GNP) Total value of a country's output produced by residents both within the country's physical borders and abroad.

Growth accounting A method of calculating how much real GDP growth results from growth of labor and capital and how much is attributable to technological change.

Growth company A company that consistently has the opportunities and ability to invest in projects that provide rates of return that exceed the firm's cost of capital. Because of these investment opportunities, it retains a high proportion of earnings, and its earnings grow faster than those of average firms.

Growth investing Emphasizes the future over apparent immediate undervaluation. Thus, usually implies buying companies with higher than average price-earnings ratios and lower dividend yields.

Growth option or expansion option The ability to make additional investments in a project at some future time if the financial results are strong.

Growth phase A stage of growth in which a company typically enjoys rapidly expanding markets, high profit margins, and an abnormally high growth rate in earnings per share.

Growth stock A stock issue that generates a higher rate of return than other stocks in the market with similar risk characteristics.

Harmonic mean A type of weighted mean computed by averaging the reciprocals of the observations, then taking the reciprocal of that average.

Hedge fund An investment vehicle designed to manage a private, unregistered portfolio of assets according to any of several strategies. The investment strategy often employs arbitrage trading and significant financial leverage (e.g., short selling, borrowing, derivatives) while the compensation arrangement for the manager typically specifies considerable profit participation.

Hedge ratio The relationship of the quantity of an asset being hedged to the quantity of the derivative used for hedging.

Hedging A general strategy usually thought of as reducing, if not eliminating, risk.

Herfindahl Index or Herfindahl–Hirschman Index A measure of market concentration that is calculated by summing the squared market shares for competing companies in an industry; high HHI readings or mergers that would result in large HHI increases are more likely to result in regulatory challenges.

Heteroskedastic With reference to the error term of a regression, having a variance that differs across observations.

Heteroskedasticity The property of having a nonconstant variance; refers to an error term with the property that its variance differs across observations.

Heteroskedasticity-consistent standard errors Standard errors of the estimated parameters of a regression that correct for the presence of heteroskedasticity in the regression's error term.

High-yield bond A bond rated below investment grade. Also referred to as *speculative-grade bonds* or *junk bonds*.

Histogram A bar chart of data that have been grouped into a frequency distribution.

Historical method A method of estimating VAR that uses data from the returns of the portfolio over a recent past period and compiles this data in the form of a histogram.

Historical simulation (or back simulation) method Another term for the historical method of estimating VAR. This method involves not a simulation of the past but rather what actually happened in the past, sometimes adjusted to reflect the fact that a different portfolio may have existed in the past than is planned for the future.

Holder-of-record date The date that a shareholder listed on the corporation's books will be deemed to have ownership of the shares for purposes of receiving an upcoming dividend; two business days after the ex-dividend date.

Holding company A company that owns the stock of other corporations. A holding company may not engage in actual operations of its own but merely manages various operating units that it owns an interest in.

Holding period return The return that an investor earns during a specified holding period; a synonym for total return.

Homogenization Creating a contract with standard and generally accepted terms, which makes it more acceptable to a broader group of participants.

Homoskedasticity The property of having a constant variance; refers to an error term that is constant across observations.

Horizontal merger A merger involving companies in the same line of business, usually as competitors.

Hostile transaction An attempt to acquire a company against the wishes of the target's managers.

Hot issue A newly issued stock that is in strong demand; often it will go to a premium over its original issue price.

Human capital The value of skills and knowledge possessed by the workforce.

Hurdle rate The rate of return that must be offered for a project to be accepted.

Hypothesis With reference to statistical inference, a statement about one or more populations.

Hypothesis testing With reference to statistical inference, the subdivision dealing with the testing of hypotheses about one or more populations.

Impairment As used in accounting, a downward adjustment.

Impairment of capital rule A legal restriction that dividends cannot exceed retained earnings.

Implicit costs Expenses that managers do not have to pay out of pocket and hence do not normally explicitly calculate, such as the opportunity cost of factors of production that are owned; examples are owner-provided capital and owner-provided labor.

Implied repo rate The rate of return from a cash-and-carry transaction implied by the futures price relative to the spot price.

Implied volatility The volatility of an asset that is implicit in the current market price of an option on that asset and a particular option-pricing model (e.g., the Black-Scholes-Merton formula).

Imports The goods and services that we buy from people in other countries.

Imputation In reference to corporate taxes, a system that imputes, or attributes, taxes at only one level of taxation. For countries using an imputation tax system, taxes on dividends are effectively levied only at the shareholder rate. Taxes are paid at the corporate level but they are attributed to the shareholder. Shareholders deduct from their tax bill their portion of taxes paid by the company.

Imputation tax system Arrangement by which investors who receive a *dividend* also receive a tax credit for corporate taxes that the firm has paid.

In the money An option that has positive intrinsic value.

Incentive A reward that encourages or a penalty that discourages an action.

Incentive system A method of organizing production that uses a market-like mechanism inside the firm.

Income approach Measuring national income by adding up all components of national income, including wages, interest, rent, and profits.

Income beneficiary A person entitled to all or a share of the income of a trust.

Income effect The effect of a change in income on consumption, other things remaining the same.

Income from continuing operations After-tax net income before discontinued operations, extraordinary items, and the cumulative effect of changes in accounting principle.

Income fund   A mutual fund providing for liberal current income from investments.

Income statement   A financial statement showing a firm's revenues and expenses during a specified period.

Income stock   *Common stock* with high *dividend yield* and few profitable investment opportunities (cf. *growth stock*).

Incremental cash flow   The changes or increments to cash flow resulting from a decision or action; the cash flow with a decision minus the cash flow without that decision.

Indenture   The legal agreement that lists the obligations of the issuer of a bond to the bondholder, including payment schedules, call provisions, and sinking funds.

Independent   With reference to events, the property that the occurrence of one event does not affect the probability of another event occurring.

Independent and identically distributed (IID)   With respect to random variables, the property of random variables that are independent of each other but follow the identical probability distribution.

Independent projects   Independent projects are projects whose cash flows are independent of each other.

Independent variable   A variable used to explain the dependent variable in a regression; a right-hand-side variable in a regression equation.

Index amortizing swap   An interest rate swap in which the notional principal is indexed to the level of interest rates and declines with the level of interest rates according to a predefined scheduled. This type of swap is frequently used to hedge securities that are prepaid as interest rates decline, such as mortgage-backed securities.

Index fund   A portfolio designed to replicate the performance of an index.

Index model   A model of stock returns using a market index such as the SP 500 to represent common or systematic risk factors.

Index option   An option in which the underlying is a stock index.

Indexing   An investment strategy in which an investor constructs a portfolio to mirror the performance of a specified index.

Indirect exchange rate   The amount of foreign currency required to purchase one unit of domestic currency.

Indirect quote   For foreign exchange, the number of units of a foreign currency needed to buy one U.S. dollar (cf. *direct quote*).

Industry life cycle   Stages through which firms typically pass as they mature.

Industry structure   An industry's underlying economic and technical characteristics.

Infant-industry argument   The argument that it is necessary to protect a new industry to enable it to grow into a mature industry that can compete in world markets.

Inflation   The rate at which the general level of prices for goods and services is rising.

Inflation-adjusted return   A rate of return that is measured in terms of real goods and services; that is, after the effects of inflation have been factored out.

Inflation premium   An extra return that compensates investors for expected inflation.

Inflation rate   The percentage change in the price level from one year to the next.

Information   An attribute of a good market that includes providing buyers and sellers with timely, accurate information on the volume and prices of past transactions and on all currently outstanding bids and offers.

Information ratio (IR)   Mean active return divided by active risk.

Initial margin   The amount that an investor must deposit to open a position in futures and some other derivatives; also used to refer to the initial equity required when a stock is purchased using borrowed money.

Initial margin requirement   The margin requirement on the first day of a transaction as well as on any day in which additional margin funds must be deposited.

Initial public offering (IPO)   The initial issuance of common stock registered for public trading by a formerly private corporation.

Innovation   Transforming an invention into something that is useful to humans.

Input list   List of parameters such as expected returns, variances, and covariances necessary to determine the optimal risky portfolio.

In-sample forecast errors   The residuals from a fitted time-series model within the sample period used to fit the model.

Inside information   Nonpublic knowledge about a corporation possessed by corporate officers, major owners, or other individuals with privileged access to information about a firm.

Insider trading   Trading by officers, directors, major stockholders, or others who hold private inside information allowing them to benefit from buying or selling stock.

Instability in the minimum-variance frontier   The characteristic of minimum-variance frontiers that they are sensitive to small changes in inputs.

Institution A retirement fund, bank, investment company, investment advisor, insurance company, or other large pool of investment buying power.

Intangible asset Nonmaterial asset, such as technical expertise, a trademark, or a patent (cf. *tangible asset*).

Interest The payment for current rather than future command over resources; the cost of obtaining credit. Also, the return paid to owners of capital.

Interest rate A rate of return that reflects the relationship between differently dated cash flows; a discount rate.

Interest rate call An option in which the holder has the right to make a known interest payment and receive an unknown interest payment.

Interest rate cap, or cap A series of call options on an interest rate, with each option expiring at the date on which the floating loan rate will be reset, and with each option having the same exercise rate. A cap in general can have an underlying other than an interest rate.

Interest rate collar A combination of a long cap and a short floor, or a short cap and a long floor.

Interest rate floor, or floor A series of put options on an interest rate, with each option expiring at the date on which the floating loan rate will be reset, and with each option having the same exercise rate. A floor in general can have an underlying other than the interest rate.

Interest rate forward (See *forward rate agreement*).

Interest rate option An option in which the underlying is an interest rate.

Interest rate parity A formula that expresses the equivalence or parity of spot and forward rates, after adjusting for differences in the interest rates.

Interest rate put An option in which the holder has the right to make an unknown interest payment and receive a known interest payment.

Interest rate risk The uncertainty of returns on an investment due to possible changes in interest rates over time.

Interest rate swap An agreement calling for the periodic exchange of cash flows, one based on an interest rate that remains fixed for the life of the contract and the other that is linked to a variable-rate index.

Intergenerational data mining A form of data mining that applies information developed by previous researchers using a dataset to guide current research using the same or a related dataset.

Intermediate Of bonds, usually five to seven years' maturity.

Intermediate goods Goods used up entirely in the production of final goods.

Internal rate of return (IRR) The discount rate that makes net present value equal 0; the discount rate that makes the present value of an investment's costs (outflows) equal to the present value of the investment's benefits (inflows).

International Accounting Standard (IAS) An accounting standard issued by the International Accounting Standards Committee. This committee has been replaced by the International Accounting Standards Board (IASB). IAS standards have been adopted by the IASB.

International Accounting Standards Board (IASB) An international standard setting body. Its principal standard-setting products are International Financial Reporting Standards (IFRSs). The IASB assumed its duties from the International Accounting Standards Committee (IASC). Existing International Accounting Standards issued by the IASC were adopted by the IASB.

International CAPM An equilibrium theory that relates the expected return of an asset to its world market and foreign exchange risks.

International Financial Reporting Standard (IFRS) A financial reporting standard issued by the International Accounting Standards Board.

International Fisher relation The assertion that the interest rate differential between two countries should equal the expected inflation rate differential over the term of the interest rates.

International monetary market (IMM) The financial futures market within the Chicago Mercantile Exchange.

International Swaps and Derivatives Association (ISDA) An association of swap dealers formed in 1985 to promote uniform practices in the writing, trading, and settlement procedures of swaps and other derivatives.

Interquartile range The difference between the third and first quartiles of a dataset.

Interval With reference to grouped data, a set of values within which an observation falls.

Interval scale A measurement scale that not only ranks data but also gives assurance that the differences between scale values are equal.

In-the-money Options that, if exercised, would result in the value received being worth more than the payment required to exercise.

Intrinsic value The value of the asset given a hypothetically complete understanding of the asset's investment characteristics; for options, the greater of zero and the amount of money realized if the option were to be exercised.

Inventory investment Changes in the stocks of finished goods and goods in process, as well as changes in the raw materials that businesses keep on hand. Whenever inventories are decreasing, inventory investment is negative; whenever they are increasing, inventory investment is positive.

Inverse floater A floating-rate note or bond in which the coupon is adjusted to move opposite to a benchmark interest rate.

Inverse relationship A relationship between variables that move in opposite directions.

Invested Capital (Private Equity) The amount of paid-in capital that has been invested in portfolio companies.

Investing Buying an asset, such as a bond, corporate stock, rental property, or farm, with reasonably determinable underlying earnings.

Investment (1) Any use of today's resources to expand tomorrow's production or consumption. Can also be viewed as spending by businesses on things such as machines and buildings, which can be used to produce goods and services in the future. The investment part of total output is the portion that will be used in the process of producing goods in the future. (2) The current commitment of dollars for a period of time in order to derive future payments that will compensate the investor for the time the funds are committed, the expected rate of inflation, and the uncertainty of future payments.

Investment Advisor (Private Equity) Any individual or institution that supplies investment advice to clients on a per fee basis. The investment advisor inherently has no role in the management of the underlying portfolio companies of a partnership/fund.

Investment bankers Firms specializing in the sale of new securities to the public, typically by underwriting the issue.

Investment company A firm that issues (sells) shares, and uses the proceeds to invest in various financial instruments or other assets.

Investment Company Act of 1940 One of several pieces of federal legislation passed after the October 1929 stock market crash and the Great Depression. This law regulated the activities and reporting requirements of investment companies, which are firms whose principal business is the trading and management of securities.

Investment constraints Internal or external limitations on investments.

Investment decision process Estimation of intrinsic value for comparison with market price to determine whether or not to invest.

Investment grade Bonds rated AAA to BBB.

Investment horizon The time period used for planning and forecasting purposes or the future time at which the investor requires the invested funds.

Investment management company A company separate from the investment company that manages the portfolio and performs administrative functions.

Investment Management Fee The fee payable to the investment management firm for the ongoing management of a portfolio. Investment management fees are typically asset based (percentage of assets), performance based (based on performance relative to a benchmark), or a combination of the two but may take different forms as well.

Investment objectives Desired investment outcomes; includes risk objectives and return objectives.

Investment portfolio Set of securities chosen by an investor.

Investment strategy An approach to investment analysis and security selection.

IPO Initial public offering.

IRR Internal rate of return.

Joint probability The probability of the joint occurrence of stated events.

Joint probability function A function giving the probability of joint occurrences of values of stated random variables.

Joint venture When companies jointly pursue a certain business activity.

Junior debt Subordinated debt.

Justified (fundamental) P/E The price-to-earnings ratio that is fair, warranted, or justified on the basis of forecasted fundamentals.

Justified price multiple (or warranted price multiple or intrinsic price multiple) The estimated fair value of the price multiple, usually based on forecasted fundamentals or comparables.

Just-in-time System of inventory management that requires minimum inventories of materials and very frequent deliveries by suppliers.

Keiretsu A network of Japanese companies organized around a major bank.

Keynesian An economist who believes that left alone, the economy would rarely operate at full employment and that to achieve full employment, active help from fiscal policy and monetary policy is required.

kth Order autocorrelation The correlation between observations in a time series separated by k periods.

Kurtosis The statistical measure that indicates the peakedness of a distribution.

Labor The work time and work effort that people devote to producing goods and services.

Labor force Individuals aged 16 years or older who either have jobs or are looking and available for jobs; the number of employed plus the number of unemployed.

Labor productivity   Total real domestic output (real GDP) divided by the number of workers (output per worker).

Labor unions   Worker organizations that seek to secure economic improvements for their members; they also seek to improve the safety, health, and other benefits (such as job security) of their members.

Land   The natural resources that are available from nature. Land as a resource includes location, original fertility and mineral deposits, topography, climate, water, and vegetation.

Law of demand   The observation that there is a negative, or inverse, relationship between the price of any good or service and the quantity demanded, holding other factors constant.

Law of diminishing returns   As a firm uses more of a variable input, with a given quantity of other inputs (fixed inputs), the marginal product of the variable input eventually diminishes.

Law of one price   The rule stipulating that equivalent securities or bundles of securities must sell at equal prices to preclude arbitrage opportunities.

Leading dividend yield   Forecasted dividends per share over the next year divided by current stock price.

Leading P/E (or forward P/E or prospective P/E)   A stock's current price divided by next year's expected earnings.

Lease   Long-term rental agreement.

Lease receivables   Amounts due from customers on long-term sales-type lease agreements.

Legal risk   The risk that the legal system will not enforce a contract in case of dispute or fraud; the risk that failures by company managers to effectively manage a company's risk exposures will lead to lawsuits and other judicial remedies, resulting in potentially catastrophic losses for the company.

Legislative and regulatory risk   The risk that governmental laws and regulations directly or indirectly affecting a company's operations will change with potentially severe adverse effects on the company's continued profitability and even its long-term sustainability.

Leptokurtic   Describes a distribution that is more peaked than a normal distribution.

Lessee   User of a leased asset (cf. *lessor*).

Lessor   Owner of a leased asset (cf. *lessee*).

Letter of credit   Letter from a bank stating that it has established a credit in the company's favor.

Level of significance   The probability of a Type I error in testing a hypothesis.

Leverage   In the context of corporate finance, leverage refers to the use of fixed costs within a company's cost structure. Fixed costs that are operating costs (such as depreciation or rent) create operating leverage. Fixed costs that are financial costs (such as interest expense) create financial leverage.

Leverage ratio   Ratio of debt to total capitalization of a firm.

Leveraged buyout (LBO)   A transaction whereby the target company management team converts the target to a privately held company by using heavy borrowing to finance the purchase of the target company's outstanding shares.

Leveraged floating-rate note or leveraged floater   A floating-rate note or bond in which the coupon is adjusted at a multiple of a benchmark interest rate.

Leveraged recapitalization   A post-offer takeover defense mechanism that involves the assumption of a large amount of debt that is then used to finance share repurchases; the effect is to dramatically change the company's capital structure while attempting to deliver a value to target shareholders in excess of a hostile bid.

Liabilities   Amounts owed; the legal claims against a business or household by nonowners.

LIFO   The last-in first-out accounting method of valuing inventories.

LIFO liquidation   A reduction in the physical quantity of an inventory that is accounted for using the LIFO method. A LIFO liquidation usually produces a nonrecurring increase in earnings because the older costs associated with the liquidated units are lower than current inventory costs.

Likelihood   The probability of an observation, given a particular set of conditions.

Limit down   A limit move in the futures market in which the price at which a transaction would be made is at or below the lower limit.

Limit move   A condition in the futures markets in which the price at which a transaction would be made is at or beyond the price limits.

Limit order   An order to buy or sell a security at a specific price or better (lower for a buy order and higher for a sell order).

Limit up   A limit move in the futures market in which the price at which a transaction would be made is at or above the upper limit.

Limited liability   A legal concept whereby the responsibility, or liability, of the owners of a corporation is limited to the value of the shares in the firm that they own.

Limited partnership   *Partnership* in which some partners have *limited liability* and general partners have unlimited liability.

Linear association   A straight-line relationship, as opposed to a relationship that cannot be graphed as a straight line.

Linear interpolation   The estimation of an unknown value on the basis of two known values that bracket it, using a straight line between the two known values.

Linear regression   Regression that models the straight-line relationship between the dependent and independent variable(s).

Linear trend   A trend in which the dependent variable changes at a constant rate with time.

Liquid   Term used to describe an asset that can be quickly converted to cash at a price close to fair market value.

Liquid asset   Asset that is easily and cheaply turned into cash—notably cash itself and short-term securities.

Liquidating dividend   *Dividend* that represents a return of capital.

Liquidation   To sell the assets of a company, division, or subsidiary piecemeal, typically because of bankruptcy; the form of bankruptcy that allows for the orderly satisfaction of creditors' claims after which the company ceases to exist.

Liquidation value   The value of a company if the company were dissolved and its assets sold individually.

Liquidity   With reference to an entity, the ability to satisfy short-term obligations using assets that are most readily converted into cash; with reference to an asset, the degree to which the asset can be acquired or disposed of quickly without loss relative to its fair value.

Liquidity discount   A reduction or discount to value that reflects the lack of depth of trading or liquidity in that asset's market.

Liquidity preference theory   Theory that the forward rate exceeds expected future interest rates.

Liquidity premium   An extra return that compensates investors for the risk of loss relative to an investment's fair value if the investment needs to be converted to cash quickly.

Liquidity risk   The risk that a financial instrument cannot be purchased or sold without a significant concession in price due to the size of the market.

Locked limit   A condition in the futures markets in which a transaction cannot take place because the price would be beyond the limits.

Logit model   A qualitative-dependent-variable multiple regression model based on the logistic probability distribution.

Log-linear model   With reference to time-series models, a model in which the growth rate of the time series as a function of time is constant.

Log-log regression model   A regression that expresses the dependent and independent variables as natural logarithms.

London Interbank Offer Rate (LIBOR)   The Eurodollar rate at which London banks lend dollars to other London banks; considered to be the best representative rate on a dollar borrowed by a private, high-quality borrower.

Long   The buyer of an asset or derivative contract. Also refers to the position of owning an asset or derivative contract.

Longitudinal data   Observations on characteristic(s) of the same observational unit through time.

Long position   The buyer of a commodity or security or, for a forward contract, the counterparty who will be the eventual buyer of the underlying asset.

Long run   (1) The time period during which all factors of production can be varied. (2) A period of time in which the quantities of all resources can be varied.

Long-run average cost curve   The locus of points representing the minimum unit cost of producing any given rate of output, given current technology and resource prices.

Long-term equity anticipatory securities (LEAPS)   Options originally created with expirations of several years.

Look-ahead bias   Bias that may result from the use of information that was not available on the test date.

Lower bound   The lowest possible value.

LP   Linear programming.

Macaulay duration   The duration without dividing by 1 plus the bond's yield to maturity. The term, named for one of the economists who first derived it, is used to distinguish the calculation from modified duration. See also *modified duration*.

Macroeconomic factor   A factor related to the economy, such as the inflation rate, industrial production, or economic sector membership.

Macroeconomic factor model   A multifactor model in which the factors are surprises in macroeconomic variables that significantly explain equity returns.

Macroeconomics   The study of the behavior of the economy as a whole, including such economywide phenomena as changes in unemployment, the general price level, and national income.

MACRS   Modified accelerated cost recovery system.

Maintenance margin   The minimum margin that an investor must keep on deposit in a margin account at all times.

Maintenance margin requirement   The margin requirement on any day other than the first day of a transaction.

Management buyout (MBO)   A corporate transaction in which management repurchases all outstanding common stock, usually using the proceeds of debt issuance; a leveraged buyout (LBO) led by management.

Management fee The compensation an investment company pays to the investment management company for its services. The average annual fee is about 0.5 percent of fund assets.

Managerialism theories Theories that posit that corporate executives are motivated to engage in mergers to maximize the size of their company rather than shareholder value.

Margin or margin deposit The amount of money that a trader deposits in a margin account. The term is derived from the stock market practice in which an investor borrows a portion of the money required to purchase a certain amount of stock. In futures markets, there is no borrowing so the margin is more of a down payment or performance bond.

Margin account The collateral posted with the futures exchange clearinghouse by an outside counterparty to insure its eventual performance; the *initial* margin is the deposit required at contract origination while the *maintenance* margin is the minimum collateral necessary at all times.

Margin call A request by an investor's broker for additional capital for a security bought on margin if the investor's equity value declines below the required maintenance margin.

Marginal benefit The benefit that a person receives from consuming one more unit of a good or service. It is measured as the maximum amount that a person is willing to pay for one more unit of the good or service.

Marginal cost The opportunity cost of producing one more unit of a good or service; the change in total cost due to a one-unit increase in production.

Marginal cost pricing A system of pricing in which the price charged is equal to the opportunity cost to society of producing one more unit of the good or service in question. The opportunity cost is the marginal cost to society.

Marginal product The increase in total product that results from a one-unit increase in the variable input, with all other inputs remaining the same. It is calculated as the increase in total product divided by the increase in the variable input employed, when the quantities of all other inputs are constant.

Marginal revenue The change in total revenue that results from a one-unit increase in the quantity sold. It is calculated as the change in total revenue divided by the change in quantity sold.

Marginal tax rate The part of each additional dollar in income that is paid as tax.

Market All of the arrangements that individuals have for exchanging with one another. Thus, for example, we can speak of the labor market, the automobile market, and the credit market.

Market analysis With respect to investing, the analysis of a the current conditions of a financial market.

Market capitalization (market cap) The number of shares a company has outstanding times the price per share.

Market demand The demand of all consumers in the marketplace for a particular good or service. The summation at each price of the quantity demanded by each individual.

Market efficiency The subject dealing with the relationship of price to intrinsic value. The traditional efficient markets formulation asserts that an asset's price is the best available estimate of its intrinsic value. The rational efficient markets formulation asserts that investors should expect to be rewarded for the costs of information gathering and analysis by higher gross returns.

Market failure A state in which the market does not allocate resources efficiently.

Market impact With reference to execution costs, the difference between the actual execution price and the market price that would have prevailed had the manager not sought to trade the security.

Market maker An institution or individual quoting firm bid and ask prices for a security and standing ready to buy or sell the security at those quoted prices. Also called a *dealer.*

Market model (1) Model suggesting a linear relationship between actual returns on a stock and on the market portfolio. (2) A method that is used in event studies. Regression analysis is used to compute the return that is attributable to market forces. It is used to compute "excess returns" that may be attributable to the occurrence of an event.

Market order An order to buy or sell a security immediately at the best price available.

Market portfolio The portfolio that includes all risky assets with relative weights equal to their proportional market values.

Market power The ability to influence the market, and in particular the market price, by influencing the total quantity offered for sale.

Market price of risk The slope of the capital market line, indicating the market risk premium for each unit of market risk.

Market return The standard (typically the SP 500) against which stock portfolio performance can be measured.

Market risk (systematic risk) Risk that cannot be diversified away. In risk management, *market risk* refers to the risk associated with interest rates, exchange rates, and equity prices.

Market risk premium   The expected excess return on the market over the risk-free rate.

Market share test   The percentage of a market that a particular firm supplies, used as the primary measure of monopoly power.

Market timer   An investor who speculates on broad market moves rather than on specific securities.

Market timing   Trying to catch short-term market movements. Extremely difficult.

Market Value   The current listed price at which investors buy or sell securities at a given time.

Market value added (MVA)   External management performance measure to compare the market value of the company's debt and equity with the total capital invested in the firm.

Marketability discount   A reduction or discount to value for shares that are not publicly traded.

Marking to market or mark to market   The settlement process used to adjust the margin account of a futures contract for (traditionally) daily gains or losses. Also known as the *daily settlement* although some futures contracts are now marked to market more frequently than daily.

Markowitz decision rule   A decision rule for choosing between two investments based on their means and variances.

Mature growth rate   The earnings growth rate in a company's mature phase; an earnings growth rate that can be sustained long term.

Mature phase   A stage of growth in which the company reaches an equilibrium in which investment opportunities on average just earn their opportunity cost of capital.

Maturity premium   An extra return that compensates investors for the increased sensitivity of the market value of debt to a change in market interest rates as maturity is extended.

Maturity strategy   A portfolio management strategy employed to reduce the interest rate risk of a bond portfolio by matching the maturity of the portfolio with its investment horizon. For example, if the investment horizon is 10 years, the portfolio manager would construct a portfolio that will mature in 10 years.

MBO   Management buyout.

MDA   Multiple-discriminant analysis.

Mean   The sum of all values in a distribution or dataset, divided by the number of values summed; a synonym of arithmetic mean.

Mean absolute deviation   With reference to a sample, the mean of the absolute values of deviations from the sample mean.

Mean excess return   The average rate of return in excess of the risk-free rate.

Mean reversion   The tendency of a time series to fall when its level is above its mean and rise when its level is below its mean; a mean-reverting time series tends to return to its long-term mean.

Mean–variance analysis   An approach to portfolio analysis using expected means, variances, and covariances of asset returns.

Means of payment   A method of settling a debt.

Measure of central tendency   A quantitative measure that specifies where data are centered.

Measure of location   A quantitative measure that describes the location or distribution of data; includes not only measures of central tendency but also other measures such as percentiles.

Measurement error   Errors in measuring an explanatory variable in a regression that leads to biases in estimated parameters.

Measurement scales   A scheme of measuring differences. The four types of measurement scales are nominal, ordinal, interval, and ratio.

Median   The value of the middle item of a set of items that has been sorted into ascending or descending order; the 50th percentile.

Merger   The absorption of one company by another; that is, two companies become one entity and one or both of the pre-merger companies ceases to exist as a separate entity.

Mesokurtic   Describes a distribution with kurtosis identical to that of the normal distribution.

Method based on forecasted fundamentals   An approach to using price multiples that relates a price multiple to forecasts of fundamentals through a discounted cash flow model.

Method of comparables   An approach to valuation that involves using a price multiple to evaluate whether an asset is relatively fairly valued, relatively undervalued, or relatively overvalued when compared to a benchmark value of the multiple.

Microcap   Refers to companies with a market capitalization in the $100 million to $300 million range.

Microeconomics   The study of the choices that individuals and businesses make, the way those choices interact, and the influence governments exert on them.

Midcap   Companies with a market capitalization in the $3 billion to $4 billion range.

Minimum-variance frontier   The graph of the set of portfolios that have minimum variance for their level of expected return.

Minimum-variance portfolio   The portfolio with the minimum variance for each given level of expected return.

Mispricing Any departure of the market price of an asset from the asset's estimated intrinsic value.

Mixed factor models Factor models that combine features of more than one type of factor model.

Mixed offering A merger or acquisition that is to be paid for with cash, securities, or some combination of the two.

Modal interval With reference to grouped data, the most frequently occurring interval.

Mode The most frequently occurring value in a set of observations.

Model risk The use of an inaccurate pricing model for a particular investment, or the improper use of the right model.

Model specification With reference to regression, the set of variables included in the regression and the regression equation's functional form.

Modern portfolio theory (MPT) Principles underlying analysis and evaluation of rational portfolio choices based on risk-return trade-offs and efficient diversification.

Modified accelerated cost recovery system (MACRS) Schedule of *depreciation* deductions allowed for tax purposes.

Modified duration Measure of a bond's price sensitivity to interest rate movements. Equal to the duration of a bond divided by one plus its yield to maturity.

Molodovsky effect The observation that P/Es tend to be high on depressed EPS at the bottom of a business cycle, and tend to be low on unusually high EPS at the top of a business cycle.

Momentum indicators Valuation indicators that relate either price or a fundamental (such as earnings) to the time series of their own past values (or in some cases to their expected value).

Monetarists Macroeconomists who believe that inflation in the long run is always caused by excessive monetary growth and that changes in the money supply affect aggregate demand both directly and indirectly.

Monetary policy The Fed conducts the nation's monetary policy by changing interest rates and adjusting the quantity of money.

Money Any medium that is universally accepted in an economy both by sellers of goods and services as payment for those goods and services and by creditors as payment for debts.

Money illusion Reacting to changes in money prices rather than relative prices. If a worker whose wages double when the price level also doubles thinks he or she is better off, that worker is suffering from money illusion.

Money market The market for short-term debt instruments (one-year maturity or less).

Money market yield (or CD equivalent yield) A yield on a basis comparable to the quoted yield on an interest-bearing money market instrument that pays interest on a 360-day basis; the annualized holding period yield, assuming a 360-day year.

Money supply The amount of money in circulation.

Moneyness The relationship between the price of the underlying and an option's exercise price.

Money-weighted rate of return The internal rate of return on a portfolio, taking account of all cash flows.

Monitoring costs Costs borne by owners to monitor the management of the company (e.g., board of director expenses).

Monopolist The single supplier of a good or service for which there is no close substitute. The monopolist therefore constitutes its entire industry.

Monopolization The possession of monopoly power in the relevant market and the willful acquisition or maintenance of that power, as distinguished from growth or development as a consequence of a superior product, business acumen, or historical accident.

Monopoly A market structure in which there is one firm, which produces a good or service that has no close substitute and in which the firm is protected from competition by a barrier preventing the entry of new firms.

Monte Carlo simulation method A methodology using a computer to generate random outcomes according to specified probability models to find approximate solutions to complex problems.

Mortgage-backed security Ownership claim in a pool of mortgages or an obligation that is secured by such a pool. Also called a *pass-through,* because payments are passed along from the mortgage originator to the purchaser of the mortgage-backed security.

Moving average The continually recalculating average of security prices for a period, often 200 days, to serve as an indication of the general trend of prices and also as a benchmark price.

Multicollinearity A regression assumption violation that occurs when two or more independent variables (or combinations of independent variables) are highly but not perfectly correlated with each other.

Multifactor model Model of security returns positing that returns respond to multiple systematic factors.

Multiple Short for price-earnings multiple.

Multiple linear regression   Linear regression involving two or more independent variables.

Multiple linear regression model   A linear regression model with two or more independent variables.

Multiple R   The correlation between the actual and forecasted values of the dependent variable in a regression.

Multiplication rule for probabilities   The rule that the joint probability of events A and B equals the probability of A given B times the probability of B.

Multiplier   The amount by which a change in autonomous expenditure is magnified or multiplied to determine the change in equilibrium expenditure and real GDP.

Multivariate distribution   A probability distribution that specifies the probabilities for a group of related random variables.

Multivariate normal distribution   A probability distribution for a group of random variables that is completely defined by the means and variances of the variables plus all the correlations between pairs of the variables.

Municipal bonds   Tax-exempt bonds issued by state and local governments, generally to finance capital improvement projects. General obligation bonds are backed by the general taxing power of the issuer. Revenue bonds are backed by the proceeds from the project or agency they are issued to finance.

Mutual fund   An investment company that pools money from shareholders and invests in a variety of securities, including stocks, bonds, and money market securities. A mutual fund ordinarily stands ready to buy back (redeem) its shares at their current net asset value, which depends on the market value of the fund's portfolio of securities at the time. Mutual funds generally continuously offer new shares to investors.

Mutually exclusive events   Events such that only one can occur at a time.

Mutually exclusive projects   Mutually exclusive projects compete directly with each other. For example, if Projects A and B are mutually exclusive, you can choose A or B, but you cannot choose both.

n Factorial   For a positive integer n, the product of the first n positive integers; 0 factorial equals 1 by definition. n factorial is written as $n!$.

NASDAQ   National Association of Securities Dealers Automated Quotations. It is the trading system for the over-the-counter market.

Nash equilibrium   The outcome of a game that occurs when player A takes the best possible action given the action of player B and player B takes the best possible action given the action of player A.

National income (NI)   The total of all factor payments to resource owners.

Natural monopoly   A monopoly that arises from the peculiar production characteristics in an industry. It usually arises when there are large economies of scale relative to the industry's demand such that one firm can produce at a lower average cost than can be achieved by multiple firms.

Negative relationship   A relationship between variables that move in opposite directions.

Negative serial correlation   Serial correlation in which a positive error for one observation increases the chance of a negative error for another observation, and vice versa.

Neoclassical growth theory   A theory of economic growth that proposes that real GDP grows because technological change induces a level of saving and investment that makes capital per hour of labor grow.

Net asset value (NAV)   (1) The market value of the assets owned by a fund. (2) The value of each share expressed as assets minus liabilities on a per-share basis.

Net borrower   A country that is borrowing more from the rest of the world than it is lending to it.

Net capital expenditures   Gross capital expenditures minus proceeds from the disposal of productive assets.

Net debt   Total debt minus cash on hand.

Net exports   The value of exports minus the value of imports.

Net income plus depreciation   Often referred to as traditional cash flow, its calculation removes an important noncash expense from net income.

Net investment   Net increase in the capital stock-gross investment minus depreciation.

Net lender   A country that is lending more to the rest of the world than it is borrowing from it.

Net operating profit less adjusted taxes (NOPLAT)   A company's operating profit with adjustments to normalize the effects of capital structure.

Net present value (NPV)   The present value of an investment's cash inflows (benefits) minus the present value of its cash outflows (costs).

Net public debt   Gross public debt minus all government interagency borrowing.

Netting   When parties agree to exchange only the net amount owed from one party to the other.

Network effect   A situation in which a consumer's willingness to purchase a good or service is influenced by how many others also buy the item.

Net working capital   Current assets minus current liabilities.

Net worth   (1) The difference between assets and liabilities. (2) Book value of a company's *common stock*, surplus, and *retained earnings*.

New growth theory   A theory of economic growth based on the idea that real GDP per person grows because of the choices that people make in the pursuit of ever greater profit and that growth can persist indefinitely.

New issue   Common stocks or bonds offered by companies for public sale.

Node   Each value on a binomial tree from which successive moves or outcomes branch.

No-growth company   A company without positive expected net present value projects.

No-growth value per share   The value per share of a no-growth company, equal to the expected level amount of earnings divided by the stock's required rate of return.

Nominal GDP   The value of the final goods and services produced in a given year valued at the prices that prevailed in that same year. It is a more precise name for GDP.

Nominal interest rate   The interest rate in terms of nominal (not adjusted for purchasing power) dollars.

Nominal risk-free interest rate   The sum of the real risk-free interest rate and the inflation premium.

Nominal scale   A measurement scale that categorizes data but does not rank them.

Nominal values   The values of variables such as GDP and investment expressed in current dollars, also called money values; measurement in terms of the actual market prices at which goods and services are sold.

Nominal yield   A bond's yield as measured by its coupon rate.

Noncontrolling interest   Generally, minority interest. However, the term is used to reflect a minority shareholder interest when the definition of control is extended beyond a simple majority share ownership interest. Any interest in an entity besides that of a controlling shareholder.

Nonconventional cash flow   In a nonconventional cash flow pattern, the initial outflow is not followed by inflows only, but the cash flows can flip from positive (inflows) to negative (outflows) again (or even change signs several times).

Nondeliverable forwards (NDFs)   Cash-settled forward contracts, used predominately with respect to foreign exchange forwards.

Nondiversifiable risk   See *systematic risk*.

Nonlinear relation   An association or relationship between variables that cannot be graphed as a straight line.

Nonparametric test   A test that is not concerned with a parameter, or that makes minimal assumptions about the population from which a sample comes.

Nonrecurring cash flow   Operating cash flow that appears infrequently or that may appear with some regularity but is very irregular in amount. In addition, even though included in operating cash flow, nonrecurring cash flow often is not closely tied to the core operating activities of the firm.

Nonstationarity   With reference to a random variable, the property of having characteristics such as mean and variance that are not constant through time.

Nonsystematic risk   Nonmarket or firm-specific risk factors that can be eliminated by diversification. Also called *unique risk* or *diversifiable risk*. Systematic risk refers to risk factors common to the entire economy.

Nontariff barrier   Any action other than a tariff that restricts international trade.

Normal backwardation   The condition in futures markets in which futures prices are lower than expected spot prices.

Normal contango   The condition in futures markets in which futures prices are higher than expected spot prices.

Normal distribution   A continuous, symmetric probability distribution that is completely described by its mean and its variance.

Normal rate of return   The amount that must be paid to an investor to induce investment in a business; also known as the *opportunity cost of capital*.

Normalized (or normal) earnings per share   The earnings per share that a business could achieve currently under mid-cyclical conditions.

North American Free Trade Agreement   An agreement, which became effective on January 1, 1994, to eliminate all barriers to international trade between the United States, Canada, and Mexico after a 15-year phasing in period.

Note   Unsecured debt with a maturity of up to 10 years.

Notes payable   Promissory notes that are evidence of a debt and state the terms of interest and principal payment.

Notional principal   (1) Principal amount used to calculate swap payments. (2) The principal value of a swap transaction, which is not exchanged but is used as a scale factor to translate interest rate differentials into cash settlement payments.

n-Period moving average   The average of the current and immediately prior $n - 1$ values of a time series.

NPV   Net present value.

NPV rule   An investment decision rule that states that an investment should be undertaken if its NPV is positive but not undertaken if its NPV is negative.

Null hypothesis   The hypothesis to be tested.

NYSE   New York Stock Exchange.

Objective probabilities   Probabilities that generally do not vary from person to person; includes a priori and objective probabilities.

Objectives   In investments, the investor's goals expressed in terms of risk and return and included in the policy statement.

Off-balance-sheet financing   Financing that is not shown as a liability in a company's balance sheet.

Offer price   The price at which a market maker is willing to sell a security (also called *ask price*).

Official reserves   The amount of reserves owned by the central bank of a government in the form of gold, Special Drawing Rights, and foreign cash or marketable securities.

Official settlements account   A record of the change in a country's official reserves.

Off-market forward rate agreement (off-market FRA)   A contract in which the initial value is intentionally set at a value other than zero and therefore requires a cash payment at the start from one party to the other.

Offsetting   A transaction in exchange-listed derivative markets in which a party re-enters the market to close out a position.

One third rule   The rule that, with no change in technology, a 1 percent increase in capital per hour of labor brings, on the average, a one third of 1 percent increase in real GDP per hour of labor.

One-sided hypothesis test (or one-tailed hypothesis test)   A test in which the null hypothesis is rejected only if the evidence indicates that the population parameter is greater than (smaller than) θ_0. The alternative hypothesis also has one side.

Open-end fund   An investment company that continuously offers to sell new shares, or redeem them, at prices based on the market value of the assets owned by the fund (net asset value).

Operating breakeven   The number of units produced and sold at which the company's operating profit is zero (revenues = operating costs).

Operating cash flow   Cash flow from operating activities computed in accordance with generally accepted accounting principles.

Operating earnings   An earnings measure that excludes selected items of nonrecurring gain, revenue, loss, and expense. This is not a GAAP measure, and its determination may vary widely among different companies.

Operating income   See *operating profit*.

Operating lease   A lease that does not transfer the risks and rewards of ownership to the lessee. Operating lease payments are expensed as incurred.

Operating profit   Core pretax profit from central operations calculated as revenue minus cost of goods sold, selling, general and administrative expense, and research and development expense.

Operating risk   The risk attributed to the operating cost structure, in particular the use of fixed costs in operations; the risk arising from the mix of fixed and variable costs; the risk that a company's operations may be severely affected by environmental, social, and governance risk factors.

Operating working capital   Current assets, including operating receivables, inventory, and prepaid expenses, that are used in operations minus current liabilities, including operating payables and accrued expenses payable that are incurred in operations.

Operations risk or operational risk   The risk of loss from failures in a company's systems and procedures (for example, due to computer failures or human failures) or events completely outside of the control of organizations (which would include "acts of God" and terrorist actions).

Opportunity cost   The alternative return that investors forgo by choosing a particular course of action; the value of something in its best alternative use.

Opportunity cost of capital   The normal rate of return, or the available return on the next-best alternative investment. Economists consider this a cost of production, and it is included in our cost examples.

Opportunity set   The set of assets available for investment.

Optimal capital structure   The capital structure at which the value of the company is maximized.

Optimal portfolio   The portfolio on the efficient frontier that has the highest utility for a given investor. It lies at the point of tangency between the efficient frontier and the curve with the investor's highest possible utility.

Optimal risky portfolio   An investor's best combination of risky assets to be mixed with safe assets to form the complete portfolio.

Optimizer   A specialized computer program or a spreadsheet that solves for the portfolio weights that will result in the lowest risk for a specified level of expected return.

Option   A financial instrument that gives one party the right, but not the obligation, to buy (for a call option) or sell (for a put option) an underlying asset from or to another party at a fixed price over a specific period of time.

Option-adjusted spread A type of yield spread that considers changes in the term structure and alternative estimates of the volatility of interest rates. It is spread after adjusting for embedded options.

Option contract An agreement that grants the owner the right, but not the obligation, to make a future transaction in an underlying commodity or security at a fixed price and within a predetermined time in the future.

Option delta Hedge ratio.

Option price, option premium, or premium The amount of money a buyer pays and seller receives to engage in an option transaction.

Options Clearing Corporation (OCC) A company designed to guarantee, monitor margin accounts, and settle exchange-traded option transactions.

Order-driven market A market without active market makers in which buy-and-sell orders directly confront each other; an auction market.

Ordinal scale A measurement scale that sorts data into categories that are ordered (ranked) with respect to some characteristic.

Ordinary annuity An annuity with a first cash flow that is paid one period from the present.

Ordinary least squares (OLS) An estimation method based on the criterion of minimizing the sum of the squared residuals of a regression.

Organic growth Company growth in output or sales that is achieved by making investments internally (i.e., excludes growth achieved through mergers and acquisitions).

Origin The intersection of the *y* axis and the *x* axis in a graph.

Orthogonal Uncorrelated; at a right angle.

OTC Over-the-counter.

Other comprehensive income Changes to equity that bypass (are not reported in) the income statement; the difference between comprehensive income and net income.

Outcome A possible value of a random variable.

Outliers Small numbers of observations at either extreme (small or large) of a sample.

Out-of-sample forecast errors The differences between actual and predicted value of time series outside the sample period used to fit the model.

Out-of-sample test A test of a strategy or model using a sample outside the time period on which the strategy or model was developed.

Out-of-the-money Said of options that, if exercised, would require the payment of more money than the value received and therefore would not be currently exercised.

Overnight A deal from today to the next business day.

Overnight index swap (OIS) A swap in which the floating rate is the cumulative value of a single unit of currency invested at an overnight rate during the settlement period.

Over-the-counter (OTC) Informal market that does not involve a securities exchange. Specifically used to refer to the Nasdaq dealer market for *common stocks*.

Overweighted A condition in which a portfolio, for whatever reason, includes more of a class of securities than the relative market value alone would justify.

P/E ratio Share price divided by earnings per share.

Paid-In Capital (Private Equity) The amount of committed capital a limited partner has actually transferred to a venture fund. Also known as the *cumulative drawdown amount*.

Paired comparisons test A statistical test for differences based on paired observations drawn from samples that are dependent on each other.

Paired observations Observations that are dependent on each other.

Pairs arbitrage trade A trade in two closely related stocks that involves buying the relatively undervalued stock and selling short the relatively overvalued stock.

Panel data Observations through time on a single characteristic of multiple observational units.

Par value (1) The principal amount repaid at maturity of a bond. Also called *face value*. (2) The officially determined value of a currency.

Par yield curve The yield curve drawn for government coupon bonds of different maturities that trade at, or around, par.

Parameter A descriptive measure computed from or used to describe a population of data, conventionally represented by Greek letters.

Parameter instability The problem or issue of population regression parameters that have changed over time.

Parametric test Any test (or procedure) concerned with parameters or whose validity depends on assumptions concerning the population generating the sample.

Partial regression coefficients or partial slope coefficients The slope coefficients in a multiple regression.

Partnership A business owned by two or more joint owners, or partners, who share the responsibilities and the profits of the firm and are individually liable for all the debts of the partnership.

Passive investment strategy See *passive management*.

Passive management Buying a well-diversified portfolio to represent a broad-based market index without attempting to search out mis-priced securities.

Passive portfolio   A market index portfolio.

Passive strategy   See *passive management*.

Pass-through securities   *Notes* or *bonds* backed by a package of assets such as home mortgage loans.

Patent   A government-sanctioned exclusive right granted to the inventor of a good, service, or productive process to produce, use, and sell the invention for a given number of years.

Payables   Accounts payable.

Payback   The time required for the added income from the convertible security relative to the stock to offset the conversion premium.

Payer swaption   A swaption that allows the holder to enter into a swap as the fixed-rate payer and floating-rate receiver.

Payment date   The day that the company actually mails out (or electronically transfers) a dividend payment.

Payment netting   A means of settling payments in which the amount owed by the first party to the second is netted with the amount owed by the second party to the first; only the net difference is paid.

Payoff   The value of an option at expiration.

Payout ratio   The percentage of total earnings paid out in dividends in any given year (in per-share terms, DPS/EPS).

Peak   The point at which a business cycle turns from expansion into recession.

Pecking order theory   The theory that managers take into account how their actions might be interpreted by outsiders and thus order their preferences for various forms of corporate financing. Forms of financing that are least visible to outsiders (e.g., internally generated funds) are most preferable to managers and those that are most visible (e.g., equity) are least preferable.

Peer group comparison   A method of measuring portfolio performance by collecting the returns produced by a representative universe of investors over a specific period of time.

PEG   The P/E-to-growth ratio, calculated as the stock's P/E divided by the expected earnings growth rate.

Per capita   Latin, meaning "by the head." Distributing to "issue per capita" means to distribute trust property to persons who take, in their own right, an equal portion of the property.

Per unit contribution margin   The amount that each unit sold contributes to covering fixed costs—that is, the difference between the price per unit and the variable cost per unit.

Percentiles   Quantiles that divide a distribution into 100 equal parts.

Perfect collinearity   The existence of an exact linear relation between two or more independent variables or combinations of independent variables.

Perfect competition   An industry structure characterized by certain conditions, including many buyers and sellers, homogeneous products, perfect information, easy entry and exit, and no barriers to entry. The existence of these conditions implies that each seller is a price taker.

Performance appraisal   The evaluation of risk-adjusted performance; the evaluation of investment skill.

Performance attribution   The attribution of investment performance to specific investment decisions (such as asset allocation and country weighting).

Performance guarantee   A guarantee from the clearinghouse that if one party makes money on a transaction, the clearinghouse ensures it will be paid.

Performance measurement   The calculation of returns in a logical and consistent manner.

Periodic rate   The quoted interest rate per period; the stated annual interest rate divided by the number of compounding periods per year.

Permutation   An ordered listing.

Perpetuity   A perpetual annuity, or a set of never-ending level sequential cash flows, with the first cash flow occurring one period from now; a stream of level payments extending to infinity.

Personal income (PI)   The amount of income that households actually receive before they pay personal income taxes.

Personal trust   An amount of money set aside by a grantor and often managed by a third party, the trustee. Often constructed so one party receives income from the trust's investments and another party receives the residual value of the trust after the income beneficiaries' death.

Pet projects   Projects in which influential managers want the corporation to invest. Often, unfortunately, pet projects are selected without undergoing normal capital budgeting analysis.

Physical capital   All manufactured resources, including buildings, equipment, machines, and improvements to land that is used for production.

PIK   Pay-in-kind bond.

Plain-vanilla   Refers to a security, especially a bond or a swap, issued with standard features. Sometimes called *generic*.

Plain vanilla swap   An interest rate swap in which one party pays a fixed rate and the other pays a floating rate, with both sets of payments in the same currency.

Platykurtic Describes a distribution that is less peaked than the normal distribution.

Point One percent (1%).

Point estimate A single numerical estimate of an unknown quantity, such as a population parameter.

Poison pill A pre-offer takeover defense mechanism that makes it prohibitively costly for an acquirer to take control of a target without the prior approval of the target's board of directors.

Poison puts A pre-offer takeover defense mechanism that gives target company bondholders the right to sell their bonds back to the target at a pre-specified redemption price, typically at or above par value; this defense increases the need for cash and raises the cost of the acquisition.

Policy statement A statement in which the investor specifies investment goals, constraints, and risk preferences.

Political risk Possibility of the expropriation of assets, changes in tax policy, restrictions on the exchange of foreign currency for domestic currency, or other changes in the business climate of a country.

Pooling of interest Method of accounting for *mergers* (no longer available in the US). The consolidated balance sheet of the merged firm is obtained by combining the balance sheets of the separate firms (cf. *purchase accounting*).

Population All members of a specified group.

Population mean The arithmetic mean value of a population; the arithmetic mean of all the observations or values in the population.

Population standard deviation A measure of dispersion relating to a population in the same unit of measurement as the observations, calculated as the positive square root of the population variance.

Population variance A measure of dispersion relating to a population, calculated as the mean of the squared deviations around the population mean.

Portfolio A group of investments. Ideally, the investments should have different patterns of returns over time.

Portfolio implementation problem The part of the execution step of the portfolio management process that involves the implementation of portfolio decisions by trading desks.

Portfolio investment The purchase of less than 10 percent of the shares of ownership in a company in another nation.

Portfolio management Process of combining securities in a portfolio tailored to the investor's prefer-

ences and needs, monitoring that portfolio, and evaluating its performance.

Portfolio performance attribution The analysis of portfolio performance in terms of the contributions from various sources of risk.

Portfolio possibilities curve A graphical representation of the expected return and risk of all portfolios that can be formed using two assets.

Portfolio selection/composition problem The part of the execution step of the portfolio management process in which investment strategies are integrated with expectations to select a portfolio of assets.

Position trader A trader who typically holds positions open overnight.

Positive market feedback A tendency for a good or service to come into favor with additional consumers because other consumers have chosen to buy the item.

Positive relationship A relationship between two variables that move in the same direction.

Positive serial correlation Serial correlation in which a positive error for one observation increases the chance of a positive error for another observation, and a negative error for one observation increases the chance of a negative error for another observation.

Posterior probability An updated probability that reflects or comes after new information.

Potential credit risk The risk associated with the possibility that a payment due at a later date will not be made.

Power of a test The probability of correctly rejecting the null—that is, rejecting the null hypothesis when it is false.

Preferences A description of a person's likes and dislikes.

Preferred habitat theory Holds that investors prefer specific maturity ranges but can be induced to switch if risk premiums are sufficient.

Preferred stock A class of stock with priority rights, both as to dividends and in liquidation, over the common stock of the same company. Corporations pay a much lower income tax on dividends from their investments in other corporations (where it has already been taxed) than on direct business earnings. Preferred stock is usually priced at the level that makes it attractive to a corporation, taking account of this tax exemption, and as a result is rarely tax-efficient for individuals.

Pre-investing The strategy of using futures contracts to enter the market without an immediate outlay of cash.

Premium   (1) A bond selling at a price above par value due to capital market conditions. (2) The purchase price of an option.

Present value (PV)   The current (discounted) value of a future cash flow or flows.

Present (price) value of a basis point (PVBP)   The change in the bond price for a 1 basis point change in yield. Also called *basis point value* (BPV).

Present value model or discounted cash flow model   A model of intrinsic value that views the value of an asset as the present value of the asset's expected future cash flows.

Present value of growth opportunities (or value of growth)   The difference between the actual value per share and the no-growth value per share.

Price controls   Government-mandated minimum or maximum prices that may be charged for goods and services.

Price discovery   A feature of futures markets in which futures prices provide valuable information about the price of the underlying asset.

Price discrimination   Selling a given product at more than one price, with the price difference being unrelated to differences in cost.

Price-driven market   A market in which dealers (market makers) adjust their quotes continuously to reflect supply and demand; also known as a *dealer market*.

Price–earnings multiple   See *price–earnings ratio*.

Price–earnings ratio   The ratio of a stock's price to its earnings per share. Also referred to as the *P/E multiple*.

Price effect   The effect of a change in the price on the quantity of a good consumed, other things remaining the same.

Price level   The average level of prices as measured by a price index.

Price limits   Limits imposed by a futures exchange on the price change that can occur from one day to the next.

Price momentum   A valuation indicator based on past price movement.

Price multiple   The ratio of a stock's market price to some measure of value per share.

Price relative   A ratio of an ending price over a beginning price; it is equal to 1 plus the holding period return on the asset.

Price risk   The component of interest rate risk due to the uncertainty of the market price of a bond caused by changes in market interest rates.

Price-setting option   The operational flexibility to adjust prices when demand varies from forecast. For example, when demand exceeds capacity, the company could benefit from the excess demand by increasing prices.

Price war   A pricing campaign designed to capture additional market share by repeatedly cutting prices.

Priced risk   Risk that investors require an additional return for bearing.

Primary market   The market in which newly issued securities are sold by their issuers, who receive the proceeds.

Prime rate   Benchmark lending rate set by U.S. banks.

Principal   The amount of funds originally invested in a project or instrument; the face value to be paid at maturity.

Principal-agent problem   The problem of devising compensation rules that induce an agent to act in the best interest of a principal.

Principal trade   A trade through a broker who guarantees full execution at specified discount/premium to the prevailing price.

Prior probabilities   Probabilities reflecting beliefs prior to the arrival of new information.

Private equity   *Equity* that is not publicly traded and that is used to finance business start-ups, *leveraged buy-outs,* etc.

Private placement   A new issue sold directly to a small group of investors, usually institutions.

Private sector surplus or deficit   An amount equal to saving minus investment.

Private trusts   A term used to identify trusts created by individuals for individuals, either during life or under will.

Pro forma   Projected.

Probability   A number between 0 and 1 describing the chance that a stated event will occur.

Probability density function   A function with nonnegative values such that probability can be described by areas under the curve graphing the function.

Probability distribution   A distribution that specifies the probabilities of a random variable's possible outcomes.

Probability function   A function that specifies the probability that the random variable takes on a specific value.

Probit model   A qualitative-dependent-variable multiple regression model based on the normal distribution.

Producer Price Index (PPI)   A statistical measure of a weighted average of prices of goods and services that firms produce and sell.

Product differentiation   The distinguishing of products by brand name, color, and other minor attributes. Product differentiation occurs in other than perfectly competitive markets in which products are, in theory, homogeneous, such as wheat or corn.

Production Any activity that results in the conversion of resources into products that can be used in consumption.

Production-flexibility The operational flexibility to alter production when demand varies from forecast. For example, if demand is strong, a company may profit from employees working overtime or from adding additional shifts.

Productivity curve A relationship that shows how real GDP per hour of labor changes as the amount of capital per hour of labor changes with a given state of technology.

Productivity growth slowdown A slowdown in the growth rate of output per person.

Profit The income earned by business.

Profit margin or Net profit margin Net income divided by sales.

Profitability index Ratio of a project's *NPV* to the initial investment.

Pro-forma earnings A measure of earnings performance that selectively excludes nonrecurring as well as some noncash items.

Program trading Coordinated buy orders and sell orders of entire portfolios, usually with the aid of computers, often to achieve index arbitrage objectives.

Project sequencing To defer the decision to invest in a future project until the outcome of some or all of a current project is known. Projects are sequenced through time, so that investing in a project creates the option to invest in future projects.

Property rights Social arrangements that govern the ownership, use, and disposal of resources or factors of production, goods, and services that are enforceable in the courts.

Proprietorship A business owned by one individual who makes the business decisions, receives all the profits, and is legally responsible for the debts of the firm.

Prospectus Summary of the *registration* statement providing information on an issue of securities.

Protective put An option strategy in which a long position in an asset is combined with a long position in a put.

Proxy An instrument empowering an agent to vote in the name of the shareholder.

Proxy fight or proxy contest An attempt to take control of a company through a shareholder vote.

Proxy statement A public document that provides the material facts concerning matters on which shareholders will vote.

Proxy vote Vote cast by one person on behalf of another.

Prudent investor rule An investment manager must act in accord with the actions of a hypothetical prudent investor.

Pseudo-random numbers Numbers produced by random number generators.

Public good A good or service that is both nonrival and nonexcludable—it can be consumed simultaneously by everyone and from which no one can be excluded.

Purchase accounting Method of accounting for *mergers*. The assets of the acquired firm are shown at market value on the balance sheet of the acquirer (cf. *pooling of interest*).

Purchased in-process research and development costs Costs of research and development in progress at an acquired company; often, part of the purchase price of an acquired company is allocated to such costs.

Purchasing power The value of money for buying goods and services. If your money income stays the same but the price of one good that you are buying goes up, your effective purchasing power falls, and vice versa.

Purchasing power parity (PPP) A theory stating that the exchange rate between two currencies will exactly reflect the purchasing power of the two currencies.

Pure discount instruments Instruments that pay interest as the difference between the amount borrowed and the amount paid back.

Pure factor portfolio A portfolio with sensitivity of 1 to the factor in question and a sensitivity of 0 to all other factors.

Put An option that gives the holder the right to sell an underlying asset to another party at a fixed price over a specific period of time.

Put–call parity An equation expressing the equivalence (parity) of a portfolio of a call and a bond with a portfolio of a put and the underlying, which leads to the relationship between put and call prices.

Put–call–forward parity The relationship among puts, calls, and forward contracts.

Put option A contract that gives its holder the right to sell an asset, typically a financial instrument, at a specified price through a specified date.

p-**Value** The smallest level of significance at which the null hypothesis can be rejected; also called the marginal significance level.

Pyramiding Controlling additional property through reinvestment, refinancing, and exchanging.

q Ratio of the market value of an asset to its replacement cost.

Qualified Institutional buyers (QIBs) Institutions that are allowed to trade unregistered stock among themselves.

Qualitative dependent variables Dummy variables used as dependent variables rather than as independent variables.

Quality of earnings The realism and conservatism of the earnings number and the extent to which we might expect the reported level of earnings to be sustained.

Quality of earnings analysis The investigation of issues relating to the accuracy of reported accounting results as reflections of economic performance; quality of earnings analysis is broadly understood to include not only earnings management, but also balance sheet management.

Quantile (or fractile) A value at or below which a stated fraction of the data lies.

Quartiles Quantiles that divide a distribution into four equal parts.

Quick ratio A measure of liquidity similar to the current ratio except for exclusion of inventories (cash plus receivables divided by current liabilities).

Quintiles Quantiles that divide a distribution into five equal parts.

Quota A quantitative restriction on the import of a particular good, which specifies the maximum amount that can be imported in a given time period.

Random number An observation drawn from a uniform distribution.

Random number generator An algorithm that produces uniformly distributed random numbers between 0 and 1.

Random variable A quantity whose future outcomes are uncertain.

Random walk A time series in which the value of the series in one period is the value of the series in the previous period plus an unpredictable random error.

Range The difference between the maximum and minimum values in a dataset.

Rate of return The future financial benefit to making a current investment.

Ratio scales A measurement scale that has all the characteristics of interval measurement scales as well as a true zero point as the origin.

Ratio spread An option strategy in which a long position in a certain number of options is offset by a short position in a certain number of other options on the same underlying, resulting in a risk-free position.

Rational efficient markets formulation See "Market efficiency."

Rational expectation The most accurate forecast possible, a forecast that uses all the available information, including knowledge of the relevant economic forces that influence the variable being forecasted.

Real assets Tangible assets and intangible assets used to carry on business (cf. financial assets).

Real Estate Traditionally, land and any structures permanently attached to the land.

Real exchange rate The exchange rate adjusted by the inflation differential between the two countries.

Real foreign currency risk The risk that real prices of consumption goods might not be identical in different countries. Also known as *real exchange rate risk*, or *purchasing power risk*.

Real gross domestic product (real GDP) The value of final goods and services produced in a given year when valued at constant prices.

Real income A household's income expressed as a quantity of goods that the household can afford to buy.

Real interest rate The nominal interest rate adjusted for inflation; the nominal interest rate minus the inflation rate.

Real options Options embedded in a firm's real assets that give managers valuable decision-making flexibility, such as the right to undertake, abandon, modify or postpone an investment project.

Real rate of interest The nominal rate of interest minus the anticipated rate of inflation.

Real risk-free interest rate The single-period interest rate for a completely risk-free security if no inflation were expected.

Real values Measurement of economic values after adjustments have been made for changes in the average of prices between years.

Real wage rate The quantity of goods and services that an hour's work can buy. It is equal to the money wage rate divided by the price level.

Realized capital gains Capital gains that result when an appreciated asset is sold; realized capital gains are taxable.

Rebalancing Realigning the proportions of assets in a portfolio as needed.

Recapture premium Provision for a return of investment, net of value appreciation.

Receivables Accounts receivable.

Receiver A bankruptcy practitioner appointed by secured creditors in the United Kingdom to oversee the repayment of debts.

Receiver swaption A swaption that allows the holder to enter into a swap as the fixed-rate receiver and floating-rate payer.

Recession There are two common definitions of recession. They are: (1) A business cycle phase in which real GDP decreases for at least two successive quarters. (2) A significant decline in activity spread across the economy, lasting for more than a few months, visible in industrial production, employment, real income, and wholesale-retail trade.

Reclassification adjustment An adjustment to reported operating cash flow that moves a cash flow item from one classification to another, such as from operating cash flow to investing cash flow or from financing cash flow to operating cash flow. An example would be the reclassification of a tax benefit from stock options from operating cash flow to financing cash flow. The goal of these reclassifications is to produce a more sustainable measure of operating cash flow.

Record date Date set by directors when making dividend payment. *Dividends* are sent to stockholders who are registered on the record date.

Recycling The reuse of raw materials derived from manufactured products.

Regime With reference to a time series, the underlying model generating the times series.

Registration Process of obtaining *SEC* approval for a public issue of securities.

Registration statement Required to be filed with the SEC to describe the issue of a new security.

Regression analysis In statistics, a technique for finding the line of best fit.

Regression coefficients The intercept and slope coefficient(s) of a regression.

Regression equation An equation that describes the average relatinship between a dependent variable and a set of explanatory variables.

Regular dividend *Dividend* that the company expects to maintain in the future.

Regulation Rules administrated by a government agency to influence economic activity by determining prices, product standards and types, and conditions under which new firms may enter an industry.

Regulatory risk The risk associated with the uncertainty of how derivative transactions will be regulated or with changes in regulations.

Reinvestment Profits (or depreciation reserves) used to purchase new capital equipment.

Rejection point (or critical value) A value against which a computed test statistic is compared to decide whether to reject or not reject the null hypothesis.

Relative dispersion The amount of dispersion relative to a reference value or benchmark.

Relative frequency With reference to an interval of grouped data, the number of observations in the interval divided by the total number of observations in the sample.

Relative price The ratio of the price of one good or service to the price of another good or service. A relative price is an opportunity cost.

Relative return A portfolio's return compared with its benchmark.

Relative strength (RSTR) indicators Valuation indicators that compare a stock's performance during a period either to its own past performance or to the performance of some group of stocks.

Relative valuation models A model that specifies an asset's value relative to the value of another asset.

Remainder The trust corpus existing at the termination of the life beneficiary's interest.

Rent seeking Any attempt to capture a consumer surplus, a producer surplus, or an economic profit.

Reorganization Agreements made by a company in bankruptcy under which a company's capital structure is altered and/or alternative arrangements are made for debt repayment; U.S. Chapter 11 bankruptcy. The company emerges from bankruptcy as a going concern.

Replacement cost Cost to replace a firm's assets. "Reproduction" cost.

Replacement value With reference to swaps, the market value of a swap.

Repo See *repurchase agreement.*

Reported operating cash flow Cash flow from operating activities computed in accordance with generally accepted accounting principles. Also see *operating cash flow.*

Repurchase agreement (RP, repo, buy-back) Purchase of Treasury securities from a securities dealer with an agreement that the dealer will repurchase them at a specified price.

Reputational risk The risk that a company will suffer an extended diminution in market value relative to other companies in the same industry due to a demonstrated lack of concern for environmental, social, and governance risk factors.

Required rate of return The minimum rate of return required by an investor to invest in an asset, given the asset's riskiness.

Reserves (1) Cash in a bank's vault plus the bank's deposits at Federal Reserve banks. (2) The fixed-income component of a portfolio, notably shorter-term highly liquid instruments.

Residual autocorrelations The sample autocorrelations of the residuals.

Residual claim Refers to the fact that shareholders are at the bottom of the list of claimants to assets of a corporation in the event of failure or bankruptcy.

Residual dividend approach   A dividend payout policy under earnings in excess of the funds necessary to finance the equity portion of company's capital budget are paid out in dividends.

Residual income (or abnormal earnings)   Earnings for a given time period, minus a deduction for common shareholders' opportunity cost in generating the earnings.

Residual income model (RIM)   A model of stock valuation that views intrinsic value of stock as the sum of book value per share plus the present value of the stock's expected future residual income per share.

Residual loss   Agency costs that are incurred despite adequate monitoring and bonding of management.

Residual risk   The specific risk contained in a security, as distinct from the general market risk.

Residual Value (Private Equity)   The remaining equity that a limited partner has in the fund. (The value of the investments within the fund.) Also can be referred to as *ending market value* or *net asset value.*

Residuals   Parts of stock returns not explained by the explanatory variable (the market-index return). They measure the impact of firm-specific events during a particular period.

Resources   Things used to produce other things to satisfy people's wants.

Restatement of the Law Third, Trusts   A book of rules and principles promulgated by the American Law Institute, concerning the conduct of a trustee in the management of a trust. It serves as a guide for lawyers, trustees, and investment advisors.

Restructuring charge(s)   Costs associated with restructuring activities, including the consolidation and/or relocation of operations or the disposition or abandonment of operations or productive assets. Such charges may be incurred in connection with a business combination, a change in an enterprise's strategic plan, or a managerial response to declines in demand, increasing costs, or other environmental factors.

Retained earnings   Earnings that a corporation saves, or retains, for investment in other productive activities; earnings that are not distributed to stockholders.

Return on assets (ROA)   A profitability ratio; earnings before interest and taxes dividend by total assets.

Return on equity (ROE)   (1) An accounting ratio of net profits divided by equity. (2) An excellent definition is profit margin × turnover × leverage, where profit margin is sales ÷ profits, turnover is sales ÷ assets, and leverage is assets ÷ equity. It is extremely high in industries with high RD that is expensed rather than capitalized and added to equity, such as pharmaceuticals.

Return on invested capital (ROIC)   The after-tax net operating profits as a percent of total assets or capital.

Return on investment (ROI)   Generally, book income as a proportion of net book value.

Return on sales (ROS)   See *profit margin.*

Revenue bond   A bond that is serviced by the income generated from specific revenue-producing projects of the municipality such as toll roads or athletic stadiums.

Reverse stock split   A reduction in the number of shares outstanding with a corresponding increase in share price, but no change to the company's underlying fundamentals.

Revolving credit   Legally assured *line of credit* with a bank.

Reward-to-variability ratio   Ratio of a portfolio's risk premium to its standard deviation.

Rho   The sensitivity of the option price to the risk-free rate.

Risk   A situation in which more than one outcome might occur and the probability of each possible outcome can be estimated.

Risk aversion   Describes the fact that investors want to minimize risk for the same level of expected return. To take more risk, they require compensation by a risk premium.

Risk budgeting   The establishment of risk objectives for individuals, groups, or divisions of an organization that takes into account the allocation of an acceptable level of risk.

Risk-free asset   An asset with a certain rate of return; often taken to be short-term T-bills.

Risk-free rate   The interest rate that can be earned with certainty.

Risk governance   The setting of overall policies and standards in risk management

Risk management   The process of identifying the level of risk an entity wants, measuring the level of risk the entity currently has, taking actions that bring the actual level of risk to the desired level of risk, and monitoring the new actual level of risk so that it continues to be aligned with the desired level of risk.

Risk premium   The expected return on an investment minus the risk-free rate.

Risk-neutral   See *risk-averse.*

Risk-neutral probabilities   Weights that are used to compute a binomial option price. They are the probabilities that would apply if a risk-neutral investor valued an option.

Risk-neutral valuation   The process by which options and other derivatives are priced by treating investors as though they were risk neutral.

Risky asset   An asset with uncertain future returns.

Rival   A good or service or a resource is rival if its use by one person decreases the quantity available for someone else.

Robust   The quality of being relatively unaffected by a violation of assumptions.

Robust standard errors   Standard errors of the estimated parameters of a regression that correct for the presence of heteroskedasticity in the regression's error term.

Root mean squared error (RMSE)   The square root of the average squared forecast error; used to compare the out-of-sample forecasting performance of forecasting models.

Roy's safety first criterion   A criterion asserting that the optimal portfolio is the one that minimizes the probability that portfolio return falls below a threshold level.

Rule 144a   *SEC* rule allowing *qualified institutional buyers* to buy and trade unregistered securities.

Rule of 72   The principle that the approximate number of years necessary for an investment to double is 72 divided by the stated interest rate.

Russell 1000 Index   The 1000 largest companies in the Russell 3000 index.

Russell 2000 Index   The 2000 smallest companies in the Russell 3000 index.

Russell 3000 Index   The 3000 largest U.S. companies, capital-weighted, which represent about 98 percent of the investible equity market.

Safe harbor   Practices that satisfy such requirements as the Prudent Investor Rule.

Safety-first rules   Rules for portfolio selection that focus on the risk that portfolio value will fall below some minimum acceptable level over some time horizon.

Sales risk   Uncertainty with respect to the quantity of goods and services that a company is able to sell and the price it is able to achieve.

Salvage value   Scrap value of plant and equipment.

Sample   A subset of a population.

Sample excess kurtosis   A sample measure of the degree of a distribution's peakedness in excess of the normal distribution's peakedness.

Sample kurtosis   A sample measure of the degree of a distribution's peakedness.

Sample mean   The sum of the sample observations, divided by the sample size.

Sample selection bias   Bias introduced by systematically excluding some members of the population according to a particular attribute—for example, the bias introduced when data availability leads to certain observations being excluded from the analysis.

Sample skewness   A sample measure of degree of asymmetry of a distribution.

Sample standard deviation   The positive square root of the sample variance.

Sample statistic or statistic   A quantity computed from or used to describe a sample.

Sample variance   A sample measure of the degree of dispersion of a distribution, calculated by dividing the sum of the squared deviations from the sample mean by the sample size (n) minus 1.

Sampling   The process of obtaining a sample.

Sampling distribution   The distribution of all distinct possible values that a statistic can assume when computed from samples of the same size randomly drawn from the same population.

Sampling error   The difference between the observed value of a statistic and the quantity it is intended to estimate.

Sandwich spread   An option strategy that is equivalent to a short butterfly spread.

Sarbanes-Oxley Act   An act of the U.S. Congress signed into law on 30 July 2002 that tightened the oversight of firms that audit public companies, added criminal penalties for earnings management activities, and took steps generally to improve company internal controls and corporate governance.

Saving   The act of not consuming all of one's current income. Whatever is not consumed out of spendable income is, by definition, saved. Saving is an action measured over time (a flow), whereas savings are a stock, an accumulation resulting from the act of saving in the past.

Scaled earnings surprise   Unexpected earnings divided by the standard deviation of analysts' earnings forecasts.

Scalper   A trader who offers to buy or sell futures contracts, holding the position for only a brief period of time. Scalpers attempt to profit by buying at the bid price and selling at the higher ask price.

Scatter plot or scatter diagram   A two-dimensional plot of pairs of observations on two data series.

Scenario analysis   A risk management technique involving the examination of the performance of a portfolio under specified situations. Closely related to *stress testing*.

Screening   The application of a set of criteria to reduce an investment universe to a smaller set of investments.

Seasoned issue   Issue of a security for which there is an existing market (cf. *unseasoned issue*).

Seats   Memberships in a derivatives exchange.

SEC Securities and Exchange Commission.

Secondary issue (1) Procedure for selling blocks of *seasoned issues* of stock; (2) more generally, sale of already issued stock.

Secondary market The market in which outstanding securities are bought and sold by owners other than the issuers. Purpose is to provide liquidity for investors.

Sector neutral Said of a portfolio for which economic sectors are represented in the same proportions as in the benchmark, using market-value weights.

Sector rotation An investment strategy which entails shifting the portfolio into industry sectors that are forecast to outperform others based on macroeconomic forecasts.

Sector rotation strategy A type of top-down investing approach that involves emphasizing different economic sectors based on considerations such as macroeconomic forecasts.

Securities Exchange Act of 1934 The federal law that established the Securities and Exchange Commission. It also added further regulations for securities markets. The law has been amended several times since its initial passage. One of the amendments that is relevant to mergers is the Williams Act of 1968.

Securities Stocks and bonds.

Securities offering A merger or acquisition in which target shareholders are to receive shares of the acquirer's common stock as compensation.

Securitization Substitution of tradable securities for privately negotiated instruments.

Security analysis Determining correct value of a security in the marketplace.

Security market line (SML) The graph of the capital asset pricing model.

Self-interest The choices that you think are the best for you.

Sell-side analysts Analysts who work at brokerages.

Semideviation The positive square root of semivariance (sometimes called semistandard deviation).

Semilogarithmic Describes a scale constructed so that equal intervals on the vertical scale represent equal rates of change, and equal intervals on the horizontal scale represent equal amounts of change.

Semivariance The average squared deviation below the mean.

Senior debt Debt that, in the event of bankruptcy, must be repaid before *subordinated debt* receives any payment.

Sensitivity analysis Analysis of the effect on project profitability of possible changes in sales, costs, and so on.

Serially correlated With reference to regression errors, errors that are correlated across observations.

Services Mental or physical labor or help purchased by consumers. Examples are the assistance of physicians, lawyers, dentists, repair personnel, housecleaners, educators, retailers, and wholesalers; things purchased or used by consumers that do not have physical characteristics.

Settlement date or payment date With reference to swaps, the date on which the parties to a swap make payments.

Settlement period The time between settlement dates.

Settlement price The official price, designated by the clearinghouse, from which daily gains and losses will be determined and marked to market.

Settlement risk When settling a contract, the risk that one party could be in the process of paying the counterparty while the counterparty is declaring bankruptcy.

Settlor The creator of an inter vivos trust; also same as *grantor, trustor,* or *creator.*

Share of stock A legal claim to a share of a corporation's future profits; if it is common stock, it incorporates certain voting rights regarding major policy decisions of the corporation; if it is preferred stock, its owners are accorded preferential treatment in the payment of dividends.

Share repurchase A transaction in which a company buys back its own shares. Unlike stock dividends and stock splits, share repurchases use corporate cash.

Shareholders' equity Total assets minus total liabilities.

Share-the-gains, share-the-pains theory A theory of regulatory behavior in which the regulators must take account of the demands of three groups: legislators, who established and who oversee the regulatory agency; members of the regulated industry; and consumers of the regulated industry's products or services.

Shark repellents A pre-offer takeover defense mechanism involving the corporate charter (e.g., staggered boards of directors and supermajority provisions).

Sharpe ratio or Sharpe measure The average return in excess of the risk-free rate divided by the standard deviation of return; a measure of the average excess return earned per unit of standard deviation of return.

Short The seller of a derivative contract. Also refers to the position of being short a derivative.

Short interest rate A one-period interest rate.

Short position The seller of a commodity or security or, for a forward contract, the counterparty who will be the eventual seller of the underlying asset.

Short run The short run in microeconomics has two meanings. (1) For the firm, it is the period of time in which the quantity of at least one input is fixed and the quantities of the other inputs can be varied. The fixed input is usually capital—that is, the firm has a given plant size. (2) For the industry, the short run is the period of time in which each firm has a given plant size and the number of firms in the industry is fixed.

Short sale The sale of shares not owned by the investor but borrowed through a broker and later repurchased to replace the loan. Profit is earned if the initial sale is at a higher price than the repurchase price.

Shortage A situation in which quantity demanded is greater than quantity supplied at a price below the market clearing price.

Shortfall risk The risk that portfolio value will fall below some minimum acceptable level over some time horizon.

Should Encouraged (recommended) to follow the recommendation of the GIPS standards but not required.

Signal (1) Action that demonstrates an individual's unobservable characteristics (because it would be unduly costly for someone without those characteristics to take the action). (2) An action taken by an informed person (or firm) to send a message to uninformed people or an action taken outside a market that conveys information that can be used by that market.

Simple interest The interest earned each period on the original investment; interest calculated on the principal only.

Simple random sample A subset of a larger population created in such a way that each element of the population has an equal probability of being selected to the subset.

Simulation Monte Carlo simulation.

Simulation trial A complete pass through the steps of a simulation.

Single-factor model A model of security returns that acknowledges only one common factor. See *factor model*.

Single-payment loan A loan in which the borrower receives a sum of money at the start and pays back the entire amount with interest in a single payment at maturity.

Sinking fund Bond provision that requires the issuer to redeem some or all of the bond systematically over the term of the bond rather than in full at maturity.

Sinking fund factor Amount that must be set aside each period to have $1 at some future point in time.

Skewed Not symmetrical.

Skewness A quantitative measure of skew (lack of symmetry); a synonym of skew.

Skill One of the three components of the standard of prudence governing trustees; familiarity with business matters.

Slope The change in the value of the variable measured on the *y*-axis divided by the change in the value of the variable measured on the *x*-axis.

Soft dollars The value of research services that brokerage houses supply to investment managers "free of charge" in exchange for the investment managers' business.

Sole proprietorship A business owned and operated by a single person.

Sovereign risk The risk that a government may default on its debt.

Spearman rank correlation coefficient A measure of correlation applied to ranked data.

Special purpose entity (SPE) A non-operating entity created to carry out a specified purpose, such as leasing assets or securitizing receivables. Also known as a special purpose vehicle (SPV).

Specialist A trader who makes a market in the shares of one or more firms and who maintains a "fair and orderly market" by dealing personally in the stock.

Specialization The division of productive activities among persons and regions so that no one individual or one area is totally self-sufficient. An individual may specialize, for example, in law or medicine. A nation may specialize in the production of coffee, computers, or cameras.

Speculation Undertaking a risky investment with the objective of earning a greater profit than an investment in a risk-free alternative (a risk premium).

Speculative stock A stock that appears to be highly overpriced compared to its intrinsic valuation.

Spin-off A form of restructuring in which a corporation separates off and separately capitalizes a component business, which is then transferred to the corporation's common stockholders; shareholders end up owning stock in two different companies where there used to be one.

Split When a stock reaches a high price, the management of the company will split it two for one, three for two, or whatever, to create a lower price per share and thus facilitate trading. The dividend may be raised at the same time.

In a "reverse split," a low-priced stock, often of a failing company, is consolidated to bring the price per share up to a reasonable level. On the Canadian exchanges such stocks are thereafter called "Consolidated Gold Bug" (or whatever).

Split-off   A form of restructuring in which shareholders of the parent company are given shares in a newly created entity in exchange for their shares of the parent company.

Split-rate   In reference to corporate taxes, a split-rate system taxes earnings to be distributed as dividends at a different rate than earnings to be retained. Corporate profits distributed as dividends are taxed at a lower rate than those retained in the business.

Spot exchange rate   Exchange rate on currency for immediate delivery (cf. *forward exchange rate*).

Spot price   Price of asset for immediate delivery (in contrast to forward or futures price).

Spot rate   The required yield for a cash flow to be received at some specific date in the future-for example, the spot rate for a flow to be received in one year, for a cash flow in two years, and so on.

Spread   With reference to options strategies, a strategy involving the purchase of one option and sale of another option that is identical to the first in all respects except either exercise price or expiration.

Spreadsheet modeling   As used in this book, the use of a spreadsheet in executing a dividend discount model valuation, or other present value model valuation.

Spurious correlation   A correlation that misleadingly points towards associations between variables.

Squeeze   The possibility that enough long positions hold their contracts to maturity that supplies of the commodity are not adequate to cover all contracts. A *short squeeze* describes the reverse: short positions threaten to deliver an expensive-to-store commodity.

Staggered board   Also called a *classified board*. This is an antitakeover measure in which the election of directors is split in separate periods so that only a percentage of the total number of directors come up for election in a given year. It is designed to make taking control of the board of directors more difficult.

Stakeholder   Any entity that is affected by the actions of a company, which may include shareholders, management, workers, communities, consumers, and so on.

Standard deviation   The positive square root of the variance; a measure of dispersion in the same units as the original data.

Standard error   In statistics, a measure of the possible error in an estimate.

Standard normal distribution (or unit normal distribution)   The normal density with mean (μ) equal to 0 and standard deviation (σ) equal to 1.

Standardized beta   With reference to fundamental factor models, the value of the attribute for an asset minus the average value of the attribute across all stocks, divided by the standard deviation of the attribute across all stocks.

Standardized unexpected earnings (SUE)   Unexpected earnings per share divided by the standard deviation of unexpected earnings per share over a specified prior time period.

Standardizing   A transformation that involves subtracting the mean and dividing the result by the standard deviation.

Standstill agreement   An agreement that a potential hostile bidder enters into with the target corporation whereby the bidder agrees, in exchange for some consideration, not to purchase more than an agreed-upon number of shares.

Start-up stage   The opening period in a company's life cycle during which operating losses often are reported and operating cash flow is consumed.

Stated annual interest rate or quoted interest rate   A quoted interest rate that does not account for compounding within the year.

Statement of cash flows   A financial statement showing a firm's cash receipts and cash payments during a specified period.

Static trade-off theory of capital structure   A theory pertaining to a company's optimal capital structure; the optimal level of debt is found at the point where additional debt would cause the costs of financial distress to increase by a greater amount than the benefit of the additional tax shield.

Statistic   A quantity computed from or used to describe a sample of data.

Statistical factor models   A multifactor model in which statistical methods are applied to a set of historical returns to determine portfolios that best explain either historical return covariances or variances.

Statistical inference   Making forecasts, estimates, or judgments about a larger group from a smaller group actually observed; using a sample statistic to infer the value of an unknown population parameter.

Statistically significant   A result indicating that the null hypothesis can be rejected; with reference to an estimated regression coefficient, frequently understood to mean a result indicating that the corresponding population regression coefficient is different from 0.

Statistics   The science of describing, analyzing, and drawing conclusions from data; also, a collection of numerical data.

Statutory merger   A merger in which one company ceases to exist as an identifiable entity and all its assets and liabilities become part of a purchasing company.

Stock   The quantity of something, measured at a given point in time—for example, an inventory of goods or a bank account. Stocks are defined independently of time, although they are assessed at a point in time.

Stock dividend   *Dividend* in the form of stock rather than cash.

Stock exchanges   Secondary markets where already-issued securities are bought and sold by members.

Stock option   A contract that gives its holder the right to buy (call option) or sell (put option) an interest in stock at a specified price through a specified date.

Stock purchase   An acquisition in which the acquirer gives the target company's shareholders some combination of cash and securities in exchange for shares of the target company's stock.

Stock selection   An active portfolio management technique that focuses on advantageous selection of particular stocks rather than on broad asset allocation choices.

Stock split   Issue by a corporation of a given number of shares in exchange for the current number of shares held by stockholders. Splits may go in either direction, either increasing or decreasing the number of shares outstanding. A *reverse split* decreases the number outstanding.

Storage costs or carrying costs   The costs of holding an asset, generally a function of the physical characteristics of the underlying asset.

Straddle   An option strategy involving the purchase of a put and a call with the same exercise price. A straddle is based on the expectation of high volatility of the underlying.

Straight-line depreciation   An equal dollar amount of *depreciation* in each period.

Strangle   A variation of a straddle in which the put and call have different exercise prices.

Strap   An option strategy involving the purchase of two calls and one put.

Strategic alliance   A more flexible alternative to a joint venture whereby certain companies agree to pursue certain common activities and interests.

Strategic asset allocation   The allocation to the major investment asset classes that is determined to be appropriate, given the investor's long-run investment objectives and constraints.

Strategy   Any rule that is used to make a choice, such as "Always pick heads."

Stratified random sampling   A procedure by which a population is divided into subpopulations (strata) based on one or more classification criteria. Simple random samples are then drawn from each stratum in sizes proportional to the relative size of each stratum in the population. These samples are then pooled.

Stress testing   A risk management technique in which the risk manager examines the performance of the portfolio under market conditions involving high risk and usually high correlations across markets. Closely related to *scenario analysis*.

Strike price   Price at which an option can be exercised (same as *exercise price*).

Strip   An option strategy involving the purchase of two puts and one call.

Structural change   Economic trend occurring when the economy is undergoing a major change in organization or in how it functions.

Structured note   A debt security with an embedded derivative designed to create a payoff distribution that satisfies the needs of a specific investor clientele.

Style analysis   An attempt to explain the variability in the observed returns to a security portfolio in terms of the movements in the returns to a series of benchmark portfolios designed to capture the essence of a particular security characteristic such as size, value, and growth.

Subjective probability   A probability drawing on personal or subjective judgment.

Subordinated debt (junior debt)   Debt over which *senior debt* takes priority. In the event of bankruptcy, subordinated debtholders receive payment only after senior debt is paid off in full.

Subsidiary merger   A merger in which the company being purchased becomes a subsidiary of the purchaser.

Subsidy   A payment that the government makes to a producer.

Subsistence real wage rate   The minimum real wage rate needed to maintain life.

Substitute   A good that can be used in place of another good.

Sunk cost   A cost that has already been incurred and cannot be reversed.

Supermajority   Provision in a company's charter requiring a majority of, say, 80 percent of shareholders to approve certain changes, such as a *merger*.

Supernormal growth   Above average or abnormally high growth rate in earnings per share.

Supplemental Information   Any performance-related information included as part of a compliant performance presentation that supplements or enhances the required and/or recommended disclosure and presentation provisions of the GIPS standards.

Supply   A schedule showing the relationship between price and quantity supplied for a specified period of time, other things being equal.

Supply curve   The graphical representation of the supply schedule; a line (curve) showing the supply schedule, which generally slopes upward (has a positive slope), other things being equal.

Supply shock   An event that influences production capacity and costs in the economy.

Supply-side economics   The notion that creating incentives for individuals and firms to increase productivity will cause the aggregate supply curve to shift outward.

Surplus   A situation in which quantity supplied is greater than quantity demanded at a price above the market clearing price.

Surprise   The actual value of a variable minus its predicted (or expected) value.

Survivorship bias   The bias resulting from a test design that fails to account for companies that have gone bankrupt, merged, or are otherwise no longer reported in a database.

Sustainable growth rate   The rate of dividend (and earnings) growth that can be sustained for a given level of return on equity, keeping the capital structure constant over time and without issuing additional common stock.

Swap   A contract whereby two parties agree to a periodic exchange of cash flows. In certain types of swaps, only the net difference between the amounts owed is exchanged on each payment date.

Swap spread   The difference between the fixed rate on an interest rate swap and the rate on a Treasury note with equivalent maturity; it reflects the general level of credit risk in the market.

Swaption   An option to enter into a swap.

Synergy   2 1 2 5 5; a combination of businesses in which the combined entity is more valuable than the sum of the parts.

Synthetic call   The combination of puts, the underlying, and risk-free bonds that replicates a call option.

Synthetic forward contract   The combination of the underlying, puts, calls, and risk-free bonds that replicates a forward contract.

Synthetic index fund   An index fund position created by combining risk-free bonds and futures on the desired index.

Synthetic put   The combination of calls, the underlying, and risk-free bonds that replicates a put option.

Systematic factors   Factors that affect the average returns of a large number of different assets.

Systematic risk   (1) The variability of returns that is due to macroeconomic factors that affect all risky assets. Because it affects all risky assets, it cannot be eliminated by diversification. (2) Market risk.

Systematic sampling   A procedure of selecting every *k*th member until reaching a sample of the desired size. The sample that results from this procedure should be approximately random.

Tactical asset allocation   Short-term adjustments to the long-term asset allocation to reflect views on the current relative attractiveness of asset classes.

Takeover   A merger; the term may be applied to any transaction, but is often used in reference to hostile transactions.

Takeover premium   The amount by which the takeover price for each share of stock must exceed the current stock price in order to entice shareholders to relinquish control of the company to an acquirer.

Tangible asset   Physical asset, such as plant, machinery, and offices (cf. *intangible assets*).

Tangible book value per share   Common shareholders' equity minus intangible assets from the balance sheet, divided by the number of shares outstanding.

Target capital structure   A company's chosen proportions of debt and equity.

Target company, or target   The company in a merger or acquisition that is being acquired.

Target payout ratio   A strategic corporate goal representing the long-term proportion of earnings that the company intends to distribute to shareholders as dividends.

Target semideviation   The positive square root of target semivariance.

Target semivariance   The average squared deviation below a target value.

Tariffs   Taxes on imported goods.

Tax adjustments   Restatements of nonrecurring items of operating cash flow to place them on an after-tax basis. For example, an outsized tax-deductible pension contribution of $50 million would be reduced to an after-tax amount of $30 million if a combined federal and state marginal tax rate of 40 percent is assumed: $50 million $\times$ (1 − 40 percent) = $30 million.

Tax bracket   A specified interval of income to which a specific and unique marginal tax rate is applied.

Tax credits   A direct dollar-for-dollar reduction in taxes payable.

Tax risk   The uncertainty associated with tax laws.

T-bill   Treasury bill.

t-Distribution   A symmetrical distribution defined by a single parameter, degrees of freedom, that is largely used to make inferences concerning the mean of a normal distribution whose variance is unknown.

Technical indicators   Momentum indicators based on price.

Technological change   The development of new goods and better ways of producing goods and services.

Technology   (1) Any method of producing a good or service. (2) Society's pool of applied knowledge concerning how goods and services can be produced.

TED spread   Difference between *LIBOR* and U.S. *Treasury bill* rate.

Temporary difference   A difference between the book and tax basis of both assets and liabilities. Alternatively, a temporary difference is a difference between book and tax return earnings that will reverse at some future point in time. Temporary differences give rise to deferred tax assets and liabilities.

Tender offer   A public offer whereby the acquirer invites target shareholders to submit ("tender") their shares in return for the proposed payment.

Tenor   The original time to maturity on a swap or loan.

Term bond   A bond that has a single maturity date.

Term structure   See *yield curve*.

Term structure of interest rates   The relationship between term to maturity and yield to maturity for a sample of comparable bonds at a given time. Popularly known as the *yield curve*.

Term to maturity   Specifies the date or the number of years before a bond matures or expires.

Terminal price multiple   The price multiple for a stock assumed to hold at a stated future time.

Terminal share price   The share price at a particular point in the future.

Terminal value of the stock (or continuing value of the stock)   The analyst's estimate of a stock's value at a particular point in the future.

Termination date   The date of the final payment on a swap; also, the swap's expiration date.

Terms of trade   The quantity of goods and services that a country exports to pay for its imports of goods and services.

Test statistic   A quantity, calculated based on a sample, whose value is the basis for deciding whether or not to reject the null hypothesis.

Testamentary trust   A trust created by will.

The Fed   The Federal Reserve System; the central bank of the United States.

Theory of contestable markets   A hypothesis concerning pricing behavior that holds that even though there are only a few firms in an industry, they are forced to price their products more or less competitively because of the ease of entry by outsiders. The key aspect of a contestable market is relatively costless entry into and exit from the industry.

Theta   The rate at which an option's time value decays.

Third parties   Parties who are not directly involved in a given activity or transaction.

Thrift institutions   Financial institutions that receive most of their funds from the savings of the public; they include mutual savings banks, savings and loan associations, and credit unions.

Tick   Minimum amount the price of a security may change.

Time deposit   A deposit in a financial institution that requires notice of intent to withdraw or must be left for an agreed period. Withdrawal of funds prior to the end of the agreed period may result in a penalty.

Time-period bias   The possibility that when we use a time-series sample, our statistical conclusion may be sensitive to the starting and ending dates of the sample.

Time series   A set of observations on a variable's outcomes in different time periods.

Time-series data   Observations of a variable over time.

Time to expiration   The time remaining in the life of a derivative, typically expressed in years.

Time value (of an option)   The part of the value of an option that is due to its positive time to expiration. Not to be confused with present value or the time value of money.

Time value decay   The loss in the value of an option resulting from movement of the option price toward its payoff value as the expiration day approaches.

Time value of money   The principles governing equivalence relationships between cash flows with different dates.

Time value or speculative value   The difference between the market price of the option and its intrinsic value, determined by the uncertainty of the underlying over the remaining life of the option.

Time-weighted rate of return   The compound rate of growth of one unit of currency invested in a portfolio during a stated measurement period; a measure of investment performance that is not sensitive to the timing and amount of withdrawals or additions to the portfolio.

Tobin's q   The ratio of the market value of debt and equity to the replacement cost of total assets.

Top-down   With respect to investment approaches, the allocation of money first to categories such as asset classes, countries, or industry followed by the selection of individual securities within category.

Top-down forecasting approach   A forecasting approach that involves moving from international and national macroeconomic forecasts to industry forecasts and then to individual company and asset forecasts.

Top-down investing   An approach to investing that typically begins with macroeconomic forecasts.

Total cash flow   The change in reported cash and cash equivalents during a reporting period.

Total cost   The cost of all the productive resources that a firm uses; the sum of total fixed cost and total variable cost.

Total fixed cost   The cost of the firm's fixed inputs.

Total income   The yearly amount earned by the nation's resources (factors of production). Total income therefore includes wages, rent, interest payments, and profits that are received, respectively, by workers, landowners, capital owners, and entrepreneurs.

Total interest paid   A term used on the cash flow analysis statement that consists of cash payments for interest on debt and capital leases, including capitalized interest.

Total probability rule   A rule explaining the unconditional probability of an event in terms of probabilities of the event conditional on mutually exclusive and exhaustive scenarios.

Total return   A return objective in which the investor wants to increase the portfolio value to meet a future need by both capital gains and current income reinvestment.

Total return swap   A swap in which one party agrees to pay the total return on a security. Often used as a credit derivative, in which the underlying is a bond.

Total revenue   The value of a firm's sales.

Total Value (Private Equity)   Residual value of the portfolio plus distributed capital.

Tracking error   A synonym for tracking risk; also, the condition in which the performance of a portfolio does not match the performance of an index that serves as the portfolio's benchmark.

Tracking portfolio   A portfolio having factor sensitivities that are matched to those of a benchmark or other portfolio.

Tracking risk or tracking error or tracking error volatility or active risk   The standard deviation of the differences between a portfolio's returns and its benchmark's returns; a synonym of active risk.

Trade balance   The balance of a country's exports and imports; part of the current account.

Trade credit   Accounts receivable.

Tradeoff   An exchange—giving up one thing to get something else.

Trading turnover   The percentage of outstanding shares traded during a period of time.

Traditional efficient markets formulation   See *Market efficiency*.

Trailing dividend yield   Current market price divided by the most recent quarterly per-share dividend multiplied by four.

Trailing P/E (or current P/E)   A stock's current market price divided by the most recent four quarters of earnings per share.

Tranche   Refers to a portion of an issue that is designed for a specific category of investors. French for "slice."

Transaction cost   (1) The cost of executing a trade. Low costs characterize an operationally efficient market. (2) All of the costs associated with exchanging, including the informational costs of finding out price and quality, service record, and durability of a product, plus the cost of contracting and enforcing that contract. Can also be viewed as all costs associated with making, reaching, and enforcing agreements.

Transaction exposure   The risk associated with a foreign exchange rate on a specific business transaction such as a purchase or sale.

Transfer payments   Money payments made by governments to individuals for which in return no services or goods are concurrently rendered. Examples are welfare, Social Security, and unemployment insurance benefits.

Transition phase   The stage of growth between the growth phase and the mature phase of a company in which earnings growth typically slows.

Translation exposure   The risk associated with the conversion of foreign financial statements into domestic currency.

Treasurer   Principal financial manager (cf. *controller*).

Treasury bill   Short-term, highly liquid government securities issued at a discount from the face value and returning the face amount at maturity.

Treasury bond   A U.S. government security with a maturity of more than 10 years that pays interest periodically.

Treasury note   A U.S. government security with maturities of 1 to 10 years that pays interest periodically.

Treasury shares Shares that were issued and subsequently repurchased by the company.

Treasury stock A corporation's issued stock that has subsequently been repurchased by the company and not retired.

Tree diagram A diagram with branches emanating from nodes representing either mutually exclusive chance events or mutually exclusive decisions.

Trend A long-term pattern of movement in a particular direction.

Triangular arbitrage With respect to currencies, an arbitrage involving three currencies only.

Trimmed mean A mean computed after excluding a stated small percentage of the lowest and highest observations.

Trough The transition point between recession and recovery.

Trust agreement or trust indenture or trust instrument The document that creates an inter vivos trust, between a grantor and a trustee, for the benefit of the beneficiaries.

***t*-Test** A hypothesis test using a statistic (*t*-statistic) that follows a *t*-distribution.

Turnover The ratio of the trading activity of a portfolio to the assets of the portfolio.

Two-sided hypothesis test (or two-tailed hypothesis test) A test in which the null hypothesis is rejected in favor of the alternative hypothesis if the evidence indicates that the population parameter is either smaller or larger than a hypothesized value.

Type I error The error of rejecting a true null hypothesis.

Type II error The error of not rejecting a false null hypothesis.

U.S. interest rate differential A gap equal to the U.S. interest rate minus the foreign interest rate.

U.S. Official reserves The government's holdings of foreign currency.

Unanticipated inflation Inflation at a rate that comes as a surprise, either higher or lower than the rate anticipated.

Unbiasedness Lack of bias. A desirable property of estimators, an unbiased estimator is one whose expected value (the mean of its sampling distribution) equals the parameter it is intended to estimate.

Uncertainty A situation in which more than one event might occur but it is not known which one.

Unconditional heteroskedasticity Heteroskedasticity of the error term that is not correlated with the values of the independent variable(s) in the regression.

Unconditional probability (or marginal probability) The probability of an event *not* conditioned on another event.

Uncovered interest rate parity The assertion that expected currency depreciation should offset the interest differential between two countries over the term of the interest rate.

Underlying With reference to derivatives, the asset on which a derivative contract is written.

Underlying earnings (or persistent, continuing, or core earnings) Earnings excluding nonrecurring components.

Underweighted A condition in which a portfolio, for whatever reason, includes less of a class of securities than the relative market value alone would justify.

Underwriter Firm that buys an issue of securities from a company and resells it to investors.

Unemployment The total number of adults (aged 16 years or older) who are willing and able to work and who are actively looking for work but have not found a job.

Unemployment rate The percentage of the people in the labor force who are unemployed.

Unexpected earnings (also earnings surprise) The difference between reported earnings per share and expected earnings per share.

Unit root A time series that is not covariance stationary is said to have a unit root.

Univariate distribution A distribution that specifies the probabilities for a single random variable.

Unlimited funds An unlimited funds environment assumes that the company can raise the funds it wants for all profitable projects simply by paying the required rate of return.

Unlimited liability A legal concept whereby the personal assets of the owner of a firm can be seized to pay off the firm's debts.

Unsystematic risk Risk that is unique to an asset, derived from its particular characteristics. It can be eliminated in a diversified portfolio.

Unwind The negotiated termination of a forward or futures position before contract maturity.

Valuation The process of determining the value of an asset or service on the basis of variables perceived to be related to future investment returns, or on the basis of comparisons with closely similar assets.

Valuation analysis An active bond portfolio management strategy designed to capitalize on expected price increases in temporarily undervalued issues.

Valuation process Part of the investment decision process in which you estimate the value of a security.

Value   The amount for which one can sell something, or the amount one must pay to acquire something.

Value at risk (VAR)   A money measure of the minimum value of losses expected during a specified time period at a given level of probability.

Value chain   The set of transformations to move from raw material to product or service delivery.

Value stocks   Stocks that appear to be undervalued for reasons besides earnings growth potential. These stocks are usually identified based on high dividend yields, low P/E ratios, or low price-to-book ratios.

Value-weighted index   An index calculated as the total market value of the securities in the sample. Market value is equal to the number of shares or bonds outstanding times the market price of the security.

Variable costs   Costs that fluctuate with the level of production and sales.

Variance   The expected value (the probability-weighted average) of squared deviations from a random variable's expected value.

Variation margin   Additional margin that must be deposited in an amount sufficient to bring the balance up to the initial margin requirement.

Vega   The relationship between option price and volatility.

Vendor financing   Amounts owed vendors for purchased goods or services, reported as accounts payable.

Venture capital   Capital to finance a new firm.

Vertical merger   Á merger involving companies at different positions of the same production chain; for example, a supplier or a distributor.

Visibility   The extent to which a company's operations are predictable with substantial confidence.

Volatility   As used in option pricing, the standard deviation of the continuously compounded returns on the underlying asset.

Volatility risk   The risk in the value of options portfolios due to unpredictable changes in the volatility of the underlying asset.

Voluntary export restraint   An agreement between two governments in which the government of the exporting country agrees to restrain the volume of its own exports.

Wages   The income that labor earns.

Warrant   An instrument that allows the holder to purchase a specified number of shares of the firm's common stock from the firm at a specified price for a given period of time.

Wealth   The stock of assets owned by a person, household, firm, or nation. For a household, wealth can consist of a house, cars, personal belongings, stocks, bonds, bank accounts, and cash.

Weighted-average cost of capital (WACC)   A weighted average of the after-tax required rates of return on a company's common stock, preferred stock, and long-term debt, where the weights are the fraction of each source of financing in the company's target capital structure.

Weighted mean   An average in which each observation is weighted by an index of its relative importance.

Well-diversified portfolio   A portfolio spread out over many securities in such a way that the weight in any security is close to zero.

White-corrected standard errors   A synonym for robust standard errors.

White knight   A third party that is sought out by the target company's board to purchase the target in lieu of a hostile bidder.

White squire   A third party that is sought out by the target company's board to purchase a substantial minority stake in the target-enough to block a hostile takeover without selling the entire company.

Wholesale Price Index (WPI)   A price index defined on a basket of goods produced.

Window dressing   Toward the end of a reporting period, particularly at year end, mutual funds and banks will sometimes round up their holdings to even thousands, or sell positions that have gone down and thus constitute an eyesore.

Winner's curse   The tendency for the winner in certain competitive bidding situations to overpay, whether because of overestimation of intrinsic value, emotion, or information asymmetries.

Winsorized mean   A mean computed after assigning a stated percent of the lowest values equal to one specified low value, and a stated percent of the highest values equal to one specified high value.

Withholding tax   A tax levied by the country of source on income paid.

Working capital   Current assets minus current liabilities.

Working capital management   The management of a company's short-term assets (such as inventory) and short-term liabilities (such as money owed to suppliers).

Workout period   Realignment period of a temporary misaligned yield relationship.

World Bank   A supranational organization of several institutions designed to assist developing countries. The International Bank for Reconstruction and Development (IBRD) and the International Finance Corporation (IFC) are the more important members of the World Bank group.

World Trade Organization An international organization that places greater obligations on its member countries to observe the GATT rules.

Write-down A reduction in the value of an asset as stated in the balance sheet.

Writer of an option A term used for the person or institution selling an option and therefore granting the right to exercise it to the buyer of the option.

x axis The horizontal axis in a graph.

y axis The vertical axis in a graph.

Yield The promised rate of return on an investment under certain assumptions.

Yield beta A measure of the sensitivity of a bond's yield to a general measure of bond yields in the market that is used to refine the hedge ratio.

Yield curve A curve showing the relationship between yield (interest rate) and maturity for a set of similar securities. For example, the yield curve can be drawn for U.S. Treasuries or for LIBOR. Typically, different yield curves are drawn for zero-coupon bonds (zero-coupon yield curve) and for coupon bonds quoted at par (par yield curve).

Yield spread The difference between the yield on a bond and the yield on a default-free security, usually a government note, of the same maturity. The yield spread is primarily determined by the market's perception of the credit risk on the bond.

Yield to maturity The total yield on a bond obtained by equating the bond's current market value to the discounted cash flows promised by the bond. Also called *actuarial yield.*

Zero-beta portfolio The minimum-variance portfolio uncorrelated with a chosen efficient portfolio.

Zero-cost collar A transaction in which a position in the underlying is protected by buying a put and selling a call with the premium from the sale of the call offsetting the premium from the purchase of the put. It can also be used to protect a floating-rate borrower against interest rate increases with the premium on a long cap offsetting the premium on a short floor.

Zero-coupon bond A bond that pays its par value at maturity but no periodic interest payments. Its yield is determined by the difference between its par value and its discounted purchase price. Also called *original issue discount (OID).*

Z-score Measure of the likelihood of bankruptcy.

$4\frac{5}{8}$ $4\frac{11}{16}$

$5\frac{1}{2} - \frac{3}{8}$

$5\frac{1}{2}$ $5\frac{1}{2} - \frac{1}{16}$

$20\frac{5}{8}$ $21\frac{3}{16} - \frac{7}{8}$

$17\frac{3}{8}$ $18\frac{1}{8} + \frac{7}{8}$

$17\frac{3}{8}$ $18\frac{1}{8} +$

$13\frac{1}{2}$ $6\frac{1}{2}$ $6\frac{1}{2} - \frac{1}{2}$

$7\frac{1}{4}$ $6\frac{1}{2}$ $31\frac{1}{32} - \frac{1}{8}$

$15\frac{1}{16}$

1 $\frac{9}{16}$ $\frac{9}{16}$

$\frac{1}{32}$ $\frac{9}{16}$

$7\frac{13}{16}$ $7\frac{15}{16}$

$7\frac{15}{16}$ $7\frac{13}{16}$

$25\frac{5}{8}$ $2\frac{11}{32}$ $2\frac{1}{2} +$

$23\frac{3}{4}$ $2\frac{1}{4}$ $2\frac{1}{4}$

$6\frac{1}{2}$ $12\frac{1}{16}$ $11\frac{3}{8}$ $11\frac{3}{4} +$

87 $33\frac{3}{4}$ 33 $33\frac{1}{16} -$

602 $25\frac{5}{8}$ $24\frac{9}{16}$ $25\frac{5}{8} +$

833 12 $11\frac{5}{8}$ $11\frac{7}{8} +$

16 $10\frac{1}{2}$ $10\frac{1}{2}$ $10\frac{1}{2} -$

78 $15\frac{5}{8}$ $15\frac{13}{16}$ $15\frac{7}{8} -$

4508 $9\frac{1}{16}$ $8\frac{1}{4}$ $8\frac{1}{2} +$

430 $11\frac{1}{4}$ $10\frac{1}{8}$

Page numbers followed by n refer to footnotes.

five forces model, V4: 135–137,
169–174
focus, V4: 15, 132, 177–178
generic, V4: 174–184
government participation, V4: 137
industry evolution, V4: 182
international competition,
V4: 213–216
multiple strategies, V4: 178–180
organizational structure,
V4: 182–183
positioning, V4: 167–168
strategic planning process,
V4: 183–184
structural analysis of industry,
V4: 131–133, 169–174
stuck in the middle, V4: 178, 179
sustainability, V4: 180–182
*Competitive Strategy: Techniques for
Analyzing Industries and Competitors*
(Porter), V4: 168
compliance
CFA Professional Standards
additional compensation
arrangements, V1: 75
candidate responsibilities,
V1: 107–108
communication, with
clients/prospective clients,
V1: 85
confidentiality, preservation of,
V1: 68
diligence and reasonable basis,
V1: 81–82
disclosure of conflicts, V1: 91–92
fair dealing, V1: 55–58
independence and objectivity,
V1: 25–26
integrity of capital markets,
V1: 39–42
knowledge of law, V1: 17–18
loyalty, prudence, and care (duty
of), V1: 50–51
material nonpublic information,
V1: 39–42
member responsibilities,
V1: 107–108
misconduct prevention, V1: 35
misrepresentation prevention,
V1: 30–31
objectivity and independence,
V1: 25–26
performance presentation, V1: 65
priority of transactions, V1: 95–98
records and record retention,
V1: 88
suitability, V1: 62
supervisors: responsibilities of,
V1: 76–78

Research Objectivity Standards
(CFA Institute), V1: 144, 151
review of, V1: 195
Soft Dollar Standards (CFA
Institute), V1: 123
composition decisions, portfolio,
V4: 14
compounded annual growth rate
(CAGR), V4: 147
compounding
continuously compounded returns,
V6: 186–187
interest, V6: 95
power of, V6: 470–472
comprehensive income, V4: 514, 518
income statement
adjustment/analysis, V2: 279–280
concentration, V4: 57–58
concentration ratio, V4: 131
concentration risk, V5: 31
conditional heteroskedasticity
autoregressive conditional
heteroskedasticity (ARCH),
V1: 395–398
defined, V1: 296
conditional prepayment rates (CPR)
auto loan-backed securities, V5: 256
CMOs, V5: 167–169, 167n3
finance charges, V5: 261
floating rates, V5: 260
home equity loans (HELs), V5: 247
conditional test: currency risk pricing,
V6: 458–459
conduct, professional. *See* Standards of
Professional Conduct (CFA
Institute)
confidence
cost of equity, V4: 291
macroeconomic risk factors,
V4: 156–157
confidence intervals: yield volatility,
V5: 85
confidence risk, V6: 390
confidentiality, preservation of
application, V1: 68–69
compliance, V1: 68
professional conduct investigations,
V1: 67
Standards of Professional Conduct,
V1: 13, 15, 67–69
conflict
agency relationship, V3: 197–200
corporate governance, V3: 197–201
director-shareholder, V3: 200–201
manager-shareholder, V3: 197–200
conflicts of interest
corporate governance, V3: 194–197,
221
disclosure of conflicts, V1: 89–94

priority of transactions, V1: 94–99
referral fees, V1: 99–101
Standards of Professional Conduct,
V1: 14, 89–101
conforming mortgage, V5: 164
conglomerate integration, V3: 249
consistency: regression parameter
estimators, V1: 293–294, 293n32
consistent estimator, V1: 322n67
Consolidated Financial Statements
(FASB), V2: 31–33
consolidation
accounting standards, V4: 116–117,
117
defined, V3: 248
consolidation method, accounting
adjustment and summary, V2: 44
conditions for use, V2: 31–33
equity method vs., V2: 35–40, 88–91
intercorporate investments, V2: 29,
31–44, 45–46
level of involvement, V2: 86–91
outside U.S., V2: 45–46
ownership influence, V2: 10
proportional consolidation vs.,
V2: 88–91
reporting requirements, V2: 28–31
variable interest entities (VIE),
V2: 103–110
constant growth
free cash flows, V4: 371, 385–386
models, V4: 349, 352–353
single-stage model residual income
model, V4: 525–526
constant maturity swap, V6: 257
constant maturity treasury (CMT)
security, V6: 257–258
constant prices, V1: 608
constant real exchange rate, V6: 439
constraints
capital rationing and budget
constraints, V3: 45
of investors, V6: 495
portfolio management, V6: 506–508
suitability standard, V1: 62
valuation, V4: 13
Consumer Price Index (CPI)
AR modeling, V1: 368–370
changes in, V1: 218n6
in-sample forecast, V1: 371
out-of-sample forecasts, V1: 372–373
testing inflation forecasts for bias,
V1: 247–248
trends, time series models,
V1: 353–355
Consumer Product Safety Commission
(CPSC), V1: 455
consumption: international trade
gains, V1: 479–481

managers for
Research Objectivity Standards,
V1: 144
Soft Dollar Standards, V1: 124
in new capital, V1: 430–431
objectives for, V6: 495
portfolio management, V4: 13
personal, V1: 144
process of, V4: 13, 14
ratio prediction for invested capital,
V1: 253–254
Soft Dollar Standards, V1: 124
strategy, V4: 13
through U.S., V4: 71–80
in working capital, V4: 35n4
investment alternatives: capital
budgeting, V3: 61
investment analysis,
recommendations, and actions
communication with
clients/prospective clients,
V1: 84–87
diligence and reasonable basis,
V1: 81–84
fair dealing, V1: 53–60
record retention, V1: 88–89
Standards of Professional Conduct,
V1: 12, 13–14, 53–60, 80–89
investment banks
credit default swaps (CDS), V6: 324
credit derivatives, V6: 317
relationships with: independence
and objectivity, V1: 23
Research Objectivity Standards,
V1: 144, 146, 149
Investment Company Act (1940),
V1: 120n1; V3: 203
Investment Company Institute,
V6: 493n1
investment decision criteria
average accounting rate of return
(AAR), V3: 18
capital budgeting methods,
V3: 10–30
discounted payback period, V3: 17
internal rate of return (IRR),
V3: 13–15
multiple IRR problem, V3: 25–28
net present value (NPV), V3: 12–13
no IRR problem, V3: 26–28
NPV/IRR ranking conflicts,
V3: 21–25
NPV profile, V3: 19–21
payback period as, V3: 15–17
popularity and usability, V3: 28–30
profitability index (PI), V3: 19
Soft Dollar Standards, V1: 124
investment horizon, V6: 450
investment management

communicating with, V6: 403
companies for, V6: 493–494
DDMs, V4: 331–333
portfolio management process,
V6: 492–494
valuation indicators, V4: 478–480
investment policy statement (IPS),
V1: 61; V6: 492, 497–498
investment risk, V4: 617–621
investment strategy, V6: 497–498
investment style, V6: 498
investment tax credits, V2: 258
investment value
of convertible security, V5: 132
defined, V4: 589
investors
institutional, V6: 493
objectives and constraints, V6: 495
portfolio constraints, V6: 506–508
invoice price, V6: 287
involuntary prepayments, V5: 241
IO. *See* interest only (IO)
IOI. *See* indications of interest (IOI)
IOSCO. *See* International
Organization of Securities
Commissions (IOSCO)
IPOs. *See* initial public offerings
(IPOs)
IPS. *See* investment policy statement
(IPS)
IR. *See* information ratio (IR)
IRP. *See* interest and interest rates,
interest rate parity (IRP)
IRR. *See* internal rate of return (IRR)
"irrational exuberance," V3: 174
irregular dividends, V3: 146n1
Irwin, John, V4: 615
ISDA. *See* International Swaps and
Derivatives Association (ISDA)
ISIC. *See* international standard
industrial classification (ISIC)
ISS. *See* Institutional Shareholder
Services (ISS)
Issue 98-3, EITF, V2: 64–65
Issue D-14, EITF, V2: 94n4
issuer-paid research, V1: 24–25
issuers
auto loan-backed securities, V5: 255
parties to securitization, V5: 235–236
SLABS, V5: 257–258
issuer-specific benchmarks,
V5: 103–104
Italy
consolidated reporting in, V2: 46
residential mortgage-backed
securities (RMBS), V5: 228–229
ITC. *See* International Trade
Commission (ITC)
ityose, V4: 50

J
Japan
consolidated reporting, V2: 46
economic growth trends in, V1: 427
futures contracts, V6: 78
futures exchanges, V6: 70
international trade patterns, V1: 475
liquidity, V4: 57
Nikkei index, V4: 60
SFAS 115, V2: 17
stock exchanges, V4: 46, 47
stock market size, V4: 54–55
trading procedures, V4: 50
yen futures contracts, V6: 78
Jarrow, Robert, V5: 41
J-curve effect, V6: 456
Jensen, Michael, V3: 125
jobs, V1: 490–491
Johnson & Johnson, V4: 291–292, 324
joint control: equity method, V2: 79
joint ventures
accounting standards, V4: 117
competitive strategies, V4: 172
consolidated vs. equity method,
V2: 39–40
proportionate consolidation, V2: 84
JPMorgan, V4: 627; V5: 41
JPMorgan Chase & Co., V6: 17, 231–233
junior tranche: credit derivatives,
V6: 318
junk bonds. *See* high-yield bonds
justified (fundamental) P/E, V4: 309
justified price multiple, V4: 414–415
justified price to book (P/B), V4: 449,
514
justified price to cash flow (P/CF),
V4: 463–464
"just say no," V3: 266
JWM Capital Management, V4: 611

K
kappa, V6: 197n35
Keene, Thomas R., V4: 89
Kellogg, V2: 251
Keynes, John Maynard, V4: 90
Keynesian policy, V4: 89
key rate duration: yield curve risk,
V5: 76–79
Kmart, V4: 182
knowledge capital, V1: 442
knowledge of law
application, V1: 18–21
compliance, V1: 17–18
global applications, V1: 20–21
Standards of Professional Conduct,
V1: 12, 15–21
Korea: economic growth trends in,
V1: 428
*k*th order autocorrelation, V1: 364